MOTOR TRADE
—————LAW—————

AN I.M.I. STUDENTS GUIDE
by
Anthea Worsdall, OBE, FIMI, Solicitor
Michael J. Pearce, MIMgt, MIRTE, MBIM
Peter Groves, FIMI, LLB, MA, PhD, Solicitor

D1149370

First published in 1989 by
The Institute of the Motor Industry
Fanshaws
Brickendon
Hertford
SG13 9PQ
Second edition 1990
Third edition 1991
Fourth edition 1993
Fifth edition 1994
Sixth edition 1995
Revised edition 1998

Printed in Great Britain by
Black Bear Press Ltd
Cambridge

ISBN 1 871880 00 9

CONTENTS

PREFACE

This students' guide to Motor Trade Law is intended to help students who are working for the IMI Certificate of Management. It is modelled very closely on the syllabus for the law modules in that course, and it is hoped it will provide a useful aid to study. Whilst the authors have taken every care as to the accuracy of the contents it is a Students' guide rather than a comprehensive statement on the law as it affects the motor trade, either as regards the range of topics covered, or the depth to which each one is discussed. It should not, therefore, be treated as a substitute for obtaining specific professional advice on particular problems which may arise in practice.

The Guide should be supplemented by reference to other reading where appropriate – for example all students of Road Transport law must have their own copy of the Construction and Use Regulations.

PART 1: PRINCIPLES OF LAW

by

Michael J. Pearce

CONTENTS

Section A
Sources of Law

What is meant by 'Law'?

In its widest sense, the word 'law' means a rule, or set of rules, that must be obeyed.

Those who have studied engineering science will have met Ohm's Law, dealing with the behaviour of electricity, Charles' and Boyle's Gas Laws, which deal with the behaviour of gases, Newton's Laws of Motion, and possibly others.

These laws state how something must behave, for example, if the volume of a gas is kept the same but its temperature is increased then its pressure **must** increase: it is a rule that it will.

The gas of course has no choice in the matter and for this reason these laws and other laws of Physics, are referred to as 'natural laws'.

When reference is made to 'the law', or, 'law studies', then the word has a narrower meaning.

It still refers to rules that must be obeyed, but this time it is the state which lays down the rules and members of the state who have to obey them.

Another difference, of course, is the matter of 'choice'.

Gases have no choice as to how they behave under different conditions, people do; but if people do not obey the law the courts are there to enforce it.

In the context of this book therefore, 'law' can be defined as "rules of behaviour, imposed by a state upon its members, and enforced by the courts".

Do all states impose the same laws?

Obviously not.

The laws of many states in the world are founded either on Roman law or English common law.

The laws of most European countries are based on Roman law, as are the laws of most South American countries, South Africa and some parts of Canada and the USA.

Whereas English common law, which has been affected very little by Roman law, is applied in most parts of the Commonwealth, and most parts of Canada and the USA (see fig. 1).

Even within a state the laws may differ. For example, in the state of the United Kingdom, Scotland, although part of the state, has substantial differences in its law from the rest of the UK because Scottish law has been affected to a considerable degree by Roman law.

For different reasons some laws passed by the Parliament in Westminster do not apply to Northern Ireland.

Where does the law come from?

There are two sources: firstly there is that body of law which has developed over the centuries and is referred to as Common Law, and secondly, there is the law made by Parliament, referred to as Statute Law.

How has the Common Law developed?

It could take a whole book to answer this question but to deal with it as briefly as possible:

Before the Norman Conquest in 1066, England consisted of a number of areas referred to as 'earldoms', each ruled by its own earl.

At the time of the Norman Conquest there were six earls,

Chapter 4.
Common Law.

Sec.
4-1. Common law declared to be in force.

§ 4-1. Common law declared to be in force.

All such parts of the common law as were heretofore in force and use within this State, or so much of the common law as is not destructive of, or repugnant to, or inconsistent with, the freedom and independence of this State and the form of government therein established, and which has not been otherwise provided for in whole or in part, not abrogated, repealed, or become obsolete, are hereby declared to be in full force within this State. (1715, c. 5, ss. 2, 3, P. R.; 1778, c. 133, P. R.; R. C., c. 22; Code, s. 641; Rev., s. 932; C. S., s. 970.)

Legal Periodicals. — For note on the role of the judiciary in the abrogation of the municipal tort immunity rule, see 5 Wake Forest Intra. L. Rev. 383 (1969).

For article, "The Rule in Wild's Case in North Carolina," see 55 N.C.L. Rev. 751 (1977).

For an article entitled, "The Common Law Powers of the Attorney General of North Carolina," see 9 N.C. Cent. L.J. 1 (1977).

CASE NOTES

I. General Consideration.
II. Illustrative Cases.
    A. Civil.
    B. Criminal.

I. GENERAL CONSIDERATION.

Historical Background. — See Resort Dev. Co. v. Parmele, 235 N.C. 689, 71 S.E.2d 474 (1952).

The term "common law" refers to the common law of England. State v. Willis, 255 N.C. 473, 121 S.E.2d 854, (1961); State v. Lackey, 271 N.C. 171, 155 S.E.2d 465 (1967); State ex. rel. Bruton v. Flying "W" Enterprises, Inc., 273 N.C. 399, 160 S.E.2d 482 (1968).

Common Law Adopted as of Date of Signing of Declaration of Independence. — This section adopted the common law of England as of the date of the signing of the Declaration of Independence. Steelman v. City of New Bern, 279 N.C. 589, 184 S.E.2d 239 (1971).

Extent of Common Law in Force and Effect. — So much of the common law as is not destructive of, repugnant to, or inconsistent with our form of government, and which has not been repealed or abrogated by statute or become obsolete, is in full force and effect in this jurisdiction. State v. Hampton, 210 N.C. 283, 186 S.E. 251 (1936).

So much of the common law as has not been abrogated or repealed by statute is in full force and effect in this State. Hoke v. Atlantic Greyhound Corp., 226 N.C. 332, 38 S.E.2d 105

(1946); Scholtens v. Scholtens, 230 N.C. 149, 50 S.E.2d 350 (1949), overruled on other grounds, Foster v. Foster, 264 N.C. 694, 142 S.E.2d 638 (1965); Henson v. Thomas, 231 N.C. 173, 56 S.E.2d 432, 12 A.L.R.2d 1171 (1949); Friendly Fin. Corp. v. Quinn, 232 N.C. 407, 61 S.E.2d 192 (1950); Ionic Lodge No. 72 F.A. & A.M. v. Ionic Lodge F.A. & A.M. No. 72 Co., 232 N.C. 648, 62 S.E.2d 73 (1950); Cooperative Whse., Inc. v. Lumberton Tobacco Bd. of Trade, Inc., 242 N.C. 123, 87 S.E.2d 25 (1955).

A common-law rule which has not been abrogated or repealed by statute in North Carolina, is still in effect under the terms of this section. Elliott v. Elliott, 235 N.C. 153, 69 S.E.2d 224 (1952); Redding v. Redding, 235 N.C. 638, 70 S.E.2d 676 (1952); McMichael v. Proctor, 243 N.C. 479, 91 S.E.2d 231 (1956); Mullen v. Sawyer, 8 N.C. App. 458, 174 S.E.2d 646 (1970), rev'd on other grounds, 277 N.C. 623, 178 S.E.2d 425 (1971). See note in 30 N.C.L. Rev. 417 (1952).

Extent to Which Common Law May Be Modified. — So much of the common law as is in force by virtue of this section may be modified or repealed, but those parts of the common law which are imbedded in the Constitution are not subject to control. State v. Mitchell, 202 N.C. 439, 163 S.E. 581 (1932).

Fig 1

The "common law" of North Carolina, USA is the common law of England.

the most powerful of whom was Harold, who was the real ruler of England and whose earldom was the south of England.

These earldoms were self-administrating and the law that was applied consisted of customs recognised generally throughout the land and also those of a local nature. The overall effect was that the law varied from one earldom to another.

When William defeated Harold at the Battle of Hastings, he considered that the country now belonged to him (a viewpoint contested by various earls for many years), had himself crowned king and set up a system of central government administered from his court.

From this King's Court, officials, and the king himself, travelled around the country dealing with administrative matters and, increasingly, judicial problems.

These judges based their decisions on the laws of the area but as they travelled about the country, hearing similar problems wherever they went, they applied the same legal remedies and the law became common throughout the land.

This common law has been developed to the present day, and is still being developed.

Does 'common law' just mean law that is common throughout the land?

That is one meaning of 'common law'. It can also mean law that is not made by Parliament – that is, to contrast it with 'statute' law and there is also a third meaning and that is to contrast it with 'Equity'.

What is 'Equity'?

Again, to put it as briefly as possible:

The remedy obtainable through the common law in a civil

case is financial compensation (referred to as 'damages').

So, for example, if a person unlawfully comes on to a landowner's land, builds a hut on the land and starts living in it, the landowner can take him to court for trespass and he will win his case. But the common law remedy is to award him damages: in other words, the trespasser would be ordered, by the court, to pay the landowner a sum of money. However, what the landowner really wants is to get rid of the trespasser: he wants him off his land.

Individuals with problems like this, that is for whom a common law remedy of damages would have been unsatisfactory, took to petitioning the king. They wrote asking him to grant a 'fairer' decision, for instance in the above example of trespass, to order the trespasser off the land.

The king handed these petitions over to the Lord Chancellor, a leading churchman, and told him to deal with the problem. The Lord Chancellor was not a lawyer, he was a churchman; consequently he dealt with the problem not from a strictly legal viewpoint, but by looking for what would be a 'fair' solution to the problem.

In the example given he would probably have ordered the trespasser to leave the landowner's land (in today's language he would have issued a mandatory injunction – an order telling someone to do something); he might also have ordered the trespasser not to re-enter that land (a prohibitory injunction – ordering someone not to do something).

The practice of petitioning the Lord Chancellor grew and special courts, Chancery Courts, were set up to deal with these problems.

For many years there were two sets of courts in the land, common law courts dispensing common law remedies and Chancery Courts, dispensing equitable remedies.

This dichotomy was ended by the Judicature Acts 1873–75, by which the two separate sets of courts were fused together, and today all courts are able to give common law and equitable remedies.

It should be noted that an equitable remedy is a discretionary remedy, which means that the courts can use their discretion whether they award an equitable remedy or not. An individual can ask for it but it is up to the court whether or not to grant it. The courts will always award a common law remedy (damages) if possible, as this is the simplest solution; only when damages are really not a satisfactory remedy will they award an equitable remedy.

What are the equitable remedies?

There are a number, but the three of most general interest are:

Mandatory injunction, a court order commanding a person to do something.

Prohibitory injunction, a court order forbidding a person to do something.

Specific Performance, this is a remedy for breach of contract and will be dealt with more fully in the Contract Law section; however, it is a court order commanding a person to carry out his side of a contract.

How is the common law being developed today?

Through what is known as 'case-law', or, to give it a more formal title, the Doctrine of Precedent.

This means that in each case the judges will apply the existing law. (Note, judges do not 'make' the law, their role is to state or interpret what the law is. It sometimes happens that their interpretation of the law almost amounts to making the law.) In applying the existing law the judges will apply the law as stated in a preceding case.

Which preceding case?

A preceding case which dealt with the same legal problem and which stated the law applying to that problem. The court dealing with the present case is bound to follow the legal principle stated by the court in that earlier case, for being the reason for coming to its decision.

Note that this applies to the **decision** reached by the court; the court hearing the present case is not bound to impose the same punishment in a criminal case, nor award the same damages in a civil case.

Is a court bound by previous decisions reached in any court?

No, it depends upon the relative importance of the two courts.

If the precedent was set in a court that is higher than the court hearing the present case, then the simple answer is that it will be bound.

It will not be bound by previous decision reached in lower courts.

If the precedent was set in a court of the same importance as the present court then it will normally follow that decision. (For more about the hierarchy of the courts, see Section B of this Part.)

How far back is a court supposed to go in the Doctrine of Precedent?

In theory there is no limit. However, in practice it is a matter of what is known of the previous case.

The doctrine probably began to develop by the end of the 12th century because of the desire of the judges of the day to create a common law. The earliest existing reports on cases were made during the period from the end of the 13th century up to the 16th century.

These reports are not considered to be sufficiently accurate; they were often merely a statement of the dispute and the decision of the court, and are seldom quoted in courts today.

By the middle of the 19th century the need for accurate law reporting was recognised and the Council of Law Reporting was established to produce detailed reports on cases heard in the House of Lords and the Supreme Court (i.e. courts which can bind lower courts). There are also reports such as the All England Law Reports, which are published privately. These present-day reports not only record the facts of the dispute and the court's decision but also give the reasons for reaching that decision.

Would it be true to say that the common law started with local and general customs, has been shaped over the years by the judges and that this is still going on today?

Yes, although there has been some input from other sources, for example, ecclesiastical law. At one time ecclesiastical disputes had been dealt with by ecclesiastical courts but after the Reformation, which made the king the head of the church in England, these problems, for example, divorce and matters concerned with wills, were handed over to the Common Law courts.

Of more relevance to these studies, Merchant Law, dealing with trading disputes and heard in the 'Courts Merchant', was also absorbed by the Common Law, although this was not completed until the middle of the 18th century.

What is 'Statute' law?

The law made by Parliament.

Why is it called 'statute' law and what has Parliament to do with making laws?

The question is best answered by explaining a little of what Parliament is and what it does.

Today the Houses of Parliament consist of the House of Lords and the House of Commons.

The House of Lords consists of:

The Lords Spiritual, senior clergymen of the Church of England.

The Lords Temporal, the hereditary peers and the life peers.

The Lords of Appeal in Ordinary, the so-called 'Law Lords'.

The House of Commons consists of Members of Parliament, each of whom has been elected by a constituency. Most, but not all, belong to one of the major political parties.

By convention, after a General Election, the monarch invites the leader of the political party which has the greatest number of Members of Parliament to form a government. Naturally, although this is not obligatory, this leader, who is then known as the Prime Minister, chooses the government from MPs in his, or her, own party.

The other members of the party become the back-benchers.

The members of the main opposition party become Her Majesty's Opposition.

There are also possibly thirty or so other members from other parties.

Although the government is formed from the party having more MPs than any other single party, there are several possibilities:

a) it may have considerably more than the combined total

of MPs belonging to the other parties. It is in a strong position.

b) it may have just more than the combined total of the other MPs. It is in a weaker position and can be under a constant strain of ensuring that all its own Members are in attendance.

c) it may have less than the combined total of the other MPs. It does not have a 'working majority' and can only function if it is supported by a number of MPs from the minority parties.

The Houses of Parliament have three main functions: executive, judicial and legislative.

The executive function, i.e. the 'running' of the country, is fulfilled by the Government.

The judicial function refers to the House of Lords in its capacity as the highest court of appeal in the land; it is of course only the 'Law Lords' (approximately ten in number) who exercise this function.

It is in its legislative capacity that Parliament 'makes laws'.

In order to achieve its political aims and to govern the country the government requires powers which it can only obtain by having laws passed. How easily it can get laws passed depends to a very great extent upon how 'strong' it is (see above).

How does Parliament introduce a new law?

A law starts life by being introduced in the form of a 'Bill'. With the exception of bills designed to raise money from the electorate, bills can be introduced in either the House of Commons or the House of Lords; the more important ones are usually introduced in the House of Commons.

A bill is introduced by being given its First Reading, this

consists merely of reading the title of the bill but has the effect of warning the House that the bill is being introduced and enabling copies of the bill to be printed so that its contents can be studied.

It then has a Second Reading.

It is at this stage that the member in charge of the bill explains the background and purposes of the bill.

A debate follows, which might last a few minutes or several days, but which can be only on the general principles, not on any detail. If it succeeds at this stage it then goes to committee.

At the Committee Stage, a committee, usually a standing committee, goes through the bill in greater details, if necessary word by word, making detailed amendments.

If the bill has been certified by the Speaker as a 'money' bill, that is, one whose main purpose is to raise money, then the committee at this stage consists of the whole House.

Once the bill has passed through the committee stage it goes back to the House for the Report Stage, during which time the committee's amendments are considered and either accepted or rejected and at this stage the House itself can also make amendments.

Usually, after passing through the Report Stage the bill immediately goes for its Third Reading.

The Third Reading, at which only minor amendments may be made, is the final stage and having passed this, the bill then goes to the other House (depending upon in which House it was introduced) and goes through the whole procedure again.

If amendments are made in the second House then the bill is returned to the first House for those amendments to be considered and either approved or rejected; it then goes back to the other House.

This can happen three or four times – until both Houses are agreed.

Once this agreement has been achieved, the bill has to receive the Royal Assent.

Nowadays this is a formality but it does serve to illustrate that laws are made by 'The King (or Queen) in Parliament', that is, that the laws are made by the monarch and the two Houses. At the present time the Royal Assent is given either by the Speaker (in the House of Commons) or the Lord Chancellor (in the House of Lords).

Once it has received the Royal Assent, the bill becomes an Act and is entered in a book known as the Statute Book for the year.

This is why Acts of Parliament are sometimes referred to as Statutes, and law made by Parliament as Statutory Law.

Supposing the two Houses do not agree, does this mean that the House of Lords could prevent something from becoming law when it has been passed by the House of Commons – the House of elected representatives?

Not any more. It used to be able to do so but when, between 1906 and 1910, 18 out of 210 Government Bills failed, either because they were turned down completely or were substantially amended, feelings ran so high that Mr Asquith, the Prime Minister of the day, threatened, with the support of the King, to create so many new life peers that they would outnumber his opponents in the House of Lords.

This was such a drastic proposal – it would have meant the creation of over 400 new peers to have the desired effect – that the Lords gave way.

Since then there have been two Parliament Acts, 1911 and 1949, effectively restricting the powers of the Lords to that of 'delaying' legislation passed by the Commons.

A 'money' bill becomes law within one month of being sent up to the Lords, whether they agree or not.

Other Public Bills can now be delayed only one year. (The actual wording, which need not concern us, is more complex than this.)

Who decides which bills can be introduced?

The simple answer is the Government, but for more than one reason.

First of all it must be realised that the Government needs to make laws in order to carry out its function of governing (for example, to enact the Finance Act which enables it to raise money) and also to implement its political aims. There is never enough time for a government to do all that it would like to. In consequence, of the time available for law making, the government appropriates about 90%.

The second reason has to do with the 'strength' of the government. If it is very strong, then it has the power and can command the support enabling it to make laws, even of a politically controversial nature.

If it is very weak, it may have to compromise with others in the laws that are made. The Government may still decide which bills can be introduced but its choice might be very limited.

Who introduces the Bills?

There is more than one kind of Bill and it depends on which kind is being introduced.

First there are Private Bills; these are not of concern to the general public, but are for the benefit of an individual, which could be a company, a corporation or a private person. For example, in the first half of the last century hundreds of private bills were promoted creating railway companies and giving them powers of compulsory purchase of land. Today, most private bills are promoted by local authorities.

A few years ago a man wished to marry his mother-in-law, which is against the law. By promoting a Private Bill he got the authority to marry; note, **he** got the authority to marry his mother-in-law, the law was not changed to enable all men to marry their mothers-in-law.

The Bills with which we are concerned are the Public Bills and these can be either Government Bills or Private Members' Bills. (Do not confuse Private Bills with Private Members' Bills.) Public Bills, obviously, are those of concern to the public and, as mentioned earlier, the government appropriates about 90% of the available time to promote its Government Bills. This type of Bill is usually introduced by the Government Minister concerned – for example, the Minister of Transport could introduce a Government Bill to nationalise (or de-nationalise) the railways; a Minister of Education would introduce an Education Bill.

The government allows some time each session (the Parliament's year) for ordinary Members of Parliament to introduce bills of their own. In practice so many MPs wish to do this, and so little time is allocated, that each year a ballot is held to decide the order of priority of members wishing to introduce a bill. Even so, less than a handful will get their bills as far as the Second Reading, and even these are unlikely to become Acts unless the government is sympathetic to the cause.

In spite of this some very important Acts of Parliament have started life as Private Members' Bills.

Do all the laws made by Parliament have to go through this whole procedure of readings, committees and reports in one House and then the other?

No, Parliament just hasn't got the time. What is done very frequently is to put a clause into an Act giving the (appropriate) Minister the power to make the detailed legislation.

This means that Parliamentary time is saved by the Houses having to discuss only the main principles; most of the members of the Houses would in any case lack the technical knowledge to discuss details, and also legislation can be introduced quickly or changed quickly without having to go back to Parliament. (For example, in a petrol shortage crisis, maximum speed limits on roads could be reduced – as a contribution towards saving petrol – and when the crisis was over, could be changed back.)

How does a Minister make these laws?

He must first of all have been given the power to do so. For example Section 41 of the Road Traffic Act 1988 says: "the Secretary of State may make regulations generally as to the use of motor vehicles and trailers on roads, their construction and the conditions under which they may be so used . . .

And, at the beginning of the Road Vehicles (Construction and Use) Regulations 1986, we find: 'The Secretary of State for Transport (hereinafter referred to as the "Secretary of State"), in exercise of the powers conferred by sections . . . 41 . . . of the Road Traffic Act 1988 now vested in him . . ., hereby makes the following Regulations:"

Delegated legislation (so-called because the Minister has had delegated to him the power to make these laws) such as the Construction and Use Regulations is made in the form of Statutory Instruments, and there may be a thousand or so of these produced each year.

(a)

Transport Act 1981

CHAPTER 56

LONDON
HER MAJESTY'S STATIONERY OFFICE
£5·45 net

(b)

STATUTORY INSTRUMENTS

1986 No. 1078

ROAD TRAFFIC

The Road Vehicles (Construction and Use)
Regulations 1986

Made · · · · · · ·	25th June 1986
Laid before Parliament · · · ·	18th July 1986
Coming into Operation · · · ·	11th August 1986

LONDON
HER MAJESTY'S STATIONERY OFFICE
1986
£10.00 net

(c)

STATUTORY INSTRUMENTS

1986 No. 2101

ROAD TRAFFIC

The Road Vehicles (Registration and Licensing) (Amendment)
(No. 3) Regulations 1986

Made · · · · ·	3rd December 1986
Laid before Parliament	11th December 1986
Coming into Operation	1st January 1987

The Secretary of State for Transport, in exercise of the powers conferred by section 16(1), (2) and (8) of the Vehicles (Excise) Act 1971(a), and of all other enabling powers, hereby makes the following Regulations:

Citation and commencement
1. These Regulations may be cited as the Road Vehicles (Registration and Licensing) (Amendment) (No. 3) Regulations 1986 and shall come into operation on 1st January 1987.

Amendment of Regulations
2. The Road Vehicles (Registration and Licensing) Regulations 1971(b) shall be further amended in accordance with these Regulations.

3. In regulation 3(1), after the definition of "tricycle" there shall be inserted the following:
"'valeting' means the thorough cleaning of a vehicle prior to its first registration by the Secretary of State including removing wax and grease from the exterior, engine and interior, and 'valeted' shall be construed accordingly;".

4. For regulation 28 there shall be substituted the following—
"**28.**—(1) For the purposes of section 16 of the Act the prescribed manner for—
(a) a motor trader to make an application to take out a licence under that section for all mechanically propelled vehicles which are from time to time temporarily in his possession in the course of his business as a motor trader and all recovery vehicles kept by him for the purpose of dealing with disabled vehicles in the course of that business;

(a) 1971 c. 10; subsections (1) and (8) of section 16 were amended by paragraph 4(2) and (8) respectively of Part 1 of Schedule 2 to the Finance Act 1986 (c. 41).
(b) S.I. 1971/450, to which there are amendments not relevant to these Regulations.

[DET 5702]

(d)

STATUTORY INSTRUMENTS

1979 No. 1198

ROAD TRAFFIC

The Motor Vehicles (Authorisation of Special Types)
General Order 1979

Made · · · ·	13th September 1979
Coming into Operation	1st November 1979

ARRANGEMENT OF THE ORDER

PART I

PRELIMINARY

[DET 33565]

An Act of Parliament (a) and three forms a Statutory Instrument can take: (b) *a "regulation"*, (c) *an "amendment"* and (d) *an "order".*

These Statutory Instruments are scrutinised by the Scrutiny Committee, a select committee set up by the House of Commons to examine every SI.

After scrutiny the Instrument may:

a) become effective without more ado,

b) be presented to Parliament and unless either House annuls it beforehand, it will become law after 40 days, or

c) require affirmation by both Houses before it becomes law.

What is a Code of Practice? Is it a law?

They are not laws, but they certainly cannot be ignored. The best way to answer the question is by looking at the example of the best-known Code of Practice there is: the Highway Code.

For example, there is no law that says that a motorist must not park his car on the brow of a hill. But the Highway Code says he should not and if prosecuted for doing so (possibly under Section 24 of the Road Traffic Act 1972, which says: "If a person in charge of a vehicle causes or permits the vehicle or a trailer drawn thereby to remain at rest on a road in such a position or in such condition or in such circumstances as to be likely to cause danger to other persons using the road, he shall be guilty of an offence") the prosecution may well say "he parked his car on the brow of a hill contrary to the Highway Code".

It is the same with any Code of Practice; the Code itself does not create legal offences but does lay down a standard against which the standard of behaviour of the 'accused' person will be compared when determining whether or not an offence was committed.

What is meant by a 'State'?

In this context a State is "a body of people occupying a defined territory and with a sovereign government"

What is a 'sovereign' government?

One with supreme power, although in a democracy it would be subject to the constitution of the State.

What is the constitution?

The rules which govern the government of a State. Some States, such as the USA and France have written constitutions. On the other hand the British constitution is partly written and partly unwritten. The written part includes Acts of Parliament which have dealt with constitutional matters, such as the Act of Settlement, 1701, which lays down the laws of succession to the throne; the Parliament Acts, 1911 and 1949, which have been discussed earlier and other constitutional documents including the Magna Carta itself.

The unwritten constitution includes that part of the common law which deals with constitutional matters and customary rules and conventions.

Are all countries States?

No, a country might be a State but it might be only part of a State or it might, on the other hand, consist of or contain States.

How can a country be only part of a State?

The following examples may help to understand this.

England, Scotland, Wales and Ireland are countries, but, the Acts of Union 1536–53 made Wales part and parcel of England and the Act of Union 1707 joined England and Scotland.

England, Wales and Scotland are collectively known as Britain. (Britain and its adjacent islands, such as the Isle of Man, are the 'British Isles'.)

In 1922 Ireland was partitioned. The six north-eastern counties, collectively known as Northern Ireland, together with Britain form the State of the United Kingdom. (The remainder of Ireland became the State of Eire.)

Although it is part of the United Kingdom, Northern Ireland has had varying power to rule itself and in consequence its laws contain differences from the law in Britain. Although it is part of Britain, Scotland's laws differ from those of England because of Scotland's 'Roman Law' heritage.

Which countries contain or consist of States?

Possibly the best example is the United States of America. The USA is a 'federation' of 50 States, each with certain political powers, each with laws of their own. By agreement between these States there is a central, or Federal, Government with political and legal powers over all the States.

A slightly different example is Switzerland which is a 'confederation' of twenty two republics, or cantons. In a confederation only limited powers are given to the central government.

The cantons of Switzerland are more independent of the Federal Government than are the States of the USA.

Is the EC a federation?

No, the European Community is a different concept although, as will be shown, there are certain similarities. This will be understood better by a brief account of its aims and functions.

The EEC was formed by the Treaty of Rome which was signed in 1957. The original Member States were France, Italy, West Germany and the three Benelux countries – Belgium, The Netherlands and Luxembourg. They have since been joined by the United Kingdom, Eire and Denmark. Greece, Spain, Portugal Sweden, Austria and Finland.

The EC is in fact only one of three European Communities, the others being the European Coal and Steel Community (ECSC) and the European Atomic Energy Community (Euratom), but all three share the same governing institutions.

The original aims of the EC were to remove economic barriers between the Member States and to integrate their economic policies. These broad aims will be implemented by the removal of national barriers which prevent the free movement throughout the Community of people, goods and money, and by establishing common policies in the key areas of the economy – including transport.

These aims have now been expanded by the Treaty of European Union ("Maastricht")

A number of bodies have been set up:

The executive function is carried out by:
The Council of Ministers and the Commission of the EEC;

The judicial function by:
The Court of Justice

The legislative function by:
The European Parliament.

It is misleading to think that the EC Parliament plays the same role as the Westminster Parliament. In fact the procedure for making laws is:

The Commission prepares and presents proposals for Community legislation.

The European Parliament is consulted and invited to give an opinion on the Commission proposals.

The Council has the power to adopt the proposals; and opinions of Parliament are not binding on the Council.

The European Parliament's role in law-making is therefore quite limited.

The Court of Justice:

a) interprets Community law,

b) reviews the legality of the actions of the Council and the Commission, and

c) hears cases where a Member State is accused of failing to comply with the obligations imposed by Community law.

In what form, or forms, is EC law made?

The legislation that is passed by the EC can be in the form of Decisions, or Regulations. These are binding on Member States without need for national legislation; for example: Regulation 3820/85, dealing with a goods vehicle's driver's hours.

It may be in the form of a Directive, which requires Member States, through their own national legislation, to implement the principles stated in the Directive within a specified time.

There are also Recommendations; these have no legal force but recommend standards the Member States should achieve in specific areas – rather like a code of practice.

Section B

DIVISIONS OF LAW

What is meant by 'divisions of law'?

For a number of reasons, perhaps procedural, perhaps to do with the sanctions that can be applied or the remedies that are available, the total body of law can be divided into a number of groups.

How many groups and what are they?

It depends upon the reason for the division; however, one basic example, which omits areas of the law outside the scope of 'motor trade' law, is shown in the following diagram:

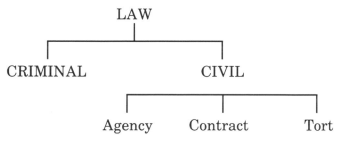

So, can both civil and criminal law be involved in the same problem?

Yes it can.
An example might make this clearer.

A person hires a taxicab. On the journey the driver drives dangerously, causes an accident and the passenger is injured.

a) The driver might be prosecuted for the **criminal offence** of dangerous driving.

b) He could be sued by the passenger for the **tort** of 'negligence'.

c) He could be sued by the passenger for the breach of an implied term (that he drive carefully) in the **contract**.

Here are three possible different legal actions, one criminal 'offence' and two civil 'offences', all arising from the driver's act of dangerous driving.

What is the difference between Criminal and Civil law?

Criminal law consists of offences against the State; the State takes action against offenders and they are punished by the State. Civil law consists of offences against individuals; the individual who has been harmed (referred to as the "injured party") has to take the action and, usually, the offender has to pay compensation to the injured party.

Are there any other differences between criminal and civil law?

Yes, for example nowadays most criminal law is statute law whereas civil law is still largely common law. Another important point is that there are different courts to enforce criminal and civil law; also the procedures for bringing an action differ.

What has criminal law to do with the motor trade?

The best way to answer is to explain what criminal law is, and this will be done in Section E of this Part.

However, the following examples of statutory legislation that give rise to criminal offences will give some appreciation of the relevance of criminal law to the motor trade:

Road Transport Law: the Road Traffic Acts, the Transport Acts, etc., and the regulations made under those Acts.

The Health and Safety at Work Act and its regulations.

The Trade Description Acts.

The Vehicles (Excise) Acts.

Various areas of Employment Legislation.

What are the differences between an action brought for a crime and an action brought for a civil offence?

The following tabular comparison shows the main differences:

Criminal Proceedings	Civil Proceedings
The State prosecutes the Accused	The Plaintiff sues the Defendant
↘	↙
who, if he loses, will	
↙	↘
be fined or imprisoned the fine going to the state	be ordered to pay damages to the Plaintiff

The purpose behind a criminal prosecution is to **punish** the offender, either by a term of imprisonment or a fine; nowadays other alternatives are being applied – for example, suspended sentences and community work.

The purpose behind a civil action is to obtain redress for a wrong committed by the defendant. Usually the plaintiff is seeking financial compensation (damages) but he might be seeking an equitable remedy, such as an 'injunction' i.e. an order issued by a court to someone to stop a certain course of behaviour, for example, publishing a libellous article in a newspaper.

How does the State bring an action – is it through the police?

By far the majority of State actions for criminal offences are brought by the police, however actions are brought by other State officials in their own areas of specialism, for example, Health and Safety Inspectors, Trading Standards Officers, Customs & Excise Officers. In addition actions may be brought by private individuals.

How does an injured party bring a civil action?

The simple answer is through his solicitor, but it might be useful to know something of the procedure.

Most actions are now started in the County Court whose jurisdiction varies according to the action, but in contract and tort is £25,000 – or up to £50,000 if the case is straightforward and the parties agree. The plaintiff must usually commence proceedings in either:

a) the court for the district in which the defendant resides or carries on business, or

b) the court for the district where the cause of action arose.

The action is commenced by the plaintiff filing particulars of the parties, particulars of the claim and the amount claimed.

A County Court summons is then served on the defendant/s.

The trial may be before a judge or a registrar. Only in cases of fraud, libel, slander, malicious prosecution, false imprisonment or seduction can a defendant claim trial by jury in a civil court.

If the action is brought in the High Court, in most cases it commences with a 'writ of summons'. A writ is a royal command to the defendant to enter an appearance in an action instituted by the plaintiff. It contains much the same information as a county court summons.

The writ is then served on the defendant/s.

The majority of civil actions never come to trial, either by agreement or by the defendant admitting liability or by the plaintiff discontinuing his claim.

It should be realised that suing someone in the County Court or the High Court can be expensive and even if the plaintiff wins the amount of damages he is awarded might be small. Also, he might not receive his costs, or not all of them; it is possible to win a case and be out of pocket.

It should also be borne in mind that there is not a lot of point in suing someone who has no money!

The procedure is more complicated than described above and although not essential, a lay person would be advised to have his solicitor act for him in both the above instances. Limited companies **must** act through a solicitor.

However, if the claim is for less than £1,000 the plaintiff can act for himself through what is known as the 'small claims procedure'. This was specifically introduced for small claims where a normal court action would not be financially worthwhile. With the small claims procedure the costs to the plaintiff are low, and would be known in advance.

The small claims procedure is simple and a guide: "Small claims in the county court" can be obtained from county courts or Citizens' Advice Bureaux – the guide is very explanatory and is well worth having.

In which court are criminal cases heard?

The courts having 'criminal jurisdiction', i.e. which can hear criminal cases are:

The House of Lords

The Court of Appeal (Criminal Division)

The High Court

The Crown Courts

The Magistrates' Courts

Why are there these different courts, all hearing criminal cases?

There are two reasons, first, in recognition that some criminal cases are more serious than others and, second, an appeal may be made to a higher court from the findings in the lower court.

Which crimes are more serious than others?

Without giving specific examples, the answer is that crimes are classed as "summary offences" or "indictable offences" (indictable is pronounced in-dite-able).

Summary offences are tried summarily, i.e. without a jury; indictable offence are tried before a jury. Indictable offences are, of course, the more serious.

The situation is a little more complicated than this, as some offences fall between the two categories, but this distinction can be ignored for the purpose of these studies.

In which courts are summary offences heard?

In Magistrates' Courts, which are the lowest level of the courts with jurisdiction to hear criminal cases (they have, in fact, jurisdiction to deal with some civil matters as well but their main role is dealing with less serious criminal cases).

A Magistrates' Court may be presided over by Justices of the Peace; these are lay people usually without legal qualifications and there must be at least two "on the bench". JPs have a legally qualified 'clerk to the justices' in the court to advise them on points of law. Alternatively there may be a 'stipendiary magistrate' (who is paid for his services). Such a magistrate is legally qualified; he sits alone and has no clerk to the justices to advise him.

The powers of magistrates are limited both with regard to the maximum length of imprisonment they may impose and the amount of fine they may exact.

Appeals may be made from a magistrates' court to the Crown Court both on grounds of fact and of law. This appeal is normally brought by the defence and in effect will result in a retrial.

A further appeal can be made to the High Court by either the defence or the prosecution. This appeal can be only on a point of law.

In which courts are indictable offences heard?

In Crown Courts, although a person cannot be tried on indictment unless he first appears before one or more magistrates. The magistrates do not try the case, they merely have to decide whether there is a case to answer. These are known as 'committal proceedings', if the magistrates do find there is a case to answer, the accused is "committed for trial" in the Crown Court.

In Crown Courts, cases are heard before a judge and jury. Appeals from the Crown Court may be made on a point of law to the High Court (Queen's Bench Division); and on points of fact and/or law, to the Court of Appeal (Criminal Division).

In certain circumstances, an appeal on a point of law can be made to the House of Lords.

In which courts are civil cases heard?

The courts which hear civil cases are:

The House of Lords

The Court of Appeal (Civil Division)

The High Court		
Queen's Bench Division	Family Division	Chancery Division

County Courts

Magistrates' Courts

Magistrates' Courts handle very little civil work. What they do handle is mainly concerned with affiliation orders and other matrimonial matters.

The County Courts are the lowest level civil courts; their jurisdiction depends upon the amount of money claimed. It varies depending upon the cause of the action, but a maximum amount is laid down in each case.

Above these maximums the action must be brought in the High Court. The High Court has three divisions, each specialising in a different area of the law. These division were shuffled and renamed a few years ago, they now are:

The Queen's Bench Division – QBD (KBD when the monarch is a king). This division handles the greatest number of cases; in particular it deals with contract and tort cases.

The Family Division, which deals with matters of divorce, wardship of infants and similar.

The Chancery Division, which deals with such matters as trusts, wills, company matters and bankruptcy.

All divisions of the High Court have appelate functions (they hear appeals), the QBD also hears appeals on criminal matters.

Appeals are possible to the Court of Appeal and to the House of Lords.

What is the difference between a "court of first instance" and an "appeal court"?

A court of first instance is a court in which a case is tried for the first time. Magistrates' Courts and County Courts are both courts of first instance for cases which come within their jurisdiction. Above those limits the Crown Court and the High Court respectively are courts of first instance, however, both the Crown Court and the High Court are also appelate courts.

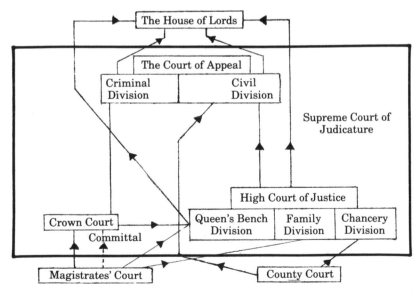

The criminal and civil courts showing the main lines of appeal.

The Court of Appeal – both divisions – and the House of Lords are only appellate courts, they hear only appeals.

What is the difference between a court of law and a tribunal?

A tribunal is not a court of law but it might, depending upon the type of tribunal that it is, hear and resolve disputes which otherwise would have had to be determined in a court of law.

What are the advantages and disadvantages of tribunals when compared with courts of law?

The advantages claimed are that they:

    are less formal,

    are less expensive;

    can hear disputes more quickly;

    can deal with disputes more quickly;

    specialise and therefore use specialists in their particular field.

The disadvantages are said to be:

    their decisions are less predictable, thus leading to uncertainty;

    some tribunals do not give reasons for their decisions, again leading to uncertainty;

    some tribunals hear cases in private;

    some tribunals will not permit representation by a professional lawyer.

Tribunals are however subject to the law. They are subject to a general supervisory jurisdiction by the QBD and they are also subject to the provisions of the Tribunals and Inquiries Act, 1971.

How many tribunals are there?

There are many but they fall into one of two groups:

Administrative tribunals and Domestic tribunals.

Administrative tribunals are concerned with administration of statute law and disputes which arise out of its operation; the following are a few examples:

Rent Tribunals, Lands Tribunals, Industrial Tribunals, Transport Tribunals.

Domestic tribunals deal with problems in particular trades or professions. The Disciplinary Committee of the General Medical Council is an example of a domestic tribunal.

What sort of problems do the Industrial Tribunals deal with?

These tribunals were set up to deal with questions, claims and complaints referred to them under various employment Acts.

The Acts under which most cases are referred to industrial tribunals are:

Employment Rights Act 1996
Equal Pay Act 1970
Health and Safety at Work Act 1974
Industrial Training Act 1982
Race Relations Act 1976
Sex Discrimination Acts 1975 and 1986
Wages Act 1986

How is a case brought before one of these administrative tribunals?

It depends upon which tribunal, but to give an example:

Industrial Tribunals. All questions, claims and complaints are made on form IT1, which can be obtained from a local Department of Employment office. The completed form is then sent to either:

The Central Office of the Industrial Tribunals (England and Wales) in London, or

The Central Office of the Industrial Tribunals (Scotland) in Glasgow.

If the Secretary of the Tribunals considers the applicant has a case, a hearing at a local tribunal will be held.

Appeals from the tribunal's decision can be made to the Employment Appeal Tribunal (EAT) and from there to the Court of Appeal and, if permission to do so is given, to the House of Lords.

Section C

CONTRACT LAW

Introduction

One of the first things to understand when studying the law of contract, is that contracts do not have to be the formal, complicated matters, involving large sums of money, that the layman often imagines them to be.

True, contracts can be all of these things, but the simple everyday activities in which we all partake – buying a ticket for a journey by public transport; buying petrol for the car; buying food, or cigarettes, or the evening paper; repairing a car for a customer, or selling a car to a customer – all these are just as much contracts as the great complicated affairs, and the same rules apply to them.

The Contract

What is a contract?

A simple, commonly used definition is: "a legally binding agreement"; another, a little more explanatory, is: "a bargain made between parties whose intention is that in the event of either failing to fulfil his part of the bargain, the other may sue him for breach of contract".

The essence is that the parties to a contract each undertake to do something, and the failure of either to carry out his part of the bargain renders him liable to a legal action by the other.

Can there be more than two parties to a contract?

It is first necessary to know what is meant by a 'party' to a contract.

The party must be a 'legal person', that is, a person whose existence is recognised by law. These persons may be 'natural', i.e. ordinary human beings, or 'artificial', i.e. non-human entities who owe their existence to a process of law. The most obvious examples of 'artificial' persons are Limited Companies which, from the moment they are incorporated, have an existence all of their own, distinct and apart from the human persons who happen to own them.

So, a contract may be between two human beings (natural persons), or two corporations (artificial persons), or one of each.

If a Company is a party to a contract, then it is contracting in its own right; it is a single legal person, even though it might be owned by a number of human persons.

It is possible for a contract to be between more than two parties but in the great majority of cases it will be found that there are only two, each of whom is a 'legal person'.

Who decides if there is a contract between the two parties?

There are two stages to this:

first, it is up to the two parties to decide if they want their agreement to be legally binding;

second, the law has certain requirements which must be satisfied if the agreement is to be legally binding.

Taking these in turn:

There is an old saying that although all contracts are agreements, all agreements are not contracts. This is just another way of saying that the agreement must be legally binding if it is to be a contract.

The parties to the agreement have the right to decide whether their agreement should be a contract or not.

The essentials of a contract

Assuming the parties intend to form a contract, there are certain legal requirements; they are frequently referred to as the "essentials of a contract" and they are:

1. That the parties intend their agreement to be **legally binding**.
2. There must be an **offer** and an unqualified **acceptance**.
3. The parties must possess **contractual capacity**.
4. Unless made 'under seal', the contract must be supported by **valuable consideration**.
5. There must be no **vitiating elements**, that is, there must be nothing that would make the contract void, voidable, illegal, unenforceable or impossible to perform.

(It should be noted that although these are the **essentials** of a valid contract, different authors will group them differently and consequently an author's list may contain any number from three to nine **essentials**. It is merely a matter of how they have been grouped.)

These **essentials** will now be considered in more detail.

Legally binding

Who decides whether an agreement is to be legally binding?

As has been stated, it is up to the parties to decide whether or not their agreement should be legally binding. A problem arises when there is a dispute on this point and the parties have not made their intention clear – or did not give the matter any thought – when the agreement was made. In such a situation the courts will try to determine what the parties had in mind when they made their agreement.

Broadly speaking the courts will presume that, if the agreement was made between parties who are connected in a business or commercial relationship, then the intention was for the agreement to be legally binding.

On the other hand, if the parties are connected in a social or domestic relationship, then the presumption is that it was not intended to be legally binding.

Both presumptions are rebuttable by evidence which shows the contrary.

Offer and Acceptance

With regard to the "offer and acceptance", does one party have to use the word "offer" and the other "acceptance"?

No, although they can: for example: "I offer you £3,000 for your car", "I accept". However in the majority of situations, the use of the words is inferred, in fact, as will be shown a little later, there is no need for anything to be said at all.

Who actually makes the offer?

Put simply, the person who takes the initiative; in the example given above, the person making the offer (known as the **offeror**) is the person who wants to buy the car, but it could just as easily have been the seller: "I offer to sell you my car for £3,000", "I accept".

Can anyone accept an offer?

It depends; if the offer is made to a specific person, then only that person may accept; if the offer is made to a specific group of persons, then only a member of that group may accept; if the offer is made "to the world at large", i.e. the general public, then anyone may accept. (The person to whom the offer is made is known as the **offeree**.)

It says above that words need not be used, how else can an offer be made?

Although it can be **expressed**, i.e. put into words (made **verbally**) – in which case it can be in writing or by word of mouth (**orally**) – it can also be **implied** by the conduct of the offeror.

For example, an evening paper can be bought by offering a coin to the seller – who will probably accept the offer by taking the coin and handing over the paper – all without a word being said.

It also says that anyone can accept an offer made to the general public, but I have heard of cases where a shopkeeper has refused to sell an article he has in his shop window; has he any right to do this?

This is an important point, not least because it appears contrary to common sense.

In the eyes of the law, when a shopkeeper displays goods in his shop window, he is not offering to sell them. Legally, he is inviting persons to offer to buy them from him; the customer is the offeror and the shopkeeper is the offeree.

As offerees always have the choice of accepting or rejecting an offer, the answer to the question is: yes, the shopkeeper does have the right not to sell goods displayed in this shop window. (Lawyers refer to the display of goods in a shop window as an "**invitation to treat**".)

Is the display of goods in a shop window the only example of an "invitation to treat"?

No, goods displayed on the shelves in a self-service store have also been held to be an invitation to treat. (The offer and acceptance take place at the cash counter on the way out.)

Rather differently, the majority of advertisements are also invitations to treat. If there is only one article being sold, then an advertisement for it is almost certainly an invitation to treat; if there is an ample supply of the goods, as for example in a mail order advertisement, then the advertisement could be an offer to sell. In such cases the advertiser will often safeguard himself by including the phrase "while stocks last" or something similar.

The problem, as can be seen, is that if a number of buyers "accept", and there is only one   or too few – article/s, the seller would be in breach of contract with those persons to whom he cannot supply, whereas if the advertisement is only an invitation to treat, then the advertiser is the offeree – and has a choice with whom he will form a contract.

When does an offer cease to exist?

There are a number of possibilities:

a) An offer will cease to exist (or "will lapse") when it is accepted, as it will then become merged into the contract.

b) It will lapse if it is revoked by the offeror. An offeror may revoke his offer at any time **before** it is accepted.

c) An offer will lapse at the end of a time that has been specified (when, for example, an offer is "kept open for one week").

d) If no time has been specified, then the offer will lapse after a "reasonable time"; what is "reasonable" will depend upon the facts in each case.

e) The death of either the offeror or the offeree before acceptance might cause the offer to lapse, but this also will depend upon the facts in each case.

f) An offer will also lapses if it is made on the basis of a state of affairs that ceases to exist. For example, if a motor trader offers a price on a part-exchange and the customer says he will go home and think about it and on the way home the car is badly damaged in an accident, the offer will have lapsed; the customer would not be able to contact the motor trader and, without telling him of the damage, accept the offer.

When does a contract come into existence?

A contract comes into existence (comes into force) at the moment the offer is accepted – as long as the acceptance is unqualified, and of course, the other essentials of a valid contract are satisfied.

What is meant by an "unqualified" acceptance?

A contract is made when the offeree accepts the offer as made by the offeror, i.e. the reply "I accept your offer", either expressed or implied, will form a contract from that moment. So, an offer: "I offer to sell you my car for £3,000" and a reply from the offeree: "I accept" will form a contract for the sale of that car for £3,000.

However, if the offeree replies "I accept if you put two new tyres on the rear wheels", then the offeree has 'qualified' his acceptance: he has introduced a new term, and no contract is formed.

In fact, what has happened is that the offeree has made a "counter-offer": "I offer you £3,000 for your new car with two new tyres"; the would-be buyer has become the offeror and the owner of the car is now the offeree and, as an offeree, he has the right to accept the new offer or reject it.

There is a further twist. A counter-offer destroys the original offer; it can no longer be accepted – and even if the would-be buyer, on having his counter-offer rejected, says "Oh, all right, £3,000 for your car as it stands", he is still not accepting the original offer, because it no longer exists; what he is doing is making yet another offer and once again, the car owner, being in the position of an offeree, has the right to accept or reject the offer – even though its terms are exactly the same as his original offer.

Apart from being "unqualified", are there any rules as to how an offer may be accepted?

No. As with the offer, an acceptance may be made orally, in writing or by implication. However, if the offeror stipulates a method of acceptance (for example "in writing"), then the acceptance must be in that form.

Supposing an acceptance, or an offer, is made by letter; is it made when the person writes it, or when the other person reads it?

A great many contracts are made by letter and the law lays down certain rules.

To be effective an **offer** must be "communicated" to the offeree, i.e. the offeree must know of the offer. As a matter of common sense (which is not always the test with law!) a person cannot accept an offer that he doesn't know about.

As a general rule, to be effective an **acceptance** must be communicated to the offeror. However, there are two important exceptions to this general rule:

a) where the requirement to communicate the acceptance has been expressly or impliedly waived by the offeror, and

b) under the so-called **post rule**.

   This states that: "when making an acceptance by letter

is the required method, or would be the normal or logical method, then the acceptance is effective from the moment that the letter, properly addressed and stamped, is placed in a post office box".

This means, of course, that the offeror will be bound by a contract without knowing it until he receives the letter but, as the alternative would be for the offeree not to know from what moment he will be bound (he would not know exactly when the offeror would receive his letter of acceptance), the law has chosen to put the offeror in the awkward position. (After all, he "caused" the problem in the first place by making the offer).

Commerce has stepped in to protect offerors and in a case in 1979 it was held that the use of the phrase "let me **know** in writing" excluded the post-rule and meant that the acceptance had to be communicated.

A **revocation** also has to be communicated to the offeree (before acceptance) if it is to be effective. Direct communication from the offeror to the offeree is not necessary, it is enough if the offeree learns of the revocation through a reliable source.

Contractual Capacity

It was stated earlier that the parties to a contract could be 'human' persons or 'artificial' persons, is there anyone who cannot form a contract?

The general rule is that any person recognised by law – whether a human person or an artificial person – may be a party to a contract. However, to this general rule there are exceptions whereby certain persons, both human and artificial, have their capacity to enter into a contract limited in some way.

As some adjectives are now going to be applied to contracts it will be useful at this point to give some definitions:

a) A VALID contract is one that is legally binding, one that the courts will enforce, one that has no defects.

b) A VOID contract; this is in effect the opposite of 'valid'; the courts will not enforce it; if a dispute arises out of a void contract the parties cannot take the dispute to court to get it resolved. (Strictly speaking, the phrase "a void contract" is incorrect, it literally means 'a legally enforceable agreement that is not legally enforceable'! However, lawyers find it convenient to use the expression, and in practice it causes no confusion.)

c) A VOIDABLE contract; this type of contract starts as a valid contract but one of the parties has the option of avoiding; more simply, he can choose to cancel it.

d) An ILLEGAL contract; obviously if a contract is illegal then the courts will not enforce it. An illegal contract will always be void.
Note that although an illegal contract is always void, the opposite is not the case, it is quite possible to have a void contract, which the courts will not enforce, but which is not illegal.

e) An UNENFORCEABLE contract; similar to a void contract in that the courts will not enforce it but this is usually because it has some technical defect; often if this is remedied the contract becomes valid.

Which human persons have limited contractual capacity?

There are several categories of which probably the most important class has been MINORS. (Minors become 'adults' on their 18th birthday.)

In the whole of living memory, minors (or 'infants' as they used to be known) have had special protection in the eyes of the law of contract.

It was considered that, because of their age, minors might unwisely enter into contracts and incur debts which would

not have been the case had they the wisdom of maturity (!)
The law could have said that minors could not form valid
contracts at all. However, such a rule could have been to
minors' detriment as they might have found it impossible to
buy anything if the seller knew that if the minor did not
pay, the courts would not enforce the agreement.

The solution (developed at Common Law and amended by
the Infant Relief Act 1874) was to make certain types of
contract void when entered into by minors. Briefly these
were:

Contracts under which minors had to repay money
loaned to them.

Contracts where minors were liable for "accounts stated",
e.g. IOUs.

Contracts of service, unless the contract was "on the
whole" for the minor's benefit.

Contracts for goods that were not "necessaries".

"Necessaries" are more than the **necessities** of life, such as
food, clothing and shelter and cover all things

". . . suitable to the conditions in life of the minor concerned and to his actual requirements at the time of sale
and delivery".

There have been many cases over the past hundred years or
so dealing with minors' contracts and most of them have
had to determine whether particular goods could be classed
as 'necessaries' for the defendant minor in the case.

Progressively over the years, young persons have matured
at an earlier age and the situation had been reached when,
far from protecting vulnerable young persons, the law was
in fact giving them an unfair advantage.

The Family Law Reform Act 1969 went some way to redress
this problem when it, *inter alia*, reduced the age of reaching
adulthood from 21 years to 18, but the Minors' Contracts
Act 1987 has taken the matter further.

This Act, which came into force in June 1987 (and which, incidentally, applies only in England and Wales) has repealed the Infants Relief Act 1874 and that part of the Betting and Loans (Infants) Act 1892 which dealt with loans made to minors.

It has also reversed the law where, in a contract of guarantee, the contract was unenforcable against the guarantor because it was unenforceable against the minor (for example, where the subject-matter of the contract was goods which were not necessaries).

The 1987 Act has not amended the Sale of Goods Act, 1979 (section 3).

The position regarding a minor's contractual capacity now appears to be:

a) Contracts of service are still binding on a minor if they are "on the whole" for the minor's benefit.

b) Contracts for goods are now binding on minors. However, if the goods are "necessaries" the minor is legally bound only to pay a "reasonable" price for them.

Minors may still enter into 'voidable' contracts but such contracts are outside the scope of this book.

Are there any other classes of human persons who have limited contractual capacity?

Yes, and for much the same reason, that is, to protect them. Persons who are mentally handicapped, or are under the influence of drink to such an extent that they are incapable of **understanding the nature of the contract** can form only voidable contracts; that is, they can affirm or reject the agreement during a lucid, or sober, interval.

A strange requirement is that for the contract to be voidable by the 'handicapped' person, that person has to prove that the other party knew of his disability.

In spite of this, if necessaries are supplied to a handicapped person,he must pay a reasonable price for them and it is not necessary for the other party to know of his disability.

Which other persons have limited contractual capacity?

Incorporated Companies, partnerships, trade unions, clubs and societies, all have rules applied to them regarding their contractual capacity, but they are outside the scope of this book.

Consideration

What is meant by 'consideration'?

In the context of a contract the word 'consideration' means something of value, each party to a contract must give and receive something of value.

If 'consideration' means "something of value", why does the essential in the list refer to "valuable" consideration?

Valuable consideration is consideration on which a monetary value can be placed. Lawyers also recognise 'good' consideration, that is, something of value that cannot be expressed in terms of money, for example, the love of a son for his mother is presumably something of value to the mother, but a price could not be put on it. In order to satisfy this essential of a contract the 'thing of value' must be capable of having a price put on it – no matter how small.

What examples are there of consideration?

Anything of value can be, but the most common examples would be money, goods and services.

It appears that consideration is not necessary if the contract is "made under seal". What does this mean?

As a general rule, English law will not enforce a contract unless it is a bargain, i.e. both parties giving and receiving something of value. The courts will not enforce a "gratuitous" promise, i.e. a promise to do something without receiving something in return.

The exception to this general rule is a relic from the past which still has its place in the law of contract today; the exception is that:

> where a promise is made in writing, is signed and sealed by the promisor, and delivered to the promisee, the promisee can legally enforce that promise.

It sounds archaic but there are situations where these SPECIALTY contracts, as they are known, are used today. (Note the spelling, the word is "specialty", not "speciality")

Is there a name given to contracts that are not "specialty" contracts?

Not to the same degree. It is usual merely to talk of 'contracts' unless a specialty contract is being referred to, in which case it is called a specialty contract.

However, the adjective 'parol' used to be applied to "non-specialty" contracts, and today the adjective "simple" might be used.
(Note the word "simple" is used to distinguish these contracts from the formal 'specialty' contracts; it has nothing to do with the content of the contract, which might be very complicated.)

(Some text-books list "contracts of record" as a further type of contract. These so-called contracts may, quite safely, be completely ignored.)

Are there any rules governing consideration?

Yes, they are collectively referred to as the 'doctrine of consideration' and can be summarised as follows:

Consideration may be **executed** or **executory** but must not be **past**, it must be **real** but need not be **adequate**, and it must **move from the promisee**.

Taking each rule in turn:

"Consideration may be executed or executory but must not be past"; this refers to the time that the consideration passes from one party to the other.

If the consideration passes from one party to the other at the time the contract is made, for example, when buying a loaf of bread, a beer or a packet of cigarettes, the consideration is 'executed', the money and the goods are exchanged at the time the contract is made.

On the other hand, a customer buying a new car for which there is a few weeks delivery delay will not receive the car, nor pay for it, until it arrives. However, the contract is binding from the moment the agreement was made (the offer was accepted). This is a point that many lay people do not appreciate; they feel that as neither party has actually done anything, i.e. parted with the car or the money, then the agreement is not binding; they feel that during that period they may 'change their mind'. In fact, informing the motor trader that they have changed their mind means they are in breach of contract.

So, a contract is valid whether the consideration passes at the time the contract is made or some time afterwards.

On the other hand, the general rule is that if the consideration has passed before an agreement is made it doesn't count, and the agreement is not legally binding.

For example, P., seeing D. drowning in a river, dives in and rescues him. On safely reaching the bank D. promises P. a reward for saving his life. P. cannot enforce D's promise because his consideration (the thing of value: saving D's life) was in the past – and past consideration is no consideration.

The law has modified the rule regarding past consideration and as it now stands if D has asked for P's services and the services are of a business nature then it is assumed that a contract will be formed in the future on the basis of that consideration.

For example, if an ordinary motorist, on seeing a fellow motorist with a car that has broken down, stops and helps to get it going, any subsequent promise of a reward would be past consideration (just as the drowning man example). On the other hand if a motorist whose car has broken down stops a motor trader's recovery vehicle that is passing, and asks for his assistance, the assumption would be that a contract would be formed to pay for that assistance.

"The consideration must be real (or "sufficient")".

The requirement is that each party puts something into the contract; he has to part with something of value whether it is money, goods, his services or something else of value.

The law will not allow him to put forward as consideration something that he would have had to part with anyway, for example, under another contract or under a public duty. In *Stilk v. Myrick (1809)* when a ship was at a foreign port, two of the seamen deserted. Being unable to obtain replacements, the captain agreed with the rest of the crew that if they did the extra work caused by their shipmates' desertion, he would share the two mens' wages among the crew. In the case that was brought when he failed to do so, it was held that the crew were not entitled to the extra pay – their original contract was to do all that was necessary to sail the ship, and that included extra work caused by the desertion – or death or sickness – of shipmates.

Hartley v. Ponsonby (1857) was, on the face of it, a similar case but this time about half the crew deserted and the court held that the men were entitled to the extra pay as it was not envisaged in their original contract that they would sail in such a dangerously under-manned state; their agreement to do so was fresh (real) consideration for the new contract for the extra pay.

"The consideration need not be adequate".

All that this is saying is that the courts do not feel that it is part of their duty to interfere with agreements that parties make.

If one party wishes to sell his new car for one penny then that is up to him; in spite of the fact that one penny is a totally inadequate payment for the new car, the courts would rule the contract to be valid.

It is true that they would take the inadequacy into account if there was an allegation of some defect in the formation of the contract, such as fraud or coercion.

"The consideration must move from the promisee".

A person may not sue another for breaking a promise unless he gave the promisor consideration for that promise. The oft-quoted case of *Dunlop Pneumatic Tyre Co. Ltd. v. Selfridge & Co. Ltd (1915)* illustrates this point:

Dunlop sold tyres to Dew & Co., a wholesaler; one of the terms of the contract being that when they resold the tyres, they should make the purchaser promise not to re-sell the tyres at less than a certain price (in the days when manufacturers could legally stipulate retail prices).

Dew sold tyres to Selfridge and duly extracted the promise from them; however, Selfridge did sell some tyres at a lower price and Dunlop sued them.

Held, Dunlop could not enforce the promise as they had given Selfridge no consideration in exchange for it.

The following diagram might make the position clearer:

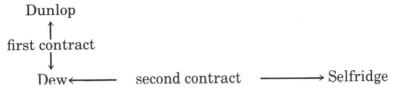

Dew did all required of them under the first contract; Selfridge was in breach of the second contract but the, in jured party' was Dew who, presumably, was not interested in enforcing the promise.

The case also illustrates another legal principle referred to as the Doctrine of Privity of Contract (loosely translated as – a contract is a private thing between the two parties) which means that only the parties to a contract have any rights or obligations under that contract.

Vitiating Elements

What else could affect the validity of a contract?

There are a number of things, collectively referred to as the "vitiating" elements, which prevent a contract from being valid and binding. Among the more important are:

a) Incorrect form in which the contract is made.

b) Duress and Undue Influence.

c) Misrepresentation.

d) Mistake.

e) Illegality.

In what *form* has a contract to be made?

Contracts can be grouped as follows:

i. Specialty contracts; these have been discussed before. The rule is that they have to be in writing, signed, sealed and delivered to the promisee, to be effective.

ii. Simple contracts which have to be in writing. There are not many examples of these but one is hire-purchase agreements. Unless these are made in writing in the prescribed way they will be unenforceable. (These contracts, unlike specialty contracts, do require consideration.)

iii. Simple contracts which, although they do not need to be in writing, cannot be enforced unless there is written evidence of their existence. Again there are few examples of these but they do include 'contracts of guarantee'.

iv. Otherwise contracts may be made orally, in writing or by implication; **they will be equally binding however made**, however, it is frequently advisable to have a written contract. The exhortation "get it in writing" is based on good common sense for a contract in writing can be produced as **evidence** in any dispute arising from the content of the contract.

What is meant by *"duress and undue influence"*?

It is fundamental principle that a contract is a legally binding agreement entered into by the parties of their own free will.

Duress and undue influence are two forms of coercion that can be applied to make a person enter a contract **not** of his own free will.

Depending upon the degree and type of coercion, the contract may be voidable or void.

What is a *Misrepresentation*?

In the course of negotiating a contract it is usual for the party trying to form the contract to make statements to the other to tempt him to enter into the contract.

These statements are known as representations; if they are

not true then they are misrepresentations.

So, a misrepresentation is a false statement of fact made to induce the other party to enter into the contract.

Could a misrepresentation be made by a representer without him knowing it was false?

Yes, in fact the law recognises three levels of 'knowledge':

i.   Innocent misrepresentation; where the person making it had reasonable grounds for believing it to be true, not only when he made it but also up to the time the contract was entered into.

ii. Negligent misrepresentation; where the person making it had no reasonable grounds for believing it to be true. There is a burden of proof on such person to prove that it was made innocently, otherwise it will be treated as a fraudulent misrepresentation.

iii. Fraudulent misrepresentation; where the person making it knew it to be false, or believed it to be false, or was reckless whether it was true or false.

A misrepresentation that a car had covered 20,000 miles when in fact it had covered 30,000 miles can be used to illustrate the forms of misrepresentation:

Innocently – the salesman genuinely believed it.

Negligently – the salesman should have checked more carefully before making the statement.

Recklessly – the salesman just quoted the reading on the odometer, having no idea whether it was the actual mileage covered or not.

Believing it to be false – the salesman quoted the reading on the odometer but believed the car had covered a greater mileage.

Knowing it to be false – the salesman quoted the reading on the odometer, knowing very well that it was not the mileage covered by the car.

What is the effect on a contract entered into under a misrepresentation?

There are two basic remedies available to a party who has entered into a contract because he was misled by a misrepresentation:

a) Rescission.

b) Damages.

To which he is entitled depends upon the type of misrepresentation.

What does "rescission" mean?

If a contract is rescinded (rescind – the verb form of rescission), it is terminated as from the beginning; it is as though it never existed; both parties are restored to the position they were in before the contract commenced.

The right to rescind is lost:

a) if the misled party has affirmed the contract. Once a contract is affirmed the misled party cannot change his mind and seek rescission;

b) if the parties cannot be restored to the position they were in before the contract was made;

c) if the misled party delays seeking rescission too long; or

d) if a third-party has acquired some right to the subject-matter of the contract.

Can a misled party rescind a contract and get damages?

The remedy available to a misled party depends upon the type of misrepresentation. Briefly, the position is as follows:

i.   If a Fraudulent Misrepresentation, the misled party may claim rescission, and damages (for fraud).

ii. If a Negligent Misrepresentation, it will be treated as a fraudulent misrepresentation unless the representer can prove he made it innocently.

iii. If an Innocent Misrepresentation, the misled party has only a right of rescission.

However, it should be appreciated that rescission is an equitable remedy (the common-law remedy is damages) and equitable remedies are discretionary remedies; in fact, in this instance, Parliament has enacted – in the Misrepresentation Act 1967 – that in cases of innocent misrepresentation the court may award damages instead of rescission.

Mistake

Can a party "get out of" a contract that he has entered by mistake?

As a general rule he cannot; however, there are some exceptions and it will be easier to follow these if some identifying labels are used:

A **"common"** mistake is where both parties are mistaken about the same thing – for example, a buyer and a seller contracting the sale of something that, unknown to either of them, no longer exists. Both parties are making the mistake of believing the thing to exist.

A **"mutual"** mistake. This time both parties are mistaken but about different things; there is no 'consensus ad idem' – no 'meeting of the minds'.

The case of *Raffles v. Wichelhaus (1864)* illustrates this quite well; the parties negotiated the sale of goods that were to be brought by ship from India; the actual terms of the contract referring to "Peerless from Bombay". There were in fact two ships called "Peerless", one sailing from Bombay in October, the other sailing from Bombay in December, although the parties did not know this. The seller had in mind the ship sailing in December, the buyer had in mind the ship sailing in October.

A **"unilateral"** mistake is where one party makes a mistake and the other party knows that he has. The majority of cases of unilateral mistake have been cases of mistaken identity – one party being mistaken as to the identity of the other party.

The last 'class' of mistake is **"documents mistakenly signed"**.

Common mistake by itself does not appear to be enough to vitiate a contract. There have been cases involving common mistake which have been declared void, but there have been others where the contract was declared valid, and a closer look at the cases which were declared void shows that there was no subject-matter to form the basis of the contract – as in the case of the buyer and seller contracting the sale of something that did not exist (*Couturier v. Hastie 1852*).

In considering a case involving mutual mistake, the courts apply an objective test: would the reasonable man on hearing the facts of the case take the agreement to mean what the plaintiff understood it to mean, or would he prefer the defendant's interpretation. Only if such an objective test failed to prefer either party's understanding would the contract be void, no agreement having been reached.

Common mistake and mutual mistake can arise quite innocently; unilateral mistake invariably has a "rogue", who either fostered the mistake or at least is taking advantage of it.

The courts' attitude towards the cases of mistaken identity is that, only where the mistaken party would not have contracted with the "rogue" had he known his true identity, will the contract be void, and it will be even more difficult for the mistaken party to have the contract declared void if he was face to face with the "rogue" when forming the contract.

As far as 'documents mistakenly signed' are concerned, for the party mistakenly signing the document to have the contract declared void, he will have to prove that not only was he not negligent in signing the document, but that the document was "fundamentally different" from the one he thought he was signing.

In what ways can a contract be *illegal*?

a) If it is to commit a crime, for example, "I will offer you £100 to break into that house and steal the television set for me"

b) If an Act of Parliament has made the contract illegal, for example, the Resale Price Maintenance Acts have made certain types of contract, e.g. where a retail price is stipulated, illegal.

Note, there are contracts where the manner of their performance is illegal under statute law, although they themselves are not illegal. The case of *Archbolds (Freightage) Ltd. v. S. Spanglett Ltd (1961)* may help to understand this:
The parties formed a contract under which the defendant was to transport 200 cases of whisky. Due to the negligence of the defendant's driver the whisky was stolen, and who was to bear the loss depended upon whether or not there was a valid contract. In order to carry goods for someone else, a haulier requires a licence to do so (nowadays referred to as an Operators' Standard Licence); the defendant had only a licence to carry goods belonging himself (nowadays referred to as an Operators' Restricted Licence). Carrying goods for someone else was therefore illegal by statute law. The plaintiff did not know that the haulier had not got the appropriate licence. It was held that in the circumstances the contract was not illegal and the plaintiff had his contractual rights. The contract was

legal: it was the manner in which it was performed that
was illegal.

c) Contracts can also be illegal at common law, if they are
"against the public good", "cause injury to society", "pre-
judicial to public policy". For example, in *Pearce v.
Brooks (1866)* a contract to hire a carriage to a prosti-
tute, knowing that she would use it to attract men, was
held to be illegal because it was "tainted with sexual
immorality".

Note, that there are also contracts which are void on
grounds of public policy although they are not illegal; one
important example of these are contracts in restraint of
trade, of which there are several forms:

a) Where an employee agrees with his employer that if he
leaves his employment, he will not work for a competitor.

Although real harm could be done to an employer if an
ex-employee of his did go to work for a competitor, the
agreement is restricting the employee's basic right to be
able to obtain employment. Such agreements are therefore prima facie void and will be upheld only:

i.   if the employee could cause real harm to his original
employer, for example, by virtue of confidential
knowledge that he possesses. A criterion often applied relates to the position the employee held; basically, the more senior the position, the more likely
that he would possess confidential knowledge – and
vice versa.

ii. the area of restraint; this must be reasonable if the
agreement is to be upheld and will depend upon the
facts in each case. For example, an agreement not to
work for a competitor within a 30 mile radius of his
original employer might be reasonable; not to work
for a competitor within a 50 mile radius might not.

iii. for the agreement to be upheld the duration of restraint must also be reasonable; not to work for a competitor for at least two years might be reasonable, not to work for a competitor for at least five years might not.

b) Another type of restraint of trade is the restriction agreed between the seller and buyer of a business is that the seller will not open up another business in competition with the buyer, as if he did, some of his original customers might follow him to his new place of business instead of dealing with the buyer. (It should be remembered that included in the price of a business is an amount for "goodwill", this takes into account the continued business from existing customers.)

The tests for validity of these contracts of restraint are similar to those for ex-employees, i.e. reasonable area and reasonable time. Once again the circumstances of each case determine what is 'reasonable' (In *Nordenfelt v. Maxim Nordenfelt Guns and Ammunition Co. (1894)* a restraint on the seller from setting up another business 'anywhere in the world' was upheld).

c) Although outside the scope of this book, "solus" agreements between petrol companies and filling stations are another example of contracts of restraint.

The terms of the contract

Now that the "essentials" of a contract have been covered, are there any other problems that can arise?

Unfortunately there are, the first possibly being that although a valid contract has been formed, it may be uncertain what it is that the parties have agreed, in other words, what the terms of the contract are.

Are there different types of "terms"?

Yes, the terms of a contract can be sub-divided in two ways:

a) The terms may be expressed or implied.

Terms that have been expressed (i.e. put into words, either orally or in writing) are referred to as "express" terms.

As well as terms that have been expressed, practically all contracts contain terms which are there by implication: neither party has mentioned them but nevertheless the law says they are present. These are referred to as 'implied' terms and they can be present through one of three ways:

i. Implied by custom.

A contract may be subject to terms which arise by custom, whether trade or otherwise, although they have not been expressly included by the parties. On the other hand, a term implied by custom can be excluded by the parties, for example, by an express term negating an implied term.

ii. Implied by statute.

An Act of Parliament may stipulate that certain terms are to be implied in certain types of contracts, for example: sections 12–15 of the Sale of Goods Act, 1979.

iii. Inferred by the courts.

The courts may look at a contract and infer that certain terms were implied to give the contract 'business efficacy'; for example, in the case of a lease for a furnished house, there is an implied term that it shall be fit for habitation at the date fixed for the commencement of the lease.

b) The terms in a contract, that is, the express terms and the implied terms together, can be sub-divided according to their individual importance:

i. Fundamental terms. A fundamental term is one that is fundamental to the contract: the main term of the contract: the one that "goes to the root of the contract".

ii. Conditions. These are important terms, essential terms in the contract.

iii. Warranties. These are the less important terms, the non-essential terms, subordinate to the main terms.

(Note, the word "warranty" in this legal usage should not be confused with the commercial use of the word where it is synonymous with "guarantee".)

What is the practical point in learning about the 'terms' of a contract?

Firstly, as was stated earlier, practically all contracts will contain both express and implied terms. These express and implied terms, all of them, comprise the obligation and rights, which arise from the contract. Unless one is aware of all the terms in a contract, one will not know fully one's obligations, or rights.

Secondly, if a party to a contract fails to comply with a term of the contract he will be in 'breach of contract' and can be sued by the injured party.

However, the more important the term is that has been breached, the more serious it is and the greater the number of courses of action open to the injured party.

What are the different remedies available to the injured party?

In the event of a breach of a condition or a breach of a fundamental term, the injured party may consider himself discharged from the contract, with no further contractual obligations, and he may sue for damages.

In the event of a breach of a warranty, the injured party may **not** treat the contract as discharged, he must continue to fulfil his obligations under the contract, but he can sue for damages.

When there has been a breach of condition, the injured party may, if he chooses, treat the breach of condition as if it were only a breach of warranty; in other words, let the contract continue with both parties bound by its terms, but sueing for damages.

In some cases the injured party **must** treat a breach of condition as a breach of warranty. The type of situation where this would apply would be where the injured party has already received some benefit under the contract and the contract is not of the type that can be severed, i.e. cut into parts, each part a contract in its own right.

Exclusion clauses

What are "exclusion clauses"?

An exclusion clause is the most common name given to clauses in contracts whereby a party attempts to exclude or restrict his liability under the contract. Other names used are "exemption clauses", "restriction clauses".

Are exclusion clauses lawful?

Some are and some are not; probably the best way to answer this question is to trace some of the background to exclusion clauses.

First, remember that a contract is legally binding on the parties because they chose to be bound by it; they have voluntarily put themselves into the position of being legally bound by an agreement.

It follows that they should be able to decide how they should be bound and, perhaps just as important, how they should not be bound.

Common law recognises the right of a person entering into a contract to limit his liability under the contract.

So, for example, A might have said to B "I offer to sell you my car for £x, as long as I am not held liable if anything goes wrong with it". B then had a choice; he could either purchase A's car on that understanding, or he need not enter into the contract, he could look elsewhere.

The underlying philosophy is that two people, having equal bargaining strength, negotiate a contract.

Nowadays however, more often than not, the private individual is not freely negotiating with another individual but is contracting with a corporation, and the corporation has a "standard form" contract with a number of clauses excluding or limiting its liability under the contract.

Although the individual has the same two choices, (he can either enter the contract subject to those terms, or not) the chances are that if he wants a particular item and decides to look elsewhere, other suppliers will also be corporations with similar standard form contracts.

As this was effectively destroying the concept of a contract as "a bargain freely entered into", for a number of years the courts have been considering the effect of different exclusion clauses in different contracts, and the following set of rules can be said to have been drawn up as a result of their findings:

1. To be effective, the other party must know of the exclusion clause. Note it is not necessary for him to have read it: it is enough that he knows of its existence. If he signs a document containing an exclusion clause, it will be almost impossible for him to claim that he did not know of it. (He might claim this if he signs a document on the front and the clause is printed on the back, so to be effective, his attention should be drawn to its presence.)

2. To be effective, the other party must know of the exclusion clause before, or at the time of, entering the contract. Exclusion clauses brought to the attention of

the other party after the contract has been formed are ineffective.

3. To be effective, the exclusion clause must be clearly worded; in fact, the greater the liability it is seeking to exclude, the clearer the words must be. If it seeks to exclude liability for negligence then, unless negligence is the only possible way the party could be liable, the words used must clearly indicate that liability for negligence is being excluded.

The following is an example of an exclusion clause which would have excluded liability for negligence, negligence being the only way the party could have been liable.

The clause is one frequently used by garages a number of years ago, often being displayed as a notice in the workshop:

"Customers' cars are driven by our staff at customers' sole risk"

(What follows is a paraphrase of a judgement in an actual case and gives an indication of the standard of reasoning of which the judge thinks the "ordinary" man is capable!)

"When confronted with the (above) clause when taking his car to a garage for work to be carried out, he knows that his car might be driven on the road by a member of the garage staff for some purpose in connection with the work.

He knows that the car might be involved in an accident, and damaged, whilst being so driven.

He knows that the accident will have occurred due to the negligence of one, or both, of the drivers.

He knows that the garage will be liable only if the garage's driver was negligent.

It follows that no sensible man could have thought that the words had any meaning except that the garage would not be liable for the negligence of their own drivers".

4. Even the breach of a fundamental term can be covered by an exclusion clause, as long as this is clearly indicated by the words used in the contract. (There has been a change in judicial opinion on this point over the years; it used to be considered that it was nonsense to have a contract to do something, with an exclusion clause saying you would not be liable if you did not do it! However, certainly after a House of Lords decision in 1980, you can exclude such liability.)

These are all common law 'rules'; hasn't Parliament had anything to say on this matter?

Parliament has played, and is playing, its part in controlling the use of exclusion clauses.

It has enacted legislation controlling the use of exclusion clauses in certain types of contract, for example, the Supply of Goods (Implied Terms) Act 1973 – (now partly incorporated in the Sale of Goods Act, 1979) – limited the use of exclusion clauses in contracts for the supply of goods. (See p. 166.)

It has also enacted legislation affecting a wider range of contracts, such as the Unfair Contract Terms Act, 1977, and the Unfair Terms in Consumer Contracts Regulations 1994.

What general contract terms are unfair?

Under the Unfair Contract Terms Act:

"s.2(1) A person cannot by reference to any contract term or to a notice given to persons generally or to particular persons exclude or restrict his liability for death or personal injury resulting from negligence"

Further, 'negligence' is defined in the Act and we find that it means more than its meaning in tort:

"s.1(1)   "negligence" means the breach –

(a) of any obligation, arising from the express or implied terms of a contract, to take reasonable care or exercise reasonable skill in the performance of the contract;

(b) of any common law duty to take reasonable care or exercise reasonable skill; . . .

Whether other liability can be excluded depends upon whether or not it was "reasonable" for such liability to be excluded.

(The Act gives "guidelines" as to the matters which are to be considered, when relevant, when testing whether an exclusion clause is "reasonable" or not.)

European law, enacted in the UK by the Unfair Terms in Consumer Contract Regulations 1994, now provides that any term in a trader's standard form contract with a consumer which creates an imbalance between the consumer's rights and those of the trader will automatically be regarded as unfair.

Discharge of Contract

What is meant by 'discharge of contract'?

Whilst a contract is in force the parties have certain rights and obligations under it. When these rights and obligations come to an end, the contract is said to be discharged,

In what ways can a contract be discharged?

There are FOUR ways in which a contract may be discharged:

a) by PERFORMANCE,

b) by BREACH,

c) by AGREEMENT, and

d) under the DOCTRINE of FRUSTRATION.

a) By Performance.

Where both parties perform the obligations they have undertaken, the contract is discharged and both parties are freed from any further liability.

b) By Breach.

Breach of contract occurs either:

i.   by a party failing to carry out his contractual obligations, or

ii. by 'repudiation'.
     Repudiation occurs when one party, by his words or actions, makes it known that he is not going to fulfil his contractual obligations when they fall due. This could be by a statement, e.g. "I am not going to carry out my part of the contract", or by his actions, e.g. a party contracts to sell his car in a week's time and, before that date arrives, sells the car to someone else.

If a contract is discharged by breach, the injured party, as long as he has completed his performance or is ready and willing to do so, is alone discharged; the party in breach remains liable.

A contract will, however, be discharged by breach only if the breach is of an important term – a 'condition' or a 'fundamental term'.
If the breach is of a 'warranty' then the injured party cannot treat himself as discharged; his only right is to sue for damages.

In cases of repudiation the injured party has the right to sue for breach of contract on learning of the repudiation; he does not have to wait until the time the performance should have been made.

c) **By Agreement.**

On the face of it, if both parties to a contract want to cancel it – to discharge themselves from it – and they both agree to do so, then that should be an end to the matter.

Legally, however, it is not as simple as that.

To start with, their contract is by definition a legally binding agreement; it follows that any agreement to cancel it must also be legally binding, in other words, would also need to be a contract.

To be a contract all the requirements would have to be satisfied, including the need for consideration.

So, for a contract to be discharged by agreement there must be consideration.

This requirement can be applied to the two situations which generally arise:

a) Neither party has commenced the performance of his part of the contract. This is the easiest situation; the parties each agree to cancel and each party thereby agrees to give up his rights under the contract in exchange for the other party giving up his rights. Both parties give something of value, each party receives something of value. This form of discharge is referred to as a 'bilateral' discharge.

b) One party to the contract has performed his part, the other has not. A simple agreement to cancel would not be sufficient, as the party who has completed his performance would be receiving nothing of value from the other to support the agreement to cancel. In order to cancel there must be what the lawyers refer to "accord and satisfaction", this was judicially defined in a 1933 case as: "Accord and satisfaction is the purchase of a release from an obligation, whether arising under contract or tort, by means of any valuable consideration, not being the actual performance of the obligation itself. The accord is the agreement by which the obligation is discharged; the satisfaction is the consideration which makes the agreement operative". This form of discharge is referred to as a 'unilateral' discharge

d) Discharge under the Doctrine of Frustration.

A contract cannot be made if its performance is impossible right from the start, for example, to walk across the Atlantic.
Such impossibility is a vitiating element.

However, it is possible to form a contract which, although quite possible to perform at the start, subsequently becomes impossible.

This is what is meant when it is said that a contract has been frustrated, but, as will be seen, a frustrated contract does not necessarily discharge the parties from their obligations.

In a case in 1647 the judges laid down what is now sometimes referred to as the rule as to absolute contracts.

Basically the rule is that if a man by entering into a contract creates a duty upon himself, then he is bound by that duty even if it subsequently becomes impossible to perform it.

The apparent harshness of this rule can be justified because the party can always protect himself by appropriate clauses in the contract, but if he fails to do so, if he undertakes an unconditional obligation then he must stand the consequences if he cannot carry it out.

The position in law is now as follows: if a prudent person could have anticipated that his obligations under the contract could become impossible to perform, then he should have guarded against that possibility in the contract. If he failed to do so then he must bear the consequences of his non-performance.

Only if the event causing the contract to become impossible to perform could not have been foreseen, will the courts rule that the contract has been "frustrated" and the parties consequently discharged from their obligations.

To put the rule in a practical situation:

An undertaking that a customer's car will "be ready by five o'clock on Wednesday" becomes a contractual obligation.

What could prevent the car from being ready?

Parts unavailable? Mechanics going sick?

If these are real possibilities then the courts expect them to be taken into account, so the undertaking should have been: "your car will be ready by five o'clock on Wednesday as long as we can get the parts . . ."

(A word of warning: making such an undertaking knowing that the parts would not be available is a criminal offence under the Trade Descriptions Act.)

If the workshop is blown down by a violent storm and the cars in it are crushed, the courts would undoubtedly hold that such a possibility could not have been foreseen and consequently the undertaking to have the car ready by "five o'clock on Wednesday" is no longer binding.

The Law Reform (Frustrated Contracts) Act 1943 changed the law which existed at the time regarding money paid under a frustrated contract.

The position now is:

If there has been a total failure of consideration from the other party, all moneys paid **before** a contract is discharged by frustration shall be recoverable and money due at the time of frustration need not be paid.

A party who has partly performed his part of the contract when the frustration occurs can obtain compensation for what he has done.

Remedies

What remedies are available to the injured party in a contract?

There are two types of remedy apparently available to the injured party:

Common Law remedies   and   Equitable remedies

Presumably the common law remedy is damages?

Yes, financial compensation for the loss suffered.

There are a number of rules applied by the courts to determine the amount of compensation to be awarded, among them, for example, is a duty on the injured party to "mitigate his loss". This means he has a duty to make his loss as small as possible; for example, if a party contracts to buy a car and then backs out, the injured party is under a duty to try to sell the car elsewhere at the best price he can get. He may not 'do nothing' and claim damages for his loss of profit.

What equitable remedies has an injured party?

First of all it should be remembered that equitable remedies are discretionary remedies, (i.e. awarded at the discretion of the court) and the courts will always award damages if they can fairly do so.

Equitable remedies are available, but not as of right.

There are, however, three equitable remedies applicable to contracts:

a) Specific Performance
   This is an order by the court ordering a party to the contract to carry out his obligations under the contract, in other words, to "specifically perform" the contract.

This remedy is not often awarded; in contracts for the sale of goods it is only likely to be awarded if the goods are unique, for example, an antique, where damages would not adequately compensate the injured party.

b) Injunctions

There are two forms of injunction: mandatory injunctions whereby the court orders the offending party to do something, and prohibitory injunctions, whereby the court orders the offending party not to do something.

In *Martin v. Nutkin (1724)* the defendant broke his agreement not to ring the church bell at five o'clock each morning! The court issued a prohibitory injunction ordering him not to do so.

c) Rescission

This remedy was discussed under 'misrepresentation'. Its effect is to cancel a contract, to have both parties return to the other what they have received from the other, so that both parties are in the position they were in **before** the contract was formed.

Extinction of remedies

Unlike criminal prosecutions, actions in civil law have to brought within certain periods of time, or the injured party will lose his right to bring the action.

The time limits are set out in the Limitation Acts which give the time from which the period starts and the length of the period for all forms of civil action.

At the end of the relevant period of time the injured party's **right of action** is said to be "time-barred".

The limitation period for breach of a 'simple' contract is six years, commencing at the breach.

The limitation period for 'specialty' contracts is twelve years, again commencing at the breach.

Claims for equitable relief, such as specific performance, do not have laid-down time-bars but in practice the courts apply similar periods.

There are also rules in equity which militate against delay in bringing an action.

Contracts of Guarantee

Is a 'contract of guarantee' a special sort of contract?

Yes, it has little in common with simple contracts and, although closer to a specialty contract it differs from them too.

In a contract of guarantee, the guarantor undertakes liability for the debts of another in the event of that other person not paying. He undertakes a secondary liability: he will be liable if the debtor defaults.

This secondary liability has meant that if the debt was for some reason unenforceable against the debtor (e.g. if he were a minor) it was unenforceable also against the guarantor.

Someone has to be primarily liable before another can have a secondary liability – if the debtor is not liable; the guarantor cannot be.

Now with the Minors' Contracts Act 1987, if the reason for the debt being unenforceable against the debtor is because the debtor is a minor then "the guarantee shall not for that reason alone be unenforceable against the guarantor" (section 2 of the Act).

Another feature of contracts of guarantee is that to be enforceable against the guarantor they have to be "evidenced" in writing.

Note that the requirement is not that the contract itself is in writing but if the creditor wishes to enforce the guarantee, then he must produce to the court written evidence of its existence.

Contracts of Guarantee v. Contracts of Indemnity

Contracts of guarantee are sometimes confused with contracts of indemnity where the indemnifier also undertakes liability for a debt.

Two simple examples may show the difference but it is important to know that it is the parties' **intentions** that make the difference, not the actual words used.

Guarantor to vendor: "Let him have the goods, if he does not pay you, I will".

Indemnifier to vendor: "Let him have the goods, I will see you are paid".

In the first example, the guarantor is undertaking a secondary liability; the vendor should try to get his money from the debtor; if he is unsuccessful he can turn to the guarantor.

In the second example, the indemnifier is undertaking a primary liability; the vendor has no need to contact the debtor at all, he can turn to the indemnifier at once.

Another difference between the two is that contracts of guarantee have to be evidence in writing to be enforceable; there is no such requirement with contracts of indemnity.

Penalty Clauses and Liquidated Damages

What is a penalty clause?

It is not uncommon for the parties to a contract to agree beforehand the amount of damages to be paid in the event of a breach. For example, a builder may agree to pay £25 a day for every day the building remains unfinished after the completion date agreed in the contract, or the supplier of a commercial vehicle may make a similar agreement regarding the late delivery of a vehicle he is supplying.

The layman invariably refers to these agreements as "penalty clauses" but in fact they could be one of two things:

a) Liquidated Damages

These are genuine pre-estimates of the loss that will be suffered by one party in the event of a breach of contract by the other.

As long as they are genuine pre-estimates then that is the amount of damages that will be paid, no more, no less, regardless of the actual loss suffered and without the injured party having to prove he suffered a loss.

b) Penalties

Penalties on the other hand, are by way of being threats, made to put pressure on the other party to perform the contract as agreed. Penalty clauses, as such, are unenforceable. Their effect in practice is to put a maximum limit to the amount that the injured party can claim in the event of a breach, and the injured party is required to prove his loss as well.

It will be evident that exactly the same words could be used for a clause for liquidated damages and for a penalty clause, and, as was stated earlier, both are popularly referred to as penalty clauses.

In fact what a particular clause is called is irrelevant. If the amount is a genuine pre-estimate then the amount is liquidated damages and is recoverable without proof of loss; if not then the amount is a penalty, which could operate against the party putting it forward as it limits the compensation he could obtain as well as requiring him to prove his loss.

Contracts Uberrimae Fidei

What is a contract uberrimae fidei?

Uberrima fides is the Latin for "the utmost good faith", therefore contracts uberrimae fidei are: contracts of the utmost good faith.

Which contracts are contracts uberrimae fidei?

There are several, the most important – if only because they are the most common – being contracts of insurance.

They are contracts where one party alone knows, or in practice could know, all the relevant facts.

How does uberrima fides apply to contracts of insurance?

It places a duty on the person seeking insurance to disclose all material facts, and failure to do so can render the contract voidable.

What is a material fact?

One that increases the risk to the insurer; a fact that if he knew it, could result in him declining to insure or at least to ask a higher premium.

Are there any material facts which do not have to be disclosed?

A fact that makes the person seeking insurance a lesser risk is not a 'material fact' and therefore does not have to be disclosed. The person seeking insurance may well want to disclose such a fact in the hope of obtaining a reduced premium.

A fact which should be known to the insurer, either because it is general knowledge or because he should know it by virtue of his type of business. For example, having described a car as a "convertible" in the proposal form, there should be no need to inform the motor vehicle insurer that it has a 'soft top', as he should know this.

A fact that the insurer has expressly or impliedly waived the need for the person seeking the insurance to disclose. For example, if the proposal form asks if the person seeking insurance has had "any motoring convictions during the past five years" the implication is that there is no need to disclose motoring convictions which occurred earlier.

Facts which can be reasonably inferred when the information given is not full. For example, it can be reasonably inferred that a man is a widower if he refers to his "late wife"; if this point is relevant, then the insurer has been 'put on enquiry' – i.e. given enough information to put on him the duty to enquire further if he wishes to, but if he does not then he cannot argue 'non-disclosure' of material facts.

Does 'disclosure of material facts' just mean answering the questions on the proposal form truthfully?

No, although that is part of it; however, the duty goes further and requires the person seeking insurance to volunteer any other material facts, even though no questions about them have been asked.

Can other contracts, for example, for the sale of a car, be made a contract uberrimae fidei?

No, in fact at common law another Latin phrase *"caveat emptor"* applies; this means "let the buyer beware" and places the responsibility on the buyer to find out all the facts about the article he is buying; there is no duty on the seller to volunteer information.

This common law duty is however subject to rules such as those applying to misrepresentation and mistake.

Section D

TORT

What does "tort" mean?

The word itself is an old Norman–French word meaning "wrong" – which, of course, tells us nothing; it could be said that all law is concerned with 'wrongs'.

(The word is also adapted for use as an adjective, hence: "tortious offence".)

How can this division of law be distinguished from other 'wrongs'?

Perhaps the key to the answer is the word 'division' for it does identify a number of the features of torts.

First, torts are civil offences. This tells us that they are offences for which the offender will be sued, not prosecuted.

Second, it is a different sub-division from the other important common-law subject "contract". Contracts impose duties upon persons, which they must fulfil or be liable to legal action. But, the duties are (technically) voluntarily undertaken by the parties when they enter the contract.

In tort, persons must fulfil duties that are laid down by the State.

In the 'Divisions of Law' section, it was said that an act can be a crime and a tort; is there any way of recognising which is which?

Many harmful acts are both crimes and tortious offences and the distinguishing feature is the result wanted.

If the desire is to **punish** the offender, he will be prosecuted by the State for the criminal offence he has committed.

If the desire is to obtain **compensation**, an injured party will sue him for the tortious offence.

There is another difference which flows from this; before an act can give rise to a civil action, someone will have had to have been harmed in some way. This is not necessary with a crime. For example, dangerous driving is a crime but it does not give rise to an action in tort unless some damage or injury is caused.

Is there a definition of "tort"?

The problem is that there are a number of definitions and even the most respected authors of books on the subject differ.

However, an acceptable "definition" can be produced by summarising the information given above:

> "A tort is a civil offence, caused by the breach of a duty laid down by the State, for which the common-law remedy is an action for damages."

(Note, lawyers call a person who has committed a tort, a "tortfeasor", meaning a "wrongdoer".)

The expression "injured party" has been used. In how many ways can a person, legally, be injured?

It might be better to say that an 'injured party' is someone who has been harmed. A person can be harmed by being physically injured; his property can be physically damaged; he can be harmed financially; his reputation can be harmed.

Does this mean that if a person has been harmed in some way then he can always sue in tort to obtain compensation?

No, it is quite possible to be harmed by someone without

having the right to sue him for compensation.

For example, a large multi-branch store opens a shop very near a small "one-man" shop.

With its 'economies of scale', the large store can charge less than the small shopkeeper.

The small shop will probably lose trade to the large store; it could be forced out of business as it cannot compete.

Without doubt the small shopkeeper has been harmed – financially – by the large store, but – on the face of it – the large store has committed no offence; it has done nothing **legally** wrong, and so the small shopkeeper has no right of action.

What sorts of "harm" do give a right of legal action?

Those in which a person has a legal right not to be harmed.

The lawyers distinguish between "harm without legal injury" and "legal injury without harm".

If a person is harmed but the person causing the harm has done nothing illegal, then the person harmed has no right of redress (the shopkeeper example above).

But, if a person's legal rights have been injured, then he has a right of action even if no actual harm has been caused.

For example, in *Ashby v. White (1703)* at an election, the returning officer wrongfully refused to allow an elector to cast his vote. The elector successfully sued the returning officer for wrongfully preventing him from exercising his right to vote. But, no harm was done, the candidate for whom the elector wished to vote was elected anyway.

What if the person causing the legal injury meant no harm?

Generally speaking, a person's motives, or intentions, are

irrelevant.

In *Bradford Corporation v. Pickles (1895)* the defendant dug wells on his land in order to harm the Corporation because they would not buy some of his land that he wanted to sell. Digging the wells reduced the amount of water that percolated through his land into the town's reservoirs, and affected the cleanliness of the water that did reach them. It was held that, although he acted with malice, the Corporation had no case against him as he was legally entitled to dig wells on his own land.

In contrast, in *Wilkinson v. Downton (1897)* the defendant told the plaintiff – a married woman – that her husband had been badly injured in an accident. It was quite untrue, the defendant intended to play a 'joke' on the wife. He had no intention of causing her harm but on hearing his 'news', the wife suffered shock (recognised in law in the same category as a physical injury). The Court held, that although he meant no harm, he was liable for the legal injury he had caused.

Are there different types of tortious offence?

Yes, there are a number but three of the most important are:

1. Nuisance, of which there are two forms: 'private' and 'public'.
2. Trespass, to the person; to land, and, to property (goods), and
3. Negligence.

Defamation (libel and slander) is another important tort but is outside the scope of this book.

What is meant by "nuisance"?

There are two forms of nuisance: private nuisance and public nuisance, and each has its own meaning.

What is the definition of Private Nuisance?

Private nuisance may be defined as: "unlawful interference with a person's use or enjoyment of land, or some right over, or in connection with it".

How can a person's 'use or enjoyment' of his land be interfered with?

In a great many ways, of which the following examples – all taken from actual cases – may help to comprehend the range:

– smells, smoke, fumes from neighbours' premises;
– noises from neighbours' premises – examples range from steam-driven pile-drivers to piano playing;
– water unnecessarily flowing from a neighbour's roof;
– interference with a person's rights over land – by obstructing a 'right-of-way';
– branches of a tree growing over the premises' boundary.

Does this mean that a person could be sued for nuisance if he had a bonfire in his back garden?

No, at least not on those bare facts.

A balance has to be struck between the right of a person to do what he likes on his own land, and the rights of his neighbour not to be interfered with by the exercise of those rights.

A compromise usually has to be made and, for instance, rarely will an isolated incident ever be sufficient to be a 'nuisance'. The essence of a nuisance is that it is continuous or recurring. (A bonfire in the back garden every weekend.)

Who can sue in private nuisance?

The key is the **land**. For example, it is not that a person objects to a smell that gives him the right of action, but that his enjoyment, or use, of his land is interfered with by the smell.

It follows therefore that the **occupier** of land can sue, that is someone who has possession of it, or has some other proprietary interest in it. This can include a tenant, even in certain circumstances a weekly tenant.

On the other hand, it would exclude lodgers or guests – and members of the occupier's family!

Who can be sued?

First, the person who created the nuisance.

Then, depending upon the circumstances, others might be liable (for example, the landlord).

What is a Public Nuisance?

Public nuisance was explained in *Attorney-General v. PYA Quarries (1957)* by Romer L.J. (Lord Justice Romer)

> "an act or omission which materially affects the reasonable comfort and convenience of life of a class of Her Majesty's subjects who come within the sphere or neighbourhood of its operation; the question whether the number of persons affected is sufficient to constitute a class is one of fact in every case, and it is sufficient to show that a representative cross-section of that class has been so affected for an injunction to issue".

For example: whenever a car is parked on a road, unless at a meter or a place designated for parking, it is causing an obstruction. It is causing an obstruction because other persons cannot use, pass over, that area of the road on which the car is parked.

Other road-users will be inconvenienced by having to go round the car, they may have to slow or wait in order to do so.

Road-users are a class of Her Majesty's subjects. All road-users will not be inconvenienced by the parked car but a representative cross-section, that is, those road-users using the road at that time, will be.

What are the main differences between 'private' and 'public' nuisances?

The first, obvious difference is that the effect of a public nuisance is more widespread: it affects a section of the public.

The same act, however, is capable of being either a private nuisance or a public nuisance; for example, excessive playing of a piano might give the next-door neighbour the right to sue in private nuisance. If that piano playing took place in a high density block of flats it could result in a public nuisance action being taken.

A second important difference is that public nuisance is a crime as well as a tort; private nuisance is a tort only.

The reason why public nuisance is a crime is probably more for the sake of procedural convenience than any other. Rather than having a multitude of private actions, all for the same set of facts, the offence is dealt with by one criminal action.

Only if an individual has suffered harm to a greater extent than other members of the "class of . . . subjects" can that individual bring a civil action.

For example in *Chesterfield Corporation v. Arthur Robinson (Transport) Ltd (1955)* the defendants were transporting an outsize load of 83 tons on a main road. Due to their fault the road was obstructed for 76 hours. All the road users who were using that road were inconvenienced and the defendants were liable for a criminal prosecution. However, the plaintiffs were affected more than anyone else – they had to re-route their omnibuses; consequently they had the right to sue.

It would appear that obstructing a public road is a public nuisance; what other examples of public nuisance are there?

The act itself could well be the same as gives rise to a private nuisance action, it is the widespread effect that is crucial; however, public nuisance actions have been brought because of noise, vibrations and dust from a quarry; because of a failure to clear up the "dead dogs and cats, vegetable refuse, fish, offal, rubbish and all kinds of filth" which people had thrown on to the defendant's land; against a golf club for having a tee and hole adjacent to the highway (balls were frequently hit on to the highway); against the organisers of a festival of pop-music which generated large-scale noise, traffic and apprehension.

Why is "trespass" an important tort? Doesn't it just mean being on someone else's land?

Most lay people probably think so, but the word 'trespass' covers more than this.

The word itself merely means "wrong", but in the sense of being a tort it implies an attack on a person's rights, whether they are his personal rights, his rights to his belongings or his right to his land.

It is convenient to look at these rights one at a time:

a) **Trespass to the person**; of which there are three forms:

    i)   **Assault**: threatening someone with, or causing them to expect, immediate violence to their person.

        Arising from this – threatening words **by themselves** are not enough to amount to an assault; the anticipation must be of **immediate** violence, and the violence threatened must be towards the person himself, not, for example, his property.

    ii)   **Battery**: unlawfully touching someone against their will. This might be directly, e.g. punching; indirectly e.g. with a stick; or with a missile, e.g. a thrown stone, or a bullet. It must be against their will, and it must be unlawful; for example, being grabbed by a police officer is probably against a 'suspect's' will but, depending upon the facts can be lawful.

It is not necessary for the 'touching' to be violent, for example, kissing someone against their will is battery.

Normally battery is combined with assault – the victim anticipates a punch on the nose before the aggressor's fist make contact; however assault is very possible without battery and it is possible to have battery without assault (for example, a blow on the head struck from behind).

iii) **False Imprisonment**: unlawfully depriving a person of his complete freedom of movement.

It is not false imprisonment merely to prevent a person going where he wants to go. In *Bird v. Jones (1845)* the plaintiff wanted to cross Hammersmith Bridge by the public footpath; he was wrongfully prevented from doing so and sued for false imprisonment. His action failed as he could have returned the way that he had come.

It is not necessary for the person to know that his freedom of movement has been prevented; e.g. locking the bedroom door of someone asleep in the room, and unlocking it before he awakes is nevertheless false imprisonment.

b) **Trespass to land**

This is the meaning of 'trespass' that most people recognise, but it also has variations:

i)   Unlawfully entering another's land, by crossing the boundary of his land or by crossing from a 'public' part of his land to a 'private' part.

For example, customers are permitted to come onto

a garage's land; in most cases they may enter the building and go to a 'reception' area. However they are often not allowed to go into the workshop unless specifically invited.

It would be trespassing if a customer entered such a workshop without permission.

ii) Unlawfully remaining on land once permission to be on the land has been withdrawn. Although someone may have entered another's land lawfully, once the permission to do so has been withdrawn, his continued presence constitutes a trespass (allowing him reasonable time to get off, of course).

iii) Placing objects on another's land, e.g. dumping rubbish.

Signs saying "Trespassers will be prosecuted" may be seen, particularly in the countryside; lawyers sometimes refer to these as "wooden lies" because they should read "trespassers will be sued", trespass being a civil offence.

There are however some situations where Parliament has, by statute, made trespassing a criminal offence.

Places where this may occur are Service establishments, such as RAF stations, Army camps, Naval dockyards; Atomic energy establishments and other government establishments.

c) **Trespass to Goods**

This means interfering with goods in the possession of another. Note that all that is necessary is for the goods to be in the lawful possession of someone else; that other person need not be the owner.

It applies therefore to goods which are in someone's possession on loan, or under a hire-purchase agreement and although a bailee can sue a bailor cannot.

The interference can amount to no more than intentionally touching the goods and a few examples from actual cases will indicate something of the scope of this tort: 'scratching the panel of a coach; 'removing a tyre from a car'; 'moving a car'; (and presumably throwing something at a car and writing in the dust on a car). Injuring or destroying goods would also come under this heading.

This tort may be committed against an animal, examples of which include: beating a dog; whipping a horse; shooting racing pigeons. It has been held that this tort can be committed, as far as animals go, without actually touching them, e.g. chasing cattle.

Conversion

Although this is a separate tort, it is so close to 'trespass to goods' that it is convenient to deal with it here.

Conversion means treating someone else's property (goods) as though it were your own. Unlike trespass to goods which is interfering with another's **possession** of the goods, conversion is concerned with the **ownership** of the goods. The owner's ownership is being challenged by someone else treating the goods as if they were theirs.

An obvious example of this would be to sell goods which belong to someone else – as could be the case when a motor trader takes a car in part-exchange from a customer who was not the legal owner (for instance when still under a hire-purchase agreement) and the motor trader subsequently sells it.

What is meant by the tort of Negligence?

Arguably this is the most important tortious offence today, books having been written on this tort alone. Part of its value is its general application, which means that it can be used in new situations as they arise.

One of its most important applications in the past has been to cover the situation where a manufacturer has been 'negligent' in producing a defective product which kills or injures someone. Since the introduction of the Consumer Protection Act 1987 Part I, a new concept of 'strict liability' in tort for defective products has been introduced (see Part 3).

Although the word 'negligence' is commonly used to mean 'carelessness' the tort of 'negligence' has a precise meaning, and to be successful in an action brought in negligence, the plaintiff must **prove** three things:

a) that he was owed a duty of care by the defendant,

b) that the defendant was in breach of that duty of care, and

c) that he, the plaintiff, suffered damage because of that breach of duty.

Who owes whom a duty of care?

A good starting point is to quote a famous passage from the judgment of Lord Atkin in the case of *Donoghue v. Stevenson (1932)*;

> "You must take reasonable care to avoid acts or omissions which you can reasonably foresee would be likely to injure your neighbour. Who, then, in law is my neighbour? The answer seems to be – persons who are so closely and directly affected by my act that I ought reasonably to have them in contemplation as being so affected when I am directing my mind to the acts or omissions which are called in question."

It is not an absolute statement of the law; we have seen earlier that it is possible to foresee that an act might harm someone but still be legally able to do it.

The statement does however establish the criteria for determining to whom a duty of care is owed. The so-called "neighbour test" is commonly applied today.

What are the facts of *Donoghue v. Stevenson* and why is it such an important case?

The facts of the case are as follows:

Ginger beer was manufactured and bottled in an opaque bottle. The ginger beer was sold to a retailer, a cafe owner. It was bought by a woman for a young woman friend who drank a glass. A second glass was poured and out from the bottle came the decomposed remains of a snail. The young woman became ill!

As she was not a party to the contract, she had no contractual rights and so the action was brought, in negligence, against the manufacturer of the drink.

The crux of the matter was whether the manufacturer owed her a duty of care – can one owe a duty of care to someone one doesn't even know exists? The answer is "yes", the manufacturer could 'reasonably foresee' that **someone** would drink that bottle of ginger beer; he should 'reasonably foresee' that if the drink was not pure and wholesome, the person drinking was likely to be 'injured'. Therefore, the young woman was owed a duty of care by the manufacturer.

To apply the principle to a motor trade situation: if a mechanic fits a wheel to a car, the law expects him to foresee that if he doesn't fit it properly then it might come off when the car is in motion. The law expects him to foresee that if it does come off when the car is in motion, then the car might be damaged, other cars might be damaged, persons in the car might be injured, persons in other cars might be injured, persons in the vicinity e.g. on the pavement, might be injured.

The mechanic owes a duty of care to all these people who might be legally injured, whether the injuries are personal or to their property. The fact that he, presumably, does not know any of them is irrelevant.

How strict is this duty, how careful must one be?

This is a critical matter, the question of how much care a person must exercise. The answer is a **reasonable** amount, the amount the 'reasonable man' would exercise in the same situation.

This concept of a 'reasonable man' has been developed over the years. He is the 'average man', the 'man in the street' and has been likened to the 'man on the Clapham omnibus'.

There is nothing special about the 'reasonable man'; he is not especially clever or wise, he is not especially strong or tough; he does have commonsense and has learned from experience.

So, when the question arises of whether the defendant was in breach of his duty of care, the amount of care that he took will be compared with the amount of care this abstract figure, the 'reasonable man' would have taken had he been in his place.

It is different if a person has, or purports to have, a particular skill or expertise.

The amount of care that a brain surgeon must take is not that of the 'average man in the street'; nor is the amount of care that a mechanic must take!

Whenever a person is exercising a particular skill then the standard of care legally expected of him is that of the average person having that skill.

The brain surgeon must observe the standard of care that the average brain surgeon has. The mechanic must show the standard of care of the average skilled mechanic. Not the best brain surgeon, or mechanic, because there is only one who is **the** best, just the average brain surgeon or the average skilled mechanic.

Note, the same standard is required if a person purports to have the skill but in fact has not (something to remember when tempted to take on a job beyond one's capability).

What is the third essential that has to be proved?

That, because the defendant owed him a duty of care – and was not careful enough – he, the plaintiff, suffered harm.

The case of *Barnett v. Chelsea and Kensington Hospital (1969)* gives a very clear example of this:

Early one morning a night-watchman called at the defendants' hospital with the complaint that he was vomiting. The duty nurse contacted the doctor on duty and reported the matter to him. Without coming to see the man the doctor said he should go home and see his own doctor in the morning. Later that day the man died of arsenical poisoning. The man's widow sued the hospital claiming that through their negligence her husband had died. She lost.

It was agreed that the doctor owed the watchman a duty of care; it was agreed that the doctor was in breach of that duty, he should have seen the man, but on the facts presented, the courts were satisfied that the man would have died anyway; there was nothing that the doctor could have done that would have saved his life.

It is not a question of 'making his last hours more comfortable' or anything like that. The issue was: was the man's death a direct consequence of the doctor's breach of his duty of care; and the answer was "no".

What is meant by "vicarious liability"?

It means that someone, other than the tortfeasor i.e. the person who actually commits the tort, is liable. The tortfeasor is always liable; vicarious liability does not introduce an either/or situation, if a person is vicariously liable, it is in addition to the tortfeasor's liability.

Why would someone else be liable for a person's torts?

Obviously there must be a good reason for this to be possible and it is because of the relationship that exists between this other person and the tortfeasor. They are related or connected in such a way that it is proper for this other person to be liable also.

What sort of relationships give rise to this vicarious liability?

There are a number, but probably the most important relationship in this connection is that of employer and employee.

Does this mean that an employer is vicariously liable for the torts of his employees?

Not quite; first of all it depends upon the type of employer/employee relationship that exists.

If the employee is under a '**contract of service**' (still referred to as a "master and servant" relationship) then the employer is vicariously liable for the torts committed by his employee – whilst acting in the course of his employment.

If the employee is under a '**contract for services**', i.e. when the employee is an 'independent contractor', then, subject to four exception given later, the employer is not vicariously liable.

What is meant by "in the course of his employment"?

Two simple cases show this quite clearly:

In *Limpus v. LGOC (1862)*; it was the days of horse-drawn omnibuses and the rivalry between the competing bus companies meant that their drivers would at times race each other and try to "cut each other up". These practices were obviously dangerous and the LGOC issued a warning to all their drivers that they were on no account to engage in such activities.

One of their drivers did; there was an accident and the LGOC was sued (Note, the driver could, of course, be sued but he would be have been unlikely to have any money. The real hope of obtaining compensation was if the LGOC – the employer – was vicariously liable).

In their defence the LGOC said that the driver was **not** acting in the course of his employment, he was not employed to drive in this dangerous manner; furthermore they, the LGOC, had issued strict instructions to their drivers not to drive in this fashion.

The plaintiffs won. The court held that the driver was employed **to drive**. He was driving. True he was driving in a manner not desired by the defendants, true he was driving in a manner they had expressly forbidden but nevertheless he was driving, and that was what he was employed to do.

In contrast, in *Beard v. LGOC (1900)* – (yes, the same London General Omnibus Company) – a bus had reached the end of its route and had to be turned round for the return journey. To be helpful the conductor got into the driver's seat and started the manoeuvre, whilst doing so he caused an accident. The company was sued.

The plaintiff's case was that he was an employee of the company, he was working for them at the time and what he was doing was intended to be for their benefit. The plaintiff lost.

The court held that the man was employed as a conductor, not a driver, therefore driving was not 'acting in the course of his employment'.

An employee may still be 'acting in the course of his employment' even if he is doing something that, strictly speaking, he is not employed to do but nevertheless is 'part of the job'.

For example, in *Staton v. NCB (1957)* an employee was held to be still within the course of his employment whilst he was cycling across his employer's site to go to an office to collect his wages.

There are several cases where employees, working away from their base, have stopped at, or gone to, a place to have a meal and have been held to have been acting in the course of their employment.

A judge, Baron Parke, in *Joel v. Morison* (1834) coined the phrase:

"... it may still be in the course of his employment even if the servant is not acting strictly in the performance of his duty provided he is not "on a frolic of his own""

a test that is still widely quoted today.

In what circumstances would an employer be vicariously liable for torts committed by an independent contractor he was employing?

The first could be where the employer told the contractor to commit the tort; or where the employer did not take proper care when selecting the contractor, and employed someone without the necessary skills. In both these circumstances the employer would be liable for torts committed by the contractor, but, as it is the employer who is really at fault he would be primarily liable, not vicariously.

The real exceptions to the rule that an employer is not vicariously liable for torts committed by an independent contractor are:

a) **Offences connected with the highway**

The highway is regarded as so important – it is the right of way for the public – that liability should attach to whoever caused the situation to arise.

In *Tarry v. Ashton (1876)*, the defendant had a lamp fixed to the wall of his house; the lamp hung over the footpath (a part of the highway). An independent contractor was employed to repair the lamp. Due to the contractor's faulty work, the lamp fell and injured the plaintiff who was passing by. Held: the defendant was liable.

b) **Where the work being carried out is intrinsically hazardous**

This is another example of the employer being liable because he has caused the situation to arise, for example, in employing an independent contractor to load or unload explosives which, if carelessly handled, will explode.

c) **Breaches of Statutory duties**

For example, under the Factories Acts it is an offence to have certain moving machinery unfenced. If a factory owner should employ a contractor to carry out some work in the factory and that contractor brought with him his own machinery of that type, which was unfenced, and in consequence an accident occurred, the factory owner would be liable.

d) **Under the Rule in *Rylands v. Fletcher***

This was a case (in 1866) where the decision was so important that it has become a tort in its own right.

The facts of the case were that a millowner employed an independent contractor to construct a reservoir on his land to provide water for his mill.

Whilst doing so, the contractor came across some old shafts and underground passages. These actually connected with mines belonging to the millowner's neighbour, although this was not realised at the time for the shafts appeared to be filled with earth. The contractor did not block them up and when the reservoir was filled with water it burst through the old shafts and flooded the neighbour's mines.

There was no argument, the contractor had been negligent and the millowner had not, however, the case went through the various courts, finally reaching the House of Lords. The final decision, the "Rule" itself is a composite of the judgment of Blackburn J. (Mr Justice Blackburn) in the (then) Exchequer Chamber and an 'amendment' by Lord Cairns in the House of Lords.

The Rule can be stated as:

"that the person who for his own purposes brings on his land and collects and keeps there (something which was not naturally there) and which is likely to do mischief if it escapes, must keep it in at his peril, and if he does not do so, is *prima facie* answerable for all the damage which is the natural consequence of its escape".

Although the original case was concerned with the escape of water from the defendant's land (it was "unnatural" for such a large quantity of water to be there) the Rule has successfully been applied to the 'escape' of: fire; gas; explosions, electricity; oil; noxious fumes; colliery spoil; rusty wire from a decayed fence; vibration; poisonous vegetation; a flag-pole; a chair-o-plane and even, although this particular decision has been strongly criticised ever since, where a landowner allowed gypsies to camp on his land, the said gypsies allegedly causing harm on surrounding land.

Is there any way that a tortfeasor can escape the consequences of his act?

Yes; there are a number of so-called "defence in tort"; some apply only to specific torts – there are three, for example, which apply only to the torts of defamation – but there are others which have a more general application.

Note that when a defendant pleads one of these defences he is in effect saying "I did it but, for the following reason, I should not be held liable". He is **not** saying "I did not do it"; a different matter altogether.

The following are the more common defences:

a) **Volenti non fit injuria**

Yes, we start off in Latin with the most important defence; but, it is always quoted in Latin so the phrase is probably worth recognising. It means that a person cannot be (legally) injured if he consented to take the risk of being harmed. (Perhaps more literally: a volunteer cannot be injured.)

A few applications if this rule will show how important it is.

If a patient did not consent to surgery, the surgeon would be liable for battery (The 'consent' form gives the surgeon written proof of the patient's consent.)

A boxer, by taking part in the fight, has, by implication, consented to being struck – otherwise battery. So has the rugby football player and indeed a participant in any "dangerous" sport.

Spectators at dangerous sports, it has been held, have impliedly consented to take the risk of being harmed; *Hall v. Brooklands Auto Racing Club (1933)*.

Persons in crowds, e.g. on the London Underground at 'rush hour', at a popular soccer match, at New Year's Eve celebrations have impliedly consented to being pushed and shoved.

Note the defence is "volenti" non fit injuria, not "scienti" non fit injuria. In other words the injured party must have "consented" to take the risk, at least by implication, not merely "known" of the risk.

In *Smith v. Baker (1891)* the plaintiff was employed on a site where a crane was swinging loads of stones over the spot where he was working. He complained to the supervisor, with no effect. Some stones fell on him and he sued. The defendants raised the defence of "volenti non fit injuria" but this was rejected there being no evidence that the plaintiff had 'consented' to take the risk and mere knowledge was not enough.

b) Unavoidable accident

This defence may be raised in the case of an accident which was not avoidable by any precautions that a reasonable man could be expected to take.

In *Stanley v. Powell (1891)* the plaintiff was working for a pheasant shooting party when he was hit by a shot which although fired (safely) forward from the party had hit a tree and ricocheted back.

c) An Act of God

The defence most easily remembered, and which seldom applies. The defence requires an **unexpected natural** phenomenon, such as a thunderbolt, a flash of lightning, an exceptionally heavy fall of rain, an earthquake, a tornado.

Although these can be described as Acts of God the majority have never been put forward in a court of law.

One that was successful, at the time – for it has since been criticised by the House of Lords – was raised when an exceptionally heavy fall of rain caused water in an artificial pond to overflow its banks and cause damage on a neighbouring property.

d) Necessity

Where the tortious act was carried out to prevent a greater harm; a simple example would be a fireman breaking down the door of a house that was on fire in order to rescue the occupants.

e) Act of a stranger

A defence available to a defendant who can show that it was a stranger e.g. trespasser, who was the cause of the tortious act; for example, where a third person deliberately blocked up a lavatory basin in the defendant's premises, thereby flooding the plaintiff's premises.

f) Statutory Authority

Where the defendant, acting in accordance with authority given him by statute, does an act which, without the authority, would have amounted to a tortious offence.

For example, digging a hole in a road is prima facie a public nuisance (obstruction of the highway) but a local authority has statutory authority to do so.

g) **Private Defence – Self Defence**
Where the defendant has used force to defend himself, or his property. It is most important to appreciate that this defence will be effective **only** if the amount of force used in defence is proportionate to the harm threatened.

A learned judge has said that one's first duty when threatened with violence is to run away!! For if one can run away then one will escape harm without having to use force onself.

It follows that if one can run away and doesn't, but elects to stay and fight then one cannot raise the defence of self-defence, for it was not necessary in order to escape harm.

What is "contributory negligence", is it another defence in tort?

Not really, although it would be pleaded by the defendant.

To make it clear; the 'defences in tort' we have been considering all have one thing in common: in all cases the defendant is admitting that he performed the act, but, for the reason he is putting forward, he should not be found liable.

If his defence is successful, the defendant will be found not liable.

Contributory negligence is different.

In these cases the defendant, having been found liable, is saying that the plaintiff would not have been harmed, or so badly harmed, if he had not been at fault himself.

If the defendant succeeds in his plea, the court will reduce the amount of damages they award to the plaintiff by the same percentage that they consider the plaintiff contributed to this own injuries.

For example, a motorist driving carelessly along a road hits a pedestrian who carelessly steps off the pavement. The pedestrian sues the motorist.

The court will first establish whether the motorist was at fault, if he is not the case would end there. Having decided that he was to blame it then considers how much the pedestrian was at fault – it could decide it was 50–50. It would decide the amount of damages, say £1,000, and say that as the pedestrian was 50% to blame for his injuries the damages would be reduced by 50%. The plaintiff would get only £500.

To sum up, a defendant would plead a 'defence in tort' in order to escape liability; he would plead 'contributory negligence' in order to get a reduction in the amount of damages that he has to pay.

Can you avoid liability for damage arising from your own negligence, e.g. by using a disclaimer?

No, not if you are trying to avoid liability for death or personal injury arising from negligence. This sort of disclaimer will have no legal effect (Unfair Contract Terms Act 1977).

Section E
CRIMINAL LAW

What is meant by a 'crime'?

Strangely enough there is no satisfactory definition of a 'crime'. The only real answer is to say that a crime is a crime because the State says so. The offence may be criminal at Common Law or because an Act describes an offence and proclaims it to be a criminal offence.

There is the view that crimes are against the State and the State will take action against criminal offenders. The State itself feels threatened by the act. Murder, obviously, is against an individual but the State feels threatened by someone killing one of its members.

With a crime as serious as murder, this particular viewpoint makes sense, but it suggests that crimes are offences which are so serious that the State as a community feels threatened. If all crimes were serious this could be true, but there are many crimes which are not all that serious – for example, parking offences.

It is not therefore, the seriousness of the offence which makes it a crime. Serious offences probably are crimes but so are minor offences which can be considered to be against the community.

As was implied earlier, the most simple definition of a crime is: "an offence which a statute designates as a crime and for which criminal proceedings are to be followed".

It said in Section B, that an act could be a crime and, for example, a tort. Can it really be 'against the State' *and* 'against an individual'?

Yes; don't forget that the State comprises individuals, so

the majority of crimes will have harmed individuals; it is really a matter of whether the State takes action on behalf of its members or leaves it to the individuals to take action themselves, and some offending acts enable both possibilities to be followed.

If we take the taxicab example in Section B:

a) The driver could be prosecuted for dangerous driving. Dangerous driving is obviously a danger to the community so the State will punish an offender. This might teach him a lesson – not to do it again; it might deter others from driving dangerously when they see that he has been punished.

b) The passenger was owed a duty of care; not because he was a passenger but because individuals are under a duty not to do something that would harm another (see the tort of negligence for a fuller explantion of this duty.)

   So, when the taxicab driver did not take sufficient care and the passenger was injured, the passenger had the right to sue the driver for compensation.

The State wants to punish him – and to deter him and others from doing it again; the injured passenger wants compensation for his injuries.

Can a person commit a crime without knowing it?

Yes, and for several quite different reasons:

a) He might not know that his act was a criminal offence. This in itself will not help his case, the lawyers have a phrase "ignorance of the law is no defence": he will be found guilty even though he did not know that his act was a crime. Although apparently unfair, this has to be the rule otherwise every defendant would be able to plead that he did not know he was doing wrong; it can be unfair because **no one** in the country knows **all** the laws by which he is bound.

b) He might have been incapacitated in some way at the time, for example, by infancy (too young); insanity (a defence subject to strict rules); diminished responsibility; drunkenness; etc.

c) It might have been what is referred to as a "strict" offence, of which more later.

What is necessary for a person to be convicted of a crime?

The prosecution must prove:

a) beyond "a reasonable doubt", that

b) the accused had **carried out the act** (actus reus), and

c) had **intended** to carry out the act (mens rea)

('c' is not always necessary with some modern statutory crimes.)

What exactly does "actus reus" mean?

The actus reus is the act or omission which constitutes the crime.

For example, if a person who is disqualified from driving is charged with "driving a motor vehicle on a road when disqualified . . ." it would have to be proved that he was "driving". What is meant by "driving"? Apart from the obvious meaning, a person has been held to have been driving when sitting in the driver's seat and steering the vehicle with someone else pushing it; similarly, when "coasting" down a hill, just operating the steering and brakes. On the other hand pushing and steering a vehicle when walking alongside it has been held **not** to be driving.

It can happen that the act must have a result before it can be the actus reus of a crime. Murder can be committed by stabbing a man, but if the man were already dead when stabbed the act of stabbing could not be the actus reus of murder.

On the other hand, perjury – telling a lie whilst under oath – is a crime from the moment the deliberate lie was told; it is not necessary to see what result the lie has.

What is the mens rea?

Mens rea is often loosely interpreted as "a guilty mind", suggesting that the defendant intended to commit the crime; that he is morally blameworthy for his action.

Nowadays the tests for mens rea are more technical and identify the following different mental attitudes:

a) Intention: if the person intends the consequences of his act, e.g. a person buys a stolen car, knowing that it is stolen.

b) Recklessness: if the person foresees the possible outcome of his act but does not care, e.g. a person buys a stolen car from a well-known car thief although he does not **know** that it is stolen.

c) Negligence: if the person does something that a sensible person could have foreseen could have undesirable consequences, e.g. a person buys a (stolen) car, for half the usual price, from "a man in a pub".

d) Blameless Inadvertence: if the person does something where a sensible person would not have anticipated the consequences of his act, e.g. a person buys a stolen car from a reputable motor trader.

Intention, obviously a person who intends the consequences of his act should be held guilty.

If he is blameless, equally obviously, he should not.

The dividing line must be between the two and at common law the line was drawn between recklessness and negligence. Nowadays there are crimes where it is sufficient mens rea for the defendant to have been negligent.

What is meant by a "strict" offence?

An offence which does not require mens rea, at least not in the full sense of the words.

An example may help.

To drive a car with faulty brakes is a strict offence.

If the driver drove the car knowing that the brakes were faulty he would have carried out the act (the actus reus) of the crime with the intention to do so (the mens rea). Quite rightly he would be guilty of the offence.

But, supposing the driver was an old lady of 90 who had no technical knowledge but did know that cars could go wrong and so had her car professionally serviced once a week.

The actus reus is present but, surely, she was quite blameless.

She might well be, but the offence is a strict offence; the only mens rea required is the intention to 'drive the car', not to 'drive the car with faulty brakes'.

She intended to drive, she did drive, the car had faulty brakes; she committed the offence of driving the car with faulty brakes. (On the facts described it is almost certain that although she would be found guilty of the offence, she would be given an absolute discharge). Other examples of strict offences are to be found in the Trade Descriptions Act 1968 (see Part 3).

What is the difference between "using, causing or permitting to be used"?

Many offences have this preamble or words that are similar. They are in fact three different ways of committing the offence.

To take an example:

"Using, causing or permitting to be used on a road a motor

vehicle or trailer with defective tyres".

The normal "use" of a vehicle is for it to be driven, therefore the driver of the vehicle is "using" it. If the vehicle is being driven for the benefit of someone else – the owner – then that person is also "using" it. Most commercial vehicles used in the course of business are therefore being "used" by their drivers **and** the businesses which own them. Less commonly, a private car could be driven by someone else for the benefit of its owner, in which case both will be "using" it.

"Causing" means that someone was responsible for – in our example – the vehicle being used. The person driving the vehicle could be regarded as "causing it to be used" but as they can already be charged with "using" it, "causing" enables someone other than the driver or owner, but who is culpable, to be charged.

A very good example is the commercial vehicle. The business owning it and the driver are both using it; the transport manager who told the driver to drive that vehicle, has "caused it to be used".

"Permitting" has a more normal meaning. If the owner of a vehicle allows – or "permits" – someone else to drive it, the person driving it is "using" it, the owner is "permitting it to be used".

Are there any other differences between these three ways of committing an offence?

Yes, "using" is a strict offence – as we saw earlier with the 'old lady' example.

In the commercial vehicle example therefore, the driver, and the owner of the vehicle when it is being used on his behalf, are both strictly liable.

They are "users" and are "using the vehicle" with defective tyres.

The offence of "permitting" and, certainly since 1974, the offence of "causing", are not strict offences.

Therefore, if a vehicle with defective tyres is used on a road, the persons using it will be guilty, but for anyone (e.g. the transport manager) to be guilty of causing or permitting it to be used, it is necessary that they knew the tyres were defective.

They are causing – or permitting – the vehicle to be "used with defective tyres".

An earlier answer suggested that although guilty, a defendant would be absolutely discharged. Why was this?

There are several reasons why a defendant might not receive the normal 'punishment' – or might not be punished at all:

a) Mitigation; before a sentence is passed the defendent will be asked if there is any reason why the normal penalty should not be imposed. His response will be a plea in mitigation – a plea to reduce the severity of the sentence – and this would be taken into consideration when determining the sentence.

b) Special reasons; sometimes the law itself provides that "unless the court for special reasons thinks fit . . . to award a lesser sentence. . . ".

c) Statutory defence; sometimes a statute states a set of circumstances which, if they apply, will be a complete defence to the charge.

Some examples of the above are:

Mitigation. Under the 'penalty points' system, once a driver has accumulated 12 points within 3 years he will be disqualified. Someone for whom a driving licence is **essential**, e.g. a doctor, may enter that fact in mitigation and the court may decide not to disqualify.

Special reason. "Driving or attempting to drive when unfit to do so through drink or drugs" is an offence which carries the penalty of obligatory disqualification for not less than twelve months.

However, s.34(1) Road Traffic Offenders Act 1988 says that the Court may "for special reasons" order disqualification for a shorter period or not at all.

Unlike a plea in mitigation the reasons looked for here are not to do with the offender, they are to do with the offence.

An example which is often given: a doctor is off duty at home during the evening and has several drinks (enough to put him over the limit). An emergency call comes for him to attend a patient. There is no alternative way to get to the patient except by his own car and there is no one else available to drive the car. He drives it himself and is stopped etc. etc.

It is suggested that the courts would consider this to be a 'special reason' for not disqualifying him.

Note, that it is not who or what the defendant is that is considered, but the circumstances of the offence.

If the doctor hoped to escape the consequences because he was a doctor and needed his car, he would put this fact forward in mitigation, which might help him if the offence carried a 'discretionary disqualification' but would not if it were an 'obligatory disqualification'.

Statutory defence. An example of a statutory defence can be seen in s.143(3) Road Traffic Act 1988, the gist of which is:

A person charged with using a motor vehicle which is not insured **shall not be convicted** if he proves that it was his employer's vehicle, he was driving it in the course of his employment, and he did not know that it was not insured.

PART 2: INDUSTRIAL AND COMMERCIAL LAW

by

Peter Groves

CONTENTS

Section A

EMPLOYMENT LAW

Contracts of Employment

Do Contracts of Employment have to be in Writing?

Not entirely. Every employee works under a contract of employment, although not all have a written contract. The law does not require the contract to be in writing, although all employees must be given a written statement setting out the main terms of their contract of employment. This written statement must include in a single document items a) to h) listed below.

When must these particulars be given?

Within two months after the employee starts work.

What must be included?

The law requires that the particulars specify:

a) the identity of the parties to the contract;

b) the date on which the employment began (and, if it is for a fixed term, the date on which it will end);

c) the date on which the employee's period of continuous employment began (this is important as it determines when the employee qualifies for protection from unfair dismissal, etc., and sometimes a previous period of employment is included);

d) the scale or rate of remuneration, or the method of calculating it;

e) the intervals at which remuneration will be paid (usually weekly or monthly);

f) hours of work (normal hours plus any required over-time);

g) holiday entitlement;

h) provisions relating to incapacity due to sickness or injury, including entitlement to sick pay;

i) pensions and pension schemes;

j) length of notice required on both sides to terminate employment;

k) job title.

If there are no particulars under g), h) or i) this fact must be stated.

Unless fewer than 20 people are employed on the date employment begins, the particulars must also include a note specifying any disciplinary rules applicable to the employee, or referring to a document which is reasonably accessible to the employee and which contains them. The note must also state who the employee must apply to if he is dissatisfied with any disciplinary decision relating to him, and who he can go to with any grievance he might have and how to apply for it to be redressed.

If he must take any other steps to appeal against a disciplinary decision or air a grievance these must also be specified, or be contained in a document to which reference is made and which is reasonably accessible to the employee.

The written statement must be provided to the employee within two months after the employment begins.

Periods of Notice

1) How much notice is an employee entitled to?

The Employment Rights Act 1996 specifies that after an employee has been in a job four weeks he is entitled to a week's notice, and thereafter he is entitled to one further week's notice for each year he has worked, up to a maximum of twelve.

If the contract is silent as to the length of notice to be given, the Courts will imply a reasonable period. This will depend on the length of the employee's service, the nature and security of his job, his age, and other factors. If the contract specifies a period of notice then, subject to the statutory minimum, that is the length of notice which must be given.

2) **How much notice must the employee give?**
The employee's obligation is to give a week's notice when he has been continuously employed for one month or more. Usually, this will be extended by the contract.

3) **What is payment in lieu of notice?**
Often, payment is made in lieu of notice. This means that rather than requiring an employee whose employment he has terminated to work out his period of notice, the employer gives him the money which he would have earned in that period and sends him on his way immediately.

What is a written statement of reasons for dismissal?

The legislation allows an employee with two continuous years of service to request a written statement of the reasons for his dismissal. If the employer unreasonably refuses to provide a statement of reasons within 14 days the employee may complain to the Industrial Tribunal which will order the employer to pay him two weeks' wages as a penalty.

What is an itemised pay statement and when is an employee entitled to one?

To answer the first question first, section 8 of the Employment Rights Act 1996 says that every employee has the right to be given an itemised pay statement in writing. It must be given at or before the time at which any payment of wages or salary is made to him. The same section specifies that it must contain the following information:

a) The gross amount of wages or salary.

b) The amounts of any deductions and the purposes for which they are made; section 9 allows a more generalised statement to be given.

c) The net amount payable.

d) Where different parts of the net amount are paid in different ways, the amount and method of payment of each part-payment.

What does the law say about how wages can be paid?

It used to be the case that the wages of what were referred to as "workmen" had to be paid in coin of the realm. This was required by the Truck Acts 1831 to 1940, which had nothing to do with commercial vehicles but were intended to stop employers giving their workers tokens to spend in the company shop, or goods instead of money. The Truck Acts were repealed in their entirety by the Wages Act 1986, along with all other legal restrictions on how wages can be paid; so the answer to the question is, "nothing".

Can an employer make deductions from wages?

Yes, in certain limited circumstances. The Attachment of Earnings Act 1971 enables creditors to get their hands on part of a debtor's wages at source, so he cannot avoid his obligations. It applies to civil debts arising from High Court or County Court judgments greater than £15 , and County Courts have the necessary powers to make attachment orders.

The Act also enables Magistrates' Courts to make attachment orders, and any court may make an order attaching an employee's earnings to secure payment under a maintenance order.

An employer upon whom an attachment order is served must comply with it within seven days. He is entitled to deduct something towards his administrative expenses – currently 50p – and must give the employee a written statement of the deductions which he has made. The order will specify how much should be attached, but will also set a level below which the debtor's pay should not (having regard to his circumstances) ever be reduced.

The Employment Rights Act 1996 expressly prohibits any deductions unless authorised by statute or contract, and makes special rules limiting deductions from workers in retail trades. (PAYE and national insurance contributions may be deducted, as may other sums by agreement.)

As well as providing that no deductions may be made unless agreed, the Act also restricts deductions from retail workers pay for stock losses and cash shortages to 10 per cent of their gross pay.

What is Dismissal?

An employee is dismissed if his employer terminates his contract of employment or, if it is a fixed-term contract, he fails to renew it.

An employee may treat a breach of the contract by his employer as reason for leaving, and this is referred to as constructive dismissal.

A dismissed employee may be able to claim against his employer for wrongful dismissal, unfair dismissal or redundancy. These provisions overlap, and it is not inconceivable that the same facts might give rise to a claim under all of them. However, the employee would not be allowed to recover twice for the same damage.

What is wrongful dismissal?

Dismissal is **wrongful** if it is done in breach of contract, for example without enough notice being given or before a fixed term contract has expired. Such action may however be justified if the employee is guilty of a breach of contract, and if his breach is serious it may even justify summary dismissal.

Note that the Courts will not order specific performance of the contract of employment; the employment relationship is obviously not one which can properly continue under legal compulsion.

Claims for wrongful dismissal must be brought in the ordinary Civil Courts and not before the Industrial Tribunal. (If he also has a claim for unfair dismissal, on which see below, the employee will have to institute separate proceedings.)

What compensation can be claimed for wrongful dismissal?

Damages for wrongful dismissal will be assessed according to the rule in *Hadley v. Baxendale* and must, so far as possible, put the employee in the position he would have been in had the contract been performed. He will normally be entitled to the wages he would have earned had full notice been given, and he is also entitled to be compensated for the loss of fringe benefits under the contract (use of company car, pension fund contribution, health insurance etc.,) which he would have enjoyed during the notice period. However the award will be reduced to account for the tax which he would have paid had he earned the money, and the employee is under a duty to take reasonable steps to mitigate his loss, which basically means trying to find a new job and if necessary taking a cut in status and salary. He must also claim any social security benefits to which he is entitled. Any earnings or benefits during the period when he should have been under notice will be deducted from the damages awarded.

Note that damages will not be awarded for distress or disappointment. A wrongful dismissal claim will be of little value to most employees, and usually the employer will give payment in lieu of notice which will completely destroy the basis for a claim. However, where the employee is entitled to long notice or is under a fixed term contract and has valuable fringe benefits the amount of the claim may be substantial.

It is conceivable that an employer could make a claim for breach of contract against an employee, but the likelihood of being able to prove loss is very small.

What is unfair dismissal?

A dismissed employee may now also complain to an Industrial Tribunal if he has been dismissed for no good reason or if the employer did not adopt a reasonable procedure. This is known as **unfair dismissal**. This is a statutory right completely separate from the contract; a wrongful dismissal may be fair, and a dismissal in accordance with the contract may be unfair.

The Industrial Tribunal consists of three members, a legally qualified Chairman with detailed knowledge of employment and two lay members one from each side of industry. Legal Aid is not available for Tribunal proceedings but Trades Unions frequently support and assist their members in bringing claims.

What does the employee have to prove?

The first stage for a claim for unfair dismissal is for the employee to prove that he is eligible. First, he must show that he is employed under a contract of employment. Secondly, he must show that he has worked for the employer for the required period of continuous employment (which for full time employees who commenced after 1 June 1985 is two years; for those who commenced work before then it is one year). Certain classes of employee are excluded from the right to bring a claim including those over normal retirement age, policemen and employees who ordinarily work outside Great Britain. No claim can be brought before an Industrial Tribunal if at the time of dismissal a strike or lockout was in progress, but if the employer sacks some strikers but not others, or sacks all but reinstates some, the Tribunal does have jurisdiction.

The second thing that the employee must show is that he has been dismissed. If the contract has been frustrated or terminated by him he will be unable to claim. If the employer is in serious breach of contract and the employee resigns he may be able to claim as this can amount to "constructive dismissal". Non-renewal of a fixed term contract is also treated as a dismissal, although provided the agreement is for a year or more and the contract is in writing the parties may contract out of the unfair dismissal provisions. If there is a dismissal the law is concerned with the reason for it and the reasonableness of dismissal for the reason. Reasons for dismissing are either automatically unfair, potentially fair, or (occasionally) automatically fair. It is up to the employer to show what his reason is for dismissing the employee and to provide that it was at least potentially fair.

When is a dismissal fair?

There are five potentially fair reasons for dismissal:

a) capability or qualification (including gross incompetence and incapacity due to ill health);

b) conduct (including theft, repeated absence or bad time keeping, or disobedience);

c) continued employment would involve breach of some statutory requirement (e.g. a foreign worker's permit has expired);

d) redundancy; and

e) "some other substantial reason". This has been held to cover the employee's refusal to accept a change in his terms of employment as a result of a business reorganisation; incompatible employees; and even making room to bring a relative into the family business.

The next stage is for the Tribunal to consider whether in all the circumstances it was reasonable to treat that reason as sufficient to dismiss. This involves not only considering whether the reason was sufficiently serious but also the procedure by which the dismissal was carried out.

What difference does it make if misconduct is gross?

Generally, a dismissal for misconduct is only fair if the employee has had a previous warning. However, his misconduct may be so bad as to justify dismissal for a first offence. What amounts to gross misconduct is a question of fact which the Tribunal must decide.

When is dismissal automatically unfair?

A dismissal is automatically unfair if it is on the grounds of: membership or taking part in the duties of a Trade Union, or (since the Employment Act 1988) for not being a member of a Trade Union; for reasons connected with pregnancy; or if the employee was selected for redundancy for an inadmissible reason or in breach of an agreed or customary selection procedure; the assertion of a statutory right by the employee (for example, to get an itemised pay statement); health and safety activities; performance of trustee duties by employee trustees of pensions schemes; a spent conviction; or refusal by a protected or opted out shop worker to work on Sundays.

What are the rights of an unfairly dismissed employee?

The main remedy for unfair dismissal is an award of compensation. The Tribunal also has the power to order reinstatement or re-engagement (reinstatement means giving the employee his old job back on the same terms whereas re-engagement means giving him a different job, or his old job on different terms). The tribunal must consider whether it is practicable for the employer to comply with such an order, and the mere fact that a replacement has been taken on will not make it impracticable. The employee's wishes will also be taken into account. Because in the circumstances of an unfair dismissal claim it is likely that any workable relationship between the parties will already have been destroyed, orders of this type are only made in about 2% of cases.

Compensation orders are made up of a basic award and a compensatory award. The basic award depends on the age, length of service and wages of the employee. The maximum basic award is £6,300 and if the dismissal is because of the employee's membership (or non-membership) of a trade union there is a minimum awards £2,770. (In that case reinstatement can be ordered too.) The compensatory award is designed to compensate the employee for wages and other benefits which he has lost as a result of the dismissal and will normally include compensation for the period up to the date of the hearing and for a limited future period. Fringe benefits, etc., may be taken into account. The employee is under a duty to mitigate his losses as with a wrongful dismissal claim. There is a financial limit to the amount of the compensatory award (currently £11,300). If the employee has caused or contributed to his own dismissal both the basic award and the compensatory award can be reduced.

If the Tribunal makes an order for reinstatement or re-engagement and the employer fails to comply an additional award of between 13 and 26 weeks' pay (and where the dismissal is concerned with a Trade Union, 156 weeks' pay with a minimum of £20,600 and no maximum) will be ordered. If the dismissal is for an inadmissible reasons (trade union activities, membership or non-membership) the employee may claim even though he has not been employed for the minimum qualifying period and the sums which may be awarded are considerably greater.

What is redundancy?

An employee who is made **redundant** may claim a redundancy payment. The right arises when the employee's job disappears and he is dismissed and not replaced. The statutory scheme is a minimum and is commonly built upon by negotiations between employers and trade unions.

The employee may only claim if he has completed two years' continuous employment and is not over the statutory retiring age or ordinarily worked outside Great Britain. The right can be excluded by agreement in writing where the employee is employed under a fixed term contract of one year or more. It is also necessary for there to be a dismissal as defined above.

The dismissal must be for reason of redundancy, which is defined as being where:

a) the employer ceases business altogether, or ceases business in the place where the employee is employed; or

b) the requirements of the employer's business for employees to do work of the kind for which the employee was employed has ceased or diminished, or have done so in the place where the employee was employed.

Any employee is regarded as being employed where the contract says he can be required to be employed, so if his employer has several establishments and closes one the employee is not redundant if his contract says he can be moved to another establishment. The work for which he was employed is also defined by reference to the contract rather than what he actually does.

If the employee is dismissed for misconduct he will not be entitled to a redundancy payment. This situation could arise if he refuses, despite his contract, to move to a different establishment of the same employer. Misconduct after notice of redundancy has been given may also effect the right to a payment. Unreasonable refusal of an offer of suitable alternative employment will also cause the right to a redundancy payment to be lost, although the law does permit the employee to have a trial period of four weeks during which time he can leave his new job and still get a redundancy payment from the last one.

A redundancy may also amount to an unfair dismissal. The employer should normally give advance notice of redundancies to individual employees and consider alternative employment for them within his organisation. He should follow any agreed or customary procedure for selecting employees for redundancy, and if there is not one he should adopt a fair procedure. "Last in, first out" is a commonly used method of selection.

What notice must be given before redundancies are declared?

Legislation prescribes periods of notice which the employer must give to any union which represents his employees who are being made redundant. The length of notice depends on the number of redundancies and the period over which they will be implemented. Failure by the employer to consult the unions may give rise to a "protective award" requiring the employer to continue to pay the wages of the employees for a period equal to the period of notice which he should have given to the union. When Leyland DAF went into receivership, the necessary notice was not given.

The employer is also required to give advance notice to the Secretary of State for Employment, the length of notice again depending on the number of redundancies. Failure to comply may result in prosecution. The employees concerned must also be given the length of notice to which they are entitled.

How is redundancy pay calculated?

The amount of a redundancy payment is calculated on the basis of the employee's age, length of service, and weekly wage at the time of his dismissal.

a) For each complete year of employment when he was aged 41 or more, the employee will receive one and a half weeks' pay.

b) For each complete year of employment when he was aged between 22 and 41, he will receive one week's pay.

c) For each complete year of employment when he was aged between 18 and 22, he will receive half a week's pay.

No more than 20 years' employment may be counted and the maximum weekly pay on which a calculation can be based is £210. This is variable from time to time. The maximum statutory award is therefore £6,300.

Where a redundancy comes about as the result of the failure of a business or its transfer the employee's rights are protected by three special rules.

a) Claims for arrears of wages and certain other payment rank as a preferential claim in the employer's insolvency.

b) Where the employer is insolvent, the employee may claim his redundancy payment and other sums in respect of payment in lieu of services, arrears of wages, etc., from the Government's redundancy fund.

c) Where a business is transferred as a going concern the Transfer of Undertakings (Protection of Employment) Regulations 1981 will apply. These provide that the contracts of employment of all employees employed immediately before the transfer are taken over by the transferee as if he had always been the employer. Any dismissal by either the transferor or the transferee for any reason connected with the transfer will automatically be unfair unless it can be shown to be for organisational or technical reasons entailing changes in the work-force.

What does the Race Relations Act 1976 cover?

In the employment field, the Race Relations Act prohibits discrimination in choosing who to offer a job to and the terms on which to offer it, and against an employee in the way the employer affords access to opportunities for promotion, transfer or training, or other benefits, facilities or services, or by dismissing or subjecting the employee to any detriment, on the grounds of race, colour, nationality or ethnic origin. Direct discrimination (not employing members of a racial group) and indirect discrimination (drawing job requirements so as to exclude a racial group) are both prohibited.

What does the Sex Discrimination Act 1975 prohibit?

The Sex Discrimination Act deals with discrimination in the same matters on the grounds of sex or marital status.

When is discrimination permitted?

Discrimination is permissible under both Acts where a genuine occupational requirement is imposed. An Indian restaurant may insist on having Indian waiters. The Sex Discrimination Act sets out several situations in which it is necessary to have an employee of the right sex (for example, as a model) and also provides that giving special treatment to a woman in respect of pregnancy or childbirth does not discriminate against men. The Sex Discrimination Act also does not apply where the employer is a partnership of less than six partners, or has five or fewer employees, and neither Act applies if the employment concerned is for the purpose of a private household.

What does the Equal Pay Act 1970 do?

The Equal Pay Act operates by implying into every contract of employment a clause to the effect that the terms of employment of men and women will be no less favourable than a member of the opposite sex doing like work, work rated as equivalent by a job evaluation scheme, or work of equal value. What exactly this means is a highly complicated matter which need not concern us here – the general principle is easy enough.

Section B
HEALTH AND SAFETY

What is the relationship between the Factories Act 1961, the Offices, Shops and Railway Premises Act 1963, and the Health and Safety at Work etc. Act 1974?

The Health and Safety at Work etc. Act 1974 deals generally with health and safety and welfare in connection with work, while the Factories Act 1961 makes special provision for a variety of premises including (but not limited to) what are normally thought of as factories, and the Offices, Shops and Railway Premises Act 1963 covers offices, shops and railway premises. With all three Acts, most of the detailed rules are contained in regulations and orders. The Workplace (Health Safety and Welfare) Regulations have been in force since the beginning of 1996. These lay down a wide range of requirements relating to the structure and organisation of the workplace, repair, maintenance, and housekeeping and facilities for staff. Large parts of the 1961 and 1963 Acts are now replaced by these regulations. There are also detailed regulations on equipment, plant and machinery used in the workplace.

Who is protected by the 1974 Act?

The 1974 Act aims to secure the health, safety and welfare of persons at work, and to protect other persons against risks to health or safety arising out of or in connection with the activities of persons at work. It also deals with dangerous substances and the emission into the atmosphere of noxious or offensive substances, so it contains something to protect everyone.

What general duties does the Health and Safety at Work etc. Act impose on employers?

The employer's general duties under the Act are set out in section 2, which says that every employer must "ensure, as far as is reasonably practicable, the health, safety and welfare at work of all his employees".

From this general duty comes a number of more specific requirements.

What specific duties does the Act place on employers?

The specific duties which the Act places on employers are still quite broadly stated. They are:

a) to provide and maintain plant and systems of work which are, so far as is reasonably practicable, safe and without risk to health

b) to make arrangements for ensuring, so far as is reasonably practicable, safety and absence of risks to health and in connection with the use, handling, storage and transport of articles and substances

c) to provide such instruction, training and supervision as is necessary to ensure, so far as is reasonably practicable, the health and safety at work of his employees

d) to maintain any place of work in a condition which is safe and without risk to health

e) to provide and maintain a working environment which is not only, so far as is reasonably practicable, safe and without risk to health, but also adequate as regards facilities and arrangements for employees' welfare at work.

The Act also requires the employer to prepare (and keep up-to-date) a written statement of his health and safety policy, and bring it to employees' attention.

Moreover, the Act goes on to say (in section 3) that employers must also ensure that they conduct their undertaking so as to ensure (so far as is reasonably practicable) that people not employed by them are not exposed to risks to their health and safety.

Employers must also consult representatives appointed by "recognised trade unions" (this is one area where the present government's reforms have not yet penetrated) in health and safety matters.

Does the law impose duties on employees?

The Act does oblige employees to take responsibility for themselves and for the safety of others. They must avoid negligent acts liable to harm their safety, or the safety of others, and must co-operate so far as is necessary to see that health and safety rules are complied with. Employees who refuse to use safety equipment or clothing can be dismissed, and if an employee is injured and brings a claim his employer may argue contributory negligence – that it is at least partly the employee's own fault.

What special rules are there for manufacturers and suppliers?

The common law has long imposed a duty on the manufacturer or supplier of articles and substances used at work to take all reasonably practicable steps to ensure that the article or substance is safe. This duty extends to those who design or import articles or substances and is in addition to the common law duty of care which such people already owe to their customers' employees.

Designers, manufacturers, importers and suppliers can discharge their duty under the Act by obtaining from their supplier a written undertaking that the supplier has taken steps sufficient to ensure that the article will be safe.

Who enforces these duties?

One of the purposes of the 1974 Act was to create a unified

inspectorate. Previously, local authorities which had the job of checking on safety at work developed local rules, so enforcement was rather variable.

The Act set up a Health and Safety Commission which has the job of promoting health and safety, partly by using Codes of Practice. It also established a Health and Safety Executive, responsible for making arrangements for enforcement. The HSE is also responsible for enforcing the Factories Act and the Offices, Shops and Railways Premises Act.

If an inspector discovers a breach of any of these Acts or of regulations made under them (of which there are many) he may:

a) serve a prohibition notice or an improvement notice;

b) seize, render harmless or destroy any article or substance which he considers is causing imminent danger of serious personal injury; and

c) prosecute, whether or not he has served a notice.

What is an improvement notice?

An improvement notice is served if the inspector thinks a provision has been or is being breached. The matters specified in the notice must be put right within the time specified in it.

And what is a prohibition notice?

A prohibition notice is stronger than an improvement notice; it prohibits the carrying on of a specified activity until the matters specified in the notice have been dealt with. The inspector can only issue one if he thinks that a provision is being or is likely to be breached, **and** involves or will involve a risk of serious personal injury.

What powers does an inspector have to prosecute?

Prosecutions may be brought whether or not improvement or prohibition notices have been served. Failure to comply with a notice of either type can also result in prosecution. Offences are punishable by fines and/or up to two years' imprisonment and the court can order that the defendant remedies the matters concerned. As a result of the decision of the House of Lords in *Tesco v. Nattrass* it can be a defence to show that the offence results from the act or omission of an employee.

Can you appeal against a Notice given under the Act?

Yes. Appeals against improvement and prohibition notices may be made to the Industrial Tribunal within 21 days (which can be extended if the Tribunal is satisfied that it is not reasonably practicable to bring the appeal within that time, provided an application has been made in writing to the secretary of the Tribunal before the 21 days expired).

Appealing against the improvement notice has the effect of suspending the notice until the appeal is determined or withdrawn. Prohibition notices are only suspended pending appeals if the Tribunal so directs, and application has to be made before the Tribunal will give a direction. If it does the suspension only becomes effective when the direction is given.

The Tribunal may cancel or affirm the notice, and may make modifications to it.

No appeal lies against a decision of an inspector to seize or destroy anything, nor can compensation be claimed.

When must employers set up safety committees and publish health and safety policy documents?

Unless the employer has only four or fewer employees (and that means throughout his business, not merely in one office) he must prepare and, as often as may be appropriate, revise "a written statement of his general policy with respect of the health and safety at work of his employees and the organisation and arrangements for the time being in force for carrying out that policy", and bring it to employees' attention. The Act prescribes no time limit for doing this; there is no latitude allowed.

Regulations issued by the Health and Safety Executive require employers to consult with appointed representatives of recognised trade unions. Even if the employer does not deal with trade unions, he is now under an obligation to consult also with the representatives of his non-unionised workers. Employers of five or more employees must set up a health and safety "organisation" which best suits their business and is most likely to produce results.

What form should a policy document take?

There can be no hard and fast rules about what there should be in a policy document. It can open with a few platitudes: "The Company regards the health and safety of its employees as of paramount importance. . .". "All levels of management are expected to give top priority to health and safety at work . . .". "Our policy is to take all reasonably practicable steps not only to protect our employees but also everyone else affected by our business . . .".

The statement must also give details of how this policy is to be carried out, which is rather more difficult. The following questions should be addressed:

a) What sort of safety organisation (if any) does the Company have?

b) Is there a safety officer? Is he properly trained? What are his responsibilities?

c) Is there a safety committee? What steps have been taken

to enable employees to make their views on health and safety known?

d) The law requires that the statement specifies the arrangements for the time being in force for carrying out the health and safety policy. What are the main hazards which employees will face? What additional rules and regulations must be observed?

e) What procedures are laid down for reporting accidents? Are the results of accident analyses made available to management and the Safety Committee?

What health and safety regulations are there which are of particular importance to the motor trade?

Many of the regulations made under the Act are of importance to the motor trade. In addition the Factories Act still sets standards for maintenance of many items of garage equipment. There are also specific regulations of importance to the motor trade such as the Abrasive Wheels Regulations and the Protection of Eyes Regulations.

I have heard a lot about the COSHH Regulations. What do they require employers to do?

The full implications of the COSHH Regulations are extremely complex. They affect all employers and employees in the retail motor industry. They are designed to protect employees and others against risks to health caused by the use of substances and processes at work. The Control of Substances Hazardous to Health Regulations 1988 impose five basic tasks on employers:

i To assess the risks to health arising from work and the precautions needed

ii To introduce measures to control or prevent the risk

iii To ensure control measures are properly used and equipment maintained and tested iv   To monitor the exposure of employees and carry out an appropriate form of surveillance of their health

v   To inform, instruct and train employees about the risk and the precautions to be taken.

What are the substances hazardous to health?

These are listed under various classifications, and can be gases, vapours, liquid, fumes, dusts, solids and components of a mixture of materials. There are certain exclusions of some substances (eg. asbestos) which are the subject of separate legislation.

Section C
AGENCY

What is an agent?

An agent is someone who negotiates and concludes contracts on behalf of someone else, who is known as the principal. A business may need an agent because it has insufficient knowledge of a new market or commodity, or simply because it is in the wrong place; companies also need agents because, although in law they are legal persons, they do not have hands and minds to make contracts even for ordering stationery and buying tea. A company's employees are therefore its agents.

How is an agency created?

Agency is a contractual relationship – there is an agreement between the principal and the agent. It may be created by a written contract, or by a contract implied from the conduct or situation of the parties. Where the agent acts gratuitously i.e. free of charge consent may be express or implied; and where the purported agent has no authority, the relationship may be ratified (expressly or implied) by the person on whose behalf he purports to make contracts.

What are the duties of an agent?

The agent's duties may well be set out in his contract with his principal, if there is a contract. If there is no contract, or if it is silent on the agent's duties (or any of them) the law will imply certain duties:

a) To obey instructions. If he is employed under a contract the agent has a duty to act and will be in breach of contract if he fails to do the job at all.

b) To exercise reasonable care. This arises under the general law of negligence; it may also be implied in the contract.

c) To perform his duties personally. The relationship between agent and principal is a fiduciary one, so unless it is specifically agreed to the contrary the agent must not delegate the performance of his duties.

d) To avoid any conflict of interest. The agent must show good faith in his dealings with his principal and must therefore avoid any situation in which his interests conflict with those of the principal.

e) Not to make a secret profit. By the same token the agent may not use his position as agent to make a secret profit over and above his commission. As an extension of this principle, the agent may not take a bribe unless it is disclosed to the principal.

f) To account to his principal. The agent must keep the principal's property separate from his own and to account for all such property held by him.

Where the agent is a commercial agent – a self-employed intermediary who has continuing authority to negotiate the sale or purchase of goods on behalf of his principal – legislation imposes further duties. Under the Council Directive (Commercial Agents) Regulations 1993 (SI No 3053) commercial agents must look after the interests of their principal and act dutifully and in good faith, conclude transactions entrusted to them; communicate information to their principal; and comply with the principal's reasonable instructions.

What are the duties of the Principal?

a) The agent has a right to be remunerated for his work if he is working under a contract of agency, as is normally the case (although the contract may be unwritten and relatively informal). If the contract says nothing about remuneration the courts will imply a term that he is entitled to reasonable remuneration. If the Regulations apply, the agent will be entitled to customary commission, or if no rate is customary, a reasonable one.

b) The agent also has the right to be indemnified by the principal against all liabilities and expenses reasonably incurred in the course of his duties. This does not apply if he exceeds his authority.

Principals too must act dutifully and in good faith towards their agents – under the Regulations. They must provide information about the goods and information needed by the agent for performance of the agreement. They must also tell the agent if there is likely to be a significant drop in sales volume.

What authority does an agent have?

The Agent may have authority to do certain things expressly given to him by the principal, or implied by the nature of the duties he has undertaken. This is known as express or implied actual authority. Where the agent is given express authority it may be that he also has incidental implied authority to do things which the main relationship requires.

The agent may also appear to have additional authority, referred to as apparent or ostensible authority. This is based on the principal's representation to a third party that the agent has some authority; the third party may rely on that unless he knows it to be false. In reality, as Diplock LJ observed in *Freeman & Lockyer v. Buckhurst Park Properties (Mangal) Limited (1964)* "it is upon the apparent authority of the agent that the contractor normally relies in the ordinary course of business when entering into contracts". The other party does not verify the agent's authority before making a contract – he takes it for granted.

How can an agency be terminated?

An agency can be terminated in a number of ways:

a) by mutual agreement;

b) by unilateral revocation (which may however be a breach of contract, giving rise to a claim for damages);

c) by expiry of a fixed period, or the death, mental incapacity or bankruptcy of either party, or by reason of supervening illegality or frustration making it impossible for the relationship to continue.

If the commercial agency regulations apply, minimum notice periods will be necessary:

- 1 month for the first year of the agreement
- 2 months for the second year
- 3 months for the third and subsequent years.

The terminated commercial agent will be entitled under the Regulations to an indemnity and/or compensation. If the parties have not agreed which, the Regulations will require compensation to be paid.

An indemnity is intended to reflect the on-going value to the principal of business introduced by the agent. The payment must be equitable, and will be capped at the average of the agent's commission over the last five years. The agent may also claim damages.

Compensation is intended to cover commission which the agent loses, and costs which he has incurred but has been unable to write off.

If the agent has terminated or broken the agreement, no compensation will be payable.

When is a motor trader an agent?

In the motor trade, agency relationships may arise in a number of situations. However, one place where they do not (usually) arise is in the manufacturer's relationship with his dealers (see below).

a) A garage's employees are its agents, and the garage is vicariously liable for their acts or omissions. If a mechanic fails to tighten the wheelnuts on a customer's car, it is the business which is liable to the customer (though the mechanic will in turn be in trouble with his employer!).

b) A garage which agrees to sell a customer's car for him rather than simply taking it in part exchange acts as the customer's agent.

c) A garage which provides mechanical breakdown insurance policies may be the agent of the insurance company, although often the garage acts merely as a retailer; if the garage fills in the forms for the customer, it is his agent.

Is a franchise holder an agent of the manufacturer?

No. Motor dealers are often incorrectly described as agents for the manufacturer. They may in certain specialised circumstances act as the manufacturer's agent, but as far as their main business is concerned they are resellers of goods which they purchase from the manufacturers.

Because of the commitments involved in setting up as an authorised dealer – investment in spares, workshop facilities, training, demonstrators, and the rest – the dealer's agreement with the manufacturer will usually stipulate that the manufacturer will not appoint further dealers in the same area. The dealer is then said to hold the "franchise" for that marque in that area.

How does the Franchise System in the Motor Trade operate?

The franchise system gives the dealer a valuable benefit – exclusivity in supplying one marque in a particular area – to compensate him for shouldering the obligations which the manufacturer insists on to promote the goods and provide after-sales service. The system therefore benefits the consumer; dealers who do not supply essential services will not be able to get supplies from the manufacturer.

However, giving exclusive rights like this also has dangers. Dealers are insulated from competition in the same marque on their patch, therefore prices can (so the theory goes) be set higher than they would otherwise. (The theory largely ignores the fact that the dealer faces competition from a dozen or more different makes of car in the same town). This underlies the arguments, still going on but less heatedly than in the early eighties, about car price differentials in the EEC.

What is the Block Exemption?

The EEC law is concerned about restrictions on competition, although it recognises that if free competition were the norm prices might be lower but promotional activities and after-sales service would suffer. So in 1985 an EEC Regulation was made, known as the motor vehicle distribution block exemption, laying down the terms on which dealer agreements which restrict competition will be tolerated. In 1995 this Regulation was updated and amended. It will last until 1 October 2002.

What does the Block Exemption Regulation say?

In order to operate his dealer agreements within the Block Exemption, the vehicle manufacturer must now permit his dealers to sell vehicles from competing franchises. The vehicle manufacturer can however insist on separate sales premises (which need not necessarily be in a different building), and also separate management for the different marques. As far as parts are concerned, the manufacturer may not require the dealer to handle only original parts. The sole permitted restriction is that the dealer may only use the manufacturer's original parts when doing free servicing warranty or recall work (when the manufacturer foots the bill anyway). Otherwise the dealer must be free to use whatever parts he likes, provided they match the quality of the manufacturer's own parts. This provision of the block exemption is, however, subject to modification in the UK by the Restrictions on Agreements (Manufacturers and Importers of Motor Vehicles) Order 1984 which prohibits **any** parts exclusivity in dealer agreements except in respect of warranty and recall work.

What is a mercantile agent?

According to the Factors Act 1889 a mercantile agent is someone who "in the customary course of his business . . . (has) . . . authority either to sell goods, or to consign goods for the purpose of sale, or to buy goods, or to raise money on the security of goods".

How does a mercantile agent pass the good title to goods?

If a motor dealer is left in possession of a car, assuming (as we may do) that he qualifies as a mercantile agent, he may sell it to a customer and provided that the customer buys it in good faith he will get title, regardless of the fact that the dealer did not have authority to sell it without referring back to the owner. The agent has to have possession in connection with a sale (it does not apply if he has the car for repair).

Section D
INSURANCE

What is the purpose of insurance?

A contract of insurance is one whereby, in consideration of the payment of a premium, the insurer agrees to take upon himself a risk borne by another person ("the insured") and to compensate him for any loss if the risk insured against occurs. The purpose of insurance is therefore to pass a risk from one party which cannot afford (or does not wish) to bear it to someone (an insurance company or Lloyds underwriters) who can afford to bear it and is willing to do so in the expectation of making a profit from it.

What is the difference between life insurance and indemnity assurance?

A life assurance contract obliges the insurer to pay certain fixed sums on the death (or in some cases the illness or accident) of the insured. Under an indemnity contract the insurer has to pay out on the insured's actual loss. Motor insurance policies are one example of an indemnity contract.

An insurer who has to pay out under an indemnity contract has what is known as a right of subrogation. This permits him to put himself in the position of the insured and to pursue whatever remedies the insured might have against whoever caused the loss, taking action in the insured's name. This is an extension of the principle that the insured cannot recover more than his actual loss.

No such right arises under a life contract. The personal representatives of the deceased may sue the person responsible for his death, and can keep any damages which are awarded as well as any policy moneys paid out by the life assurance company.

What sort of indemnity policies are encountered in the motor trade?

Probably the most familiar of all types of indemnity insurance is the motor policy, which is dealt with in greater detail below. Other common types of policy cover against fire and burglary, and are as applicable to garage premises as they are to private houses.

All employers are required to have in force policies covering their liabilities to their employees (on which see Section B, on Health and Safety, above) and to display a certificate at the premises which it covers. Occupiers' liability (governed by the Occupiers Liability Act 1956 which makes the occupier liable for injuries to third parties caused by defects in premises) can also be insured against, as can public liability.

Manufacturers commonly take out insurance against defective products, though since the new product liability laws came in making manufacturers liable without proof of fault this has become expensive and many companies will carry a certain amount of the risk themselves. This is exactly the same principle as an excess on your car insurance; you are bearing the risks up to a certain limit.

A relatively new species of indemnity insurance covers legal expenses. Individuals can insure against incurring legal costs, for example following a road accident; companies can also cover themselves against legal costs in a variety of areas. Defending an action concerning a defective car could cost a garage many thousands of pounds and make a big dent in one year's accounts; legal expenses insurance could help avoid this.

It is also possible that a businessman in the motor trade will encounter professional indemnity insurance, if, for example, his accountant messes up his accounts or his solicitor advises him wrongly (it does happen occasionally). Because of the grave implications of such an error, these professions (and others) are required by law to be insured.

What on earth does *uberrimae fidei* mean, and what has it got to do with insurance law?

Uberrimae fidei is Latin for "of the utmost good faith". In the law of contract it used to describe contracts where something more than an ordinary duty of good faith must exist between the parties.

This is particularly important in an insurance contract. No insurer could undertake to investigate every risk which he is asked to cover. He relies entirely on the information disclosed by the insured in the proposal.

So the proposer must take care to disclose every "material fact" of which he is aware or should have been aware. If he fails to reveal any such material fact (even if he was unaware of it, if it was one of which he should have been aware) the insurer may at any time avoid the contract.

So what is a "material fact"?

A fact is material if it would influence the judgment of a prudent insurer in deciding whether to accept the risk and, if so, in setting the premium. The proposer may not think a fact is material, but that makes no difference. He has to ask himself whether the insurer would think it material.

What duty is there to disclose material facts?

What an insurer, with years of experience, may consider material may appear to be of no importance to the proposer. Nevertheless if he fails to disclose it he could lose all his protection. Merely answering all the questions on a proposal form is not enough; if the proposer knows another material fact, he must disclose it. Refusal of a proposal of insurance in the past is a material fact, sometimes even if the refusal was of a completely different type of policy.

However, there is no duty on the proposer or insured to disclose facts which diminish the risk, or facts which the insurer knew or ought to have known.

Motor Vehicle Insurance

What types of motor insurance are there, and what does the law require?

There are four main types of motor vehicle insurance:

a) Road Traffic Act Policies (now superseded by new legislation).
b) Third Party Policies.
c) Third Party, Fire and Theft Policies.
d) Comprehensive Policies.

The law used to require only minimal cover, provided by a Road Traffic Act policy; now a third party policy is the minimum.

What does each of these cover?

Any risk which a motorist may face can in theory be insured against. Since the Road Traffic Act 1930, insurance against third party risks (causing death or bodily injury to a third party – i.e. not the insurer or the insured) has been compulsory. The law is now in the Road Traffic Act 1988. It is now also necessary to be insured against damage to property arising out of the use of a vehicle, so the old "Road Traffic Act Policies" which covered only the compulsory risks will no longer be allowed.

Usually, the minimum cover which a motorist would buy is a third party policy, covering the compulsory risks as recently extended. He might also wish to cover himself against the theft of the vehicle, or its destruction or damage by fire, or he may wish to have comprehensive cover, insuring against not only damage to third parties and their property but also against his own loss.

What is the significance of a motor insurance policy?

A policy of insurance is what the Road Traffic Act requires to be in force before a vehicle is used on the highway. A policy is a document containing all the terms and conditions under which the insurer agrees to indemnify the policy holder; but the operative document in a contract of motor insurance is in fact the certificate by which the insurer certifies that a policy is in force.

What is the significance of the certificate and what are the details which it shows?

The certificate is the document which proves that a car or driver is insured. It is the document which must be produced to the Police if they want to see it; it must also be produced in support of an application for a Vehicle Excise Duty Licence. Section 147 of the Road Traffic Act 1988 provides that a policy is only in force for the purposes of the Act if a certificate has been delivered to the insured.

The certificate shows the limitations on the cover which the insurer has imposed (usually at the request of the insured). These will include use (social, domestic, pleasure, business, to and from work, etc.), drivers (insured, insured and spouse, named drivers, any drivers), and extensions such as permitting the insured to drive other cars.

If the vehicle is used outside these limits – by a driver not included in the policy or on business where use is restricted to social, domestic and pleasure – the policy does not apply and, unless the compulsory risks are covered by another policy (for example, where the policy only applies when the insured himself is driving, by another driver's own policy) an offence is committed.

What is the role of a cover note?

Temporary cover notes are provided by insurers either on new policies or when old ones have expired, until they are renewed. They are acceptable for some purposes in place of insurance certificates, but are not quite the same.

A certificate shows that a policy is in force: a cover note merely shows that the insurer is willing to issue a policy, but it is ineffective unless accepted by the insured either by communication with the insurers or by his actions – for example, taking the car out on the road. On such an event, the insurer's offer is accepted by the insured and a binding contract is created. The insured is liable for the premium, although whether he has actually paid it is immaterial.

Why does a renewal notice sometimes have a cover note on it?

A cover note may come attached to a renewal notice. This is simply to facilitate continuing cover while the premium is paid. If the insured does not intend to renew, he may not drive on the strength of the cover note; if he does, he is bound by contract and must pay the premium.

What defences are there to driving without insurance cover?

One little-known alternative to motor insurance is to deposit £500,000 (the sum remained constant from 1930 until quite recently at £15,000) with the Supreme Court. This only applies where a vehicle is driven under its owner's control (presumably including by his or her chauffeur) and does not provide an indemnity – it merely secures the payment of the first £500,000 of any damages awarded against the driver, who may well have to pay out much more to anyone injured.

It is also possible to obtain a certificate of security from an authorised insurer or other person specified in section 146(2) of the 1988 Act. This replaces a certificate of insurance: it shows that if the owner cannot discharge his liabilities to third parties the insurer or whatever will do so instead.

Section E

DANGEROUS SUBSTANCES

What regulations govern the transport, storage, receipt and supply of petrol?

Transport, storage and sale of petroleum spirit and certain other inflammable substances are regulated principally by the Petroleum (Consolidation) Act 1928. County Councils are empowered to issue petroleum spirit licences and carry out certain other functions including enforcement. Petroleum spirit is defined as such petroleum as, when tested in the prescribed manner, gives off an inflammable vapour at a temperature of less than 73 degrees Fahrenheit.

The 1928 Act (and Orders made under it) now have effect as if any requirement or prohibition imposed by or under them was imposed by or under health and safety regulations (Health and Safety at Work, etc, Act 1974). It is an offence to contravene any health and safety regulations or any requirement or prohibition imposed under them.

Conveyance of dangerous substances (including petrol) by road in road tankers and tank containers is (except in certain circumstances set out in schedule 2 of the regulations) governed by the Carriage of Dangerous Goods by Road Regulations 1996 (SI 1996 No 2095) which came fully into force on 1 September 1996. Regulation 3(8) says (the name of the instrument notwithstanding) that it matters not whether the vehicle is on the road. The Regulations also deal with deliveries to "petroleum filling stations".

The Health and Safety Executive is charged with producing an approved list of dangerous substances which may be carried by road. The list specifies identification numbers for the substances, emergency action codes and other matter.

Unless excepted by the Regulations, an operator may not use a vehicle or tank container for the conveyance of dangerous substances unless it is properly designed and constructed and is suitable for the purpose. For road tankers and tank containers first used after 1st June 1992 the operator must also possess specified written information about its design, construction, examination and maintenance and any repairs which have been done to it. The road tanker or tank container concerned must have been duly examined and tested.

Certain information has to be available during carriage and the operator is required to keep specified documents and to have information about the substance carried. The tank must not be over-filled, and every person involved must observe all precautions necessary to prevent fire or explosion. Openings and valves must be securely closed before the journey starts. When it is not being driven, the driver must (in most cases) ensure that it is either parked in a safe place or supervised by a competent adult.

The HSE is empowered to issue exemption certificates if it believes classes of persons or dangerous substances can safely be exempted from the Regulations. Conditions may be attached.

What is the procedure when petrol is delivered to a filling station?

Regulation 20 and Schedule 12 to the Regulations lay down special requirements relating to the unloading of petroleum spirit at petrol filling stations and certain other premises licensed for the keeping of petroleum spirit:

The Regulations distinguish between licensee-controlled and driver-controlled deliveries, but in either case the licensee – the person licensed under the Petroleum (Consolidation) Act 1928 – is responsible for the correct procedure being observed. The licensee must ensure that:

a) every storage tank at the premises is clearly labelled with
 i. a number, letter or combination of both which cannot be readily altered or defaced; and
 ii. its maximum capacity, and the grade of petrol permitted to be stored in it; (the operator of the vehicle must ensure its tanks are marked too);

b) every dipstick other than those permanently fixed to a storage tank and any other device used to check the quantity of petrol contained in a storage tank is marked in the same way as the tank for which it is to be used;

c) any pipe leading to a filling point not on or immediately adjacent to the storage tank is also marked in the same way as the relevant tank, and that a vapour balance pipe (if used) is clearly marked as such;

d) so far as practicable, delivery does not start until he has taken reasonable steps to ensure that the pipe is properly and securely connected to the tank and to the filling point.

e) where petrol vapour given off during delivery is returned to the tanker by way of a vapour balance pipe connected to a hose attached to the tanker, the vapour balance pipe must be marked accordingly.

f) before delivery begins a competent person who is not the driver of the vehicle or the attendant on it is in charge of the storage tank for the purpose of the delivery.

The competent person appointed by the licensee must be adequately trained. He is in charge of deliveries, whether they are licensee-controlled or driver-controlled.

For licensee-controlled deliveries the competent person must ensure that delivery does not commence until the pipe is connected (as above), the contents of the tank have been measured, any dipping opening has been closed again, and (if necessary) the tank has been isolated from other tanks at the premises.

The competent person must then fill in and sign two copies of the prescribed form showing the number of the storage tank and the quantity and grade of the petrol being delivered. Each copy must then be completed and signed by the driver, to whom one copy is handed after delivery is complete. Both the proprietor and the petrol supplier are required to keep their copies for 12 months.

The driver must take care to ensure that the pipes are properly connected before beginning delivery.

During the delivery the competent person must keep a constant watch to ensure no hazardous situation arises; and the driver must ensure that the vehicles engine is not run and keep a watch on the hose. Both must ensure the tank does not overflow.

The procedure for driver-controlled deliveries may only be used if the licensee has a special licence from the petroleum licensing authority (the County Council) and a written agreement with the operator of every road tanker likely to make deliveries to the premises.

Under this procedure, the licensee has to ensure that the filling points for his storage tanks are padlocked. Each storage tank must have a suitable measuring device and there must also be a ticket printer, an alarm, adequate illumination, emergency telephones, a suitable fire extinguisher, 25 kg of dry sand, a plan of the licensed premises, and a cut-off switch for the fuel pumps.

The licensee or competent person is still required to complete and sign a specified form which is handed to the driver.

The road tanker used under this procedure must have a bottom-operated foot valve fitted to each compartment, which can be shut off in emergency. It must be loaded in such a way that the contents of one of its compartments will not need to be split between two storage tanks.

The driver must comply with conditions attached to the licence, which the licensee is required to tell him about. He must complete his part of the specified form and sign it, then check that he has the right padlock key, that there is enough "ullage" (spare capacity) in the tank and that there is a dialling tone on the emergency telephone(s). He must place the fire extinguisher in an accessible position, test the alarm and take all reasonable steps to ensure that the hoses are properly connected.

During delivery, the driver must ensure that the engine stays off and the tanker remains stationary. He must as far as is practicable ensure that no petrol overflows the tank or escapes from the hose and keep a constant watch on everything.

After delivery, he must remove the hoses and close everything up. He then gives one copy of the certificate to the licensee and the other to the petrol supplier.

Anyone prosecuted for committing an offence under the Regulations has a good defence if they can show that they took all reasonable precautions and exercised all diligence to avoid committing the offence.

What are the rules concerning other dangerous substances?

The Regulations provide that a vehicle or tank container used for the conveyance by road of dangerous substances must have prescribed hazard warning panels showing:

a) the emergency action code for the substance;

b) the substance identification number;

c) the appropriate hazard warning sign; and

d) where specialist advice can be obtained at all times.

Similar provisions apply to tank containers and to multi-loads (two or more dangerous substances in separate tanks or compartments) which must also bear labels showing the substance identification number and the appropriate hazard warning sign for each tank or compartment.

It is the operator's duty to obtain the necessary information to enable him to comply with these requirements and to be aware of the risks. He must also ensure that the driver has been properly instructed and trained about the substance.

What does the law say about storing petrol?

A label conspicuously declaring "Petroleum Spirit" and "Highly Inflammable" must be displayed on or near any vessel containing petroleum spirit which is:

i.   being kept at any place (except for the first seven days after importation);

ii. sent or conveyed between any two places in Great Britain (except where it is being used to propel the motor vehicle, ship or aircraft carrying it); or

iii. sold or exposed or offered for sale.

The name and address of the consignee or owner, the sender or the vendor respectively must also be shown. These provisions do not apply to the conveyance of petroleum spirit by road in a road tanker or tank container.

A dangerous substance prescribed by the classification Packaging and Labelling of Dangerous Substances Regulations 1984 (SI 1984 No 1244) – including petrol – may not be supplied to any person unless:

i.   it is in a container designed, constructed and secured so as to prevent any of the contents escaping under normal handling, and

ii. the container and its fastener, insofar as they are likely to come into contact with the substances, are made of materials which are neither liable to be adversely affected by the contents nor liable in conjunction with the contents to form any other substance which is a risk to health or safety.

The container must also show the name of the substance, the name and address of its manufacturer, importer and wholesaler or supplier, prescribed words and a prescribed symbol indicating the general nature of the risk, prescribed words indicating the particular risk and the safety precautions required.

Petroleum spirit may be kept in small quantities without a licence. This may be for private use or sale, and it must be kept in separate glass, earthenware or metal containers, securely stopped, containing not more than a pint each and three gallons in aggregate. For petroleum mixtures not susceptible of measurement as liquids, the figures are one pound and thirty pounds. Special rules apply to calcium carbide, and general lighthouse authorities (you will be pleased to know) may keep as much as they need.

These rules do not apply to petroleum spirit kept and used for the purpose of any internal combustion engine and not even partly for sale. The rules for these situations are that it must be kept in plastic or metal vessels so constructed and maintained as to be secure against breakage and to prevent leakage of liquid or vapour. No such vessel may exceed 2 gallons in capacity, unless it is the fuel tank for the engine or unless it is kept in a storage place situated more than 20 feet from any building, highway or public footpath, provision has been made to prevent petroleum spirit from flowing out in case of fire, and written notice has been given to the local authority. Any vessel other than such a fuel tank must be marked indelibly and conspicuously with the words "petroleum spirit" and "highly inflammable".

No storage place may contain more than 60 gallons of petroleum spirit at any time; if it is within 20 feet of any building, stack of timber or other inflammable substance, it may only be kept in the fuel tank for an internal combustion engine and in not more than two other vessels (not exceeding 2 gallons each) carried on the vehicle propelled by the engine, unless written notice has been given to the local authority.

The storage place must be in the open air or be well-ventilated and have an entrance direct to the open air. There must be effective means for extinguishing fires and the place must not form part of or be attached to any building used as a dwelling or a place where persons assemble unless it is separated from it by a substantial floor or partition. If it is in any building it must not be situated under any staircase or other means of exit likely to be required in case of fire, unless separated by a substantial floor or partition. All reasonable precautions must be taken at every storage place to prevent any fire or artificial light liable to ignite inflammable vapours being so near any vessel in which petroleum spirit is kept as to be dangerous.

Petroleum spirit may not be used in any storage place otherwise than as fuel for an internal combustion engine except as fuel for lighting or heating apparatus constructed and maintained so as not to be able to ignite inflammable vapour (other than as such fuel), or for cleaning or as a solvent for repair purposes in quantities not exceeding one gill at any one time.

No operation involving the exposure of petroleum spirit may be carried on in the neighbourhood of any fire or artificial light liable to ignite inflammable vapour. Emptying petroleum spirit into a sewer, or permitting petroleum spirit to enter a sewer is prohibited.

Where a fixed container which has been used for the storage of petroleum spirit is no longer used for such purpose the occupier (or the owner, if the premises are unoccupied) must take all steps which are reasonably necessary to prevent danger from it. The local authority may require the occupier or owner to show them such derelict tanks and permit them to ascertain the measures taken to make them safe, and may by notice require him to take reasonable steps to prevent danger.

How do you get a licence to store petrol?

Unless storage is permitted without a local licence, petroleum spirit may not be stored unless a licence granted by the local authority is in force.

The local authority may grant licences for such term and make such provisions relating to renewal, and attach such conditions, as it thinks necessary and expedient. If a licensee contravenes any condition of his licence he commits an offence. Licences may be transferred by the local authority.

A person aggrieved by the decision of a local authority to refuse to issue or transfer a licence, or to impose conditions, may appeal to the Secretary of State. The Secretary of State or the person (if any) he appoints to hear the appeal may direct the HSE to grant a licence (conditionally or unconditionally) or modify the conditions attached by the local authority.

PART 3: CONSUMER LAW
by
Anthea Worsdall

CONTENTS

Section A
SALE OF GOODS

How does a contract for the sale of goods differ from other contracts?

The basic principles of contract will still apply, i.e. the rules as to offer, acceptance, consideration and so on. (For a reminder on these points, refer back to the section on Contract Law.) However, it is important to understand that we are talking in this section about contracts for the SALE of GOODS only. In other words, contracts which do not involve a sale of goods, e.g. hiring or leasing contracts or gifts, and contracts to supply something other than goods, e.g. a contract to sell a service such as repairing a car, are not included. This is an important distinction because Parliament has decided to control the content of contracts for the sale of goods by means of the legislation in the Sale of Goods Act 1979, and therefore we need to know which contracts are covered by its provisions.

The Sale of Goods Act defines a contract for the sale of goods as

The Sale of Goods Act defines a contract for the sale of goods as

> "A contract by which the seller transfers or agrees to transfer the property in goods to the buyer for a money consideration, called the price".

This means that where no money changes hands at all, for example if goods are simply exchanged, there is no contract for the sale of goods.

Does that mean that a contract for the sale of a motor car where part of the price is paid by means of a part exchange of the customer's car is not covered by the Sale of Goods Act?

No. The Sale of Goods Act will apply in this situation, as part of the price is paid in money.

Is a written contract necessary to create a contract for the sale of goods?

No, in common with most other contracts (there are only a few specific exceptions), contracts for the sale of goods can be made in writing, orally, or partly orally and partly in writing, or in some cases implied from the way the parties behave. While a written contract is not therefore essential, its use makes the rights and obligations of the parties clear, and enables the parties to vary some of the provisions of the Sale of Goods Act.

Where a motor vehicle is being sold to a customer, it is very likely that the motor trader will use a standard form of printed contract (e.g. the form recommended by the RMI.)

The terms used in this type of standard form contract in a transaction with a consumer will now be caught by the Unfair terms in Consumer Contracts regulations 1994 (see page 65) if any of the terms create an "imbalance" between the rights of the trader and the rights of the consumer. Standard terms which are ambiguous, or not printed clearly, or are not drawn to the customer's attention, may also be regarded as "unfair" and therefore unenforceable. A 'consumer' in this conext means a 'natural person' acting for purposes outside his business. This means that a company is not a consumer for this purpose.

Does the Sale of Goods Act say anything about how the goods should be paid for?

The Act provides that if no fixed price has been agreed by the parties, then the buyer must pay a reasonable price for the goods, depending on all the circumstances.

An order form used by a motor trader will normally provide a fixed price for the vehicle, but with clauses which will enable the price to be increased if the price charged by the manufacturer goes up. This sort of clause would normally be accompanied by a further one which would let the customer cancel the deal if the price increased by more than a certain amount.

If the buyer is to pay delivery charges, these must be specifically included in the contract, otherwise the Sale of Goods Act provides that they must be met by the seller.

What is the situation where the buyer has paid a deposit but the purchase does not get completed?

Where the buyer has paid a deposit on signing the contract, the question as to whether this will be returnable if he fails to complete the purchase will depend on whether the contract contained any clause dealing with this situation, and otherwise on the facts. If he has simply changed his mind, then the deposit would normally be forfeited, at least to the extent of covering expenses. If the cancellation is due to the default of the seller, then the deposit would be repayable.

What happens if the buyer does not complete the purchase by paying for the vehicle?

The Sale of Goods Act provides that time of payment for goods will not be "of the essence". This means that failure to pay on time would not enable the seller to cancel the contract, only to sue for damages.

The damages which he would be able to recover would be based on the "available market" for the vehicle. In other words, if he is easily able to resell, the damages will be very small. The seller cannot recover damages simply because he is only able to make one sale rather than two.

What is the position if there is a delay in the delivery of the vehicle?

If a specific date is fixed for delivery, failure to deliver the goods on that day will amount to breach of contract enabling the other party to cancel the whole deal.

The Sale of Goods Act provides that if no time for delivery is fixed, then the goods must be delivered within a "reasonable" time. The practice in the motor trade would normally be not to commit to a specific date for delivery, using words such as "as soon as possible". In this situation, the Sale of Goods Act would apply to require that the goods are delivered within a reasonable time.

What happens if a vehicle sold by a motor trader turns out to have been stolen, or the subject of a hire purchase agreement?

The rule is that a person cannot pass the legal ownership of the goods (a good title) to something if he does not own it (nemo dat quod non habet). For example, if a vehicle has been stolen then no one who subsequently buys it, even if innocent of the theft, will be able to become the legal owner. This remains the true owner who would be able to take an action against a buyer to recover the vehicle.

There are some exceptions to this rule which are relevant to the motor trade:

a) The sale of a motor vehicle subject to a hire purchase or conditional sale agreement.

This is a statutory exception to the normal rule, so that the private purchaser who buys the vehicle in good faith, i.e. without knowing of the existence of the hire purchase agreement, will be protected from claims made by the original owner. It is important to note that a dealer does not get this protection.

b) Sale by a mercantile agent

This will arise where the motor trader has a vehicle in his possession in the course of his business as a 'mercantile agent', i.e. someone who in the course of his business has authority to sell or buy goods. Therefore, a motor trader who has a car in for repair in the workshop will not be covered by this exception.

c) Sales where the owner will be "estopped" (legally prevented) from denying the seller's right to sell

This can arise, for example, where the true owner negligently allows someone else to appear to be the owner of a vehicle.

d) Sale by the seller or buyer in actual possession of the goods

This could arise where the seller purports to sell goods twice over when he still has them in his possession. The innocent second buyer will be protected. Similarly, a buyer in possession of the goods but over which the seller still has some rights, for example if the buyer has not yet paid for them, can pass good title to a buyer who is unaware of the true facts.

What remedy does the buyer have against the seller if it turns out the goods did not belong to the seller after all?

The Sale of Goods Act (s. 12) provides that there is an implied term in every contract for the sale of goods that the seller has the right to sell the goods, or that he will have the right at the time when the "property" in the goods is going to pass. It also implies a term that the goods are free from any third party interests, for example an agreement with a finance company. This will mean that the customer who fails to reveal an existing hire purchase agreement on a vehicle which he is selling or part exchanging with the dealer will be in breach of his contract.

This term may be partially limited by the seller writing into his contract a term that he will only contract to pass on the title that he actually has.

What other terms does the Sale of Goods Act write into a contract for the sale of goods?

The Sale of Goods Act writes in or "implies" three other terms, which may never be excluded or limited when the buyer under any contract is a consumer.

These implied terms are

a) that where the contract is for a sale of goods by description, the goods will comply with that description (S. 13).

b) that where the seller is selling in the course of a business, there is an implied condition that the goods will be of "Satisfactory" quality. This provision came into force on 3 January 1995 and replaces the concept of "Merchantable" quality. (Sale and Supply of Goods Act 1994).

c) that where the seller is selling in the course of a business, and the buyer expressly or by implication makes known any particular purpose for which the goods are being bought, there is an implied condition that the goods will be reasonably fit for that purpose, whether or not this is a common purpose for which the goods are supplied, unless it can be shown that the buyer did not rely, or that it was unreasonable for him to rely, on the seller's skill or judgment. (S. 14(3)).

What does "satisfactory" quality mean?

The Sale of Goods Act now states that goods will be of satisfactory quality if they meet the standard that a reasonable person would regard as satisfactory, taking account of any description of the goods, the price (if relevant) and all other relevant circumstances. The quality of goods includes their state and condition, and aspects of quality will include:

a) fitness for all the purposes for which goods of the kind in question are commonly supplied
b) appearance and finish
c) freedom from minor defects
d) safety
e) durability.

Are there any circumstances in which this implied term does not apply?

Yes. If matters making the goods unsatisfactory have been pointed out to the customer before the contract is made, or where he examines the goods before the contract and those unsatisfactory matters should have been revealed by the examination, the implied term does not apply. In other words, the customer will have no legal remedy under the contract of sale in these circumstances.

Can the seller attempt to vary or reduce his liability in relation to these implied terms?

No, not if he is selling to a consumer. Such an exclusion clause would be completely useless, and would also involve the seller in the commission of a criminal offence because the use of exclusion clauses in consumer sales was made illegal by an order made under the Fair Trading Act 1973.

Is there a legal definiton of "consumer" in this context?

Yes. The Unfair Contract Terms Act 1977 defines a consumer as a person who is buying goods of a type normally bought for private use or consumption, and who is not buying, or holding himself out as buying, in the course of a business.

This definition has been interpreted widely to mean that many business buyers of motor vehicles will be treated as consumers, unless buying vehicles is an integral part of their business e.g. a car hire company, another motor trader etc. Sale of cars to companies e.g. of shipping brokers or estate agents for the use of the employees on business will be treated as consumer sales.

Can the seller exclude the implied terms if he is selling to a non-consumer?

If a sale is made to a non-consumer (see above), the crucial test of an exclusion clause will be to see if it is 'reasonable'. This means that a court would look into all the circumstances surrounding the contract, for example, whether one person has a stronger bargaining position than the other, to see if it meets the test. If it does then it will be enforceable.

What is the buyer entitled to claim if he buys something which is unsatisfactory or unfit for purpose?

Under the Sale of Goods Act the buyer has two basic rights

a) to cancel the contract, reject the goods and get his money back

and

b) to claim damages for breach of contract against the seller

The right to reject is however limited, and the buyer will not be entitled to use it once he has "accepted" the goods.

How does "acceptance" take place?

This may happen in a number of ways

i.   where the buyer actually informs the seller he is accepting the goods e.g. by signing an acceptance note

ii. where a reasonable time has elapsed after delivery, the buyer will be deemed to have accepted the goods if he retains the goods without telling the seller he is rejecting them even if at that point in time he is unaware that they are faulty. In the case of *Bernstein v. Pamsons Motors (Golders Green) Ltd 1986,* a period of 3 weeks and 140 miles was held to be too long — the buyer had accepted the vehicle.

However, the recent amendment to the Sale of Goods Act now provides that the reasonable time must be calculated by reference to whether the buyer has had a chance to examine the goods to see if they are satisfactory. Allowing the seller to carry out a repair will no longer on its own amount to "acceptance".

If, the buyer has lost his right to reject, he may still be entitled to claim damages for breach of contract.

How will damages for breach of contract be calculated?

The buyer will be entitled to a sum calculated on the difference between the value of the vehicle in its unmerchantable state at the time of sale and what it would fetch if merchantable, plus all consequential losses arising from the breach of contract e.g. hiring charges for alternative transport, towing and repair bills.

Does the seller of goods have any other obligations other than those which arise under the contract if he sells goods which are faulty or dangerous?

Yes, under the Road Traffic Act 1991, the seller of an unroadworthy vehicle is committing a criminal offence in selling or offering for sale a vehicle which is unroadworthy i.e. does not comply with the Construction and Use Regulations.

It is also an offence to sell or fit parts which will make the vehicle no longer comply with the requirements of the Construction and Use Regulations.

In addition, the Consumer Protection Act 1987 Part II imposes criminal liability on the suppliers of unsafe goods. Motor vehicles are excluded, but parts and accessories for motor vehicles are included. The retailer will be liable for supplying an unsafe product unless he can prove to the court that he had reasonable grounds for thinking that it was safe.

The General Product Safety Regulations 1994 apply to all products supplied to or for use by consumers except where specific European safety legislation applies. Goods must be safe when placed on the market, and producers must provide safety information to consumers and monitor any risks associated with the product in use. The distributor also has to play a part in monitoring the safety of goods supplied. Non-compliance is a criminal offence.

Section B

CONSUMER CREDIT

It is very common for the customer who is buying a motor vehicle not to finance the whole cost of it out of his own cash resources. He may obtain the money from the bank or a finance company, and the type of legal contract he enters into may be for hire purchase, conditional sale, credit sale or straightforward loan.

The Consumer Credit Act 1974 had the objective of getting rid of the variety of legal rules which applied to these different forms of contracts where goods were bought on credit, and setting out one legal framework which would apply, at the same time as introducing more protection for consumers. The Act took a long time to come fully into force because there are a very large number of complex regulations which have been introduced to deal with particular aspects, for example advertising credit and the content and form of consumer credit agreements.

What is the difference between the different types of consumer credit agreement?

Loans

A loan will enable the customer to enter direct into an ordinary sale of goods contract with the retailer so that he gets immediate legal ownership of the goods, while at the same time taking on obligations as to the repayment of the loan to the bank or finance company. Normally, the lender will not be concerned if the goods turn out to be faulty – he will still be entitled to be repaid his money and the buyer would have to enforce his rights against the retailer (see Section A). If however, there is a business connection between the seller and the lender the Consumer Credit Act provides that the lender will share responsibility with the retailer if the goods turn out to be defective. This shared responsibility also applies where goods are bought with a credit card.

Credit Sale

The buyer gets ownership of the goods immediately although he is paying for them by instalments.

Hire purchase

Here the contract is for the hire of goods, normally from a finance company who has bought the goods from the retailer, with the hirer being given an option to buy the goods at the end of the hire term.

Conditional sale

Here the full legal ownership does not pass to the buyer until some condition has been fulfilled. This will usually be the payment of all the instalments.

Hiring

Where the consumer simply hires goods this may also be caught by the Consumer Credit Act where goods are hired leased or rented to an individual for a period of more than 3 months for a rental not exceeding £15,000. This is known as a consumer hire agreement and is dealt with in more detail in Section I.

Are all credit agreements caught by the Consumer Credit Act?

The Act only applies to regulated consumer credit agreements, that is an agreement made after 1 April 1977 providing an individual with credit not exceeding £15,000. An individual includes one man businesses, partnerships and other bodies which are not limited companies. Credit agreements with corporate bodies, i.e. private and public limited companies, are not included.

The £15,000 is calculated by excluding the charge for credit and any deposit taken.

How does the Consumer Credit Act control these agreements?

The Act requires that in order to be enforceable all consumer credit agreements must conform with the requirements of the Act so far as the content, legibility, signature, and availability of copies is concerned.

The agreement must contain the following:

a descriptive heading showing the nature of the agreement, e g "Consumer Hire Agreemont rogulatcd by thc Consumer Credit Act"

the name and address of the parties

financial details of the transaction

other terms of the agreement e.g. description of the goods, provision for payment etc

statements about the consumers rights under the 1974 Act

The consequence if an agreement does not conform to these rules is that it will be unenforceable.

What rights does the consumer have to cancel the contract?

The consumer's rights are regulated by the cancellation provisions of the Act. These broadly give him the right to cancel unless he signed the agreement on trade premises (i.e. the premises at which the other party to the transaction or anyone else linked to the transaction carries on business).

What controls are there over those who offer consumer credit?

This is a very important part of the Consumer Credit Act. The Act requires that anyone carrying on consumer credit business must have a licence. Consumer credit business included all sorts of activities as well as actually lending money, for example credit brokerage and debt counselling. Most motor traders will require a standard consumer credit licence in order to carry out their businesses – for example activities such as giving customers time to pay, introducing customers to sources of credit, and hiring vehicles for more than three months are all caught and require a licence.

An applicant for a licence must satisfy the Director General of Fair Trading that he is a fit and proper person to be granted a licence. He has wide powers, and so can refuse a licence e.g. to a motor trader who has been convicted of offences under the Trade Descriptions Act. He can also revoke or suspend a licence.

What happens if consumer credit business is carried on without a licence?

This is a criminal offence carrying penalties of fines or imprisonment. In addition any contracts entered into by an unlicensed business will be unenforceable.

How does the Act apply to advertisements of consumer credit?

One of the main principles of the Act is that consumers should be able to find out the true charge for credit that they are being offered. This means that there are detailed regulations which cover the way in which the cost and availability of credit may be advertised or stated in contract documents.

The basic rules about advertisements are

    that they must not give misleading information

they must not offer to supply goods and services on credit if they are not also available for cash

they must comply with one of the types of advertisements created by the Consumer Credit (Advertisements) Regulations 1989.

What types of advertisements are allowed?

The advertisement may be simple, intermediate or full. In a simple advertisement all that may be stated is that the advertiser is prepared to provide credit or hire facilities and include his name and occupation in the advertisement. An intermediate advertisement must add more information to this basic amount e.g. that written terms are available. A full advertisement must include a great deal of information including the annual percentage rate of interest charged (the "APR").

The practical effect of these rules is that if someone intending to put out only a "simple" advertisement in fact adds more information about credit than is permitted, he must then add all the details required to bring the advertisement up to the next category.

When a customer buys a vehicle on hire purchase who is his contract with?

In this type of transaction, the customer is entering into a contract, not with the motor trader, but with the source of the money he is "borrowing" – usually the finance company.

Does this mean that a customer who has bought a vehicle on hire purchase has no come-back on the retailer if it breaks down?

This is strictly speaking correct. The customer must bring his claim against the person he entered into the contract with i.e. the finance company. In addition, the Consumer Credit Act provides that any representations made by a retailer about the goods before a hire purchase agreement is made will be the responsibility of the finance company, because the retailer will be treated as its agent.

However, the retailer will still be involved in any dispute because, of course, he sold the goods to the Finance Company, and that contract is subject to the normal Sale of Goods Act rules.

In addition, he may be liable to the finance company under the terms of a "recourse agreement" where it is agreed that the finance company can recover from the motor trader the loss on any transaction negotiated through him.

If the customer buys a vehicle on hire purchase, does this mean that the terms implied under the Sale of Goods Act do not apply to the contract?

No. Although a hire purchase contract is not a contract for the sale of goods, the implied terms that the goods are merchantable, fit for purpose, and meet any description applied to them are also specifically implied into hire purchase contracts, so the customer will have the same rights as if he were a cash buyer.

Section C
TRADE DESCRIPTIONS

What is meant by a trade description?

"Trade description" is the term used by parliament to mean the sort of statement used by people in business to describe goods or services which they are selling. Until 1968 a trade description which was incorrect was covered only by the civil law and the consumer who suffered as a result would only be able to bring an action for misrepresentation or breach of contract. In that year however, parliament passed legislation which makes both the actual application of a false trade description to goods or services or the supply of goods or services which have been wrongly described, a criminal offence. Note that the main provisions of the Act do not apply to false descriptions made by private individuals, although they may be prosecuted in certain circumstances or be liable for misrepresentation to the buyer (a civil action). This Act is called the Trade Descriptions Act.

Does this mean that anything that is said about goods is caught by the Act?

The Act only catches false or misleading statements about the goods which fall into certain categories. These are listed in the Act as follows:

quantity size or gauge

method of manufacture production processing or reconditioning composition

fitness for purpose strength performance behaviour or accuracy any physical characteristics not included in the preceding paragraphs testing by any person and the results of those tests

approval by any person or conformity with a type approved by any person

place or date of manufacture production processing or reconditioning

person by whom manufactured produced processed or re-conditioned other history including previous ownership or use

As you can see, this list is very comprehensive and there-fore in practice most statements about goods can fall into one of these categories. The following are all examples of statements about vehicles which can be trade descriptions and therefore give rise to potential problems if the state-ment is wrong:

Describing a car's condition e.g. as in "beautiful condi-tion"

Making an incorrect statement about fuel consumption

A statement about the engine capacity

The year of manufacture

That a car is "new"

The identity of the manufacturer e.g. where a spare part is in fact counterfeit

Approval by a particular body e.g. "BS approved"

Mileage

Previous ownership e.g. "director's car"

How is an offence under the Act committed?

The Act creates two types of offence. The first category is what are called "absolute offences" and relates to goods and is contained in section 1 of the Act. This makes it an offence to

a) apply a false description to goods

or

b) supply goods to which a false trade description has been
   applied.

An offence can only be committed by someone acting in the
course of a trade or business. This means that the consumer
who clocks his own car cannot be prosecuted under this
section of the Act, although this may be possible under a
later section if it can be shown that he has caused someone
else e.g. the innocent motor trader to commit the offence of
"supplying" goods to which the false description has been
applied.

**Is someone who buys car and does them up for sale on
a regular basis caught by the Act if he does it as a
hobby in his spare time?**

This is a very grey area. Generally, the courts are strict
about their approach and if it can be shown that he does
this on a fairly regular basis, he will probably be treated as
being "in the course of a business".

How does a trade description get "applied" to goods?

The Act sets out the circumstances where a person will be
applying a description to goods. This includes a description
on the goods themselves, or on anything the goods are supplied with (e.g. packaging, labels), placing the goods in on
or with anything to which a description has been applied
(e.g. a notice in the showroom), or using the trade description in a manner likely to be taken as referring to the goods
(this could include oral statements and statements in
advertisements). There will also be a "deemed" trade description where goods are supplied in response to a request
for goods corresponding to a particular trade description.
This would arise, for example where a customer places an
order for a "new" car.

How does the offence of supplying goods to which a false trade description has been applied get committed?

The crucial point to note is that this offence can be committed without the trader being aware of the fact that the description is false. This means for example that a trader can commit an offence if he sells a car which has been clocked even if he is quite unaware of this himself. This means that great caution has to be exercised in particular when used cars are taken in for sale.

Does this mean that there is no defence to a prosecution under the Act even if the trader is unaware that a trade description is false?

There are defences to a prosecution under the Act.

a) It may be possible to avoid conviction by use of a disclaimer. This is particularly helpful when used car sales are involved and the trader fears that the car may have been 'clocked'. However, in order to be effective the disclaimer must be worded properly, and must be applied at the right time and in the right way. The idea is that it should be brought to the buyer's attention at the same time that he would otherwise have seen the actual trade description e.g. the false mileage reading. If it is later than that, if for example the disclaimer notice is only displayed in the showroom or on the vehicle invoice the disclaimer will not be effective.

A disclaimer will only be effective to the person who has been charged with the offence of supplying. The person who has actually applied the false trade description e.g. clocked the car, is not entitled to use it as a defence.

Example of disclaimer wording which was effective:

"Trade Descriptions Act 1968. Dealers are often unable to guarantee the mileage of a used car on sale. Please disregard the recorded mileage on this vehicle and accept this as an incorrect reading".

b) It would of course be a defence to a charge under the Act that either the trade description complained of was not false or was not false to "a material degree" (for example a very minor mis-statement)

c) There is in addition to these points a statutory defence under s.24 of the Act. There are two parts to this defence:

i. The person being prosecuted must show that his committing an offence was due either to a mistake, or to the "act or default" of someone else.

and

ii. He must show that he took "all reasonable precautions and exercised all due diligence to avoid committing an offence". It is this second part of the defence that causes problems because the standard of precautions and diligence that the court requires has been held in many cases to be very high because the courts take the view that liability should not be easily avoided.

For example, in cases involving the level of due care and diligence in relation to mileage readings the courts have held that traders should check with previous owners, check the service records of the vehicle, use a disclaimer which is appropriately worded, and of course carry out a careful inspection of the vehicle.

The defence has been used in cases where an employee has failed to carry out his duties properly and it can therefore be argued that he/she is the "other person" which has caused the employer to commit an offence. For example this was successfully used in a case involving a false description of the service supplied when servicing was not carried out in accordance with the manufacturer's service schedule. It was proved that the mechanic had failed to do the job properly, and the employer was able to satisfy the court that he did have adequate training and supervision and that this was an isolated incident.

Does this mean that an employee can be personally prosecuted under the Trade Descriptions Act?

Yes, employees have been successfully prosecuted although normally it will be the employer who is charged, unless, for example, the facts showed that there was deliberate fraud or dishonesty on the part of the employee.

Does the Act apply to false or misleading statements about pricing?

Section 11 of the Act did apply but has now been replaced by Part III of the Consumer Protection Act 1987 which makes it an offence to use misleading pricing. This is a much broader idea, and will be backed up by a Code of Practice which will give guidance on what misleading price is. (For more details on pricing refer to Section H.)

How does the Act apply to services?

Section 14 of the Act will apply to statements about servicing and repairs made by motor traders and makes it an offence to make a false statement knowingly or recklessly about

i.   the provision of a service in the course of a trade or business (e.g. "Engine tuning")

ii. the nature of any service in the course of a trade or business (e.g. "Ford 12,000 mile service")

iii. the time a service is to be provided, or the way in which it is to be provided, or the person who is going to provide it (e.g. "all servicing by fully trained mechanics")

iv. the examination, approval or evaluation by any person of services (e.g. "AA approved")

This offence DOES require either knowledge or recklessness, and does not impose such a heavy burden on the motor trader as offences in relation to goods under section 1 of the Act (see above).

What are the penalties if an offence is committed?

Penalties are a fine of up to £5,000 (in a magistrate's court), or an unlimited fine and up to two years imprisonment if prosecuted in the Crown Court.

Does the consumer bring an action under the Trade Description Act himself if he has a complaint?

The Act creates criminal liability rather than civil rights. This means that in theory the consumer could bring a private prosecution by applying to the magistrate's court for a summons. In practice this is vary rare, and the enforcement authority in the vast majority of cases is the local trading standards authority. This is run by the local council which employs trading standards officers to enforce not only this Act but also a number of other statutes, e.g. relating to food and drugs, calibration of petrol pumps, overloading of vehicles etc. The prosecution will normally be brought in the magistrate's court, unless the case is very serious in which case it might be started in the Crown court or sent there for sentencing after conviction.

Do I have to let trading standards officers on to my premises to carry out inspections of my vehicles?

The trading standards officer is given wide powers under the Act to enter business premises at all reasonable times to inspect goods, and if he has reasonable cause to think an offence has been committed require the production of books and records for inspection. He can also in these circumstances seize goods for examination or testing, and books and records which he believes will be needed in evidence. He may also require containers or vending machines to be opened. If he thinks entry to the premises is likely to be refused or if the proprietor is absent or evidence is likely to be destroyed he can obtain a warrant from a magistrate to allow him to enter. It is an offence to wilfully obstruct a trading standards officer or refuse to give information.

Section D

SERVICE AND REPAIR

What effect does the law have on the contracts that a motor trader has with his customers to repair or service their vehicles?

These contracts are contracts for the supply of a service (the act of repairing or maintaining the car), together with the supply of goods, i.e. the spare parts and other materials needed to carry out the work. Other contracts which are also treated as contracts for the supply of a service are those which do not involve the supply of any goods at the same time, but literally just the service involved, for example, a car wash, or car park for which a parking charge is made.

The usual rules about the formation of a contract will apply, for example as regards offer, acceptance, consideration and so on. This means for example that in order for the contract to be enforceable the parties must be in agreement about exactly what work has been agreed as the subject matter of the contract. This point has considerable practical significance as all too often problems can arise in the service department when the receptionist has noted down what the customer thinks needs to be done on the job card, and then the necessity for further work is discovered by the workshop. If the customer's authority is not obtained for the additional work to be done it will not be possible to recover the cost of the additional items from him unless it can be shown that he had agreed for all necessary items to be attended to, either expressly or by implication from previous contracts with you.

Does this mean that there is no legislation controlling what you can and can't say in this type of contract?

Up until 1982, there was no statute which applied to these sorts of contracts and the only terms of the contract would be those agreed between the parties and those implied in the contract by the common law, for example a duty on the person providing the service that he will act with reasonable care and skill, that the work will be done within a reasonable time, and that the person requesting the work will pay a reasonable amount.

The Supply of Goods and Services Act 1982 now applies and provides that in addition to the express terms agreed between the parties to this type of contract and the terms implied at common law, there will also be certain statutory implied terms rather like those implied into contracts for the sale of goods by the Sale of Goods Act 1979.

These are

a) That where the supplier of a service is acting in the course of a business, there will be an implied term that the supplier will carry out the service with reasonable care and skill (s. 13).

   This provision absorbs the old common law rule, and does not stop the law implying a stricter standard of care in some cases. For example, an undertaking by a garage that a car when repaired will be fit for use on the road goes beyond the implied term that he will exercise reasonable care and skill.

b) Where there is no time agreed in the contract for the performance of the service, there will be an implied term that it will be carried out within a reasonable time (s. 14)

c) Where no sum has been agreed as payment for the service, there is an implied term that a reasonable charge will be paid. This will be a question of fact, so a court will be able to take into account the usual charges for work of this type. (s. 15)

If a garage gives an estimate of the cost before carrying out a job for a customer, does this mean that the cost has been fixed?

There is a legal distinction between "quotations" and "estimates". A quotation is a promise to do the work at a particular price, whereas an estimate is what it says it is – an assessment of what the cost of the work may be. It follows that where a quotation has been given that cost is then binding on the parties to the contract. It is the contract price. On the other hand an estimate need only be close to the final price and only if the final bill exceeds the estimate by more than a reasonable amount, could the customer refuse to pay and argue that he is only bound to pay what the Act provides for, i.e. a "reasonable" amount for the work concerned. He would no doubt then be able to produce the estimate as evidence of what was a reasonable amount for the job.

Can the motor trader write in to his contracts for servicing and repair a term which excludes or changes any of these terms?

These sorts of contract are now caught by the Unfair Contract Terms Act 1977 (s. 3). This provides that clauses which try to limit or exclude contractual liability altogether will be tested by the court to see whether they are "reasonable".

Terms which will be affected in this way are those which

a) limit liability for breach of contract (e.g. by trying to avoid consequential losses which are caused by a defective spare part supplied under the repair contract)

b) suggest that the repairer will be complying with the contract if he does something substantially less than might have been reasonably expected (eg "all cars driven at owner's risk")

c) would allow no performance of the contract at all

In deciding whether any particular clause was reasonable or not, a court would look at all the circumstances, and also to a number of points set out in the Unfair Contract Terms Act, such as the relative bargaining power of the two parties, whether the parties had always contracted on these sorts of terms, and whether the work could have been done on more favourable terms elsewhere.

In addition, s. 2 of the Unfair Contract Terms Act will apply. This makes any contract term which excludes liability for death or personal injury caused by negligence completely ineffective.

The Unfair Terms in Consumer Contracts Regulations will also apply (see page 66).

If a garage subcontracts repair work to someone else, who is liable if the subcontractor's work is not up to scratch?

The rule is that the garage who originally contracted to do the work will be liable for the subcontractor's mistakes unless the customer nominated the subcontractor.

What is the position if a customer's car is damaged while it is on the motor trader's premises?

The motor trader who has a customer's car in his possession for work to be done is known as a bailee. This means that he is under an obligation to look after the customer's property, and will be liable for any damage unless he can prove that it was not caused by negligence on his part. What amounts to negligence will depend on the facts in each case. In one case where a car was left on the road overnight by the trader and it was stolen and recovered later damaged, it was held that the trader was not liable because in the circumstances the court was satisfied that he had proved that he was not negligent. The customer was aware that overnight storage facilities at the dealership were limited, and the vehicle itself had been disabled.

What rights does the motor trader have if the customer refuses to pay the bill for the work that has been done?

The unpaid repairer is allowed by the law to retain the vehicle until such time as the bill is paid. This is known as a lien, and the rules about how it can operate are contained in the common law. The lien is in theory limited to cases where there has been improvement or repair of goods, rather than simply routine maintenance. This suggests that the motor trader cannot exercise his lien for his unpaid bill for servicing work alone. However, in practice it may be difficult to distinguish between cases where only maintenance has been done, and other cases where in the course of the maintenance work some parts have been replaced and therefore it could be argued that the vehicle has been "improved".

Does the lien last indefinitely until the bill has been paid?

No. The lien will be lost if the customer lawfully takes the vehicle away from the repairer's premises, and it cannot be revived even if the car comes in again on a later occasion for work to be done, if the customer pays for the later work, the lien cannot be enforced for the earlier unpaid part.

How long must a motor trader keep a vehicle if a customer fails to come back for it and pay the bill?

The Torts (Interference with Goods) Act 1977 lays down the rules which will apply in this situation. It allows the unpaid bailee to sell the goods to recover his money and then account to the owner for the balance of any money raised after deducting the money owed to him.

The diagram below shows how the rules work, and this should be looked at with the notes that follow.

Torts (Interference with Goods) Act 1977
Uncollected goods in possession of Bailee

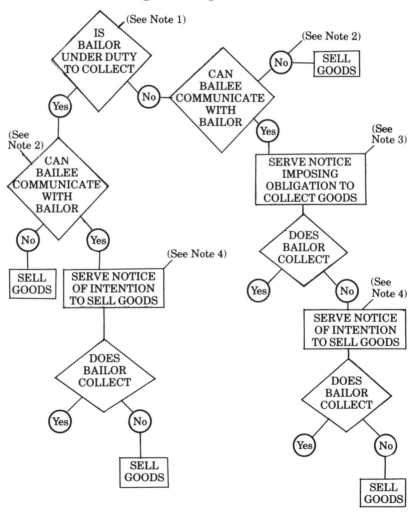

NOTE 1
The duty to collect can be imposed in the original contract of bailment. For example, a specific agreement that the customer will collect a motor vehicle on completion of the work.

NOTE 2
If the bailee is unable to communicate with the bailor or to trace him (e.g. no correspondence address or 'gone away'), and has taken reasonable steps to do so and is reasonably satisfied that the bailor does own the goods, the bailee can go straight ahead and sell the goods.

NOTE 3
The power to impose an obligation to collect the goods applies in the following cases:

where goods have been accepted for repair or other treatment and the work has been carried out

where goods have been accepted for valuation or appraisal, and that has been carried out by the bailee

where the goods have been stored by the bailee – whether or not he has been paid to do so – and either the term of storage has come to an end, or is being brought to an end by notice at the same time as the notice imposing the obligation to collect. This does not apply to goods held by a person as a mercantile agent.

Requirements of the notice

a)   It must be in writing and either delivered to the bailor or left at his address or posted to him.
b)   It must specify the name and address of the bailee, particulars of the goods and where they are held.
c)   It must state that the goods are ready for collection, or will be ready when the contract of bailment is brought to an end (see above).
d)   It must specify how much money if any the bailor owes the bailee.

NOTE 4
The Notice of Intention to Sell the goods may be combined with the Notice Imposing an Obligation to Collect Goods (see above). It must be in writing, and sent by registered or recorded delivery letter.

Requirements of the Notice

a)   It must specify the name and address of the bailee, particulars of the goods and the address or place held.
b)   It must specify the date on or after which the bailee proposes to sell (this must allow a "reasonable" period for collection or if money is owed by the bailor to the bailee, not less than 3 months notice must be given).
c)   It must specify the amount payable.

The bailee cannot sell the goods if he knows that the bailor is disputing all or part of the bill.

What does the trader do if he is not 'reasonably satisfied' that the bailor does own the goods?

In this situation the bailee can take advantage of rules set out in the Act which allow him to apply for a court order authorising the sale, and allowing him to deduct his costs and any amount due from the proceeds. Any balance can then be paid into court to be held for the credit of the bailor.

Section E

MANUFACTURERS' LIABILITY

If a product is faulty and causes injuries or kills someone, what rights do they have so far as compensation is concerned?

There are two categories of people who may be injured by a defective product. First there are those who bought it, and secondly those who did not buy it but came into contact with it. If the person who has been injured was the buyer of the product then he will of course have rights under the Sale of Goods Act against the seller if the product is not merchantable or fit for purpose (see Section A). In addition he may be able to sue the manufacturer for compensation either under the Consumer Protection Act 1987 which makes manufacturers strictly liable for defects in their products, or by proving that the manufacturer was negligent in producing the product with a defect in it (see below).

An obvious example of the second group would be the passengers in a car which is involved in an accident caused by, for example, defective brakes. Until recently this second category of people would have had a much more difficult time recovering compensation than the person who had actually bought the car. This is because they would have had no rights under the contract of sale of the car (even if they were all part of the family of the purchaser) and they would have had to prove that the manufacturer was negligent before they could get any compensation. This has now changed because of the passing of the Consumer Protection Act 1987 which makes manufacturers strictly liable for defects in their products. This means that the manufacturer will be liable even if he can show that he was not negligent.

As far as manufacturers' liability is concerned, does this mean that the law of negligence has been abolished by the new law?

No, the law of negligence will still exist although it will not be used so frequently. It will however continue to be relevant for some time because the Consumer Protection Act only applies to products which are supplied after 1 March 1987.

What is the manufacturer's liability so far as the law of negligence is concerned?

The principle of manufacturer's negligence was first established in the case of *Donaghue v Stevenson* in 1932. This involved a dead snail which had got into a bottle of ginger beer. The House of Lords decided that the manufacturer of the ginger beer was liable for the injuries caused to someone who drank the ginger beer, even though they had not themselves bought it, because the manufacturer had a duty to take care that his product did not injure anyone who he might reasonably have foreseen would come into contact with it. This category obviously included anyone who ultimately drank the ginger beer even if they had not bought it. If the manufacturer failed to take care, he was said to be negligent and therefore liable to pay compensation. This principle has been followed in many later cases, but has caused problems to consumers because it can be difficult and expensive to obtain the evidence which will prove that the manufacturer was actually negligent.

What types of defect may the manufacturer be liable for in a motor industry situation?

Defects in a motor vehicle may arise at different stages of its life. There may be a basic fault in the design – for example the petrol tank may be fitted in a position where it explodes if the vehicle is involved in a rear end collision. This type of defect is one of the most worrying for a manufacturer because it may mean that a very large quantity of vehicles may be affected. Secondly, faults may arise at the manufacturing stage because some part is missed out or wrongly fitted, or defective materials are used. This type of fault may be relatively less serious because it may be a one-off problem or may only affect a small batch of vehicles. Thirdly, the warnings and instructions given with the vehicle may be inadequate or wrong, and may be treated as defective. For example instructions for child proof rear door locks which had been inadvertently reversed so that they were unlocked rather than locked would undoubtedly be a defect.

What steps can a manufacturer take to avoid liability for negligence?

He has to show that he has taken all reasonable steps to ensure the safety of his product and that it will not kill or injure anyone. This will include not only taking care at the design and manufacturing stage but also once the vehicle is on the road making sure that the necessary recall action is taken if a problem comes to light.

How does the Consumer Protection Act change the situation

The object of the Act is to ensure that anyone who is injured or killed by a defective product will be able to recover compensation without having to prove that anyone was negligent. All he has to prove is that the product had a defect which caused the damage which he has suffered.

The basic principle of the Act is therefore to make the "producer" of a defective product strictly liable for this sort of damage, and also damage to consumer's property caused by the defective product.

"Producer" is defined very widely so that it includes:

a) The actual manufacturer – if it is a defective component

that has caused the damage then both the vehicle manufacturer and the component manufacturer will be liable.

b) The importer of the product into the EEC. The intention is that the consumer will always have someone to sue inside the EEC, and so this means, for example, that even though an importer of Japanese vehicles may not have done anything to a vehicle he will still be treated as the producer if it turns out to be defective.

c) The person who puts their own name or trade mark on a product will be treated as its producer unless they can identify the actual producer within a reasonable time of being asked to do so.

d) The retailer of a product will be liable as a producer if he is unable within a reasonable time to identify his supplier. This has very important implications for the motor trader who is selling spare parts. If for example he is sourcing the same component from a number of different factors it will be essential that records are kept so that the source of any part can be identified.

"Product" will include the finished product and the parts that have gone into it.

"Defective" in the Act has a special meaning. It is defined in s. 3 of the Act as follows: "There is a defect in a product . . . if the safety of the product is not such as persons generally entitled to expect".

In deciding what standard of safety a person is entitled to expect a court will take into account the way in which a product is marketed, any warnings or instructions with the product, reasonable use of the product and the time when it was supplied.

Does the Act mean that a manufacturer will be liable for his products until they are scrapped?

The Act has a ten year cut-off period after the date of supply of the product by the producer. After this time strict liability will not apply, but there could still be the possibility of bringing an action of negligence providing the action is brought within three years of the injury.

Is any financial loss caused by a defective product covered by strict liability?

No. The Act only applies to losses of more than £275 arising from personal injury or death, and damage to consumer property, but not damage to the defective product itself. It does not cover what is known as "pure economic loss" which means items such as loss of use claims, repair costs, towing charges etc. The retailer will therefore continue to be liable under the Sale of Goods Act 1979 (see above) for these types of claims if the vehicle is not merchantable or fit for purpose.

Does the fact that the law creates strict liability mean that the manufacturer will not have any defence to a legal action for compensation?

There are defences in the Consumer Protection Act s. 4. These are:

a) That the product was not defective when it left the producer. This would enable a vehicle manufacturer to argue for instance that the person making the claim had failed to service and maintain a vehicle properly and it was this that gave rise to the problem rather than a basic fault in the vehicle.

b) That the defect arose because it complied with a regulation or standard imposed by UK or EEC legislation (e.g. Construction and Use Regulations) Note – this is not the same as saying that a product is not defective because it complies with a regulation. This would not be a good defence.

c) That the producer did not in fact supply the product.

d) That the supply was not in the course of a business.

e) That the state of scientific and technical knowledge at the time the product was supplied was such that the producer could not be expected to have discovered the defect.

This last defence is the so-called "development risk" defence and has been widely criticised, but it seems unlikely that a vehicle manufacturer would have such a defence available very often.

How does the law affect the manufacturer's attitude toward recalls?

Although the manufacturer's liability will be strict in future for defects, recalls will still be a very important way in which he may be able to reduce his liability. This is for two reasons:

1. because recalling defective vehicles will help to prevent accidents occurring

   and

2. because the Consumer Protection Act does allow compensation to be reduced if it can be shown that the person claiming in fact contributed to his injuries ("contributory negligence"). The fact that a recall notice had been ignored by the person making the claim would therefore be relevant in any subsequent legal action if an accident occurred due to the problem.

The administrative procedure for recall of motor vehicles is now governed by the various Codes of Practice for Vehicle Recalls approved by the Department of Transport. Different Codes relate to different types of vehicle e.g. passenger cars, motor cycles etc and also to parts and accessories, but the basic provisions are the same. Whilst manufacturers are not legally required to follow the Codes, failure to do so would undoubtedly lead to further legislation and it is generally accepted that the Codes operate well.

The Codes apply when there is evidence of the existence of a safety defect in a significant number of vehicles some of which have already been sold for use in Great Britain. The manufacturer has responsibility to decide when a defect is notifiable under the terms of the Code. When he notifies he must tell the Department of Transport the nature of the defect and hazard involved, the estimated number of vehicles affected, and the planned action.

As soon as a manufacturer has decided on action, he must notify all owners/registered keepers of the affected vehicles by any method he chooses. He will be able to obtain details of the names of registered keepers in appropriate cases from the DVLC at Swansea on payment of a fee.

The Department must be kept informed at all stages of the recall and they publish details of all recalls at regular intervals.

Is there any other legal control over products which are unsafe other than giving people who are injured the right to sue?

Part II of the Consumer Protection Act 1987 creates a specific criminal offence of supplying an unsafe product. This liability will rest on anyone in the chain of supply including manufacturer, wholesaler, importer and retailer. It does not apply to motor vehicles but will apply to parts and accessories for motor vehicles.

A product will be "unsafe" if it is not reasonably safe having regard to a number of points including the way the product is marketed, the normal use of the product, and any relevant safety standards.

A product that does conform with safety standards will be regarded as safe in relation to the features of the product covered by the standard.

The retailer will have a defence if he can show that he had

reasonable grounds for believing that the goods were safe and so it will be sensible practice for the retailer to check that parts he sells do conform to relevant standards.

Offences are punishable by fines of up to £5,000 and/or imprisonment.

Any supplier may be issued with a "Notice to Warn" potential or previous customers about an unsafe product which he must carry out at his own expense.

A "Prohibition Notice" may also be issued which actually prohibits sale or supply of a particular unsafe product.

The General Product Safety Regulations 1994 will also apply (see p. 170).

What about controls over the safety of motor vehicles?

These are to be found in the Construction and Use Regulations, and the requirements of the Road Traffic Acts.

Section F
GUARANTEES

What is the difference between a manufacturer's warranty and a guarantee?

Both these expressions are used to describe the promise given by a manufacturer, or retailer when he sells goods that he will meet the cost of putting right defects in goods within a certain time or amount of use, but it is unecessarily confusing to use the word "warranty" in this context at all. This is because in legal terms a warranty has a very precise legal meaning as a minor term in a contract. It is therefore better to refer to manufacturers' or retailers' "guarantees", and this is the word which the Office of Fair Trading is now recommending should be adopted.

Now that the retailer cannot get out of his liabilities under the Sale of Goods Act to sell goods which are of satisfactory quality and fit for purpose, what is the point of a manufacturer's guarantee?

Its main function now is to serve as an additional benefit for the customer, which can obviously be seen as commercially very useful. The Consumer Transactions (Restrictions on Statements) Orders 1976 and 1978 apply to guarantees so that it is not possible for them to be used as a way to take away any of the consumer's rights under the Sale of Goods Act 1979. Any promises they make must therefore be over and above the liability of the retailer. This is very relevant where, for example, a manufacturer's guarantee excludes liability for items such as hiring of alternative transport when a vehicle is off the road. This is perfectly acceptable as an exclusion from the guarantee, but as it cannot have any effect on the retailer's liability, the question of whether the customer is entitled to recover the cost of alternative transport will have to be decided by looking at the question of whether the vehicle was merchantable or not (see above Section A).

Other exclusions such as tyres, windscreens and so on will be treated in a similar way.

Are there any other exclusions which a manufacturer is not allowed to put in his guarantee?

The Unfair Contract Terms Act 1977 provides that the manufacturer may not include in the guarantee any term which would exclude his liability for any loss or damage while the vehicle the subject of the guarantee is in consumer use which arises from a defect caused by his negligence or death or injury arising from negligence.

Are there any items which a manufacturer must include in his guarantee?

There are two aspects to this question. First, what the law says, and secondly the provisions of the Motor Industry Code of Practice.

There must be a statement in the guarantee that it does not affect or alter any of the consumer's rights against the retailer under the Sale of Goods Act 1979. (Consumer Transactions (Restrictions on Statements) Orders 1976 & 1978.)

The Code of Practice also lays down various requirements:

a) The terms of the guarantee must be easily understandable particularly when items are included or excluded from it

b) manufacturers and dealers should give advice to consumers as to who is responsible and what to do if they have a problem regarding parts and accessories not covered by the manufacturer's guarantee

c) the manufacturer should permit the transfer of the

unexpired portion of any warranty to a second or subsequent owner

d) the manufacturer must make clear that rectification work may be done under warranty by one of his franchised dealers who was not the selling dealer

e) manufacturers must operate fair and equitable policies to permit the extensions of the guarantee in the event of a car being off the road for an extended period for rectification of guarantee faults, or of repetition of a fault which had previously been the subject of rectification work during the guarantee period.

Is a manufacturer's guarantee legally enforceable by the consumer if something goes wrong?

The legal status of a guarantee is rather unclear. It seems likely that in the event of a dispute being brought to court, it would probably be accepted that the manufacturer must honour his guarantee even though there is no contract direct between him and the consumer. It would probably be treated as an enforceable promise if it could be proved that the consumer knew of the existence of the guarantee before he entered into the contract to buy the goods.

The Office of Fair Trading have made it clear that they believe that guarantees which are not intended to be legally binding should not be offered.

How do these rules apply to guarantees offered by a dealer, for example on sale of a used vehicle?

Exactly the same rules apply as to the items which can and cannot be included, and as to their legal effect. This means that a three month/3,000 mile guarantee offered with a used car can not be used by the retailer as a way of limiting liability if the car is in fact unsatisfactory or not fit for purpose (see Section A above). In other words, he may still be liable after the period of the guarantee.

Does that mean that when I sell a second hand car I have to accept liability for defects even if I am selling it for scrap and without any guarantee?

Whatever the condition of what you are selling, the Sale of Goods Act will apply. Obviously the standard of satisfactory quality for something sold as scrap will be totally different from that of a new car, and that would be taken into account, as would the price and "all other relevant circumstances" (see Section A above). If the trader goes beyond describing the goods e.g. "sold as scrap" and adds words such as "no warranty or guarantee" then hs is running the risk of criminal prosecution under the Consumer Transactions (Restrictions on Statements) Orders because this type of statement may be treated as an illegal exclusion clause if it is used in a sale to a consumer. This does not, of course, prevent the use of this type of exclusion if the sale is to a trader, where the only test in the event of a dispute will be to see whether the exclusion is "reasonable".

Section G

FAIR TRADING

The Fair Trading Act 1973 was an important piece of legislation because for the first time Parliament decided to appoint a Director General of Fair Trading whose job it would be to look after consumers to make sure that manufacturers and traders selling goods and services to consumers were not acting unfairly, or illegally.

How does the Director General of Fair Trading do this job?

He has various responsibilities imposed on him by the Fair Trading Act (and also other pieces of legislation as well). He must, for example, keep an eye on activities by those doing business with consumers to make sure that they are not trading in an undesirable way. If he finds practices which he does not like, he can recommend to the government that new laws should be introduced to stop them, and this may be done by way of regulation which creates criminal liability.

Regulations

There have been several regulations made under the Fair Trading Act. The most significant from the point of view of the motor trade are the Consumer Transactions (Restrictions on Statements) Orders 1976 and 1978, and the Business Advertisements (Disclosure) Order 1977. The first regulations makes it a criminal offence for traders to continue to use clauses which exclude the seller's responsibility to supply goods which are of satisfactory quality and fit for purpose when selling to consumers. These clauses have no legal effect, but many traders have continued to use them, and because the implied terms that the goods are merchantable and fit for purpose do not apply to private sales, consumers may be deterred from enforcing their rights under the Sale of Goods Act if the goods they have bought turn out to be defective. Motor traders in particular have been prosecuted widely under this regulation for statements like "no warranty given", and "as seen tried and approved" when used in relation to consumers.

The second regulation makes it an offence to advertise goods for sale in a way which make it appear that the seller is a private individual when in fact he is a trader. The reason for this regulation is very similar to the Restrictions on Statements Regulation, and is to ensure that consumers are not deterred from enforcing their rights under the Sale of Goods Act by thinking that they do not exist.

Undertaking

An alternative control is that he can require a trader who is not treating his customers properly to give him an undertaking under Part III of the Act that he will behave in a more acceptable way in future. These undertakings can be enforced by court order, and breach of a court order can mean a fine or even imprisonment for contempt of court. There have been quite large numbers of undertakings given since the Act was passed, many of them by motor traders.

Codes of Practice

In addition, the Fair Trading Act requires him to encourage industries to introduce Codes of Practice which lay down rules of behaviour covering that industry. These Codes are operated through the various trade associations. In the Motor Industry, there are various Codes. The main ones are:

The Code of Practice for the Motor Industry which was first

launched in 1976 by the Motor Agents Association, the Society of Motor Manufacturers and Traders, and the Scottish Motor Trade Association.

The Code of The Vehicle Builders and Repairers Association

The Motor Cycle Code introduced by The Motor Cycle Association

The Codes are revised from time to time.

These Codes of Practice are all approved under the Fair Trading Act provisions. In addition to these Codes there are also various Codes of Practice on Vehicle Safety Defects. These have been drawn up by the Society of Motor Manufacturers and Traders and the Department of Transport and lay down the procedures to be followed when vehicle manufacturers and concessionaires become aware of safety defects in vehicles, parts, accessories, and trailers sold in Great Britain.

Does this mean that the contents of the motor codes are legally binding on all garages and manufacturers?

No, strictly speaking the Codes are what is called "self regulatory" which means that the trade associations are responsible for enforcing the Codes amongst their members. However, the law has been used in some cases to enforce the Code, e.g. by a prosecution under the Trade Descriptions Act of a motor trader who displayed the RMI logo, but failed to follow the Code which is obligatory for all RMI members. In practice, failure to follow an agreed Code means that the Director General will consider whether legislation would be a more effective way of dealing with particular problems.

Section H
PRICING AND ADVERTISING

Advertisements

Up until relatively recently there has been very little specific legislation controlling advertising generally. However, controls have been gradually developed so that there are now a number of statutes and regulations which control the content and style of advertisements. In addition, there is a code of practice introduced by the Advertising Standards Authority which controls advertising on a voluntary basis, and reference to this code is also included in the Code of Practice for the Motor Industry.

What laws do apply to advertisements?

One of the most important is the Trade Descriptions Act 1968 (see Section C). This makes the application of a false trade description to goods or services a criminal offence. The Act will catch statements made in advertisements, e.g. mileages on used cars, statements about condition and so on.

Do these provisions also apply to sales literature, brochures and so on?

Yes, the Trade Descriptions Act applies equally in this situation, and even the existence of a disclaimer in the brochure as to the accuracy of the information may not help if it can be shown that the inaccuracy in the brochure was known about at the time the buyer was influenced to enter into the transaction.

What specific regulations apply to information in motor trade advertisements?

The Passenger Car Fuel Consumption Order 1983 applies to the quoting of fuel consumption figures in any material issued to the general public with a view to promoting sales of cars. It requires that such material must include specified information as to the results of official fuel consumption tests carried out in accordance with government requirements. The object of the regulation is to make sure that this information is available to the general public in a variety of ways. The manufacturer must make sure it is included in any manual or handbook issued to the first owner, the motor trader who deals in new cars must make the results of the official tests available to customers, and any new car displayed on his premises must have a label on it giving the results of the fuel consumption test in a specified form.

Advertisements by businesses are controlled by the Business Advertisements Disclosure Order (for details see Section G).

The content of Consumer Credit advertisements are controlled by regulations under the Consumer Credit Act (for details see Section B).

Are there any other general controls over advertising?

Yes. The Control of Misleading Advertisements Regulations 1988 came into effect on 20 June 1988. These are intended to supplement and back up the existing rules by giving the Director General of Fair Trading power to step in if it is in the public interest that certain misleading advertisements should be stopped by a Court Order.

Pricing

An important part of controlling advertising relates to the pricing of goods as this may be a powerful incentive to buyers to choose a particular motor car or television set. The law therefore regards it as very important that goods are priced accurately and in a way which is not misleading.

Does this mean that the Trade Descriptions Act will also apply to statements about prices?

Section 11 of the Trade Descriptions Act 1968 made it an offence to apply a false price to goods. This has now been replaced by Part III of the Consumer Protection Act 1987 which makes it an offence to apply a "misleading" price to goods to consumers where it is likely that consumers will rely on the misleading price indication and there have been no steps taken to stop them doing that.

What does "misleading" mean?

The Act sets out various tests as to when a price will be considered to be misleading for example:

if it is suggested that the price is less than in fact it is

if it is suggested that the price covers matters in respect of which an extra charge is made (e.g. delivery charges, number plates)

if a price comparison is made on incorrect facts

The Act backs up these provisions by the introduction of a Code of Practice which gives practical guidance, and the Act contains power to make specific regulations when necessary.

Is there any legal requirement to give written price information to customers?

Yes. Since 1 September 1991, The Price Marking Order 1991 has made it a legal requirement that almost all goods offered for retail sale – that is to consumers rather than to businesses – are accompanied by a written indication of the price. When the goods are on display, this means that the price must be marked either on the goods, or on a price list, notice or price ticket close by which clearly relates to the goods.

What about goods not on display, such as in the Parts Department?

Where goods are not on display, the law requires that the written price information is given to the customer either by showing him a price list or catalogue with the price indicated, or by showing him the price on a VDU screen.

Does this mean that the service department has to give customers a written price in advance for parts to be supplied when a vehicle is in for repair or service?

No. The legislation does not apply to goods supplied as part of a contract of service.

What items must be included in the written price indication?

Where sales from the premises are mainly to private consumers rather than to businesses, the price must include VAT. Where sales are mainly to businesses, VAT may be shown separately and with equal prominence to the exclusive price, or VAT exclusive prices may be shown with a prominent general notice that VAT is payable at the current rate. The cost of any ancillary goods or services (for example the cost of delivery from the manufacturer to the dealer) which the consumer must pay for in order to obtain the goods must also be included, or if excluded the price of those items must be shown with equal prominence to the main price. If number plates are excluded from the price, then this fact must be specifically stated.

Does the legislation apply to advertisements?

Advertisements by retailers are covered by the legislation, and if price information is included then it must comply with the rules. Manufacturers' advertisements are not covered so long as they just include a general indication of the recommended price at which the goods may be available from retailer.

Are there any penalties for not complying with the law?

Yes. Failure to comply is a criminal offence punishable by fines of up to £5,000 in the Magistrates' Court, or of an unlimited amount in the Crown Court.

Aren't there special rules which apply to pricing of petrol?

Yes. Petrol pricing is also controlled by the Price Marking Order 1991 which contains special rules on petrol pricing. It applies to all retailers who indicate that petrol is for sale from their premises who must give a written indication of the price of the petrol they are selling in a specified way, and if the price display signs can be seen from the road, certain additional information must be included.

The price displayed on the pump must be clear and legible and identify the grade of fuel it relates to and include a statement of the unit of measurement i.e. litres or gallons.

Section I

CONTRACTS FOR THE SUPPLY OF GOODS

Section A discussed in detail the legal rules which apply when goods are sold to a customer in exchange for a payment which he makes before the goods change hands. These contracts include straightforward case sales where the buyer produces the money himself, and situations where he gives the seller cash but he has obtained the money from another source such as a bank through a load or overdraft, or by using his credit card.

There are other types of contract where ownership of the goods may change hands which are not covered by the Sale of Goods Act. For example where a garage carries out a repair on a customer's car, and in the course of doing so supplies and fits parts to it that is not a contract for the sale of goods but for work done and materials supplied. Those contracts are now caught by the Supply of Goods and Services Act 1982 which writes into those contracts similar terms to those in the Sale of Goods Act about quality and fitness for purpose.

Finally, there are contracts where the customer may get the use of the goods in exchange for money, but where either he will never own the goods for example when he hires or leases them, or the ownership of them will only pass to him when he has finished making a series of payments as in the case of a hire purchase contract.

Hiring and leasing contracts

As the Sale of Goods Act does not apply does this mean that the consumer has no rights when he hires a car if it turns out to be faulty?

The Supply of Goods and Services Act 1982 provides that implied terms similar to those in the Sale of Goods Act 1979, shall apply to hiring contracts. The terms are:

a) That the person hiring out the goods (the bailor) has the right to transfer possession to the hirer (the bailee) for the period of the hiring agreement.

b) That the goods hired out will correspond to its description i.e. a contract to hire a "Bedford Tipper" meant that only a Bedford truck and tipper would do, and it must be driveable and suitable to receive and tip loads of materials.

c) That where the bailor is acting in the course of a business the goods are satisfactory and reasonably fit for purpose.

d) That where the goods are hired by reference to a sample, the goods will match the sample.

What obligations does the customer have when he hires goods?

The Supply of Goods and Services Act does not impose any obligations on the customer, but the common law will apply and provides that he must take reasonable care of the goods, and return them when the hiring period has finished. If the agreement is a regulated consumer hire agreement (see below), special rules apply if the bailor wants to get the goods back before the end of the agreement.

Are there any other statutes which apply to hiring and leasing contracts?

Any hire or lease agreement which is a "consumer hire"

agreement is now regulated by the Consumer Credit Act 1974. A "consumer hire" agreement is defined as one where goods are hired or rented to an individual (this includes sole traders and partnerships), which can last for more than three months, and does not involve payments of more than £15,000.

What are the consequences of an agreement being a "consumer hire" agreement?

The agreement will not be enforceable unless it complies with the requirements of the Consumer Credit Act 1974. These are very similar to those required in hire purchase contracts, and cover points such as the inclusion of all relevant terms, the fact that the agreement must be legible and contain various statutory statements about the hirer's rights. The hirer has the right to copies of the agreement, and will have cancellation rights similar to those in hire purchase contracts.

What can the owner of the goods do if the hirer does not keep up the payments or breaks the agreement in some other way?

His rights are now affected by the Consumer Credit Act. He has to serve a default notice giving at least seven days warning if he wants to terminate the contract, recover possession, demand early payment, enforce any security, or do anything which alters the hirers rights under the contract.

Hire Purchase

What terms are written into a contract for hire purchase?

These contracts are covered by the Supply of Goods (Implied Terms) Act 1973 which provides that the same implied terms that apply to sale of Goods Act contracts will apply to contracts where the goods are sold on hire purchase.

Who is liable if a vehicle supplied under a hire purchase agreement turns out to be faulty?

The contract in this situation will not normally be between the customer and the motor trader, but between the customer and the finance company which will have bought the vehicle from the trader and then entered into the hire purchase agreement with the consumer. This means that the consumer's rights if the car is faulty are against the finance company who in turn would generally bring in the motor trader as the supplier to him.

If the customer can show that a vehicle he bought under hire purchase was unsatisfactory or unfit for purpose does he then have the same remedies against the finance company as he would have against the seller if he had bought it for cash?

No. Because the Sale of Goods Act does not apply to these contracts the situation is different. Whereas the consumer had brought goods for cash may be able to recover the whole of the money paid (see section A) together with any consequentional losses, the buyer under a hire purchase agreement will only be able to recover instalments he has paid less a deduction for actual use of the vehicle. However, whereas the cash buyer has to act very quickly if he wants to get his money back and will lose this right if more than a "reasonable" time has elapsed since he took delivery, the buyer under a hire purchase contract has a reasonable time to act from discovering the fault.

PART 4: ROAD TRANSPORT LAW (GENERAL)

by

Anthea Worsdall and Peter Groves

CONTENTS

Section 4A and 4B

TYPE APPROVAL AND CONSTRUCTION AND USE

Road Vehicles (Construction and use) Regulations 1986 (No 1078)

Motor Vehicles (Type Approval) Regulations 1980 (No 1182)

Motor Vehicles (Type Approval for Goods Vehicles) (Great Britain) Regulations 1982 (No 1271)

Motor Vehicles (EC Type Approval) Regulations 1992 No 3107)

How does the law ensure that motor vehicles are constructed to safe standards?

The law deals with the safe construction of motor vehicles in two ways:

1. It imposes *type approval requirements* before a vehicle can be registered: and

2. It controls the *construction and use* of vehicles once they are on the road.

The Road Vehicles (Construction and Use) Regulations (or C&U Regulations for short) are constantly being updated and amended, and every student should have their own copy and familiarise themselves with them. The current basic Regulations date from 1986 (Statutory Instrument No 1078) but there are several amending Regulations too.

The C&U Regulations also require that in some instances vehicles or parts of vehicles bear marks showing that they conform to certain specific requirements. Furthermore, certain vehicles have to be "type approved" before they can be registered for use on the roads in Great Britain. Type approval also applies to some vehicle parts.

C&U Regulations apply to goods vehicles and passenger cars. There are separate type approval requirements for commercial vehicles and passengers cars.

How does "type approval" for passenger cars operate?

All vehicles to which EC Type Approval applies must either be approved by the Secretary of State for Transport in the UK, or be approved in another EC member state. The vehicle manufacturer holding the approval must issue a Certificate of Conformity in respect of each vehicle to which the approval applies. He must also keep records for ten years of the serial number of the certificate issued, the vehicle identity number, and the reference numbers of the EC Directives with which the vehicle conforms. Special arrangements known as Single Vehicle Approval (SVA) apply for the approval of single vehicles such as kit cars, personal imports and very low volume vehicles.

At present, there are two means for obtaining type approval:

1. A manufacturer may obtain a national type approval certificate from the Secretary of State. This shows that the type vehicle conforms with the relevant require-ments. The manufacturer must also demonstrate to the Secretary of State that series production of the vehicle will conform with the type vehicle. The manufacturer then issues *certificates of conformity* to show that vehicles of that type which it makes subsequently conform with the approval. This system is primarily suitable for domestic manufacturers but has also been open to manufacturers from other EC Member States. Few of them have used it.

2. Alternatively, manufacturers may obtain a Minister's Approval Certificate. Initially, a Primary Minister's Approval Certificate (PMAC) is issued, then Subsequent Minister's Approval Certificates (sub-MACs) are issued

for each vehicle subsequently imported. The manufacturer does not certify conformity in this case.

The manufacturer or importer quotes this type approval number on the application for first registration of a motor vehicle when using the so-called "secure route" (Forms V55/ 1–4). When the vehicle is first registered outside the secure route procedure (using a V55/5), which is the case with a personal import, this does not happen. This number is the evidence required by the licensing authority that the vehicle is type approved.

The detailed technical requirements for approval have since 1970 been the subject of a process of harmonisation within the European Community. This came to fruition in 1992, and since 1996 EC type approval has replaced the existing national system for vehicles made in the EC. First registration is obtainable on production of evidence that an EC certificate of conformity or a Minister's Approval Certificate has been issued in respect of the vehicle.

What vehicles need type approval?

From 1 January 1998, EC Type Approval applies to all "light passenger vehicles". These are vehicles, excluding some specialised vehicles, with four or more wheels, and an internal combustion engine, which are constructed or adapted for the carriage of passengers and are not goods vehicles, with no more than eight seats in addition to the driver's seat, and having a maximum design speed exceeding 25 kph.

What exclusions are there?

The regulations do not apply to

a) to vehicles where the user can show that EC Type Approval was not necessary for registration
b) to vehicles used under a trade licence

c) a motor vehicle brought temporarily into Great Britain by a resident abroad;

How does type approval for goods vehicles operate?

The scheme is almost identical to that relating to passenger cars. However, it only applies to those parts of the vehicle produced by the original manufacturer, e.g. the chassis, and not parts or conversions added afterwards in a number of different stages by different manufacturers. Evidence that the chassis conforms to the type approved will be required when the vehicle is plated for the first time.

How does type approval relate to the Construction and Use Regulations?

All vehicles have to comply with aspects of the C&U Regulations and the Lighting Regulations (see below). These regulations require that certain components of certain vehicles should be marked with an "E" or "e" mark to show that they have been manufactured to the required standard. A type approved vehicle will either comply with or be exempt from these marking requirements.

What is an "E" mark?

An "E" mark shows that the component to which it is applied complies with the requirements of regulations made by the United Nations Economic Commission for Europe (UNECE). This body has various committees of experts, which produce technical regulations in a variety of fields.

ECE regulations are made under an agreement made in Geneva in 1958. They are intended to ensure that motor vehicles can be exported from one country to another and legally be used on the roads abroad. The aim is very similar to that of the European Community, with its harmonised technical legislation.

Every country which has signed the Geneva Agreement, and which agrees to adopt an ECE regulation, will accept vehicles on its roads so long as they comply with the technical standard. They must also be marked with the "E" mark which is the manufacturer's certificate that the vehicle or part conforms with the one that was tested.

What does the "E" mark look like?

The "E" mark comprises a circle enclosing a letter "E", the relevant mark for the regulation complied with and the identification number of the country where the approval was granted. 11 identifies the UK: "E" marks are most readily seen on lamp lenses and window glass.

How can I find out which "E" marks are required by British law?

Any ECE regulation which has been adopted in Great Britain has been included in a regulation made under the Road Traffic Acts.

What is an "e" mark?

An "e" mark means that a vehicle or a part of it complies with a construction requirement laid down in a European Community directive. These may be an alternative to either an "E" mark or an approved British Standard – BS – approval mark. For example, rear reflectors on vehicles first used on or after July 1970 must conform with ECE regulation 3, or BS AU 40 part 2, or the equivalent EC standard.

What happens if the type approved vehicle is converted or altered in some way?

If the alteration is made before the vehicle is first registered and affects the approval certificate in specified respects then the alteration must be notified to the Department of Transport. If the alteration is made after first registration, the approval will not be affected, but C&U regulations will apply.

How does the law ensure that the user of a vehicle maintains it in a safe condition?

Apart from the regular testing of vehicles (see section C), the law makes it a criminal offence to use a vehicle on the road if it is "unroadworthy". This is defined as failing to comply with any of the legal requirements as to braking, steering gear, tyres or lighting equipment, the construction weight or equipment of vehicles, or the state of general maintenance of the vehicle.

What responsibility has a motor trader under the road traffic legislation for the condition of vehicles he is selling?

It is an offence for a trader to supply an unroadworthy vehicle or to alter it or fit defective or unsuitable parts or accessories which will make the vehicle unroadworthy. It is also an offence to sell a vehicle or part which is subject to type approval but for which no certificate is in force.

Section C

ANNUAL TESTING

How does the law ensure that vehicles on the road remain in a safe condition?

Apart from the "use" part of the Construction and Use Regulations which require the owner of the vehicle to ensure that it complies with the requirements at all times, vehicles over a certain age must undergo a test to ensure that certain items are still safe.

What requirements are there for vehicles to be tested?

The Motor Vehicles (Tests) Regulations 1981* require specified motor vehicles registered for more than three years to be tested on an annual basis. Any vehicles to which the regulations apply must have a current test certificate in force at any time it is used on the road.

The classes of vehicles covered by the Regulations are:

I   Light motor bicycles

II   Motor bicycles other than light motor vehicles

III Light motor vehicles

IV   Motor cars and heavy motor cars not covered in other categories

V   Large passenger carrying vehicles and certain specified PSVs

VI   Other public service vehicles

VII Goods vehicles of which the design gross weight is more than 3000 kg but does not exceed 3500 kg

*S.I. 1981 No 1694 as amended.

Are there any exemptions?

There is a long list of exempted vehicles in the Regulations. These include:

locomotives and motor tractors

tracked vehicles

goods vehicles over 3500 kg gross – not dual purpose vehicles or caravans

an articulated vehicle not being an articulated bus

works trucks

pedestrian controlled vehicles

certain invalid carriages

licensed metropolitan taxis

vehicles going to a port for export

vehicles of visiting forces

vehicles temporarily in GB

vehicles licensed in N Ireland or which have a N Ireland test certificate

vehicles exempt from duty due to travelling less than 6 miles per week on public roads

certain taxis

certain hire cars

police vehicles maintained in approved workshops

imported military vehicles

electrically propelled goods vehicles not over 1525 kg unladen

agricultural motor vehicles

In addition a test certificate is not required in a number of other situations when a vehicle is being used on the road, for example:

a vehicle being taken to a previously arranged test

a vehicle authorised under a Special Types Order

an imported vehicle while travelling from the port of importation to the home of the owner

a vehicle being removed under a statutory power

a vehicle seized or detained by police or Customs and Excise

a vehicle being tested by a motor trader after repair.

Who may carry out the test?

These must be carried out by an authorised examiner who might be a firm or a company. An authorised examiner has to comply with any conditions specified in his authorisation and in the regulations and, after 1 January 1977, no one may carry out or supervise a test or sign a test certificate unless he has successfully completed an approved course of instruction. The examiner must arrange for the test to be carried out or personally supervised, and the test certificates signed, by someone who fulfils these requirements.

The examiner has to display a notice of all those authorised to supervise tests or to sign test certificates, together with the authorisation of the testing station. A sign in the form prescribed in the Regulations must be displayed on the wall outside the testing station. The examiner must submit to inspections by the Secretary of State, given notice.

Authorisation is not usually granted to carry out examinations on all classes of vehicles covered by the Regulations.

Authorisation may be withdrawn, usually on 35 days' notice, at any time. The examiner may make written representations to the Secretary of State.

What procedure is to be followed to submit a vehicle for testing?

The vehicle may be submitted to either an authorised examiner or to certain local authorities who have been approved to carry out tests, either by prior appointment, or on the spot. The time and date of an appointment must be recorded by the examiner.

The applicant must produce evidence of the date of first registration of the vehicle, and if he does not do so the examiner is not under an obligation to carry out the test. Similarly, the examiner may refuse to carry out the test if the vehicle is so dirty that it would be unreasonably difficult, where the vehicle must be driven for the test and it has insufficient fuel and oil, where the examiner has required goods to be removed or secured and this has not been done, or where the fee has not been paid in advance.

What items are required to be tested?

These are set out in Schedule 2 of the Regulations (as amended) and specify the requirements which must be met by the various categories of vehicles.

SCHEDULE 2

THE PRESCRIBED STATUTORY REQUIREMENTS FOR VEHICLES IN CLASSES I AND II

1. (a) The requirements contained in the following provisions of the Construction and Use Regulations:

Item No.	Regulations	Affecting
1	16 and 18	Braking
2	24, 26, 27 and 100(1) (insofar as it relates to the condition of the road wheels)	Wheels and Tyres
3	29	Steering
4	37	Audible Warning Instrument
5	54, 57 and 100(1) (insofar as it relates to the condition of the pipings, attachment brackets and mounting of the exhaust system)	Exhaust
6	100(1) (insofar as it relates to the condition of the vehicle structure, the chassis, frame and any subframe or any mounting or connection or part of the suspension, to the extent that such condition may prejudice the steering or braking of the vehicle)	Structure and Suspension

(b) The requirements contained in the following provisions of the Lighting Regulations:

Item No.	Regulations	Affecting
7	18 and 23	Front Position Lamp
8	19 and 23	Dipped Beam Headlamp
9	18 and 23	Main Beam Headlamp
10	18 and 23	Rear Position Lamp
11	18 and 23	Rear Retro Reflector
12	18 and 23	Stop Lamp
13	18 and 23	Direction Indicator

THE PRESCRIBED STATUTORY REQUIREMENTS FOR VEHICLES IN CLASS III

2. (*a*) The requirements specified in items 2, 3, 4 and 7 to 13 in paragraph 1 above.

(*b*) The requirements contained in the following provisions of the Construction and Use Regulations:

Item No.	Regulations	Affecting
14	15, 16 and 18	Braking
15	30	Glass and Field of Vision
16	33	Mirrors
17	34	Windscreen Cleaning
18	39 and 100(1) (insofar as it relates to the security and condition of the fuel system components or, as the case may be, their maintenance so that no danger is likely to be caused)	Fuel Tanks and Pipes
19	46, 47 and 48	Seat Belts and Anchorages
20	54 and 100(1) (insofar as it relates to the condition of the pipings, attachment brackets and mounting of the exhaust system)	Exhaust
20A	66	Plates
21	67	Vehicle Identification Number
22	22 and 100(1) (insofar as it relates to the condition of the vehicle structure, the body, the chassis, frame and any subframe or any mounting or connection or part of the suspension, to the extent that such condition may prejudice the steering, braking or seat belt mounting of the vehicle or may otherwise cause danger)	Structure and Suspension
23	100(1) (insofar as it relates to the condition of seats, doors and other openings, to the extent that such condition may cause danger)	Seats, Doors and Other Openings

(*c*) The requirements contained in the following provisions of the Lighting Regulations:—

Item No.	Regulations	Affecting
24	18 and 23	Rear Registration Plate Lamp
25	18 and 23	Rear Fog Lamp
26	18 and 23	Hazard Warning Signal Device

(*d*) The requirements contained in the following provisions of the Road Vehicles (Registration and Licensing) Regulations 1971:—

Item No.	Regulations	Affecting
27	17, 18, 19 and 20	Registration Marks

THE PRESCRIBED STATUTORY REQUIREMENTS FOR VEHICLES IN CLASS IV

3. (*a*) The requirements specified in items 2, 3, 4, and 7 to 27 in paragraphs 1 and 2 above.
   (*b*) The requirements contained in the following provision of the Construction and Use Regulations:—

Item No.	Regulations	Affecting
28	61	Emissions

THE PRESCRIBED STATUTORY REQUIREMENTS FOR VEHICLES IN CLASS V

4. (*a*) The requirements specified in items 2, 3, 4, 7 to 13, 16 to 20, 22, and 24 to 26 and 28 in paragraphs 1 and 2 above.
   (*b*) The requirements contained in the following provisions of the Construction and Use Regulations:

Item No.	Regulations	Affecting
29	15, 16, 17 and 18	Braking
29A	25	Tyre Load and Speed Ratings
30	30, 31 and 32	Glass and Field of Vision
31	35 and 36	Speedometer
32	36A and 70A	Speed Limiter
33	100(1) (insofar as it relates to the question whether the particulars opposite are fitted or, as the case may be, maintained so that no danger is likely to be caused)	Seats, driving controls, body, doors and other openings

THE PRESCRIBED STATUTORY REQUIREMENTS FOR VEHICLES IN CLASS VI

5. (*a*) The requirements specified in items 2, 3, 4, 7 to 13, 16 to 20, 22, 24, 25, 26 and 28 to 33 in paragraphs 1 to 4 above.
   (*b*) The requirements contained in the following provisions of the Construction and Use Regulations:—

Item No.	Regulations	Affecting
35	60	Radio Interference Suppression

Item No.	Regulations	Affecting
36	62	Closets, etc.
37	100(1) (insofar as it relates to the question whether the particulars opposite are fitted or, as the case may be, maintained so that no danger is likely to be caused)	Spare wheel carrier, means of coupling trailers, chassis, wiring, engine mounting, transmission, battery, shock absorbers, bumpers, doors, seats, driving controls and security of glass in windows and mirrors
38	109	Television sets

(c) For those vehicles certified in accordance with the Public Service Vehicles (Conditions of Fitness, Equipment, Use and Certification) Regulations 1981, the requirements contained in the following provisions of those Regulations:—

Item No.	Regulations	Affecting
39	8	Guard Rail
40	13	Fuel Tanks, Carburettors, etc.
41	14	Exhaust Pipe
42	15	Luggage Racks
43	16	Artificial Lighting
44	17	Electrical Equipment
45	18	Body
46	20	Steps, Platforms and Stairs
47	21	Number, Position and Size of Entrances and Exits
48	22	Width of Exits and Entrances
49	23	Doors
50	24	Marking, Positioning and Operation of Emergency Exits
51	25	Access to Exits
52	28	Seats
53	29	Passenger Protection
54	30	Ventilation
55	31	Driver's Accommodation
56	32	Windscreens
57	33	Passengers' Communication with Driver
58	34	General Construction

Item No.	Regulations	Affecting
59	35	Fire Extinguishing Apparatus
60	36	First Aid Equipment
61	38	Obstruction of Driver
62	39	Body Maintenance
63	44	Carriage of Inflammable or Dangerous Substances

(*d*) For minibuses of a type mentioned in regulation 41 of the Construction and Use Regulations, the following requirements specified in Schedules 6 and 7 to those Regulations:

Item No.	(Schedule 6)	Affecting
64	1	Exhaust Pipes
65	2	Doors
66	3	Emergency Doors
67	4	Power-operated Doors
68	5	Locks, Handles and Hinges of Doors
69	6	View of Doors
70	7	Access to Doors
71	8	Grab Handles and Hand Rails
72	9	Seats
73	10	Electrical Equipment and Wiring
74	11	Fuel Tanks
75	12	Lighting of Steps
76	13	General Construction and Maintenance

Item No.	(Schedule 7)	Affecting
77	I	Fire Extinguishing Apparatus
78	II	First Aid Equipment

(*e*) The requirements contained in the following provisions of the Lighting Regulations:—

Item No.	Regulations	Affecting
79	18 and 23	End Outline Marker Lamp

(*f*) The requirements of the Community Recording Equipment Regulation insofar as they relate to the installation of recording equipment and the seals to be affixed to such equipment.

THE PRESCRIBED STATUTORY REQUIREMENTS FOR VEHICLES IN CLASS VII

6. The requirements specified in items 2, 3, 4, 7 to 13 and 15 to 29A in paragraphs 1 to 5 above.

How are the results of the tests notified?

The examiner must notify the results of the tests on the prescribed forms. If the vehicle passes the test a certificate in the prescribed form is issued. If it fails, a notification of refusal of a certificate is issued with reasons. In the case of vehicles in Classes III, IV and V an inspection check list must also be issued.

What Forms are used to notify the results of the tests?

VT20   Test certificate
VT21   Refusal of Test Certificate
VT22   Refusal of Test Certificate (incomplete test)
VT12   The Register
VT29   The Check List

Is there any way that an appeal can be made against a refusal of a test certificate?

An appeal by a person aggrieved by a refusal may be made to the Secretary of State and must be lodged with an area traffic office not later than 14 days after the refusal. The fee is the same as for a test.

Section D

CHECKING THE MECHANICAL CONDITION OF VEHICLES

What powers do the police and examiners have to examine a motor vehicle on the road?

The Road Traffic Act 1988 provides that an authorised examiner may test a motor vehicle on the road, by driving it if necessary, to find out whether the C&U and lighting requirements are being complied with, and whether the condition of the vehicle is dangerous.

Who is an authorised examiner?

The Act defines this as being a DOE examiner, a Metropolitan taxi examiner, an authorised police officer, and someone appointed for this purpose by the Secretary of State.

Does this mean that any of these people may stop a vehicle on the road to examine it?

No. Only a police officer in uniform can require a vehicle to stop.

Does the driver have to consent to the test?

Yes, it is an offence to obstruct the examiner. However, the driver can elect to have the test deferred unless it seems that the vehicle has caused an accident or it is seriously defective. If he chooses this option he must specify a period of not less than seven days in the next thirty days when the test may be carried out. The examiner then has to give at least 48 hours notice.

What if the driver is not the owner of the vehicle?

He must inform the examiner of the name and address of the owner of the vehicle and the owner will then have the opportunity of specifying the period within which the test should take place, as above.

What happens if a defect is found?

If a motor vehicle is tested under the Act and a defect is found, the owner can be served with a notice specifying the defect and requiring him to put it right within a specified period and produce a certificate from a testing station to that effect.

What powers do the police and examiners have to inspect vehicles on premises rather than on the road?

An authorised examiner can test brakes, silencer, steering gear, tyres, lights and reflectors of a motor vehicle or trailer on premises if the owners of the premises and of the vehicle consent or have been given 48 hours notice. Notice is not necessary if the vehicle has been involved in a notifiable accident. Wider powers exist in relation to goods vehicles where an authorised examiner may enter premises at any reasonable time.

What powers exist in relation to vehicles being kept on premises for sale?

An authorised examiner may at any reasonable time enter premises where vehicles or used vehicles are kept for sale to examine them to make sure they can be used on the road legally. He can test the vehicles on the road for that purpose.

What special rules apply to goods vehicles?

S.68 of the Road Traffic Act 1988 lays down special rules to ensure that goods vehicles are maintained in a fit and serviceable condition. This allows a goods vehicle examiner or certifying officer to examine a vehicle on the road or enter premises at any reasonable time. Obstruction of an examiner is an offence.

What is meant by a "prohibition notice"?

If an examiner finds that a goods vehicle is defective and is unfit to be driven or is likely to become so, he can prohibit the driving of that vehicle on a road by issuing a Form GV9. This will take the form of a prohibition either with immediate effect, or delayed for not more than ten days from the date of the inspection. The notice will be given to the person in charge of the vehicle.

A prohibition remains in force until removed by an examiner, and the notice must be kept with the vehicle and presented when the vehicle is submitted for re-examination. If on re-examination the vehicle is still not serviceable a Form GV9C will be issued, subject to a right of appeal to the Licensing Authority for an inspection.

A notice may be removed by the issue of a GV10 when the vehicle is serviceable.

Once issued, the notice may be varied either by amending the list of defects, or by suspending or deferring its date of operation. This is done by a GV9A.

If the vehicle has to be moved for repair, a Form GV9B may be issued permitting this movement if the examiner is satisfied that certain conditions are met e.g. it will be proceeding to the nearest specified garage; the load will be removed before proceeding; or to be towed away with a solid tow-bar. However, it should be noted that the issue of a GV9B does not cover any possible infringements of Construction and Use Regulations.

What happens if only minor defects are found?

The examiner may issue a GV219 (a 'defects notice'). This notifies the operator of the minor defects and these should be rectified immediately. There is, however, no need to inform the Licensing Authority when they are rectified, although the LA will have received a copy of the GV219. The use of the vehicle is not prohibited.

What about overloaded vehicles?

A Form GV160 can be issued to an overloaded vehicle, ordering the excess load to be removed before the vehicle can proceed.

Section E

LIGHTING REGULATIONS

LEGISLATION – ROAD TRAFFIC ACT 1988 ROAD VEHICLES LIGHTING REGULATIONS 1989 (as amended)

What lights are required to be fitted to motor vehicles?

The basic requirements for most vehicles are:

Two front position lamps which are used to indicate the presence and width of a vehicle when viewed from the front. The Regulations lay down the maximum distance of these lamps from the side of the vehicle, and maximum height above the ground. These lights must be white, unless incorporated in a headlamp only capable of emitting yellow light in which case they may be yellow.

Two headlamps with a dipped and main beam. A headlamp is a lamp used to illuminate the road in front of a vehicle, and does not include fog lamps. Headlamps may emit only white or yellow light, and must conform with the positioning requirements in the regulations as to height and distance from the side of the vehicle.

Two rear position lamps which are used to indicate the presence and width of the vehicle when viewed from the rear. The lights must be red and fitted in conformity with the regulations for that type and age of vehicle.

Two stop lamps used to indicate to other road users that the brakes of a vehicle are being applied. The lamps must be red and fitted in conformity with the regulations for that type and age of vehicle.

Two pairs of rear reflex reflectors are required on most vehicles to indicate the presence and width of the vehicle when viewed from the rear. The reflectors must be fitted at or near the rear of the vehicle, face to the rear and be red.

Two or more pairs of side reflex reflectors may be required on goods vehicles depending upon the date the vehicle was first used and its overall length. The object is to make the vehicle more visible from the side. The reflectors must be amber in colour, and fitted in conformity with the requirements in the regulations.

At least one but not more than two rear fog lamps must be fitted to vehicles first used on or after 1 April 1980. The lamp must be red and be fitted in conformity with the regulations.

At least one rear number plate lamp must be fitted where a rear number plates must be displayed. It must be capable of illuminating the rear number plate without causing undue dazzle or discomfort to other road users.

A dim-dip lighting device is required for vehicles first used on or after 1 April 1987. The European court ruled that this mandatory requirement by the UK is contrary to EEC law and an exemption was made to this requirement for vehicles complying with the EC Lighting Installation Directive. But since this requires self levelling headlamps, in practice few cars qualify.

Direction indicators to indicate to other drivers that a vehicle intends to change direction. On vehicles first registered after September 1965 these must be flashing amber in colour, and fitted in conformity with the regulations.

A hazard warning light is required on vehicles first used on or after 1 April 1986. It is a device which is capable of operating all the direction indicators of a vehicle simultaneously.

Projecting trailers and loads must be lit if they are wider than the preceding or carrying vehicle.

Note that the Regulations prescribe lights to be carried by all manner of road vehicles, including bicycles and handcarts. The requirements are not, however, all the same. All light prescribed must be in good working order and clean.

What additional lights may be carried?

In addition to the basic requirements, additional lamps and reflectors may be fitted provided that they conform with the requirements for the obligatory lights of that type.

They must also not contravene the restrictions on the colour of lights to be carried, i.e. no vehicle may be used on the are not required by law, if they are fitted they must comply with the requirements of the Regulations.

They must also not contravene the restrictions on the colour of lights to be carried i.e. no vehicle may be used on the road readily capable of showing a red light to the front, except a red light from an authorised traffic sign attached to the vehicle, or a red and white light from a fire service vehicle. Lights to the rear may only be red except for authorised exceptions e.g. white reversing lights, amber indicators, taximeter lights etc.

When must lights be used?

It is an offence to use, cause or permit to be used a vehicle on a road

– between sunset and sunrise,

– between sunrise and sunset in seriously reduced visibility unless every obligatory front position lamp, rear position lamp, rear registration plate lamp and side marker lamp is kept lit.

In addition, a vehicle with obligatory dipped-beam headlamps must keep them lit during the hours of darkness except when on a road lit by street lights not more than 200 yards apart, and in seriously reduced visibility (except in this instance fog lamps may be used instead).

It is also an offence to allow a vehicle to remain at rest on a road during hours of darkness unless the obligatory lamps (other than headlamps) as above are lit. A concession to this requirement is granted where the vehicle is parked in a 30 mph limit, in a designated parking place, or on the left hand side of the road (the right if the road is one-way) not less than 10 m from any junction, but this concession does not apply to goods vehicles which exceed 1,525 kgs unladen weight (nor to large passenger carrying vehicles).

What are the hours of darkness?

This is defined as being the time between half an hour after sunset and half an hour before sunrise.

What is seriously reduced visibility?

This is not defined in the regulations, so it is up to the driver to decide.

What additional lights may be used?

Any number of front fog lamps may be used on a vehicle, providing they show a white or yellow light, do not dazzle other road users, and are not used except when visibility is impaired, or when the vehicle is parked. They must be fitted at a maximum distance of 400mm from the side of the vehicle, and can be used in place of dipped beam headlamps in conditions of seriously reduced visibility.

Reversing lights may be used while reversing the vehicle if they are white, not more than 24 watts and fitted so that they will not dazzle at a reasonable distance.

In addition certain vehicles are permitted to be fitted with warning beacons and warning lamps. These include amber beacons on a breakdown vehicle, a blue beacon on an emergency vehicle, and a yellow beacon on vehicles used at airports. No vehicles other than those specially permitted shall carry such warning lights or beacons.

Amber beacons on recovery vehicles may be used at the scene of the breakdown/accident and when towing the broken-down vehicle. NB. It may not be used when going to the scene of the breakdown/accident.

Recovery vehicles may also be fitted with 'searchlights' referred to in the regulations as 'work lamps'.

These may only be used for the purpose of illuminating the area in the vicinity of the recovery vehicle when at the scene of the breakdown/accident and must not be used so as to dazzle or cause discomfort to the driver of the vehicle.

Section F

EXCISE LICENCES

Vehicle Excise and Registration Act 1994.

Duty is charged on any mechanically propelled vehicle used or kept on a public road. Any person who uses or keeps it must ensure that it has a current excise licence, unless it is an exempted vehicle.

When a vehicle is licensed for the first time, a unique registration mark is allocated to that vehicle and must be displayed on it (see below) together with the current excise licence.

What exemptions apply?

There are various exemptions set out in the Act and other legislations. They include:

invalid carriages not exceeding 508 kg unladen
fire engines
Crown vehicles
vehicles brought temporarily into Great Britain by an overseas resident (exempt for three months)
ambulances

How is a vehicle first licensed?

Applications for first licences may be made at local vehicle licensing offices not more than 14 days before the licence is to come into effect.

How is a vehicle first registered?

On the issue of a first licence for a vehicle the Secretary of State must register it and assign a registration mark to it. A vehicle to which a mark has already been assigned may have another one assigned to it, or a mark previously assigned may be re-assigned. The mark has to be fixed to the vehicle in the manner prescribed by C&U (see below).

A registration can be transferred on payment of a fee.

Before issuing a registration book for a vehicle, the owner can be required to produce the vehicle so that the details can be checked. Once issued the owner must produce the registration book when required at any reasonable time by the police or representatives of the Department of Transport. The book must not be altered or defaced except by the new owner entering his name and address in it.

How is a vehicle's licence renewed?

Where a licence is being renewed, application may also be made at a post office which issues licences within 14 days before the expiry of the old licence, provided: the application is made on Form V11; any change of address or ownership has been noted on the registration document; and no alteration has been made to the vehicle which would involve a different rate of tax being payable.

Applications for renewal must be accompanied by the certificate of insurance, and a test certificate if the vehicle is over three years old and is required to be tested.

How can a refund be obtained?

A holder of an excise licence may surrender it at any time. He may then apply for the duty to be refunded. The refund will be allocated on the basis of one twelfth of the duty for each complete and unexpired month of the licence, and for a three month trade licence one third of the duty paid.

What legal requirements are there for the display of the registration mark and the licence?

The registration mark allocated on first registration must for most vehicles be displayed at the front and the rear of the vehicle and on any trailer which it draws. The lettering must be of a specified size and must be on a flat rectangular plate or surface. In the case of vehicles first registered on or after 1 January 1973 (subject to some exceptions – notably vehicles over three tons unladen fitted with reflective rear markings) the number plate must be of a reflex reflecting material and marked as conforming with BS AU 145:1967. For vehicles first registered on or after 1 October 1938 the plate need not be displayed vertically, but it must be easily legible and comply with conditions as to visibility set out in the regulations. The mark must not be obscured.

The excise licence must be displayed on a vehicle which is kept or used on a public road in a holder to protect it, normally on the nearside of the windscreen. It is an offence to alter or deface a licence, or to display anything else which may be taken for a licence.

How are the different types of vehicle taxed?

Different rates of tax apply depending on the "type" of vehicle. These are in the Vehicles Excise and Registration Act 1994 which sets out the applicable rate of duty in various extremely detailed schedules.

Main licensing categories are:

light vehicles such as motorcycles and tricycles

rigid and articulated vehicles over 3.5 tonnes revenue weight where the rate of duty will vary according to the number of axles with which the vehicle is fitted
vehicles not falling within other schedules (including cars and light commercial vehicles).

"Revenue weight" means the confirmed maximum weight of the vehicle (if it has one) or its design weight. A vehicle has a confirmed maximum weight if at any time it has a plated gross weight or plated train weight and that weight is the maximum laden weight at which the vehicle may be used lawfully in Great Britain.

In addition, there are special rules for special types of vehicle e.g. tractors, showman's vehicles, farmer's vehicles, motor cycles, articulated vehicles and draw bar trailers, and since 1988 recovery vehicles also have their own class of excise duty.

If a goods vehicle is used partly for private purposes and partly for carrying goods in connection with a trade or business or for hire or reward, then the appropriate rate of duty will be the higher of the private or goods vehicle rate.

Similarly, if a goods vehicle taxed as a private one is used to tow a trailer carrying goods in connection with a business, then a higher rate of duty may be payable.

How is a recovery vehicle defined?

A recovery vehicle is defined in the Vehicles Excise and Registration Act 1994 as one which is either constructed or permanently adapted primarily for the purposes of lifting, towing and transporting a disabled vehicle.

A recovery vehicle may only be used to recover disabled vehicles, to remove them from where they became disabled or from premises where taken for repair to a place where they are to be repaired or scrapped, and to carry fuel, tools, lifting apparatus etc.

A vehicle that can carry several disabled vehicles from one place to another is not a specialised recovery vehicle because it is not used for helping individual broken down vehicles.

Section G

TRADE LICENCES

What is a trade licence?

A trade licence is a vehicle excise licence issued at a lower rate than a normal licence.

Who is able to apply for a trade licence?

A motor vehicle trader, or vehicle tester can apply to the Secretary of State for Transport. If the application is refused the trader may ask for a review of the decision. A motor trader is defined for this purpose as a manufacturer or repairer of, or dealer in, mechanically propelled vehicles. In addition, traders who modify vehicles prior to first registration and vehicle valeters are also covered. A person is regarded as a dealer if his business is mainly one of collecting and delivering vehicles.

Changes in name and address of the licence holder must be notified.

Trade plates will be issued with the trade licence which must then be displayed in the same manner as ordinary licence plates. They must be returned when the licence expires.

On what vehicles can trade plates be used?

A motor trader may use the licence on vehicles temporarily in his possession, in the course of his business as a motor trader.

A motor vehicle tester may use it on vehicles submitted to him for testing.

A motor trader who is a manufacturer (see above) may use it on vehicles (including those lent by other manufacturers) used by him for research and development.

A licence cannot be used on more than one vehicle at a time except when a recovery vehicle draws a disabled vehicle.

Are there any restrictions on the use of a trade licence by a motor trader?

Yes. A motor trader may only use his trade licence for a business purpose being one of the following:

a) for test or trial of a vehicle or its accessories and equipment in the ordinary course of construction modification or repair

b) for going to or from a public weighbridge for registration purposes

c) for its test or trial for the benefit of a prospective purchaser

d) for its test or trial for a person interested in promoting publicity in regard to it

e) for delivering it to a place where the purchaser intends to keep it

f) for demonstrating its operation to a purchaser when delivering it

g) for moving it between his premises and those of another motor trader

h) for going to or from a workshop where a body, special accessories or equipment is going to be fitted or where it is to be painted or repaired

i) for going from the trader's premises to where it is to be transported by train, ship etc

j) for going to or from its place of sale, where it is habitually used as such

k) for going to or from a place where it is to be tested, broken up or dismantled

What can be carried on a vehicle being used for one of these purposes under a trade licence by a motor trader?

No goods can be carried other than

a) a load used for demonstrating the vehicle or its equipment (NB the load must be returned to where it started from unless it consists of water, fertiliser or refuse)

b) in the case of a vehicle which is being delivered or collected, a load consisting of another vehicle used or to be used for travel from or to the place of delivery or collection

c) a load built in as part of the vehicle or permanently attached to it

d) parts accessories or equipment to be fitted to the vehicle, and the requisite tools

e) a load consisting of a trailer other than a disabled vehicle (which includes an abandoned vehicle or one which is scrap). When a trailer is attached so that a substantial part of its weight is borne by the vehicle they are treated as one vehicle

Who is allowed to travel in a vehicle bearing trade plates?

No passengers may be carried other than a person carried in connection with a purpose for which the vehicle can be used on trade plates (see above).

Section H
ACCIDENT PROCEDURE

What does the law say that a driver of a vehicle which is involved in an accident has to do?

Where an accident due to a mechanically-propelled vehicle has occurred and

a) anyone other than the driver of the vehicle has been injured, or
b) damage is caused to any other vehicle (including, for example, a bicycle) or
c) damage is caused to any animal (as defined in the Road Traffic Act – horses, dogs, asses, mules, sheep, pigs, goats, and cattle are included but not e.g. cats) other than one carried in that vehicle or
d) damage has occurred to any property constructed on, growing in or otherwise forming part of the land on which the road runs or adjacent land

the driver must STOP.

He must give his name and address, and also that of the owner of the vehicle, and its registration number to a policeman or anyone else having reasonable grounds for requesting it.

If he does not give his name and address on this occasion, then he must report the accident personally at a police station as soon as possible and at the latest within 24 hours.

Where the accident involves personal injury to another person the driver must also produce his certificate of insurance to the police or someone else reasonably requiring its production. This must be done when he reports the accident to the police, or within seven days at a specified police station.

A driver who can prove that he was unaware that he had had an accident cannot be convicted of failing to stop. (*Harding v Price (1948)*)

Section I

TRAFFIC OFFENCES

What punishments are available to the courts when someone has been convicted of a road traffic offence?

The offending driver may have details of the offence written on his driving licence (an endorsement), or may be disqualified from driving altogether for a specified period. In addition a fine may be imposed.

The Transport Act 1981 introduced a system of penalty points for road traffic offences. Under this system drivers who are convicted of an endorsable offence but not disqualified will incur penalty points which are then endorsed on their licence.

What are the consequences of having penalty points endorsed on your licence?

If twelve or more penalty points are incurred within three years then the driver will be disqualified unless the court is satisfied that there are mitigating circumstances. The three year period is measured backwards from the date on which the most recent offence was committed.

For what offences must a court endorse a driving licence?

There is a list in the Road Traffic Offenders Act 1988 of the offences for which the courts must endorse the driver's licence.

How long does an endorsement remain on a driving licence?

Endorsements remain on a licence for a period of four years after conviction, except for drink/driving offences where the period is eleven years.

When will a court disqualify for a road traffic offence?

Disqualification may be either "obligatory" or "discretionary". Where the Act provides that disqualification is obligatory, the court may only exercise a discretion not to disqualify in very exceptional circumstances connected with the offence. In other cases, the courts may disqualify at their discretion if the offence was considered serious enough.

With effect from 1 June 1997, a scheme has been introduced which requires drivers who accumulate 6 or more penalty points within 2 years of passing their test to be retested.

"What offences carry "obligatory" disqualification?

These are defined in the Road Traffic Act 1988:

Causing death by dangerous driving

Reckless and dangerous driving, if committed within three years of another conviction for this offence, or causing death by dangerous driving.

Driving or attempting to drive while unfit through drink or drugs

Driving or attempting to drive with blood alcohol concentration above the legal limit

Failing to provide a specimen of blood or urine for a laboratory test if at the relevant time the accused was driving or attempting to drive a motor vehicle on the public road or other public place

Motor racing and speed trials on the highway

How long is the period of disqualification?

This varies depending on the offence. Where the offence is one where disqualification is "obligatory" the minimum period is one year unless the court exercises its discretion.

In what circumstances can a driver apply to have a disqualification removed?

The disqualified driver can apply to the Clerk of the Court which imposed the disqualification to have it removed. Application may be made as follows:

Period of disqualification	*Application*
Less than four years	Two years from date of disqualification
More than four but less than ten years	When half period has expired
In any other case	When five years have expired

What is the fixed penalty system and how does it work?

This system was introduced to take the pressure off the court system by introducing fixed fines for certain offences. The offender is handed a ticket or it is affixed to the vehicle, and he then has 28 days in which to pay the fine, or seven days if it is an excess parking charge. Failure to pay incurs a further fine.

Who issues the ticket?

This may be either a traffic warden, or the police.

Who is liable to pay the fine?

The registered owner of the vehicle is responsible for payment if the driver does not pay within the specified time. If the fine has not been paid, the registered keeper of the vehicle will be sent a statement giving details of the offence and requires him to pay unless he is able to complete a "statutory statement of ownership". This can be used if, for example, the registered keeper was not actually the owner at the time of the offence e.g. he had sold it, or had not yet acquired it. He may also avoid having to pay if he can show that although he was the registered keeper, the vehicle was in possession of someone else without his consent. The owner of a vehicle which has been hired out can avoid the fine by declaring that the vehicle was on hire and producing a statement signed by the hirer acknowledging responsibility for any fixed penalties or excess parking charges.

What offences can incur fixed penalties?

There are over thirty listed, including a number of moving traffic offences such as speeding, where only the police are entitled to issue a fixed penalty ticket.

Other offences include:

    parking at night without lights

    contravening parking restrictions

    failing to display a current excise licence

    making an unauthorised U turn

    driving the wrong way down a one way street

Section J
DRIVING LICENCES

The Road Traffic Act 1988 provides that no one may drive a vehicle on the road otherwise than in accordance with a licence authorising them to drive a vehicle of that class, or cause or permit a vehicle to be used on the road by someone who is unlicensed. Anyone who drives a vehicle otherwise than in accordance with a licence commits an offence.

Does that mean that employers have to make sure that their employees have a current driving licence?

Yes. In *Ferry Masters Ltd v Adams (1980)*, a company was prosecuted for "permitting" when they had no system for checking that licences were still current.

What is the position for companies which hire out their vehicles for other people to drive?

The same rule applies. If a vehicle is hired out to someone without a driving licence the hiring company would be committing an offence.

What types of driving licence are permitted by the Road Traffic Act?

A licence means a licence to drive a motor vehicle granted under the RTA. This includes:

a) A full licence issued to someone who during the 10 preceding years has passed a driving test, or held a licence for the class of vehicle concerned.

b) A full licence issued to someone who holds an "exchangeable" licence and who, although normally resident here has not lived here for more than a year. An exchangeable licence is one issued either in another member state of the EEC, or in a specified list of countries.

c) A provisional licence issued to someone with a view to them passing a driving test.

d) In the case of a person who resides outside the UK, who is in Great Britain temporarily, an international driving permit, or a domestic driving permit of another country, or a British forces licence is accepted for a period of twelve months following his last entry into the UK. If he acquires a provisional licence during this period he is exempt from complying with its conditions (see below).

A person who holds a Community licence who becomes resident in UK may drive in UK (and Gibraltar) on it.

What conditions attach to the use of a provisional licence?

Various conditions apply to the use of such a licence, for example

a) the provisional licence holder must not drive unless supervised by a full licence holder, who must be at least 21 and have held a full licence for three years

b) the vehicle being driven must display "L" plates to the front and back

c) No trailer may be drawn except an agricultural trailer or in the case of an articulated vehicle

The restriction in (a) above does not apply if

i.   the driver is taking his test

ii.   if the vehicle is not constructed to carry another person, so long as the vehicle is not a motor car

iii. an electric goods vehicle not over 16cwt constructed to carry only one person

iv.   a goods carrying road roller not over 3 tons unladen

v.   it is on the road in an "exempted island". This is defined in the Act but does NOT include the main off-shore islands of the UK.

What age limits are there for holding a full driving licence?

The minimum ages for driving the main different classes of motor vehicles are now:

	years
Invalid carriage	16
Motor cycles	17
Mopeds, mowing machines, pedestrian controlled vehicles	16
Small passenger or goods vehicle	17
Agricultural tractor	17
Medium sized goods vehicle	18
Other vehicles	21

A "small" passenger vehicle is one constructed solely to carry passengers and their belongings, and is adapted to carry no more than 9 people inclusive of the driver.

A "small" goods vehicle is a motor vehicle constructed or adapted to carry or haul goods, not adapted to carry more than nine people inclusive of the driver, and its permissible maximum weight does not exceed 3.5 tonnes.

A "medium" goods vehicle is as above, exceeding 3.5 tonnes but not exceeding 7.5 tonnes maximum permissible weight.

"Other" vehicles are those for more than 9 passengers, and those over 7.5 tonnes. The age limit of 21 for this type of vehicle may be reduced to 18 if the driver is registered under a training scheme if the vehicle is owned by his employer or training establishment.

These rules may also be waived in other specified cases and reference should be made to the regulations for details.

In addition to considering the age requirements for a driving licence for different vehicles, it is also necessary for anyone driving an LGV to have an appropriate licence. It is an offence to drive, or cause or permit another person to drive an LGV if they are under 21 or if they are without an LGV licence.

How is an LGV defined?

An LGV means either

a) an articulated goods vehicle i.e. a motor vehicle so designed that a trailer can be partially superimposed on it

   or

b) a large goods vehicle which is constructed or adapted to carry or to haul goods of which the maximum permissible weight exceeds 7.5 tonnes.

For further details of the requirements please refer to the section on HGV law.

Does EEC law have any impact in relation to driving licences?

Yes. An EC Directive introduced a harmonised driver licensing system under which licences are the responsibility of one authority (the Secretary of State). It puts vehicles into one of five groups with each one having its own test standards. The categories are

(A) Motor cycles
(B) Cars
(C) Goods vehicles larger than cars ("large goods vehicles")
(D) Passenger vehicles larger than cars ("passenger carrying vehicles")
(E) Articulated vehicles or those drawing tractors

PART 5: ROAD TRANSPORT LAW (HGV)

by

Anthea Worsdall
and Peter Groves

CONTENTS

Section A

PLATING AND TESTING

Goods Vehicles (Plating and Testing) Regulations 1988 (SI 1988 No. 1478)

as amended by SI 1989/1693
SI 1990/448, SI 1991/252
SI 1992/564
SI 1993/2048
SI 1994/328
SI 1995/1456

What is plating in regard to goods vehicles?

This is a way of indicating by means of an official plate (of paper laminated in plastic) attached to a vehicle the maximum axle and gross weights, and other particulars beyond which that vehicle may not be operated. In the case of a trailer, it must be displayed in a conspicuous position on the nearside of the vehicle.

Why is there a plate and a plating certificate?

The plate – the VTG6 – and the plating certificate – VTG7 – are similar but not the same. They are both paper and plastic laminates and the position of a number of the panels on the documents coincide. When they are being completed the panels are aligned and the information on one is a carbon copy of the other.

The VTG7 is the certificate. It has more information than the plate. It should be kept with the vehicle's documents in the operator's office and in the event of a discrepancy between the information entered on it and the information entered on the plate it is the VTG7 that is taken to be correct.

The plate, the VTG6, has the information on it that is most likely to be required when on the road.

The VTG6A is replacing the VTG6 and contains additional information, on weights and dimensions, required by the EEC.

What are the requirements with regard to testing of goods vehicles?

Most vehicles will be subject to a first examination at a Department of Transport Testing station 12 months after first registration, or in the case of trailers, 12 months after being sold retail. The vehicle must then be retested regularly every twelve months, not later than the anniversary of the date by which it had to be first tested, or (if earlier) the expiry date of the certificate.

How is plating carried out?

A plating certificate and plate will be sent to the operator of the vehicle when the vehicle is first registered and the appropriate type approval certificate has been produced to the licensing authorities in Swansea. The plating certificate will show the gross and unladen weights at which the vehicle may operate and the plate showing this information must be displayed by the operator in the cab of the vehicle.

Which vehicles are required to be plated and tested?

The regulations apply to articulated vehicles (both parts, the tractive unit and the semi-trailer, are plated), rigid goods vehicles over 3,500kg, design gross weight, draw-bar trailers over 1,020kg unladen and converter dollies. There are several exemptions including:

dual purpose vehicles not being part of an articulated vehicle

breakdown vehicles

engineering plant

works trucks

electrically propelled vehicles

agricultural vehicles

licensed taxis

In addition, a vehicle otherwise subject to plating and testing may be used legally on the road without a certificate in specified circumstances, i.e.

when submitting it for an examination

when a certificate is refused, delivering it to a place for repair or breaking

when being driven or drawn unladen by a vehicle driven under a trade licence

when the vehicle is imported, when it is being driven to the place where it is going to be kept

while being used under a Special Types Order

while seized or detained by the police or Customs and Excise

when being removed under statutory powers.

It is also possible for a certificate of temporary extension to be issued if exceptionally a test cannot be completed by the prescribed date.

What is the purpose of testing?

The purpose of the test is to ensure that the construction and use requirements applicable to the vehicle are complied with. The requirements are set out in detail in the various Regulations.

What is the procedure for applying for a test?

Applications for a test must be sent at least one calendar month before the desired date with the correct fee to the

Goods Vehicle Centre at Swansea. The fee (which varies from £16.70 to £34.70 according to the vehicle) will be retained and the application passed to a testing station nominated by the operator. The test will then be booked and the operator informed of the date and time of test. The driver must remain with the vehicle while it is tested and be available to drive it if requested by the examiner.

Can the examiner refuse to carry out the test?

The examiner can refuse to carry out the test for a variety of reasons including late arrival, non-production of the appointment card or registration document, where a trailer booked in does not accompany the drawing vehicle, or where the vehicle is unreasonably dirty.

What items are examined on the first test?

The first examination covers both plating and testing. If the vehicle is subject to type approval, which will now almost always be the case, the plating certificate issued on registration must be produced and the particulars are checked to see that they are correct and that no notfiable alteration has been made – see below. If the examiner is not satisfied it will be subject to a normal plating examination.

If the vehicle is not subject to type approval – see above – it is checked to make sure that it is a make, model and type to which the Standard Lists apply, and the construction particulars are complied with, and the weights in the Standard List apply to the vehicle. If the Standard List does not apply, the examiner will determine the plated weights having regard to all the relevant circumstances about the construction etc of the vehicle. A plating certificate will then be issued containing the plated weight, the date and tyre size of the vehicle.

The testing part of the examination is then dealt with to see if the vehicle complies with those set out in the Regulations.

Broadly speaking, the test is in four stages:

Stage 1 carried out on hard standing

The examiner inspects those items that he can when walking around the vehicle and getting into the cab.

Stage 2 a pit inspection, the pit being provided with a jack for raising the steered wheels.

Stage 3 a check on lights, headlamp setting, reflectors etc.

Stage 4 a brake test using a roller brake test machine whenever possible.

The Goods Vehicle Tester's Manual lists each test carried out, exactly how it is carried out and the reasons for which the item might fail.

What happens if the vehicle fails the test?

The vehicle can either be submitted for a re-test or an appeal can be made against the refusal of a test certificate, or the determination of the plated weight. The procedure to be followed on a re-test depends on the time when the test is being carried out, and whether it is to be carried out at the same testing station.

An appeal can be made to the Secretary of State. It must be lodged at the Goods Vehicle Centre not more than 14 days from the examination, and must be accompanied by the fee.

What happens if the vehicle is modified after plating?

If the modification comes into the category of a notifiable alteration an operator must give this information to the Goods Vehicle Centre at Swansea before the vehicle can legally be used on the road.

What is a notifiable alteration?

A notifiable alteration is a modification which

alters the carrying or towing capacity

alters the braking or steering system

alters the vehicle or its equipment so that it is unsafe to travel on the road at its plated weight.

What is the difference between the plate that has been discussed and a manufacturer's plate?

The plate that has been discussed, the VTG6 or VTG6A, is normally referred to as the Ministry Plate. It is the plate that is required under the Plating and Testing Regulations.

A Manufacturer's plate is a metal plate required by the Construction and Use Regulations to be attached to a vehicle in a "conspicuous and readily accessible position".

The information that is required on this plate is similar to the information on a Ministry plate, one difference being that if the vehicle is powered by a compression ignition engine then the type and power of that engine must be shown.

Section B

EXCISE LICENCES

Vehicle Excise and Registration Act 1994

How are goods vehicles taxed for road fund purposes?

The general basis of calculation of duty for goods vehicles is now the revenue weight and the number of axles fitted.

The basic rate of duty – currently £150 – applies to a vehicle which has a plated revenue weight over 3.5 but not over 7.5 tonnes and then on a sliding scale ranging up to £4,250 for a vehicle over 31 tonnes but not over 44 tonnes revenue weight, and which has four or more axles. There are special rules for some vehicles for example: Showmens' vehicles, island goods vehicles and draw bar trailers.

The procedure for licensing and first registering a heavy goods vehicle is referred to in Section A, Plating and Testing.

Section C

DRIVING LICENCES

**Road Traffic Act 1988
Motor Vehicles (Driving Licences) (Heavy Goods
Vehicles and Public Service Vehicles) Regulations
1990. (No. 2611). Motor vehicles (Driving Licences)
(Large Goods Vehicles and Passenger Carrying
Vehicles) Regulations 1990 (No 2612) as amended**

When is an HGV licence required?

From 1 April 1991, the requirements for separate HGV and PSV licences were abolished. Existing HGV licences remain in force. Now, the driver of what is referred to as a large goods vehicle (LGV) or passenger-carrying vehicle (PCV) will be issued with a normal licence which include these vehicles.

It is an offence to drive or cause or permit another person to drive an LGV if they are under 21 or without an appropriate licence. An LGV means either

a) an articulated goods vehicle i.e. a motor vehicle so designed that a trailer can be partially superimposed upon it

  or

b) a motor vehicle (not articulated) which is constructed or adapted to carry or to haul goods of which the maximum permissible weight exceeds 7.5 tonnes.

Like ordinary driving licences, there are full and provisional HGV licences, and full licences have provisional effect for other classes of HGV than those for which they are issued.

Can a trainee under the age of 21 drive an LGV?

A trainee over 18 years and under 21 can apply for a full or provisonal licence which will permit him to drive LGVs. Conditions will be attached to the licence.

The conditions prescribed for a provisional licence holder are:

i. he must be supervised by a holder of a full licence for that class of vehicle; and

ii. the vehicle must carry the required "L" plates.

Where the licence is a trainee's licence, the trainee may drive (provided he is the registered employee of a registered employer) vehicles within the scope of his training contract owned or operated by the employer or a registered LGV training establishment.

Special provisions apply to part-time members of the armed services.

Can a trainee drive any HGV?

The trainee licence only permits the trainee to drive an HGV for his employer or when on a full time training course. The trainee starts, at the age of 18, on Class 3 vehicles and can progress at yearly intervals to Class 2 and then Class 1. The trainee may still not drive an articulated vehicle or rigid and draw-bar combination until he is 21 years of age except under supervision.

What is the procedure for obtaining a licence?

The application must be made on the appropriate form not more than three months before the date when the licence is needed. The Secretary of State must be satisfied that the applicant is a fit person to hold a licence, and the traffic commissioners have the task of assessing this. A medical certificate in the prescribed form must also be provided.

What other requirements must the applicant fulfil?

He must take a test appropriate for the type of vehicle he wishes to drive and produce a pass certificate before a full licence can be granted.

Can the application be revoked or suspended?

Yes. A licence must be suspended or revoked if the holder's conduct makes him unfit to hold the licence. Other provisions relative to normal driving licences also apply. Revocation or suspension means that the driver is disqualified.

What happens if a driver is disqualified from driving?

The effect of disqualification (where, for example, the offence is committed in a car) means that the driver loses his new unitary licence, and is not allowed to drive any vehicle at all. When the period of disqualification is over a licence will only be granted when the licence holder has passed the appropriate test to drive an LGV.

Can an appeal against the decision of the Secretary of State be made?

An appeal against the Secretary of State's decision to revoke or suspend a licence or to order disqualification may be made to a magistrates court under the Road Traffic Act 1988.

What are the different classes of HGV licence?

There are six different classes of licence depending on the type of vehicle

Class 1/1A   An articulated vehicle without/with automatic transmission

Class 2/2A   A heavy goods vehicle without/with automatic transmission other than an articulated vehicle designed and constructed to have more than four wheels in contact with the road surface

Class 3/3A   A heavy goods vehicle without/with automatic transmission other than an articulated vehicle designed and constructed to have not more than four wheels in contact with the road surface.

What licence is required to drive a breakdown vehicle?

An HGV licence is not required if the maximum permissible weight of the breakdown vehicle is not more than 7.5 tonnes.

Section D

DRIVERS' HOURS AND RECORDS

Transport Act 1968
Council Regulation 3820/85
Community Drivers' Hours and Recording
Equipment (Exemption and Supplementary
Provision) Regulation 1986/1456

I   Drivers' Hours

What regulations govern the number of hours a goods or passenger vehicle driver may work?

The rules governing drivers' hours are found in both national and EEC law. The rules which apply to any particular driver will vary depending on what vehicle he is driving, and where he is driving. The EEC rules are contained in EC Regulation 3820/85, and the national rules in the Transport Act 1968.

Do drivers have to worry about obeying both sets of rules?

No. The national rules apply to all drivers of goods vehicles used in connection with a business, but if the vehicle is one covered by the EEC rules, the driver does not also have to follow the national rules.

What sorts of driver are covered by the rules?

Any person who drives a goods vehicle in the course of his employment is covered, so this means that not only regular drivers are covered but also people who may drive vehicles from time to time.

What does "driving" mean in this context?

This is defined as sitting at the controls of a goods vehicle for the purpose of controlling its movement when it is either moving or stationary with the engine running.

The EC Regulation

What journeys does the EC Regulation apply to?

The EEC Law applies to "carriage by road" on any journey or part of a journey made within the EEC, whether or not the vehicle is registered in the EEC or in a third country. Carriage by road means any journey by road of a vehicle, whether laden or not, used for the carriage of passengers or goods.

What vehicles does the EC Regulation apply to?

The Regulation applies, with various exceptions, to goods vehicles over 3.5 tonnes maximum permissible weight. Maximum permissible weight means the maximum authorised operating weight of the vehicle fully laden.

What vehicles are excepted from the EC Regulation?

There is a long list of exceptions which include

– passenger vehicles constructed to carry not more than 9 passengers inclusive of the driver

– goods vehicles under 3.5 tonnes

– vehicles used by the emergency services, postal authorities, armed forces, refuse collection and various other services of a public nature

– vehicles used to carry sick and injured and rescue material

– specialised breakdown vehicles.

In the case of *Universal Salvage Ltd v Boothby (1984)* it was held that this last category means a vehicle specially adapted or built, and kept for the purpose of going to the assistance of a broken down vehicle. A car transporter/trailer was not a specialised breakdown vehicle within this definition because although it was equipped with a winch and ramps to lift disabled vehicles, its main purpose was to carry a number of vehicles from one place to another. This interpretation may now be in doubt following a judgment of the European Court in 1986 (*Hamilton v Whitelock*).

What are the maximum driving periods permitted by the Regulation?

The Regulation restricts drivers in the amount of time they spend driving without a break in three ways:

a) in a day

b) in a week

c) in a fortnight

The maximum limits are:

for continuous driving without a break	Four and a half hours
for daily driving	Nine hours or Ten hours on two days in the week
for weekly driving*	6 continuous daily shifts
for fortnightly driving	90 hours

*If a driver spends the maximum possible in one week, i.e. 4 days of nine hours and two of ten, then in the following week he may drive for only 34 hours.

When does a "day" start?

A case in the Court of Appeal (*Kelly v Shulman (1988)*) has confirmed that a day is the twenty four hour period commencing when the driver starts or resumes driving after his last weekly rest period.

What is meant by a week?

The period from 00.00 hours Monday to 24.00 hours Sunday, in other words Midnight Sunday/Monday to Midnight Sunday/Monday.

What is a "break" from driving?

A break is a period of at least 45 minutes taken after four and a half hours driving. The break may also be taken as three breaks of at least 15 minutes each taken during and immediately after the driving period.

The break requirement does not apply if immediately after driving the driver is going to start a rest period.

What is a "rest period"?

In a 24 hour period a rest of 11 hours must be taken except

a) this may be reduced to 9 hours three times in a week but the time must be made up by additional time taken before the end of the following week

b) the period may be split if it is not reduced as in a) above, and taken in 2 or 3 periods during the 24 hours provided one period is of at least 8 hours duration, the others are at least 1 hour and the total rest period is increased to 12 hours.

What is a "weekly rest period"?

Once in each "week" a daily rest period must be joined with a weekly rest period to make a total of 45 hours.

This can be reduced to 36 hours when taken where the vehicle is based, or 24 hours when taken elsewhere, but in both cases the reduced time must be made up by additional time taken together before the end of the third week following the week in which the reduced weekly rest period is taken.

What happens if a vehicle is double manned?

When the vehicle is double manned, the daily rest requirement is that each man must have at least 8 hours rest in each period of 30 hours.

Can a rest be taken in the vehicle?

Daily rest periods can be taken in the vehicle if it is stationary and fitted with a bunk.

National Rules

Which vehicles are covered by national rules?

Only drivers of vehicles not covered by the EC Regulations (see above) have to apply the national rules.

What are these rules?

The daily limits are as follows:

Daily driving	10 hours
Daily duty	11 hours

What does "duty" mean?

Being "on duty" means being on duty for driving or other purposes in the course of employment.

What exemptions are there?

Certain light goods vehicle drivers are exempted from the duty requirements, for example the medical profession, those in the employment of one of the motoring organisations, and those employed mainly in connection with carrying out services of inspection, cleaning, maintenance and repair.

II Drivers' records of work

Council Regulation 3821/85 as amended

What rules are there governing the records which a driver must keep?

There are national rules requiring drivers' record books and in addition those vehicles covered by the EC Regulation must also comply with those requirements which include the fitting of a tachograph. Those who are exempt from EC law but covered by national law may use a record book instead of a tachograph.

Which vehicles are covered by the EC Regulation?

Vehicles over 3.5 tonnes are covered by the Regulation subject to the same exemptions which apply in relation to drivers' hours (see above), and in addition the following exemptions:

passenger vehicles used on regular services where the route covered exceeds 50km

vehicles on national transport operations constructed to carry not more than 15 passengers including the driver

vehicles used within Great Britain on local road tests for purposes of repair or maintenance

vehicles on national transport operations for moving live animals from farms to local cattle markets or for transporting carcases and waste not for human consumption

specialised vehicles used within Great Britain at local markets, for door to door selling, for mobile banking exchange or savings transactions, for purposes of worship, for the lending of books, records or cassettes, or for cultural events or mobile exhibitions.

What is a tachograph?

A tachograph is a device which records the distance travelled by a vehicle, its speed, driving time, periods of other work, breaks in work and daily rest periods. The record of the time, speed and distance is made by styli pressing on a chart. The chart rotates with a clock, and the vehicle's movement activates the styli. Each record covers a 24 hour period. If the vehicle has more than one driver, the tachograph must be capable of recording all this information on two separate sheets for each driver.

What information does the driver have to insert on the record chart?

Each driver has to complete the chart by inserting his name; date and place of commencement and finish of chart; registration number of the vehicle used; the odometer reading at the start of each working day, at the start of the first journey recorded, at the finish of the working day, and at the finish of the last journey recorded and if more than one vehicle is used during the day the readings on each vehicle; the time of any change of vehicle. If the driver changes vehicles during the day, he therefore has to take the chart with him.

What should the driver do with the completed charts?

He must keep them for the current week and also for the last day of the previous week he drove and give them to his employer within 21 days.

How long must the employer keep the chart?

He must keep them for at least a year.

What happens if a tachograph breaks down during a journey?

The driver must mark on the chart or on a temporary one all the relevant information that is required. Repairs must be carried out by an approved tachograph centre as soon as possible.

What are the requirements on calibrating tachographs?

The tachograph must be calibrated after any repairs which necessitated breaking the seals, if the tachograph fails, if different size wheels or tyres are fitted. In any event, the calibration must be checked every six years.

What are the requirements on fitting and maintenance of tachographs?

The tachograph may be fitted only by an approved fitter who must place his special mark on the seals which he uses. An installation plaque certifying that it has been properly installed must be displayed.

The tachograph must be checked on installation, after each repair and after every two year period.

As it is essential that the instrument records accurately, it is the responsibility of the employer and crew member to make sure that it works properly and that the seals placed on the equipment remain unbroken, except in case of extreme necessity which must be justified to the authorities.

What about vehicles which are not covered by the EC Regulation?

A tachograph can be fitted and used voluntarily. If its fitting and use comply with EEC law then the operator would have a defence to a charge that he was not using the books and record required by UK law.

What are the national requirements for vehicles not covered by the EC Regulation?

A driver's record book must be in a prescribed form and comprise a front sheet, instructions for use, daily sheets, an example of a completed daily sheet, weekly reports. The driver of a goods vehicle is required to make the entries in the driver's book.

What exemptions are there?

A driver who in a 24 hour period from midnight to midnight only drives a vehicle exempted from operators licensing, or who during a similar period does not drive a goods vehicle for more than 4 hours and does not drive it outside a radius of 25 miles from its operating centre, is exempted from the record keeping requirements.

In addition, see the situation when a tachograph is fitted and used voluntarily – see above.

Section E

OPERATORS' LICENSING

Goods Vehicles (Licensing and Operators) Act 1995

What is the purpose of Operators' Licensing?

The Transport Act 1968 established new basic procedures in the licensing of road haulage operators to ensure control over matters such as record keeping, drivers' hours, and suitability of applicants.

Who requires an operator's licence?

Any person who uses a goods vehicle on a road for the carriage of goods for hire or reward or in connection with a trade or business carried on by him must have it authorised by an operator's licence. A licence is not required for a small goods vehicle or for an exempted vehicle.

A small vehicle is defined as one which has a plated weight not over 3.5 tonnes or, if unplated, an unladen weight not over 1,525kg.

What exemptions are there?

There are numerous specific exemptions from the requirements. These include:

a dual purpose vehicle

a public service vehicle

a police, fire brigade or ambulance vehicle

a vehicle being used under a trade licence

a vehicle used for naval, military or air force purposes by the Secretary of State for Defence

What types of Operator's Licence are there?

A licence maybe either a restricted operator's licence or a standard operator's licence.

What is a restricted operator's licence?

This authorises the carriage of goods in connection with the holder's trade or business, but not for hire or reward.

What is a standard operator's licence?

A standard operator's licence covers both the carriage of goods for the operator's business, and also covers hire or reward. The standard licence may apply only nationally, or both nationally and internationally, and a statement must appear on the licence showing which it is.

How is a licence obtained?

An application for a licence is made to the Licensing Authority for the area in which the vehicle operating centre is located. An operator may have more than one licence for different areas but not more than one in the same area.

What is an operating centre?

An operating centre is the centre at which the vehicle is normally kept when it is not being used, and the authority will want to be satisfied that it is suitable for that purpose. This is not necessarily the same thing as the operating centre for business purposes. The operating centre will be specified in the licence and a place may not be used as an operating centre unless it is so specified.

What is the procedure for applying for a licence?

The applicant must apply to the appropriate Traffic Commissioner at least nine weeks before the date on which it is to take effect. The application must include details of the vehicles, and the number and type of trailers that will be used. He must also supply any other information the Authority may require. This may include:

the proposed use of the vehicle

arrangements for ensuring that drivers' hours and records rules are kept

facilities for maintaining the vehicles

details of any other vehicle operations that the applicant has been involved with

any relevant convictions that the applicant has had

After receipt of an application, the Traffic Commissioner must make details of it available at his office to relevant persons such as the police, or anyone entitled to oppose the grant of a licence. It must also advertise details of the application.

What are the main criteria that the applicant must satisfy to be successful?

The Traffic Commissioner must satisfy himself

a) as to the good repute of the applicant, i.e. that he is a fit person to hold a licence having regard to any relevant notified convictions

b) that the applicant has made satisfactory arrangements for maintaining the vehicles and the operating centre is suitable for that purpose

c) that the applicant has made satisfactory arrangements for ensuring drivers' hours and overloading rules will be complied with

d) that the applicant is of sufficient financial standing to ensure that all of the above are dealt with

and that in the case of a standard licence application, that the applicant is professionally competent or employs a transport manager who is of good repute and professionally competent. If it is not satisfied then it must refuse the licence.

The application form also includes a detailed "statement of intent" by the operator that he will comply with these requirements.

Who can object to the grant of a licence?

The following can object:

The police,

a local authority,

a planning authority,

a prescribed trade union i.e. National Union of Railwaymen, Transport & General Workers Union, Union Shop Distributive Allied Workers, United Road Transport Union, General & Municipal Workers Union, or association of persons holding operators' licences or employees of such persons, i.e. Road Haulage Association, Freight Transport Association, British Association of Removers, on the grounds that the applicant does not meet the criteria set out above.

In addition, anyone owning or occupying land in the vicinity can also object on environmental grounds.

If objections are received, the Authority will hold a public enquiry at which both sides can present their case before making a decision.

How is professional competence established?

A person will be considered professionally competent if he holds a certificate issued by an approved body, e.g. the Royal Society of Arts, to the effect that he possesses the requisite skills; or is a member of a specified professional institute such as the Chartered Institute of Transport or the Institute of Road Transport Engineers (those in higher grades of membership are deemed competent for national and international standard licences as those in the lower grades for national only) or Member or Associate Member of the Institute of Traffic Administration.

Can the applicant appeal against refusal of a licence?

The applicant can appeal to the Transport Tribunal. Any objectors also have a right of appeal against the grant of a licence.

Must an operator already possess the vehicles for which he applies for a licence?

No, the operator can apply for vehicles that he possesses and vehicles he intends to acquire. If his application is granted then he can add new vehicles to his fleet without having to submit a new application; all he needs do is to notify the Traffic Commissioner.

The numerical difference between the number of vehicles on an operator's licence and the actual number he possesses is colloquially referred to as the "margin".

What happens if the operator wants to vary the terms of the licence e.g. by adding a new vehicle not covered by the margin?

The holder of a licence can apply to the Traffic Commissioner that granted the licence for a variation. The licence may then be increased to take account of new vehicles. The Authority must go through the same provisions as to advertisement of the application as on the first grant of a licence.

What disciplinary powers does a Traffic Commissioner have once it has granted a licence?

The Commissioner has wide powers to revoke, suspend, terminate or curtail licences.

These are various grounds on which this may be done including:

a) the holder has contravened a condition of the licence

b) that in the preceding 5 years there have been relevant convictions

c) that a false statement was made to get the licence, or a promise made has not been fulfilled

d) that the licence holder is bankrupt or in liquidation

e) that there has been an important change of circumstances relevant to the grant of the licence

f) where the holder of the licence has been disqualified.

When a licence is revoked, it is taken away altogether and the holder is disqualified from holding another licence for any period that is thought fit. Where the holder of a restricted licence is convicted on more than one occasion in a 5 year period of using a vehicle for hire or reward the Traffic Commissioner must revoke the licence.

When a licence is curtailed, the duration of the licence will be reduced, or the number of vehicles covered by the licence is reduced.

When the licence is suspended, it will be inoperative for a certain period.

A licence holder who objects to the decision of the Traffic Commissioner can appeal to the Transport Tribunal.

TURNED OUT NICE

MAREK KOHN

Turned Out Nice

How the British Isles Will Change as the
World Heats Up

faber and faber

First published in 2010
by Faber and Faber Limited
Bloomsbury House, 74–77 Great Russell Street,
London WC1B 3DA

Typeset by Faber and Faber
Printed in England by Mackays of Chatham, Chatham, Kent

A CIP record for this book
is available from the British Library

ISBN 978-0-571-23815-6

2 4 6 8 10 9 7 5 3 1

For Sue and Teo, and so on

'Future generations may well have occasion to ask themselves, "What were our parents thinking? Why didn't they
wake up when they had a chance?" We have to hear that
question from them, now.'

Al Gore, *An Inconvenient Truth*

Contents

I

Atlantic Shade

At the time of writing, the weather is mild. By turns it is cool, damp, fair or fresh. There are sunny periods and scattered showers. The rain may set in for a season, or the sky may stay its hand for weeks on end. In winter and summer there are moments in which the weather throws off its island blanket and hints at its true strength. But by and large, over the couple of years during which this book was researched and written, conditions have remained in that reassuringly familiar zone of mild discomfort known as 'typical British weather'. After a period of unease, aroused by disordered seasons and startling bouts of heat and storms, the reversion to type has revived the appeal of the well-worn line: 'Climate change? Chance would be a fine thing!'

There are plenty of other inducements to set climate change aside: prices, earnings, savings, loans, mergers, acquisitions, profits and losses, all the pressing concerns that arise from the six-billion-player game of human industry and the turbulent concentrations of power within it. Citizens, states and corporate bodies all have immediate costs to weigh against bills that may not arrive for decades or centuries, and are not even certain to arrive at all. They will be tempted to disregard the shadow of the future if the future does not seem to be making its presence felt. The risk they will run – that they are running – is that they will turn those possibilities into certainties.

People in Britain and Ireland have always been insulated from what climate is really like by the Atlantic. On the Continent, away from the ocean, people know that summers are parched, winters are frozen, and both are punishing. On the offshore islands, the seasons are mild and muffled. Vast circular processions of water around the North Atlantic bring warmth north from the tropics; westerly winds blow in air warmed and moistened by the sea. In the millennial mood around the beginning of the century, storms, floods and heatwaves seemed to be warnings that the cosy mists were being blown away. Since then the shocks have abated and people have stopped noticing that it is getting warmer. The novelty of green shoots in autumn wore off years ago, and the odd winter frost seems to do them little harm. Central England has warmed by a degree Celsius since the 1970s, but that is startling to meteorologists rather than the general public. As Al Gore noted in his film *An Inconvenient Truth*, change needs to be big and abrupt to be noticed. Drop a frog into hot water and it will leap out; put it in slowly warming water and it will not notice it is being brought to the boil.

The North Atlantic may have been concealing the truth about global warming not just from the British Isles but from the rest of the world as well. Its circulating currents go through cycles, weakening and then growing in strength again. There is evidence that a natural ebbing in the Atlantic circulation, reducing the transport of heat northwards, may be cooling the ocean surface, keeping the lid on global temperatures. At the same time, greenhouse gas emissions are increasing.

This coincidence could have profound and irreversible consequences. We may be in the moment that decides the future. What happens in the next few years may determine whether human activities steer the planet onto a course that avoids more than a glancing blow from the climate, or commit it to centuries of rising seas and temperatures that remain raised for millennia. There seems to be widespread agreement among those focused on the problem that between five and ten years are about what we've got. Anything that draws attention away from this possibility, be it distractions caused by economic crisis or delusions caused by wholly natural processes in the ocean, could change the world for ever and for the worse. Human beings will live with the consequences for as long as any civilisation might be expected to last. Countless other species will not survive at all.

If the Atlantic circulation has indeed been offsetting global warming, the effect will wear off in a few more years as the currents recover their strength, revealing the impact of all the greenhouse gases emitted while the ocean was giving them cover. Economic disorder has reduced greenhouse gas emissions, because the world's industries burn less fuel as they slow down. Emissions fell by about three per cent in 2009, largely because of the effects of the previous year's financial crisis; as emissions have risen around three per cent a year since the 1950s, that is equivalent to a two-year pause in emission increases. But a temporary slowdown at this critical moment could lead to a rise in temperature that to all human intents and purposes would be permanent. In his review of the economics of climate change for the British government, Nicholas Stern pointed out that investments made in the next few years will determine whether the world's economy moves to a more sustainable path or stays locked into high emissions for the next half-century. That would probably take the world's climate past the point of no return.

With the onset of recession, Stern urged investment in low-carbon infrastructure as a strategy that would both revive the economy and prevent dangerous climate change. But that would require capital, which is likely to be in short supply after the disastrous stock market falls, and the demands on it from bankrupt banks. Enterprises need capital for the technologies that will be needed if the global economy is to change course away from the greenhouse. Technology companies need capital to fund research into making photovoltaic devices – solar panels or films that turn light into electricity – cheaper and more practical. Power utilities need capital to develop carbon-capture equipment for coal-fired power stations, and to find places to put the captured carbon dioxide. They will also want to make up for the extra costs of running such plants, which will have to use a significant fraction of the energy they generate to pump the gases deep underground. Carbon dioxide from a coal-burning station in Wales, for example, might have to be pumped up through Scotland and down into an exhausted oilfield in the North Sea. Businesses will protest about being loaded with costs, and governments will be wary of passing the costs on to the voters. Executives and ministers will be tempted to drag their feet until things get better, thereby increasing the risk that things will become irreversibly worse.

Politicians' timescales are geared to electoral cycles of five years or so. Economic cycles are not so predictable but their timescales are similar. So is that of the cycle in which the Atlantic circulation waxes and wanes from decade to decade. These are numbers that people can grasp properly. Up to ten is child's play; tens are manageable. But grasping the implications of climate change involves thinking on a scale of a hundred or a thousand years. We can do the arithmetic, but these numbers are just abstractions to us. We need to care about the people of the future and the planet they live on: to feel emotionally entwined with people who do not yet exist.

This makes 2100 a natural horizon. Many children alive today will still be living then: caring about what kind of world we are leaving for our children and grandchildren is not so difficult, and pointing to a time when many of them will still be in that world, or will not long have left it, can give parental consciences pause for thought. A 2100 horizon also allows enough time for the effects of climate change to mount up in the scientific models, and their projections typically run up to that date. A line drawn at the end of the century helps to give our picture of the future a frame.

Drawing a line at 2100 verges on denial, though. For one thing, it disregards the likelihood that, however bad things might be by then, they will get still worse for a generation or two after that. Much of the energy trapped by greenhouse gases is at first drawn into the sea, which warms and cools more slowly than the air. In 2000, the world had warmed about 0.7°C since 1880, but the slow rate at which the oceans release heat they have absorbed still left an additional 0.6°C rise in the pipeline. There will probably be plenty in the pipeline come 2100 as well. And when the focus is on Britain and Ireland, where the impact of climate change is likely to be felt more through its indirect effects upon the world's nations and economies than through its direct effects on warmth or rain in the British Isles, the water will be warming more slowly on the hob than almost anywhere else. The sketches and discussions of the future in this book are mostly set around the end of the century – except for the final one, which peers beyond that horizon and sees an ominously different prospect. While the mainstream climate science projections on which they are based offer a wealth of data on what could happen up to 2100, few studies extend to what might happen after that. The mainstream projections also avoid possibilities that are hard to model, such as the sudden collapse of major ice sheets.

Although the scenes from the end of the century that appear in the following chapters are intended to be climatically credible, they do not represent the only possible climatic future, and they only represent the beginning of the story. If the world's climate changes to the extent supposed in these accounts, which is within the range of consensus projections, the prospects for the next and subsequent centuries will be forbidding. The only end that 2100 is likely to mark is that of the period in which people in Britain and Ireland could still imagine that it had turned out nice after all. If a complete history of climate change is ever written, the problems of a couple of generations will rate no more than a footnote. The most ominous warning from the scientists' graphs is that once the temperature goes up, it stays up. Even if humankind did not burn a single gram of carbon after the turn of the twenty-second century, the world's mean temperature could stay where it was for at least another thousand years. Human activities have left about half a trillion tonnes of carbon in the atmosphere since the start of the industrial revolution. If the world continues its business as usual, accumulated emissions could reach 2,000 gigatonnes by 2100. That could keep the global temperature raised by more than three degrees for a thousand years; and it could still be more than a degree and a half higher after ten thousand years. The last of the carbon emitted by today's industry may not sink into the ocean until hundreds of thousands of years have passed.

The oceans take centuries to absorb heat and centuries more to release it again; not just because of their immense volume, but because their uppermost hundred metres or so form layers that separate the surface waters from the deep. Nor will they be able to absorb all the emitted carbon: a substantial proportion – perhaps a fifth, or possibly most of it – will remain in the air. It will take geology, acting on a geological timescale, to remove it. Carbon dioxide will react with the calcium oxide in igneous rocks to form calcium carbonate, the stuff of chalk and limestone, which will hang in the seas like motes in the air, but eventually sink to form sediments on the ocean floor.

Reviewing the evidence for the long slow death of greenhouse carbon dioxide, climate scientists David Archer and Victor Brovkin draw a comparison between the debates over climate change and the controversies over nuclear power. The fact that some forms of radioactive waste will take tens of thousands of years to decay is a source of outrage among opponents of the nuclear industry, who not only question the idea that these materials could be securely sealed away for such an immense span, but are also affronted by the very idea of producing waste that takes such an unconscionable time to die.

Ethically speaking, carbon dioxide in the air compares poorly with plutonium in a container. While the radio-active substance will do no harm as long as whatever it is kept in does not leak or disintegrate, the greenhouse gas will remain an active pollutant, helping keep the heat up for longer than many of the planet's vital systems may be able to stand. Ice sheets and rainforests might be able to cope with temperatures that went up several degrees and then subsided as quickly as they had risen, but their prospects under sustained periods of heat at such levels must be doubtful, if not dire. Even if an ice sheet managed to survive a thousand years, Archer and Brovkin observe, it would not last through ten thousand years of warmth. Going on evidence from the distant past, they suggest that an extra three degrees could raise the seas by fifty metres, if the melting had enough millennia to run its course.

Could the effects of the actions people take, or don't take, in the next few years really stretch that far into the future? Do our responsibilities really stretch that far too? A future so impossible to imagine is perhaps impossible to take seriously. But there is serious scientific reason to believe that choices made in the near future could have effects that dominate the next thousand years. That leaves us with two horizons that we have to strain to see, one a hundred and the second a thousand years away. The authors of a scientific paper that pointed to these lines in the distance called the first the 'political time horizon', meaning that it marked the limit – set by human lifespans and 'our (limited) ability to consider the world we are leaving for our grandchildren' – within which current decisions could be influenced by their possible effect on future events. The second line was the 'ethical time horizon', implying that we should factor considerations about events that far away into our decisions, but we probably won't. They drew the line at a thousand years because on historical form it seemed like a good innings for a civilisation.

People in the British Isles have another ethical climate horizon to look at, or turn away from. It lies to the south, where the human impacts of climate change will be concentrated. The poorer the region, the harder its inhabitants will be hit. Many areas that are already poor because they are harsh and dry, from southern Africa to northern China, will become harsher and drier still. The jolts and spasms from a disturbed climate will bear down hardest upon lands that are already the least generous to those who try to cultivate them. Africa as a whole is worst placed: its people are likely to lose five hundred times as many years of healthy life to climate change as Europeans will. The Democratic Republic of Congo, one of the very poorest countries in the world, has been identified, together with Tanzania and Mozambique, as one of the African countries most likely to suffer hunger because of climate change within a couple of decades. By the 2090s, half of southern Africa's crop seasons may fail. Worsening storms will batter the coastlines of countries where people are least protected, such as Bangladesh, which is one of the poorest in Asia and whose inhabitants

9

are already the most vulnerable in the world to tropical cyclones. The average death toll from disasters caused by floods, storms and droughts is over a thousand in poor countries; in rich ones it is under twenty-five. Climatic changes in the British Isles will be more moderate physically, because they will be softened by the Atlantic, and less severe in their human impacts, because they will be falling upon affluent societies.

This will leave Britain and Ireland in a position that the rest of the world – with one or two possible exceptions, such as New Zealand – will envy. They will not only be shielded from the full blast of climate change, but may find themselves enjoying conditions that in many respects are more benign than before. There will be obvious challenges, particularly the need to conserve water, to adapt cities to increasing heat, and to work out how best to respond to rising sea levels. Many of the challenges will not be so obvious. There will be losses to which most people may be oblivious, but which matter nevertheless, such as the disappearance of alpine plants from the slopes of Snowdonia or of the curlew from Irish skies. There will be shifts in ecological balance – trees climbing higher up hills, grass shrivelling under the summer sun – that will alter the quality and tone of landscapes. The moods of places will change.

There will be ethical questions that can be evaded, such as the responsibilities affluent and climatically lucky nations have towards poor and climatically stricken ones, and others that cannot, notably how to treat people from such countries who come looking for a place in the Atlantic's shade where they can live and work. Climate change will pose searching questions for the people of the British Isles about who they are and what their relations with the rest of the world should be.

It would be easier for them to find answers to those questions if they were going through what the rest of the world was going through. Alexis de Tocqueville, the nineteenth-century French author of *Democracy in America*, observed that Americans liked to explain almost all their actions on the principle of self-interest properly understood. They saw that it was in their own interests to help others and to make sacrifices for the common good. But they could see for themselves that in a community where people helped others, they would themselves be helped when they needed it, and they trusted that the state they supported would support them. For much of this century the benefits of helping distant strangers in foreign countries will not be so obvious to people in the British Isles, who will be reminded of their relative good fortune every time they look out of their windows or step outside.

All in all, they may consider, it has turned out nice. The narrower their horizons, the nicer it will seem to have turned out, and the harder it will be to see where their interests really lie.

With 2100 as the horizon, the British Isles present an opportunity to think about climate change in ways that are inevitably sidelined when the focus is global and the burning question is how catastrophic it can get. There will be heat-waves and floods, for sure, but nothing to compare with the kind of shocks that will hit Spain, half of which could become semi-desert, let alone Bengal. Without threats of devastation to worry about, there is room to look at other ways in which climate change will shape peoples and places.

Climate change will not just be a physical process. It will influence people's relations with each other – possibly even their most intimate relationships – and rearrange human communities as well as plant and animal communities. It will change people's sense of who they are and what the places they live in mean to them. In the British Isles, changes like these may be among the most far-reaching consequences of changes in the climate during this century. The most important effect of climate change for Britain and Ireland will be that it will change the political and economic relationship between the British Isles and the rest of the world.

Britain was the country that started climate change, being the first to use coal to power industry, but by a quirk of history and geography, it will be among the countries that will suffer least from it. People in Britain are accustomed to thinking of the industrial revolution as something that happened in the north of England a couple of hundred years ago. The extinction of mills, mines and factories adds to the sense that this chapter of British history closed long ago. That is a rather parochial view, though. The industrial revolution that erupted first in Britain was just the beginning of a global process of industrialisation that is still under way. When asked about the impact of the French Revolution, the story goes, the Chinese communist premier Zhou Enlai replied, 'It is too early to tell.' With the advent of climate change – and the studies warning just how long that change may last – it is becoming clear that the same goes for the industrial revolution.

With the revolution's eastern fronts ablaze and its western ones quietened, the gap between industrially mature nations and their emerging competitors could prove the undoing of international attempts to reduce carbon emissions. Developed countries look at China and see the world's largest emitter of greenhouse gases. China looks at developed countries and sees the gases that have accumulated in the atmosphere during the course of their development; it looks at its own factories and sees them producing the goods that the developed countries want. The countries that have emitted the most carbon into the atmosphere are the ones that should take the lead in cutting emissions, in China's view – after all, thanks to those emissions, they can afford it.

Industrialisation continues after the furnaces go out and goods are replaced by services, or information. The economies of Britain and Ireland will continue to develop. Globalisation, digital networks, migration, visions of an economy based on selling knowledge: these are all features of the permanent revolution that is the industrial age, and so is climate change. It's futile to try to think about the possible effects of climate change on the British Isles without thinking about other forms of change, and how the climate will interact with them. Climate change is one among a number of forces of change that have all arisen from industrialisation. In the short run it may be less visible than some of the others; in the long run it may be the only one that lasts.

During this century, the greatest impact of climate change on British and Irish society may be through migration. Since the British Isles will change less than most other parts of the world, their economies will be burdened less than others by the costs of adapting to a warmer climate.

That should improve their buoyancy, and their appetite for extra labour. Many of the climatic changes Britain and Ireland do undergo will make them more attractive as a place to live, visit, work or invest in. This new appeal will grow as other places become costlier and harsher under the stresses imposed by climate change.

Meanwhile, the population will be burgeoning under its own steam. Projections already suggest that by the end of the century, Britain will contain half as many people again as it did at the beginning. The graphs climb to different heights, depending on the assumptions made about fertility, mortality and migration, but the best estimate is that the population will rise from sixty million today to eighty-five million by 2081. That point is on a steadily rising slope, heading for a figure of ninety million by 2100. As the climate improves by comparison with the overheated climates of other regions, increasing numbers of people will want to immigrate to the British Isles, and those already here will be less inclined to emigrate. Britons will no longer retire to the costas of Spain to enjoy their leisure in the Mediterranean sun. Summer temperatures in Spain and southern France may rise by more than six degrees. By the late twenty-first century, heatwaves in much of France could become ten times more intense than they are now; in parts of Spain they could become twenty times more intense and last twenty times as long. As the heat in Spain and southern France becomes stifling, the trend will be reversed: the villages of the Lake District and the seaside towns of the West Country will be colonised, and restyled, by free-spending Spanish and French settlers. By then, south coast towns like Torquay, Bournemouth, Eastbourne and Hove will long since have shrugged off the old jibes that they were places where people went to die and forgot why they had come. Older people in the north or the Midlands will find the climate more equable; when they retire, they will be more inclined to remain in the communities where they spent their working lives.

Other migrants will be drawn to Ireland, whose population is a tenth of Britain's, and which would consider itself densely settled at a tenth of what Britain's population is likely to be. It could well increase to a significantly higher percentage. Projections by the two Irish governments' statistical departments suggest that the island's total population could reach nine million before the middle of the century, a million more than it supported before the Great Famine of the 1840s. But even if that rate of increase were sustained for the rest of the century, sending it within sight of fifteen million, Ireland would still be only about half as densely populated as Britain could be by then. Britain will still be the crowded island.

Far greater numbers of migrants will make their way to the British Isles not from choice but from lack of it. If the desiccation of the Mediterranean perimeter leaves the European side parched, it will leave the African shore barren. Egypt, a rectangle of desert a million square kilometres in size, is divided by the Nile and its delta, a stem and its flower, along which the country's population is crowded. There are already twice as many people in Cairo as in London, packed twice as closely together, and living on perhaps a twentieth of what Londoners earn. Rising seas will claim the coast, threatening the city of Alexandria and poisoning fertile farmland with salt water; efforts to get more out of the remaining land will exhaust it, allowing the desert to encroach into what the sea hasn't taken.

South of the Sahara, the mass of the continent will be stricken at least as badly and likely worse. The impact of climate change on societies will be determined by degrees of temperature and millimetres of rainfall, but most of all by dollars of per capita income. Africans will be forced to migrate in search of a living, on a scale which their efforts today, however desperate, can only hint at. They will compete in the struggle for economic survival with migrants from other regions, across the breadth of southern Asia, where conditions have gone from marginal to impossible. People living on low-lying coasts, such as the Ganges–Brahmaputra–Meghna delta in Bangladesh and the Mekong delta in Vietnam, will be threatened by rising sea levels. Two million people could be forced to leave the Mekong delta for Ho Chi Minh City, two-thirds of which could also be at risk from floods by the end of the century. The Philippines will become increasingly vulnerable not only to cyclones and floods but also to droughts and landslides. The snows and ice-sheets of the Himalayas are so vast that the Tibetan plateau is known as the 'Third Pole': at least ten countries, including China and India, rely on it for water. As the Himalayan glaciers melt, the basins of the great rivers that they feed in India, China and Indochina could be threatened first by floods and then by droughts.

Although many or most of those displaced by climatic pressures will remain within their national borders, great numbers will be drawn abroad by the demand for their labour in wealthy countries. The migrant poor will continue to do the work that the well-off are unwilling or unable to do, and the amount of such work to be done will grow steadily. More people will be unwilling to do menial work because more people will be well off, and more people will be unable to do things for themselves because they will be older: by 2100, nearly half the population of western Europe may be over sixty.

The climate will create the supply of refugee labour that meets the demand created by western European affluence: a tidy economic solution, perhaps, but not a pretty human picture. Whatever good fortune the Isles enjoy will stem from the rest of the world's misfortune. And there will be only hollow victories for the winners in a losing world. Being part of a crowd on its feet is better than standing out from a crowd on its knees. Though they stand to gain some secondary compensation because climate change will deal them a better hand than most, the states of the British Isles – however many of them there may be by the end of the century – will be losers along with the rest. They may enjoy being envied, but they will be less prosperous and less secure than they would have been if the world had kept its climate under control.

The contrast will not be just between these northern islands and the global south, but between the Isles and the Continent. Around the northern Mediterranean, water will become ever more precious. The Iberian peninsula may become more like north Africa; southern France may become more like today's southern Spain. Across the Continent as a whole, land and people will be exposed to climate change in full swing; in the British Isles, the effects will be damped. The contrast leaps out from a map of Europe showing projected temperature increases for the latter part of the century. Rises are shown in darkening shades running across the red arm of the spectrum, from a watery cream, under two degrees, to an ominous maroon, over four degrees. The continent is darkest to the south and east, following an arc that runs from Finland to the Balkans, and reappears to cover the interior of the Iberian peninsula; a dry-land archipelago within Spain goes beyond red into indigo, indicating a temperature rise above 5°C. Almost the entire mainland is scorched red or orange, except for a golden coastal strip running from Brittany as far as the Danish peninsula. It is mirrored across the Channel by a golden British heartland extending into Wales and reaching as far north as Yorkshire. The rest of the British Isles are a pale cosmetic pink, with flecks of ivory.

The intensity of the contrast this map shows between the temperate British Isles and the torrid Continent is, of course, an artefact. A different colour key, a different climate scenario and a different computer model would have produced a different effect. Within this map, each colour has different implications at different places. A temperature rise of four degrees will thaw Finland, but bake Greece. Nevertheless, the implication stands. Political and economic forces have been bringing the British Isles and the Continent together: climate change will conspire to drive them apart again. It will exert its greatest effects upon the south of Europe, already the hottest and historically the poorest part of the continent. By then, moreover, economic and political Europe may have extended to Turkey and other parts of Eurasia that will also be hot, dry and relatively poor. Britain and Ireland, insulated by the Atlantic, may become reluctant to share the costs of climate change that will fall so much more heavily upon the Continent.

As well as accentuating differences between the British Isles and the European mainland, climate change is also likely to sharpen contrasts between different parts of Britain. A division already exists between southern England, where the wealth collects, and north Britain, whose towns and cities are overlooked by stern and unprofitable uplands. 'By northern Britain I mean a country rather more like Wales or Ireland than southern England,' writes the landscape historian Christopher Smout. 'It begins with the Pennines. Doncaster, Derby and Manchester are frontier towns.' North Britain in this sense covers not just Scotland and the north of England, as far south as the Peak District, but much of Wales, which is similar in character. A map of Britain's uplands, forty per cent of the island's area, shows north Britain in relief. The greater south, which includes the Midlands, is drained, fenced and closely packed. North Britain's high moors and mountains were once dismissed, if not detested, as wastelands; now they are where people go to find something resembling wilderness. They are blustery, misty, cool expanses of peat and bog. They are Atlantic lands.

Smout goes on to reflect that it would have made good geographical sense if the medieval wars between England and France had gone differently, with a settlement that left the Stuart monarchs in power north of the Humber, and French kings ruling England to the south of it. 'Whereas the south would have had the mega service-cities Paris and London, the heavy clays and chalk, the marshes and the majestic woods of . . . oak and beech of southern England

and northern France, the north would have had most of the wild land of Britain . . .' That wild land contains most of what makes Britain's nature special.

Paris and London are now connected by a railway while the French state has a stake in many of south-east England's lesser train services, and ultimately owns much of the region's electricity infrastructure. Changes in the climate will take the region further in the same direction, accentuating the divide with the north. Southern England will become much more obviously an offshore climatic outpost of the Continent, of warmth-heavy nights and sunburned ground.

Under the Atlantic's shade, north Britain will become a milder version of its traditional self. It will change, in subtle and significant ways; its people will face stresses and will change the ways they use the land in response, but its peaty character will remain. The same will be true of western Ireland, where the climate will be buffered more by the Atlantic than anywhere else. People will hold north Britain and western Ireland all the more dear if these lands seem to be capable of maintaining their connections to their past while other places are torn away from their roots.

Climate change will cause the countryside to be not only more loved, but more valued. This is a matter of elementary economics. As goods becomes scarcer, their value increases. Britain's grass will look greener from the other side of the Channel as the Continent undergoes the stresses of summer drought and winter storms; and in fact it will be greener. Buffered by the Atlantic, the British Isles will start to resemble a northern Arcadia, and their climate will be an object of envy rather than derision. Fewer and fewer places on Earth will remain like them. People will pay more to live in or to visit these pleasant lands. And the lands will be, for the most part, pleasanter than at any time since before observers began to make observations such as that of the Roman historian Tacitus: 'The sky is foul with continual rains and mists; severe cold is absent.'

As the pressures and the demands on the landscape grow, so will the management requirements. Visitors will have to be encouraged, in order to put the landscape on something like a business footing; but they will have to be skilfully controlled, like livestock, to restrict their numbers while cultivating the revenues they provide. The environments of the British Isles are overwhelmingly artificial, and their protection in an increasingly complex world demands more artifice than ever. They will be more crowded than ever before, with lairds and lords turning their estates over to outdoor leisure industries, property companies, new money buying out old, conservation leviathans and county naturalist groups, farmers as preoccupied with reinventing themselves as with the look of the sky, National Parks authorities, utility companies, partnership projects, joint committees, environmental consultants, incomers, week-enders and sundry others with views to be canvassed.

Together they will follow the ways that have made the British landscape what it has been since the Normans arrived. 'Most of England is a thousand years old,' wrote the landscape historian W. G. Hoskins. That means, above all, a thousand years of bureaucracy. William the Conqueror began it with the Domesday surveys he conducted to produce a detailed inventory of land and property in the territories he had conquered. He also brought the forest to England –

not by planting trees, but by instituting the forest as a legal category of land in which the king enjoyed a monopoly of hunting rights. (Trees do not form part of the definition, and large tracts of forest, such as the New Forest, may be heath or other open land.) Those of lower rank might be assigned other rights to make use of the forest, such as estovers (the right to gather wood), turbary (the right to dig turf) and pannage (the right to let pigs forage in the woods). The exercise of these rights and the general good order of the forests were policed by an array of officials, including verderers, agisters, beadles and regarders; the forests were administered through a battery of courts: eyres, swani-motes and woodmotes. A medieval verderer transported to the twenty-first century would find the jargon equally pecu-liar – except in the New Forest, where a Verderers' Court still holds sway – but would soon realise that with their scoping studies and habitat action plans his successors were faithfully upholding the ancient bureaucratic traditions.

This book looks towards the horizon at the end of the century, about a lifespan away, and at certain points tries to see to the far horizon – the thousand-year stare. The future it imagines is what might happen if the world carries on the way it is going. This is partly because the world does look as though it is going to carry on the way it has been going, at least until it's too late, and partly because this is about the consequences of our own actions. The least we can do is think what our actions will mean for people who are already among us.

The rough dimensions of climate change in this future come from a set of scenarios, developed by scientists working for the Intergovernmental Panel on Climate

Change (IPCC), that have become the standard toolkit for climate modellers. The figures that appear in the media for temperature rises or rainfall changes over the course of the century are almost invariably from these scenarios, though it's rarely explained that the range of figures represent different storylines about the future. When it is reported that global mean temperatures will probably rise by between 1.8 and 4°C by 2100, the lower end of the range comes from scenarios in which the world moves to a more sustainable path, and the higher end from ones in which the world carries on business as usual. Temperatures rise the most under the storyline in which the world carries on exactly as it is: going for growth, globalising, burning all the fossil fuels it can lay its hands on. Although 4°C is the best estimate for this scenario, the maximum is 6.4°C – a figure with apocalyptic implications, and especially shocking coming from the IPCC, which is known and criticised for its cautious, consensus-minded approach. A four-degree rise seems a more likely prospect to climate scientists than it did when the last IPCC report came out in 2007, and a closer one too: simulations suggest that if the world continues on its present course, it could be four degrees warmer by the 2070s or even earlier.

In an alternative business-as-usual scenario, the countries of the world also go for growth, but they turn away from globalisation. Temperatures rise somewhat less, but the world's population rises far higher than in other storylines, reaching fifteen billion at the end of the century. Because regions keep their wealth to themselves, it is a highly unequal world. Having to pull themselves up by their bootstraps, poor regions are slow to achieve the levels of wealth that induce people to limit their families. In the storylines that combine growth with globalisation, the world's population reaches a peak of nine billion around the middle of the century, but falls to seven billion by the end of it. There they part company with UN projections, which show the world's population reaching nine billion by the middle of the century and then staying at that level.

If the world did carry on just the way it started the century, it would follow the steepest tracks in the IPCC's graphs, with greenhouse gas emissions right at the top of the range projected in the climate models. It cannot keep that up all the way, though. There will be more economic shocks like the one that hit the world less than ten years into the century. Emissions from burning oil will decline because there will be less oil to burn. And the world will make attempts to set itself on another path. Most industrialised nations now talk the talk of sustainability. The emerging industrial powers are only too aware that they are poised on the horns of a dilemma, between the rewards of a dash for growth and the pain that climate change may inflict on them before they have escaped from poverty. As seas rise, people on rich coasts may fear drowning and the loss of their homes; on poor ones, such as India's, they will fear cholera as well. Some deniers may remain vocal, particularly with corporate backing in the United States, but as the possible consequences of climate change loom larger, many sceptics may come to feel that even if they are still not entirely convinced, they ought to take the risks seriously. As time goes by and the consequences start to mount, governments and societies will react. But by then it will probably be too late.

Although climate change is a global process, it will divide the world. At present the nations of the world are failing to take the steps necessary to avert dangerous climate change because they cannot reconcile their individual short-term interests with those of humankind and the planet as a whole. As the consequences of that failure make themselves felt in economic shocks and shortages of essential resources – fuel, food and water – tensions between nations will rise. Globalisation could fragment into a nervous and grudging competition between individual nations, or gangs of them.

Putting these possibilities together, we can imagine that the history of this century will be a combination of the IPCC's storylines. The one that sets the scene is business as usual, carrying on exactly as we are; then there is a shift towards ways of using energy that do not release carbon; but because this comes too late in the day, nations and regions begin to pull apart and follow their own courses. Carbon emissions grow in the earlier part of the century; in the later part birth-rates grow, because wealth is not shared equally around the world. By 2100 the world's mean temperature has risen by between three and four degrees, and its population has stayed around the peak of nine billion it reached in the middle of the century. In Britain, average summer temperatures have risen five degrees in the south of England and nearly four degrees in northern Scotland. Winter rainfall has increased by more than a quarter in southern England and the Midlands; summer rainfall is down by nearly half in parts of the south-west. In London, summer temperatures regularly climb into the forties.

The standard scenarios all confidently expect that wealth will grow along with warmth, predicting annual world growth rates of between two and three per cent over the period from 1990 to 2100. That would be a slacker pace than the twentieth century set, with an average annual rate of 3.6 per cent a year. The disasters of the twentieth century were the kind that either boosted economies, one way and another, or left them unruffled. Wars drove armament production; the devastation the armaments caused drove reconstruction afterwards. The battlefields of Flanders were soon green fields again – and the First World War had a negligible effect on the world's economy, despite the terrible destruction in Europe.

Climate change will not knock things down so that they can be built up again. It will change the world for good. The fields will not turn green again. Spiteful climatic outbursts will deliver shocks to the world economic system, which may be plunged into crisis if the climate strikes at a number of weak points around the world in quick succession. Markets could topple like dominoes if confronted with drought on one continent, floods on another and failed harvests in the grain belts. Shortages and uncertainties will induce chronic stress and debility. Climate change will bankrupt businesses, destroy jobs, raise prices, push up interest rates and empty shelves in shops. People in the British Isles may enjoy the nice weather, but they will not be able to escape these impacts of climate change. They may be in their shirtsleeves, but they won't be able to relax. In the long run, the British Isles will not be able to escape the direct impacts of climate change either. The land will inexorably change as the air stays warm. The Isles will shrink and their outlines will alter as the seas continue to rise. There seems little doubt that this will inevitably happen once temperatures rise by more than a couple of degrees; the question is whether it will happen over hundreds of years, or start much sooner.

It will start during this century if meltwater from the Greenland and West Antarctic ice sheets starts contributing to sea-level rise. The IPCC did not attempt to factor these ice sheets into the projections for its 2007 report because how they will respond to warming remains a mystery. It cut its headline figure for maximum global sea-level rise to fifty-nine centimetres from the previous estimate of eighty-eight, which had included a consideration for the Greenland ice. Experts take the risk of melting in Greenland seriously, though, and the United Kingdom's environment ministry decided not to alter its recommended sea-level allowances for coastal defence planning, based on the earlier figures.

A global rise in temperature of 1.5 degrees above the level at the start of the century, which may already be unavoidable, could be enough to start the thaw in Greenland. The seas might also rise by a metre simply by expanding as they warm, without a contribution from Greenland. By comparing sea-level and temperature data going back to 1880, the climate scientist Stefan Rahmstorf has calculated a rate of temperature-induced rise that produces an increase of between 0.5 and 1.4 metres by 2100. Another modelling study pushed the upper limit to two metres by turning the knobs up to ten, the amount by which they multiplied the rates at which glaciers melted. Whatever level the seas reach by 2100, though, they will not stop there. The Dutch government's official flood-protection committee warns that the Netherlands should be ready for the North Sea to rise between two and four metres by 2200. One prominent climate-change authority, James Hansen, has argued that the ice sheets may melt suddenly and quickly, through what he and his colleagues call 'albedo flip'. Albedo is the proportion of light that the Earth or part of it reflects; the albedo of ice is high and that of water is low. As bright ice turns to dark water, less incoming energy from the sun is reflected back and more is absorbed, warming the planet even faster. This acceleration, Hansen predicts, is likely to tip the ice sheets into a cataclysmic meltdown; he has suggested that ice-sheet loss could raise sea levels by metres within this century. Fissures and rivulets have appeared in the Greenland glaciers, splitting the ice and lubricating it at the base so that it slides more easily towards the sea. Ice sheets may be more likely to disintegrate catastrophically, like an ice lolly falling in chunks from its stick, than to melt gradually like an ice cream upon a plate.

If the Greenland ice sheet were to melt, sea levels could rise by seven metres; the West Antarctic could add another three – or twice that, by some estimates. Fast or slow, the loss of either of these ice sheets would change the shape of Britain and threaten its largest city. Without defences on a scale to match, large areas of London – much of the east, as far inland as West Ham and Barking, most of the inner southern basin from Rotherhithe to Lambeth, western reaches including Battersea, Fulham and Barnes – could find themselves below the waterline. The Wash would distend into a great pouch of seawater that might approach the outskirts of Cambridge and Peterborough. Grimsby and Skegness could go the way of Dunwich in Suffolk, lost offshore; the North Sea could advance along the Humber and spill out over the low-lying hinterland, turning Doncaster and Selby into coastal towns. In Somerset, Glastonbury Tor might overlook the sea. The south-eastern tip of England could be cut off, leaving Margate, Ramsgate and Broadstairs on a new island.

To pursue the storyline as far as the end of the century, I've gone to places around the British Isles, some familiar to me and others new. I learned about how they got to be the way they are now, and about the forces and factors acting on them today, in order to try to imagine how climate might change them in the future. I thought about the places in the light of climate change, and thought about climate change in the light of the places. It seemed to me that what might not change could be as significant as what might.

These sites vary in character and their stories vary likewise. The one that starts in central London and works outwards into a broader discussion of cities and towns is urban and edgy in its suggestions about how people may live in future. The Sussex one that follows it is pastoral and serene. Both are essential parts of the picture. The vast majority of people will live in towns and cities, as they do today, but the future of idealised rural landscapes will be at the heart of many people's feelings about what climate change means to them.

Different places bring different questions to mind. A cameo from the Suffolk coast is about energy and the politics of power: a small migrant wading bird connects the nuclear plant at Sizewell with the new industrial frontier of the Russian Arctic. Two upland scenes, from the Black Mountains and the Yorkshire Dales, are reminders that moors and meadows are vulnerable to climate change;

and also reflections on the uses that might be found for marginal areas like these as the climate combines with the other forces that are changing them. As elsewhere in these stories, they tend more towards social satire than science fiction, but they are serious nevertheless.

The northernmost site is a Scottish glen that has become the focus for a vision of a resurgent Caledonian forest in which nature would be allowed to take its course, restoring much of the Highlands to a condition similar to that in which its first human settlers found it. A climate changed by human activities may make a mockery of the idea of nature taking its course; though advocates of 're-wilding' do favour assisting nature by reintroducing animals that humans drove to extinction, such as wolves. That provocative idea leads on to others that environmentalists are wrestling with as they consider how to help species threatened by climate change, and what role the British Isles can play as a refuge for them.

The final location is on the west coast of Ireland. I went to contemplate the Atlantic – if I was to tell a story based on the influence of the ocean, it seemed proper to go and look at it – and found myself transfixed by the 'fertile rock' I found myself standing on in the Burren area of County Clare. Its features all spoke of scarcity and struggles over resources, so it seemed an apt place to think about climate change; and its paradoxical qualities encouraged me to glimpse in it an unexpectedly optimistic image for the future.

But nothing I saw anywhere I went, or read, or heard from the experts I talked to, tempted me to think that we might be off the hook after all. We have to recognise that the next ten years could determine the next thousand. And in the British Isles we also have to recognise that the more the climate changes, the worse off our children and grand-children will be, no matter how nice it may sometimes seem to have turned out.

The Isle of London

When the lands west of the city of London were still left to their own devices, they were crowded with 'dense woods and forests', according to a charter issued in 785 on behalf of the Anglo-Saxon King Offa of Mercia. To the west of this belt, which ran from the Fleet river to what is now Mayfair, the Ela burn, later known as the Tyburn, made its way south and then turned east below the woods, losing its thread in marshes before entering the Thames. In doing so it formed an island, upon which Edward the Confessor built Westminster Abbey. At spring tides the marshland was flooded.

Later in the Saxon period, fourteen 'leprous maidens' founded a hospital on the northern margin of the swamp. Pious as well as leprous, the women dedicated their hospital to St James the Less. It survived until Henry VIII deported the lepers to Suffolk, built St James's Palace upon the site and drained its southern hinterland so as to create 'a nursery for deer'. In Henry's day this area was apparently an open field, with a central avenue forming the embryonic spine of a park.

Further steps in that direction were taken in the early seventeenth century by James I, who ordered a decorative arch to carry the Tyburn into a reach known as Rosamond's Pond. This pool later gained a reputation as a trysting place for lovers, particularly doomed ones, which gave rise to its alternative name: Suicide Pond. The park quickly acquired a pastoral mythology too. During the reign of Charles I, a French courtier named de la Serre reported that the park 'is full of wild animals, but as it is the place where the ladies of the Court usually take their walk, their kindness has made the animals so tame, that they all submit to the power of their charms rather than to the pursuit of the dogs'. The fauna of the park included the exotic inmates of a royal menagerie, among them a crocodile and an elephant.

Charles I passed through the park on his last procession, from St James's Palace to the scaffold at the Palace of Whitehall. The republican Commonwealth government stripped it of some of its ornament, renaming it James Park and felling for fuel many of the trees that had grown up in it – de la Serre had remarked upon 'the shade of an innumerable number of oaks' – but re-stocking the deer. It was Charles II who finally made the park modern, turning it into a playground for Restoration fashion, frivolity, gossip and intrigue. The menagerie had gone, but there were aviaries instead, giving a name to Birdcage Walk and introducing the strain of exotic birdlife that flourishes in the park today. A Russian ambassador initiated pelican diplomacy, presenting a pair of the birds to the king and starting a tradition that foreign envoys still uphold. By this time Britain was into the 'Little Ice Age'; the diarist Samuel Pepys recorded skaters in St James's Park, the first he had seen in his life, on 1 December 1662.

Charles had the park geometrically remodelled on the

lines favoured by French royalty, with the trees parading along avenues and the water tidied into a ruler-straight canal that bisected the park from east to west. In plan view, St James's Park now resembled a kite. It is said, however, that even the landscape architect André le Nôtre, who laid out the gardens at Versailles and Fontainebleau, declined to impose a similar degree of order in this pastoral enclave, maintaining that 'the natural simplicity of this Park, its rural and in some places wild character, had something more grand than he could impart to it'. The park continued to impress visitors with its rural charms, including milkmaids stationed at the Whitehall gate selling milk straight from the cow, twice daily, at noon and evening. A throwback to earlier sporting traditions occurred in 1739, when an otter, said to be five feet long, was hunted with hounds and speared to death; but the harmonious relationship with wild animals developed by the ladies of the first Charles's court appears to have endured, for a foreign visitors' guide of the period advised that stags and deer would feed from the hand.

In 1771 a French observer noted that on the southern side of the park, 'nature appears in all its rustic simplicity: it is a meadow regularly intersected and watered by canals, and with willows and poplars without any regards to order'. This insistent theme of natural simplicity was taken up in the late 1820s by John Nash and incorporated into the grand design that linked St James's Park to Marylebone Park, refashioned and renamed Regent's Park, via the new Regent Street. The canal was softened and widened into a lake with a plausibly irregular shape. Avenues were replaced by winding paths and flowerbeds by

shrubbery. The Ornithological Society of London contributed birds and a cottage for their keeper; both the building
and the post remain in existence. As a landscape the park
is much as Nash left it, and current management aspires to
be faithful to his spirit.

Many of the 1,700 trees in St James's Park and its neighbour Green Park are planes: some date back to Nash's
day, and could possibly last the course of this century too.
Within the parks the trees are generally in good condition,
but on the edges they are not. Along Pall Mall, the cere-
monial boulevard that runs westwards from Buckingham
Palace along the northern edge of St James's Park, the trees
suffer from poor soil, vehicle exhaust pollution and salt
spray from the road in winter.

For the public, the park remains the amenity it has been
since Charles II first allowed them in. It offers sun, shade,
space and an intimation of nature. The animals that feed
from the hand are grey squirrels rather than fallow deer,
but the sensation for the feeder must be much the same.
Many of the birds also approach their benefactors with
a swagger, and some may even perch as well. It may not
amount to a vision of the harmony between man and beast
before the Fall, but it does offer a welcome suggestion that
even in the heart of a huge city, interactions usually dominated by anxiety and suspicion may turn out better than
expected.

The value of the park to people in central London will
grow with the heat. By the 2080s average summer temperatures in the Greater London area are projected to rise
by up to 5.5°C, an increase of more than a third over the
present average of just under 16°C, according to a study by

35

the UCL Environment Institute. With daily highs pushing thirty degrees, London summers will be as hot as those of Naples or New York today. Winters will be nearly 3.5°C milder. Rainfall will be reduced in summer to half the levels of a hundred years before, but will increase in winter by over a fifth; over the year as a whole, rainfall will decline (by over twelve per cent from its current levels of around 700 millimetres) and snow will be seen only in Dickensian Christmas images – which might maintain their nostalgic appeal. Under these pressures the soil in London's parks and back gardens would lose a quarter of its moisture, measured over the year, and nearly forty-five per cent in summer.

By the later stages of the twenty-first century London could have a climate similar to that of Marseille in the twentieth century, and Mediterranean leanings in its character too. As the city heats up, people in central London will seek shade rather than opportunities to sunbathe. Indoors they will be comfortable, because of the measures that will be taken to adapt buildings to the heat, but they will still want open air. For visitors, the parks will be oases; and St James's Park will be the oasis at the capital's heart, between the Palaces, Parliament and the centre of the city.

The park's daily rhythms will alter. Already there are signs that in hot summers, visitors are starting to prefer the evenings. The fashionable parades of the Restoration park might in time reappear as an evening *paseo* like those performed by smartly dressed families and keen youth in the towns of southern Europe. Opening hours, entertainments and security arrangements could adjust over time to the new routine.

Underlying the new social opportunities offered by warm summer evenings, however, is a phenomenon that poses serious challenges for health as well as comfort in cities. In the countryside, much of the sun's energy is absorbed by plants, which draw water from the ground and release it into the air. As water molecules absorb the heat from the air that they need to escape from liquid to vapour, they lower the temperature. In cities, the balance is shifted towards warming. Rainwater is channelled into drains instead of soaking into the ground. Artificial materials store the heat from the sun, especially when they are concentrated in the massive structures of large buildings, and release it slowly back into the air. They may also absorb heat from the myriads of motors and electronic circuits that swarm in cities, though how much all those devices contribute to the warming effects is unclear. Pollution from engines can also contribute to urban warming by creating a local greenhouse gas cloud that traps the sun's heat. And where tall buildings form 'urban canyons', they trap the sun's energy within them. All this adds up to what is known as an urban heat island, in which there is a marked difference between temperatures in a city and in the surrounding countryside.

The island reaches its maximum at night, between about 11 o'clock and three in the morning, as the city fabric releases the heat it has absorbed from the sun during the day. London is Britain's most prominent heat island, with temperatures on average four to six degrees higher than in nearby rural areas. It also has some effect during the daytime, as commuters may notice when they get off their trains at their home stations. The difference between the city temperature and the out-of-town site used as a reference point is known as the urban heat island intensity. During the 2003 heatwave, London's heat island intensity reached nine degrees. In a warmer climate, the heat island could also make itself felt earlier, when people are in their offices, as well as later when they are in their bedrooms.

Within cities, parks act as counter-islands. They cool down more quickly in the evenings than the streetscapes in which they are set, and their cooler climates may spread into the surrounding streets. Their effect is visible in a thermal map of London showing temperatures in the summer of 2000: Richmond Park in south-west London was a degree cooler than its surroundings, with a temperature close to that of its comparison site outside London. (Temperatures were highest at a point just south of the British Museum, with an average heat island intensity of three degrees, though the position of the city's thermal centre depends on the wind direction; a study conducted the previous year located the central hotspot in the canyons of the City of London.) The central London parks are not visible on this map, but that does not mean their effect is imperceptible on the ground. Parks and the banks of the Thames are typically about half a degree cooler than the paved interior. A study in the Swedish city of Gothenburg, which is around the same latitude as Inverness but has similar summer temperatures to those of London, found that even a small park 3.5 hectares in size was a couple of degrees cooler than surrounding areas. Temperature differences between the city's largest park and a built-up area reached nearly six degrees at their maximum, and the park's cooling effect reached over a kilometre beyond its boundaries. At 156 hectares, however, that park is considerably larger than London's Hyde Park, which in turn is about six times the size of St James's Park.

Heat islands reduce the costs of heating (by twenty-two per cent, according to a study of two dozen buildings within the London heat island) but increase the costs of cooling (by twenty-five per cent, in the same study). Their major impact, however, is on health. In a heatwave, the island that surrounds the city at night denies relief after a long day of simmering stress. It seems likely that this extra thermal load contributed to the 600 excess deaths, above the mortality that would normally be expected during the period, recorded in London during the heatwave of 2003. The mortality rate in the capital was more than double that of the country as a whole; deaths among the elderly, the main victims, rose by seventeen per cent across England and Wales, but forty-five per cent in London. Even that leap was overshadowed, though, by the fifty-four per cent rise in France, which confirmed the rule that climate hits the Continent harder than the offshore islands. Across Europe, the total death toll was estimated at between 22,000 and 35,000.

The London heat island seems bound to grow as summers become hotter and sunnier. By the 2050s, greenhouse gas emissions at medium levels could increase London's heat island intensity in August by half a degree, leaving average night-time temperatures in London about three degrees higher than those in what survives of the green belt around it. On the hottest nights, the difference could reach more than ten degrees.

The hazards to health will probably ease, however, as the

city adapts. Deaths among elderly people in the 2003 heat-wave were so high because it came as a shock. People were unused to such heat and their homes were not adapted to cope with it. In Mediterranean towns, elderly people can wait out the stifling afternoons behind heavy shutters, in narrow streets that shoulder out the sun. Southern countries set the bar for heatwaves higher than northern ones. In Latvia the official threshold is 33°C, but in Malta it is 40. At present, heat seems to cause deaths in London when average temperatures rise above 19°C, but that threshold may rise as society adjusts to a hotter climate. The necessary adjustments would include steps to ensure that older people have the funds and the guidance they need to get their homes adapted, and a general shift in the direction of neighbourliness. Cities in affluent countries ought to be able to protect their elderly people from heatwaves and heat islands. But sprawling megacities in poor countries, growing ever larger and hotter, will not be capable of much kindness towards their old, their sick and their very young. Buildings in wealthy cities will be made of materials not yet invented and adjust automatically to the weather; megacity slums will probably still have tin roofs and open sewers.

Heat island effects can be very sensitive to local conditions. A step as simple as painting a building white can make a real difference. Measurements taken in typical central London street gorges one sunny lunchtime showed that a matt white wall was six to ten degrees cooler than dark brick surfaces: if the buildings in the gorge had been entirely painted white, the air temperature in the street could have been three or four degrees lower. Up on the roofs, temperatures may well pass 50 or 60°C, building up heat to be diffused into the night. Painting roofs white would help: a start has been made on London's buses. As well as reducing the supply of heat to the island, reflective roofs would ease discomfort and demands for cooling. They would also last longer, suffering fewer strains from the cycles of expansion and contraction that go with heating and cooling.

They could also make a significant contribution to the planet's heat balance. Urban surfaces are twenty to twenty-five per cent roofs and forty per cent pavements; reflective materials applied at roof level and street level together could increase the albedo, or reflectance, of urban areas by about a tenth. On a typical new house with a garage, a cool roof could offset ten tonnes of carbon dioxide. Applied globally, that could have a similar effect to removing 44 gigatonnes of carbon dioxide from the atmosphere, an amount equivalent to about a decade's worth of growth in carbon emissions. And these materials are not only available in white. Over half the sun's radiation is in the near-infrared band, with wavelengths just a little too long for the eye to see. Paints that reflect this part of the spectrum, while absorbing radiation in the visible band, are both coloured and cool.

Energy absorbed from the sun can also be put to use on the spot. Solar panels that heat water are the simplest way to tap solar energy; solar arrays that convert sunlight into electricity – photovoltaic systems – are commonplace but not yet versatile enough to realise their potential as a kind of artificial chlorophyll, covering any built or manufactured surface with a sun-harnessing skin. That may happen as and when photovoltaics become more like skin, taking the form of thin films rather than rigid arrays. If these become sufficiently cheap, and practical to apply on small scales, surfaces from vehicle roofs to lamp-posts and the backs of road signs could be mobilised in a drive for energy efficiency comparable to, but much more far-reaching than, the drive to grow food on urban land during the Second World War. Cities could be solarised, like deserts being greened.

Cities themselves can be greened too. In the later decades of the twentieth century, environmentalists and community activists created an urban wildlife movement that took over unwanted waste ground, such as the old Camley Street coal yard on the Regent's Canal behind King's Cross Station, and turned them into nature reserves. Camley Street Natural Park has survived the redevelopment of the area, and now has the St Pancras International Eurostar terminus for a neighbour, but its history of struggle suggests that claiming waste ground for nature is a strategy that has had its day. As Tom Clarke of the London Wildlife Trust points out in a politically candid reflection, the site became a reserve because it became a focus for an activist movement which secured support from local politicians, because the environmentalists' aims struck a chord with the left-wing Greater London Council administration of the early 1980s, and because, being at the derelict back end of an area with a vicious reputation, it was worth little to developers. Soon after the park opened in 1985, however, it lost its political patrons when the Conservative government abolished the GLC. Within a few years, the immense regeneration plans for the King's Cross area threatened to send the northern end of the Channel Tunnel rail link through the site, and rekindled the struggle to assert the reserve's value in the midst of the new concentration of capital. The park's defenders succeeded in steering the tracks away from the site and preserving this humble monument to the politics of a bygone era.

Camley Street shows that existing reserves may survive with political support and thrive under the care of devoted volunteers, but the odds are now heavily against the annexation of new green enclaves. Pressure to preserve green fields in the countryside leads government to favour the redevelopment of derelict land within cities, and developers will seize opportunities to take advantage of high urban property values. Volunteers may be allowed to manage a site as a nature reserve at times when nobody else has a use for it, but when the economy picks up, the bulldozers will move in. As Camley Street's supporters were uncomfortably aware when its future was under threat, urban wildlife sites cannot usually claim antiquity or biological rarity. Their claim to authenticity is social rather than natural: Camley Street stood for the efforts of the community that created it, but the political climate has changed, and will only become more unfavourable as cities grow denser. The Olympic Park in east London is an exception that proves the rule. Its hundred hectares of open space, anticipating climate change with 'cool island' shade trees and flood-preventing wetlands, will only be made possible by the immense international prestige of the Olympics, which are not likely to come round more than once a century.

Instead, the greening of the city will continue above the ground. There is an example in St James's Park, though by design an unobtrusive one. According to the Royal Parks organisation, the Inn the Park café, opened in 2004 and run by the restaurateur Oliver Peyton, 'blends into the original intentions of Nash's 1828 park design'. It achieves this by covering itself with a grassed roof, which makes it invisible from the Mall; underneath is a smooth glazed ellipse supported by columns of Austrian larch. Whereas its predecessor, like other conventional buildings in such a setting, was the analogue of a crag or large boulder, this is an artificial cliff. The green roof defers to the grassed space in which the building is set, fulfilling a brief to 'continue the park up and over the top of the building in one seamless curve', while at the same time creating a new rooftop view over the lake.

It will also play its part in reducing the London heat island, replacing as it did the conventional roof of the late-1960s Cake House which preceded it on the site. Green roofs insulate the buildings beneath them, helping to keep the interior cool in summer, and may reduce the energy needed for heating in the winter. Vegetation on roofs cools its surroundings in the same way as vegetation growing in the ground, by releasing water which draws heat from the air as it evaporates. The effects of extensive roof greening are hard to estimate, but they could be significant. Modelling studies in North America have calculated that if half Toronto's roofs were greened, the streets might be cooled by 1°C, and that green roofs could bring temperatures in Los Angeles down by about 1.5°C.

The greenness of a roof can vary considerably in quality and extent, from something resembling a weed-stippled railway trackside to a passable imitation of a meadow. Even a roof stocked with potted plants can be counted as green, but the term is generally taken to mean a layer of vegetation. The most basic covering is sedum, a short succulent plant that requires only a couple of centimetres of bedding and can be laid in mats, like rolls of turf. At the other end of the scale, the most intensive installations require irrigation and structural support. While these furnish prestige developments with elevated parks, more modest green roofs in residential streets and suburbs blur the boundaries between homes and gardens. Almost any flat roof can be greened, as can pitched roofs whose slope is less than thirty degrees, though the giant sheds that serve as warehouses or out-of-town megastores are not strong enough to carry the weight. In Victorian terraces roof greening will amount at most to spreading a rug of plants over the flat-roofed back additions, and nothing at all can be done with most pitched-roof houses of later date. It is the modernised areas – the office-block forest of central London, or the unloved shopping parades of the suburbs – that are best suited to, and most in need of, an organic covering.

There is no need for it to stop at the eaves. Walls can be greened too – not just by growing creepers up them, but also by covering them with envelopes of ersatz soil in which vegetation can be planted vertically. While green roofs will put gardens on top of homes, green walls will transform streetscapes. Exotic tendrils and blooms can make a glass-walled office block look like a botanical greenhouse with the plants on the outside. Deciduous vegetation covering glass walls will shade the interior in summer, then shed its leaves in autumn, allowing as much sunlight as possible to enter in winter. Thanks to this winter light, the glass building will use less energy over the course of the year than if it were made of brick. Its appearance will change from vegetable to mineral, and back again in spring. A building that is seasonal will seem closer to nature.

On the other hand, some passers-by may find a tussocky meadow growing perpendicular to the ground disconcertingly unnatural. Some green-wall initiatives will set out to unsettle people's perceptions about plants, buildings and the proper places of each. Others will encourage the fantasy that the country is taking over the city, or play on the familiar cliché of the flower-clad cottage. Laundrettes could be festooned with wisteria and council offices could have roses round the door. What might seem whimsical today might become conventional, like ornamental trees or hanging baskets, if green walls become a favoured means to manage energy efficiently. Buildings will come to look bare without a cladding of vegetation. Economic pressures will shape aesthetic preferences.

As well as moderating temperatures, green cladding can help to conserve water, which is the problem around which London's responses to climate change will revolve. Urban surfaces are mostly hard and impervious, ushering water as quickly as possible into the drainage system and onward to the sea. Rainfall is wasted at best and turned into a hazard at worst. In storms, water cascades off roofs and down gutters at rates that can overwhelm the system, spilling over into flash floods. Water that runs into a river from the drains of a town upstream may cause the river to overtop its banks further downstream. And as water pours over asphalt and concrete, it may sluice an urban seasoning of oil, metals and other noxious chemicals into watercourses.

The chronic debility that the capital faces is that of drought. London is constitutionally short of water to start with, maintaining the country's highest population density in one of its driest regions. The result is that it is among the world's driest capital cities, and has about as much water available for each of its inhabitants as Israel. Demand may exceed supply in nearly the whole of the Greater London area in a dry year. A city conspicuously short of water nevertheless consumes it conspicuously. Londoners use 168 litres of water per head each day, well above the national average of 150 litres a day.

At present London's water stress is compounded by gross inefficiencies in supply. Half the pipework is more than a hundred years old, a third is over 150 years old, and a quarter of the water that enters the mains leaks out of them. The ground does not let the Victorian pipes rest easy: the London clay that covers the ancient floodplain is particularly corrosive and elastic. Although the brightly coloured plastic tubes that are replacing the original cast-iron pipes will be less vulnerable to London's subsurface chemistry, and readier to bend as the ground flexes, the swelling and shrinking of the clay is likely to unsettle the city with increasing insistence as the climate becomes more extreme. When London clay absorbs water it swells, causing what is known as heave; when it dries out it shrinks, causing subsidence. London clay is a distinctly unfortunate substrate for a city so obsessed with property prices.

Urban surfaces need to become softer and more pervious, to accept water instead of deflecting it. In the future new materials may alter and enrich urban textures, but in the meantime there is plenty of scope for more prosaic measures. Few will be more prosaic than the measure taken nationally in 2008 to deter householders from concreting over their front gardens by requiring planning permission for impermeable surfaces, but not for permeable ones such as gravel or porous asphalt. Rain will be subject to increasing bureaucratic regulation.

London's water foundations lie far below the surface, underneath the great slab of clay, in the chalk bedrock and some sandy layers above it. The clay, bluish and stiff, acts as a seal over the London Basin that reaches a thickness of 150 metres in some areas; the aquifer underneath is filled from the rim of the basin, the chalk hills of the Chilterns and the North Downs. As industry developed in the London area during the nineteenth and twentieth centuries, drawing off increasing amounts of water, groundwater levels fell. By the 1960s they were sixty-five metres lower in the middle of the London Basin than they had been in the 1840s. When the manufacturing tide began to recede, in the 1950s and 1960s, groundwater levels began to rise again, by as much as three metres a year in the central area.

Under London, rising water pushes itself into the clay, which is prone to fissure. As the water approaches the surface, it may threaten to stress or flood deep-set buildings and the many tunnels that have been driven through the obliging clay. To avert the risk in central London, London Underground, Thames Water and the Environment Agency drew up a programme of groundwater management, aiming to pump out an extra fifty million litres of water a day. The strategy worked, perhaps too well: water levels are falling by five metres a year in south-west London, and are also dropping in the centre of the city, prompting the authorities to refuse permission for new wells. Too low, then too high, then too low again:

the last thing London's water supply needs is a change in the climate that exaggerates the highs and lows of rainfall within the course of each single year.

As the search for renewable energy soures becomes more urgent, London's aquifer will increasingly be used for heating and cooling as well as washing and drinking. A ground heat pump reduces a building's dependence on the electrical grid by drawing on energy stored in the earth. The temperature in a building with thick walls will change more slowly than the temperature in a more lightly built one, because the mass in which heat can be stored is greater; under the ground, within the mass of the Earth itself, the temperature at any point tends to stay the same all the year round. At 10 to 15°C, water pumped from an aquifer in winter will be warm compared with surface temperatures and can contribute to the warmth of a building, while in summer it can help to keep the building cool. The water can be pumped back into the aquifer, so there need be no net loss of water. But if too many pumps are returning water that has warmed or cooled above ground, the temperature of the aquifer may change, spoiling the pumps' efficiency.

Competition between boreholes is likely to intensify as landowners decide that they need their own private water supplies for times of drought. John Nash pioneered such an arrangement in St James's Park, switching the lake's supply from the culverted Tyburn to boreholes within the park that reach down into the gravel layer beneath the clay. An independent water supply could become a valuable asset as the city heats up, but its value may diminish if everybody has a straw stuck into the same bowl.

And on top of that there will be the sheer weight of numbers. London's population has been growing continuously since 1988: it reached 7.56 million in 2007 and is projected to add another million by 2026. It has been there before, having reached its peak of 8.6 million in 1939. Household sizes have declined since then – nationally, the average has fallen from 3.6 in the post-war years to 2.4 – and so has the density of dwellings in London. The architect Richard Rogers has described the densities in current London developments as 'ridiculously low': the average for new buildings in central London is seventy-eight dwellings a hectare, whereas more than two hundred dwellings per hectare may be packed into the grand but subdivided nineteenth-century terraces of Bloomsbury or Notting Hill. Around 25,000 new homes a year are needed to keep up with demand. London is under mounting pressure to increase the efficiency of its accommodation as well as of its water and energy use.

For architects and planners, the obvious answer is that cities should become denser; for the public, the obvious objection is that cities were blighted by the high-density tower blocks built in the 1960s and 1970s. This time round it will be different, the designers insist: 'compact' cities are not to be confused with crammed cities. Carefully designed and properly managed, they can be good to live in as well as efficient. People will walk or cycle more and drive cars less. They will use less energy to heat or cool their homes; and they will be better neighbours. New dense neighbourhoods could help to recreate something of the sense of community that tower blocks did so much to destroy. And if these things turn out to be true, planners and architects will have redeemed themselves in the eyes of the public for their professions' earlier experiments in dense packing.

Encouraged by planning guidance, urban designers are already thinking and building dense. In London, they are reinventing the Georgian terrace – and looking beyond historic density levels to 'superdensity'. The London Plan envisages that densities in central areas could reach more than four hundred dwellings per hectare. Parisians would not be especially impressed, with densities in the centre of their city already reaching three hundred per hectare, and what seems superdense in London might seem almost sub-urban to residents of central Barcelona, rubbing shoulders in five hundred dwellings per hectare. Nevertheless, this kind of living cheek by jowl will demand high standards of design and operation if it is to foster communities rather than exercises in packing. One long-established constraint is the requirement that windows of principal rooms should be at least twenty-two metres (seventy feet) from equiva-lent rooms in neighbouring homes: the distance is said to have been set in the early twentieth century on the basis that at that range, any inadvertent glimpses of neighbours in a state of undress would not be detailed enough to com-promise decency.

With homes in central city areas far out of most people's reach at market prices, planning authorities try to redress the social balance by requiring that a proportion of homes in new developments are 'affordable'. This improves balance only in the accounting sense, by bringing down the average income. It leads to incongruous and jarring juxta-positions of people who cannot imagine ever having to call on the welfare state and people who cannot imagine ever living without its support. The middle is missing: genuine social balance requires the inclusion of families that are basically self-reliant and can contribute to the life of an emerging community.

Families can live happily in flats, and may be encouraged to do so if they have reasonably good access to open space. The greening of city roofs could allow children to play on roof lawns, with glazed walls keeping them safe while allowing the sunlight to reach the greenery. But householders with children generally prefer houses. A denser London of the future will still have to rely on terraces, as did the denser London of the past.

Houses can reach a density of 120 homes per hectare, but apartment blocks will be needed to attain superdensity. These will provide opportunities for efficient energy use, such as combined heat and power schemes, or even anaerobic digesters in which microbes generate combustible methane from waste, that may never be practical for individual homes. Machinery of this kind, like other communal installations such as lifts and security systems, will require capital to buy it and high service charges to keep it running. In theory, residents could manage their collective arrangements collectively, but community life in capital-intensive urban blocks is more likely to be limited to the exchange of pleasantries between the concierge and the residents as they bustle in and out. In buildings managed by service companies, contractors take care of communal interests. The green roofs and walls will be maintained by specialists – and the job may become more specialised if climate change makes the care of plants more difficult for amateurs.

Residents might well like the idea of contributing to the ecological life of their buildings, though. One Brighton, a housing development on former railway land adjoining Brighton Station, offers home-buyers a lifestyle that is smart and metropolitan, but incorporates opportunities to grow their own vegetables. It takes its name from the One Planet Living initiative, which claims that 'if everyone in the world lived like an average European we would need three planets to live on'.

A computer-generated image of how One Brighton development might look when finished gives an impression of bustling vegetable rather than human life, with plants climbing walls and crowding roofs. At one stage the vision included 'vertical allotments', glazed stairwells in which householders would be encouraged to grow food, though it later quietened down into a promise to provide space for gardening. The sales pitch, however, is of 'a contemporary mix of studio, 1 and 2 bedroom eco apartments moments from Brighton Station'. These are small flats that will appeal to child-free commuters, or to affluent Londoners in search of a weekend place only an hour from Victoria on the train. The plant life will largely depend upon hired hands. And on the hoardings that shielded the buildings as they took shape, the developers dropped the one-planet slogans to spell out the selling point: 'For a unique second home . . . there's only One Brighton'. One planet, two homes – who really cares that it doesn't add up?

Over the road, dwarfed by the bulk of One Brighton, is a pocket estate made of small brick-built blocks arranged in a rectangle. The landings outside many of the flats have been decorated with ornaments and pictures by the residents, their homeliness spreading beyond the front door like flowers spreading beyond the gardens in which they are planted. Ever since council managers realised that personal touches do more for estates than standardised sterility, householders like these have shown how convivial blocks like these can be. People who are around their homes a lot of the time, because they are retired, or not working for other reasons, or working locally rather than commuting to another city, have time and incentive to care for their surroundings. Social housing residents are better placed to make their homes green, and tread more lightly on this one planet we all share, than busy professionals with windowless schedules.

Architects and urban planners will become increasingly preoccupied with making the most of limited space and energy. The two go together: making the most of one will generally make the most of the other.

The basic principles of energy efficiency are illustrated by the school textbook example of the elephant, whose bulk stores warmth so well that its ears have enlarged in order to increase the surface area from which it can shed excess heat. Increasing the area of an object creates a larger surface from which heat can be lost, while increasing the volume creates a larger space in which heat can be retained. Six detached houses in a row will have ten external walls separating them; six houses in a terrace will have none, and so will lose heat to the outside air less quickly. Large buildings warm and cool more slowly than small ones, so the need to keep them warm or cool artificially is reduced. Mass has a similar effect to volume: a building with thick walls will tend to warm up in daytime and cool down more slowly at night than one with thin walls. This may become less of a consideration as new insulating materials come into use, but until then mass will be the greatest asset an old building can have in the struggle to meet the demands the twenty-first century makes of it.

The new drive for density will shape suburbs and average towns as well as city cores, although the superdense properties will be concentrated in the super-expensive central districts of London and a few other major cities. There is more to the familiar density gradient, from apartment blocks and terraces in urban centres to small detached houses and then on to the lawns of suburbia, than the high value of central locations. It is also the result of the way that wealth and aspirations intertwined with the expansion of towns and cities. Suburbs have become almost synonymous with detached houses and gardens, but in the nineteenth century they were terraced ranks advancing through the fields. In the twentieth century, between the wars, it became possible for people to aspire to detachment. More people were able to afford houses, and local authorities began to build ones for those who could not. Families wanted gardens for their children to play in, and space between themselves and their neighbours.

Some of the reasons they wanted that space have faded. Close packing was life-threateningly unhealthy in a period when there were still few defences against infectious disease, and coal smoke streamed from every chimney. The status that detachment confers is still a powerful draw: whatever the size of an Englishman's home, he can regard it as his castle if it stands within its own plot of land. But detachment is not a requirement for high status: the penthouse apartment is a byword for luxury. Encouraging people to aspire to homes with party walls doesn't seem like an especially difficult marketing challenge, especially if these new homes are rich in advanced technological features that synthesise comfort and efficiency.

One factor that may weigh more heavily with householders in the future than in the past is noise. A 1930s family would have had a wireless in the living room that fell silent when everybody went to bed; a family today is likely to have televisions, music players and video game consoles throughout the house, with different rooms under the control of different family members, keeping different hours. Even here, however, energy-efficient design helps people live close together comfortably. Insulation keeps warmth in and noise out. Timber-framed buildings seem to be quieter than ones built of concrete; timber comes from a renewable source and is carbon kept out of the atmosphere, whereas cement production emits 900 kilograms of carbon dioxide for every 1,000 kilograms of cement, and is responsible for about five per cent of global carbon dioxide emissions. Greener homes are more peaceful homes.

The most important consideration for householders, however, will be the rising cost of energy, which will gradually force them to huddle together. New suburban developments everywhere will resemble those of the nineteenth century rather than those of the twentieth century. From the remaining fields, the views will be of rows and blocks, urban profiles, rather than the evenly spaced boxes of twentieth-century suburbia. Suburban householders will be faced with a prospect not unlike the one that faced the cowherds and milkmaids of Portobello Farm in the mid-nineteenth century, as they gazed down the lane leading to the Notting Hill turnpike gate and the massing ranks of streets.

London's housing stock includes terraces, towers, villas, mansion blocks, Georgian town houses and mock-Tudor suburban ones, estates with each home on its own small patch and estates full of homes packed into blocks. Although the density of flats is high, and the variety of styles is wider than in the average town, London's housing mix is typical of the country's as a whole, which is dominated by three massive waves of construction: Victorian, inter-war and post-war.

Since most of these buildings are still standing, much of the country's housing stock belongs to the age of the steam engine, in which coal was taken for granted and so were draughts. Over a fifth of English homes were built before 1919, in the great building boom that obliterated huge expanses of farmland between the later decades of the nineteenth century and the 1900s; more than four million Victorian and Edwardian homes are still occupied. Another seventeen per cent were built between the world wars, a phase of suburbanisation in which London swallowed up the entire county of Middlesex. More than a quarter of the dwellings in London itself were built before 1918, and more than half before 1945. Less than a fifth of the national housing stock dates from 1980 or later. Altogether, Britain's homes are responsible for over a quarter of the country's greenhouse gas emissions. The oldest buildings tend to be the least efficient with energy, and the newest are the most efficient.

Old homes will remain standing because they belong to

the people who live in them. Nearly seventy per cent of all British homes are owned by their occupiers. For many if not most of these householders, their homes are their principal or only source of capital. If they wanted to demolish and rebuild their houses, they would need another source of capital to pay for the work, as well as another place to live in while it was going on. With most households moving every five to ten years, few of them would enjoy the benefits in reduced electricity and water bills that would require such outlay and disruption. It would also be difficult to pass the costs of rebuilding on to the next owners, since most of them would likewise expect to be there for only a relatively short period.

While people may not be committed to any particular home for long enough to make major improvements in its energy efficiency worthwhile, they are deeply committed to owning each successive home that they live in. Homes are seen as the basis of financial security, and people are likely to count on them still more in the future as they lose confidence in other sources of security, such as jobs, pension funds or the welfare state. During times of uncertainty and periodic turbulence – some of which will be the result of climatic shocks, such as floods and failed harvests, in other parts of the world – people throughout the British Isles are likely to sleep easier in their beds for the knowledge that they own the homes in which those beds are housed. The more uncertain the world becomes, and the less confident people become that they can rely on their states or their governments, the more they will invest in their own four walls.

People will build their lives upon the capital embodied in

58

their homes. For future generations home ownership will be the principal source of inherited wealth. Despite attrition from the increasing costs of care for the elderly, inherited property wealth will capitalise millions of families. It will play an increasingly strategic role in plans and choices that span generations. And it will be increasingly necessary for ordinary families, because by making the British Isles relatively attractive places to live, climate change will push house prices up. All in all, the effect will be to embed owner occupation still more deeply into the fabric of the housing stock, and so to preserve dwellings that have already been built. At current rates of demolition, eighty-five per cent of the United Kingdom's twenty-four million existing homes will still be there in 2050; and at current rates of construction, they will amount to seventy per cent of the national housing stock.

For the most part the housing stock will remain divided up into individual homes, individually owned. Homeowners of the 2090s will be living in houses built to meet the aspirations of homebuyers in the 1930s for space, or of homebuyers in the 1960s for light, and subjected to a continuous succession of overhauls throughout the course of the twenty-first century in efforts to stop those profligate old buildings from leaking carbon.

The sealing and padding has been under way for some time, lofts stuffed with insulating fibres and foam injected into the cavities between the double layers of outside walls. Rotting and grumbling wooden window frames are replaced with tight-fitting plastic, sometimes doubly glazed. Chimney flues were sealed long ago when central heating came in; only a minority have been opened up again. The alterations have been piecemeal, though, and many of them have been done for the sake of appearance or convenience rather than energy saving. Radiators installed under windows, ideally positioned to warm the air outside rather than the room, epitomise an indifference to efficiency that shaded into plain stupidity. Dramatic savings do not require advanced materials or technologies. What they need is thoroughness, not just a few hanks of fibreglass in the loft and an energy-saving bulb in the spare room. In Germany, a pilot programme called *Zukunft Haus* (Future House) insulated thirty-four blocks of flats inside and out, including the windows, and installed efficient energy systems. Modifications to make the most of sunlight included solar collectors, essentially rooftop pipework that absorbs sunlight to heat water, and south-facing balconies. Energy demand was reduced by four-fifths, mainly through the meticulous application of common sense. In south London, the showpiece BedZED eco-village has cut water use to half the national average, which gives a hint of how much rigorous design, and conscientious habits, could reduce London's copious water consumption.

Blocks of flats are likely to be among the more promising candidates for improvement to twenty-first-century standards. They have substantial mass, which buffers them against extremes of temperature, and they lend themselves to energy systems that would be impractical or too expensive for individual homes. Many of them are also unprepossessing in appearance at best. In some cases almost any alterations to exteriors would be regarded as improvements, and few original features are worth preserving.

By and large, houses dating from the first half of the twen-

tieth century or earlier will be better suited to the requirements of the twenty-first century than ones built between
the 1950s and 1990s, for the simple reason that their mass
tends to be greater. Two-storey Victorian houses may be
an exception, but on the other hand they are packed into
terraces, the architectural form of the future. The fifth of
the current housing stock that was built before the 1920s
is at a disadvantage, however, in lacking a double-layered
wall with a cavity. Applying insulation to the outside walls
may fall foul of conservation regulations, or put off potential buyers. Walls can also be insulated on the inside, with
heating pipes embedded in the extra layer, but that inevitably makes the rooms smaller.

On the horizon, householders can look forward to the
benefits of nanomaterials, based on particles around a mil-
lionth of a millimetre in size, which have properties unat-
tainable in conventional materials. Instead of lagging a wall
with a thick layer of foam or fibre, householders might be
able to achieve the same results with a coat of paint. If
nanotechnology fulfils its prophets' visions, a house could
combine its nineteenth-century appearance with twenty-
first-century performance. It's a seductive promise: change
that can be trusted, but can't be seen. With changes in the
climate on top of all the other changes that make modern
life a constant flux of agitation and uncertainty, people may
cling gratefully to homes that look as though they have
never changed.

Something will have to be done about the windows,
though. No longer does it suffice to set a pane of glass into
a wooden frame and seal it with putty. Now at least two
panes are needed, if not three, with inert gases – argon,

krypton or xenon – filling the spaces between them. In the future windows will be required to be smart, controlling the entry of light and air, and may use the light that shines on them to generate electricity. It should be possible to combine these subtle powers with the cords, pulleys and weights boxed into the frame of a traditional sash window – though perhaps not at a price that many householders could afford. From an engineer's point of view, using a system of pulleys and weights devised in the seventeenth century to open windows that could generate electricity from sunlight would be like installing satellite navigation on a stage coach. It would be quite British, however, in its combination of nostalgia for old technologies and hope placed in new ones.

Offices, shops and other buildings will be replaced more briskly than homes, their fates decided by owners with access to capital and unburdened by sentiment. The standards of efficiency and environmental sensitivity their replacements reach will be set by the authorities, local and national, but these may fall far short of what could be achieved. Efficiency is expensive, and governments are always under pressure to limit the costs they impose on businesses. Every time the economy slows down, the pressure to relax standards increases. Building regulations may prove to be another example of how recessions can reduce greenhouse gas emissions in the short term, as the world economy takes its foot off the accelerator, but increase them in the long run, by discouraging green spending on buildings or machinery that will be in use for decades.

Nor should the formidable inertia of British buildings be underestimated. Despite the Blitz, the bulldozers of post-war redevelopment and the inexhaustible appetites of consumerism, over half of London's shop floorspace dates back to before the Second World War; the national level is forty per cent. Children are still taught in those hulking brick monuments to universal education that first loomed over awed pupils in the late nineteenth century. Schoolchildren in the early twenty-first century were still being accommodated in prefabricated concrete Horsa huts, erected as stopgap classrooms in the austerity years after the Second World War. They are a warning that a building can be crude, inefficient, uncomfortable, ugly and unsuitable for changed conditions, yet still be standing decades after it should have been replaced as originally intended. And, like motorway maintenance and the railways, they are a reminder that Britain's track record in public works doesn't entirely inspire confidence in its ability to adapt to climate change.

By contrast, the grand style in which nineteenth-century municipal schools were built speaks of an unshakeable confidence that the principles on which they were founded would be enduring. In one practical sense that has turned out to be true. Schools will be increasingly susceptible to overheating as summer temperatures combine with the heat emitted by electronic equipment, as well as the heat given off from other sources – including emissions from the occupants, estimated at about 75 watts per teacher and 60 watts per pupil. Old school buildings that have survived rebuilding programmes, thanks to their heritage status, will be relatively easy to adapt to climate change, thanks to their mass. Given a degree of ingenuity and a few technological advances, children of the late twenty-first century could yet be having lessons in classrooms that are two hundred years old. The windows will darken and lighten of their own accord, discreetly adjusting the shade like attentive servants. As it grows dark outside, the lofty rooms will be illuminated not by lamps but by their own glowing walls and ceilings. Information technology will fill the space with fantastical images but no perceptible heat, obtaining the modest stream of electricity it requires from photovoltaic tiling on the roof. But unless school funding is elevated to a higher plane of timeliness and adequacy – which climatically induced economic turbulence will do its best to prevent – the adapted Victorian school will not be as sleek or neat as the technology on which its efficiency depends. The walls will be ribbed with ducts, veined with pipes, and studded with the remains of disused fittings, which together will tell the story of a century's muddling through.

So will Britain's buildings as a whole. Some will be as elegant in appearance as they are in efficiency. Some will be quirky relics of a succession of design enthusiasms – houses made from car tyres, or hemp, or holes in the ground. Many are likely to be uninspired exercises in ticking building-regulation boxes, or gimcrack constructions thrown up to take advantage of passing grants and tax breaks. Many will be neglected and some will be falling down. By 2100, homes built before 2000 will probably have undergone as many generations of climate-minded alterations as they have had new owners, and many will have the scars to show for it. But those that are in good repair will certainly be efficient. As green buildings and refurbishments have shown, fuelled and electric heating can already be reduced to small fractions of twentieth-century levels. In a warmer climate, and with advanced technology, buildings should be able to take care of their heating and cooling needs without having to draw in energy through pipes or cables.

When the Romans built the town of Londinium, they chose a site by the Thames but beyond its reach. As London grew outwards from its Roman kernel, it spread along lower banks. On today's map the zone at risk from tidal floods is a broad blue riband across the city's middle, from plush Richmond in the west to the creek-dissected flatlands out towards Sheerness and Southend. It spreads north of the river's snaky bends between Mortlake and Wandsworth, into Hammersmith and Fulham, and has a claim on the former marshlands of Pimlico and Westminster, including St James's Park. The whole of inner south London between Wandsworth and Deptford is at risk, as are the Isle of Dogs and Greenwich. Large tracts of east London are vulnerable on the north bank, reaching inland as far as Stratford and East Ham. Further upstream, the flood-risk zones spill across broad swathes either side of the river. London came into being because of the Thames: the blue sash warns that the river could be the city's undoing.

Two hundred billion pounds' worth of property, home to a million and a quarter people, stands within the 350 square kilometres of the Thames tidal floodplain. So does the centre of government at Westminster and much of the cityscape that forms the world's image of London. If the Thames brimmed over in this central band, it would paralyse the capital. Railways above and below ground would be halted, roads blocked and electricity supplies disrupted. London's transport system would be overwhelmed

by the evacuation rush even before the water shorted out
the rails that supply electricity to the trains. The London
Underground would have to be shut down well ahead of
the tide if the risk of its becoming a tomb for thousands of
passengers were to be avoided. Although people would be
safe on the upper floors of buildings, many could be trapped
in the chaos at ground level and drown. The towers of the
City of London, built on the site of Roman Londinium,
would be above the water, but they would be marooned.
Even if their lights stayed on, their offices would be empty.
Judging by the disarray in which moderate snowfalls and
similar bouts of challenging but normal weather leave
London's transport system, those offices could stay empty
for a long time.

London is too important and too self-conscious to let
that happen. It has cultivated the idea that it is a 'world
city', and with an elected mayor as a pseudo-president it
is inclined to act as though it is a city-state. Its real rulers
in Westminster are profoundly aware that a great national
capital cannot be allowed to collapse. America lost face
when New Orleans was left looking like the scene of a
Third World disaster in the wake of Hurricane Katrina.
If London were to be crippled by a major flood, Britain's
international prestige would be dealt a crippling blow
too. So might its economy. If London is to safeguard its
position as a leading global finance centre, it will have to
do what is necessary to reassure international corporations that its flood defences are sound and sufficient. Sir
Hermann Bondi, the mathematician and cosmologist who
wrote an influential report on Thames flood defences for
the government in 1967, observed that 'it is almost irrel-

evant whether the probability of such an event striking in the next 100 years is 10 or 1 or 1/10 per cent'. This 'knock-out blow to the nerve centre of the country' was such an unthinkable prospect that it simply had to be ruled out. (Not all governments are so protective. New York, with a greater wealth of property at risk than any other port city in the world except Miami, is only defended against a once-in-a-century surge; whereas London's defences are supposed to be able to withstand the kind of event that would only happen once in a thousand years.)

With national prestige and income both at stake, there should be little doubt that Britain will spend whatever it takes to keep the Thames from spilling over into London. Yet even in the capital, where the stakes are higher than anywhere else, the response has lagged well behind the threat. Bondi's report was commissioned in the course of the ponderous official response to the 1953 floods, caused by a storm surge, that killed 300 people on the east coast of England and 1,800 in the Netherlands. It took the British authorities thirty years to digest the lessons of the disaster and complete the Thames Barrier.

What happened in 1953 was the work of the Atlantic, abetted by the North Sea. When an atmospheric depression forms above the sea, the reduced air pressure on the water allows it to bulge upwards, and as the water is whipped up further by the winds, a storm surge develops. At the end of January 1953, a depression formed south-west of Iceland and passed over the top of Scotland, whereupon an encounter with another system tumbled it down into the North Sea, which funnelled the bank of water southwards towards the narrow, shallow corner edged by eastern England and the Low Countries. The sea level rose by two metres in the region of the Humber estuary and three metres off the Dutch coast. Fifty-eight people died on Canvey Island in the Thames Estuary, west of Southend, and the river almost brimmed over the parapet on the Embankment in central London.

Atlantic depressions will continue to roll into the North Sea, and the risks of tidal flooding will rise with the sea level. Another metre would increase the area of the Thames Estuary flood-risk zone, which includes much of the Thames Gateway development area as well as large parts of London, to 650 square kilometres. Nevertheless, the Thames Estuary 2100 project, whose purpose is to plan flood defences up to that date, is confident that London itself will remain adequately protected for most if not all of the century without the need for a new river barrier. The findings from the six-year study are upbeat. Modelling studies produced no signs that climate change would make North Sea storm surges larger or more frequent. With upgrades, the existing defences could resist a 2.7-metre storm surge, the worst-case scenario. Maintaining and improving these defences, which include 330 kilometres of embankments and walls as well as the centrepiece barrier, will not be cheap: £4.5 billion for the first sixty years, and over £4 billion more for the remainder. There will be environmental costs too, with mudflats and saltmarsh squeezed out of existence between rising tides and river walls, but the project judges that building on existing defences would do less harm to the environment than building new ones. The plan envisages that around 2070 a decision will have to be taken on whether to build a new barrier; it recommends a site near Gravesend, twenty kilometres downstream from the one that went into service in the early 1980s. Later still, after 2135, the defences could be tightened by fitting the barriers with locks, or converting them into tide-blocking barrages.

Meanwhile the risks of flooding from the other direction will rise too, as the river upstream is swollen by increased winter rains. By 2080 the peak flow at Kingston, near London's western limits, may have grown by forty per cent. The degree of protection that the Thames Barrier can provide for the western suburbs against floods from upstream, by blocking the tidal contribution from downstream, will diminish as the demand for protection against high tides increases. The barrier is limited by design to seventy closures a year, to ensure that it stays in working order in case of tidal surges. Westminster and Canary Wharf will take priority over Richmond and Twickenham. Upstream Thames towns like Windsor, Reading and Oxford also face a future of increased flood risks, wrangles between local authorities and developers over whether to build on the lucrative but vulnerable Thames Valley floodplains, and recriminations over failures to build defences in time.

*

It is 2100. Londoners and their guests need a pastiche of Arcadia in the heart of the capital more desperately than their forebears could possibly have imagined. Peak summer daily temperatures are nearly seven degrees hotter than they were in 2000, and the city is far more crowded. By mid-afternoon the day's heat is starting to hang heavy, and will not disperse until the small hours. Evenings are febrile and nights fitful. Shaded open spaces draw people out of doors like a magnet summoning iron filings. They travel less far than they used to, and open country is farther away than it used to be. The natural appearance of St James's Park, noted by the landscape architect le Nôtre in the seventeenth century and developed by John Nash in the nineteenth, is the kind of vision that Londoners now crave.

They have to shut their eyes and imagine it when they wander between the Mall and Birdcage Walk, though. The features of the park are still in place: the lake, the shade of the trees, the pelican colony, less incongruous now that the climate has warmed. But the glades have shrunk to enclaves no wider than the branches of the trees beneath which they survive. There are wild flowers, but they are confined to beds. It is not that the climate has become too hot and dry for green glades to survive, but that the heat has filled the park with people while starving it of water.

For many years, the park's managers and gardeners tended Nash's Arcadian legacy, confident that it could be sustained and that it was the most appropriate form that the park could take, symbolically asserting that nature was present even here, between the teeming West End and the government quarter of Westminster. As a stylised open woodland, it resonated with the modern ideal of woods sensitively managed to provide space for a wide variety of species, in much the same way that it had once played upon the ancient ideal of forests as spaces in which kings on horseback could hunt deer. But while the climate would have permitted the park's keepers to sustain a vision that Henry VIII might have appreciated, it proved impossible to combine with the activities that had formed much of the park's raison d'être since Henry's Stuart successors took it over. People flocked there to promenade, to see and be seen, to court and to gossip, to escape from streets where heat was oppressive to a place where warmth was at once balmy and electric. As the summers grew drier and the visitors' footfall heavier, the grass wilted and the open spaces turned to a baked beige.

It might have been possible to keep the grass going with irrigation, but that would have involved a great deal of wrangling over limited water supplies with neighbouring estates and property owners. The park's natural appearance also discouraged moves to keep it drizzled and springy underfoot. It was not a bowling green, after all. Public bodies were supposed to set good conservation examples, using water as sparingly as possible. And although it was a royal park, it was unquestionably a public space. The green sward could have been protected by restricting access, in the way that access to many rural areas of outstanding natural beauty had become restricted. But the London parks were felt to be special precisely because they were open. When people had to wait their turn to enter the great art galleries in central London, and wait their turn likewise to enter beauty spots out in the countryside, it seemed all the more important to keep restrictions on visiting parks to a minimum. In a gesture affirming that even park keepers can have enough of regulations, children are permitted to splash around in St James's shallow lake once the Met Office has declared a heatwave.

Gradually, the park's managers accepted that its visitors overwhelmingly wanted it to be the promenade-ground it had been when Charles II first allowed the public in. The daytime spectacle of the ducks and squirrels had become overshadowed by the buzzing throngs of the new hot evenings. Now that central London had the kind of climate formerly enjoyed in southern Europe, Londoners had developed southern European habits, and had decided that St James's Park was the best place to practise them. Many southern Europeans themselves found London's climate more congenial than the one they endured at home, where temperatures had risen from vibrant to vicious. Spanish and Italian voices are prominent in the hubbub of Continental tongues. Many are settlers, many are visitors. Although intercontinental tourism has largely withered away, now that people really do fly only when their journeys are really necessary, a vigorous railway network keeps travellers criss-crossing Europe.

The park's managers drew a lesson from the idea of 'desire paths', the trails people make across open spaces following courses that suit them. Planners had sometimes suggested that built paths should follow these 'desire lines'. Instead of simply regarding areas that had lost their grass as damaged, the park's planners began to appreciate them as areas in which the public had shown that it wanted to gather, and to make them more comfortable to gather in. The expanses of Hyde Park were left to become bare and dusty, as many of their Continental counterparts had always been. Green Park was left to the same fate, and was renamed Piccadilly Park when the irony became too glaring, but St James's Park was felt to deserve special treatment to make up for the loss of its special character. Large areas are covered with the soft artificial surfaces used to protect paths in rural beauty spots, their tones sensitively chosen to respect the remaining vegetation. White furniture offers contrasts and sophistication is added by discreet motifs worked into the surfaces. The park looks as though it has put on a suit.

Londoners and visitors do still have a place nearby where they can stroll across well-sprung turf to woods and a small lake. Buckingham Palace Garden is no longer the one secret island in the archipelago of parks that follow the buried courses of lost rivers from Bayswater to Westminster. The Royal Family has had to make a number of compromises in order to maintain its position. In one of these, Charles III followed Charles II's example by letting the public into the grounds behind the palace in which he was born. Combining his long-held apprehension of environmental doom with shrewd political foresight, Charles calculated that this move would secure Buckingham Palace's garden against climate change. In conditions of chronic water shortage, supplying the sixteen-hectare garden with all the water it required would be justified as a public good, instead of being criticised as an unfair private privilege. As in the Second World War, when Charles's grandmother Queen Elizabeth declared that the bombing of the Palace allowed her to look the bomb-ravaged East End in the face, there was now a sense that the whole of the nation was in it together.

And so the palace garden is kept in the style to which it has been accustomed, in return for controlled public access. Visitor numbers and hours of admission are restricted, which preserves the lawn and suits the royals. In the summer evenings, while Mediterraneanised Londoners enact the adopted ritual of the *paseo* in St James's Park, the

Royal Family gets the garden back to itself again. Their circumstances may be somewhat reduced, but it will take more than climate change to dislodge the Windsors.

London has become softer and greener as it has grown hotter and drier. From above, much of it looks like a mosaic of tiny gardens separated by chalky thoroughfares. The gardens are green roofs, which are as common a covering on flat-topped buildings as tiles are on pitched roofs. The roads look chalky because asphalt has been replaced by new materials that are light in colour, to reflect solar radiation instead of absorbing it and releasing it as heat later. They show up the dirt, but their job is to make the city cooler rather than smarter.

Almost all urban surfaces are now pervious to water. Road and pavement surfaces are porous at the edges, creating invisible strips through which rainwater soaks into the ground. Since the new materials combine strength with elasticity, pavements are springy underfoot. With many areas off limits for motor vehicles, older streets now look and feel a little more like they must have done before the roads were surfaced and the pavements raised up, but the new pseudo-organic surface doesn't turn to mud when it rains. Surface flooding is common in winter, though. The porous soakaways cannot drain water away as fast as the old gutters did, but water pooling in the winter streets is the price that has to be paid to save every possible drop in the parched summers. It also does less damage than flash floods from overloaded drains.

Among their other properties, the new surfacing materials lend themselves to colouring and texturing. Streets can be designed as if they were interiors, with shading, patterning and detail. Soft surfaces have encouraged urban planners to explore the possibilities of soft control. Tense neighbourhoods are coated in calming tones, though not necessarily to much effect; avenues and squares are patterned with bright islands of colour that encourage pedestrians to gather, while contrasting shades induce them to keep moving through zones that the planners have decided should be kept clear. Urban designers have seized on the illusion that urban surfaces are organic and intensified it by innervating the streets with fibres that control colour-changing particles. Not only can the authorities alter the surface tones to change the mood of public spaces as they see fit, but they can also send explicit messages that light up on the ground, telling the public what it must and must not do. No longer do the authorities have to rely on standing orders such as 'no entry' or 'no loitering': now they can issue instructions as they go along, orchestrating public behaviour from minute to minute. This signalling system is exploited with even greater enthusiasm by advertisers. Patterns erupt and sweep in shoals over the skins of busy streets like the evanescent ink-blots that pulse across the skins of squid, illustrating how extravagantly adaptations to climate change can be adapted for other purposes.

London is run as a tight ship in other ways. Air conditioning was banned decades ago, in a belated and ineffectual attempt to reduce greenhouse gas emissions, and remains prohibited in order to help maintain energy discipline. Buildings are expected to rely on their own resources to cool themselves. Some householders do flout the ban, often concealing the illegal equipment behind shrubs on their green roofs, but the thermal surveillance satellites generally find them out.

There are separate arrangements for the rich, as always. The wealthiest residents are able to have their rooms at whatever temperature they please, usually by securing privileged access to groundwater sources, or living by the Thames. Many of them have apartments in a belt of skyscrapers that has sprung up along the north bank, which offers both the water supply and the south-facing riverside frontage that can absorb maximum sunlight without any other buildings getting in the way. Elsewhere the drive for density has created forests of tall buildings that shade each other out, reducing their ability to make use of solar surfaces. As buildings have risen taller and sunlight has become an increasingly fundamental source of energy, litigation over access to light has become increasingly common. Some district authorities have capped building heights in order to put a stop to such disputes.

Although London's thirst is more gargantuan than ever, because of increased temperatures and increased population, its residents consume a small fraction per head of the water that their predecessors got through at the turn of the century. They import less water too. Schoolchildren enjoy hearing about how water for drinking used to be transported hundreds of kilometres in bottles, and people would pay as much for it as for flavoured drinks. This example of bygone irresponsibility and foolishness strikes an agreeable chime of superiority. People do see a period charm in some twentieth-century enthusiasms, though. Thousands of tiny gardens in London and the suburbs beyond have been covered in boards and blue paint, in a 2090s imitation of the 1990s craze for decking and do-it-yourself. Gardeners see it as a form of naive folk design that lends itself nicely to drought-choked modern summers.

A more striking and significant respect in which the colours of London in the late twenty-first century resemble those of a previous century is on the map of poverty. In the 1880s, the philanthropist Charles Booth compiled a map of London colour-coded according to the assessments of living standards that he and his colleagues made as they surveyed the capital street by street – a little like Google Street View with value judgements. The dominant tones were rosy-cheek pinks and reds, indicating that most neighbourhoods in London were occupied by the 'comfortable' or the 'well-to-do'. An ominous minority, however, were shaded dark blue, for 'chronic want', or black, denoting the presence of the 'vicious, semi-criminal' classes. By the late twenty-first century, the social reformers' notebooks and legwork can be replicated with a few moments' work on a computer, producing a pattern that remains true to Booth's original. Overall living standards have risen far beyond the Victorians' wildest dreams, and most of the population is comfortably off by anybody's standards, but there are still districts that defy stability. Some of them are the same pockets of notoriety charted by Booth two hundred years ago, rebuilt and relapsed again.

The places where the social fabric is frayed are also gaps in the city's environmental fabric. The zones of disorder are heat outcrops that consume water and mains electricity at unusually high rates. Anybody who ventures into one of these neighbourhoods can see why: solar films coated with grime, windows boarded up after breakages or against intruders, roofs that might have been green once but are now more like pocket deserts, clods of electronic circuitry lying discarded and unreplaced. The packaging that insulates homes from heat and cold is tattered. In summer people sit out the night heat on steps and roofs, simmering and never far from boiling over. If the social fabric is unhealthy, the environment will be too. That is as true for the planet as it is for a neighbourhood.

The blighted districts are the ones to which the most desperate climate refugees have found their way. Decades of struggle to build up the resources of the belt that runs across Africa south of the Sahara desert withered as growing seasons shortened or failed altogether. Many of the refugees from that region were left not only destitute but stateless, as struggles over resources tore their countries apart, leaving them without passports issued by recognised states. They have been joined by other impoverished migrants from around the world. Though most migrants remain within their countries or regions, the numbers are so huge that the ripples of all crises reach the British Isles: even Central Americans driven off the land by drought and South-East Asians driven off their coasts by flood have found refuge here. Most of them were handicapped by coming from outside the greater European bloc and by being the first major groups of immigrants from their countries of origin. Europeans are free to live and work anywhere in Europe, which has provided relief to people from regions of Turkey and the Caucasus that have been hit hard by climatic upheavals, but are now part of an expanded Europe. Those lacking rights or connections have been left with the kind of places, and in some cases the actual places, that Charles Booth had warned his fellow Victorians about.

These climate ghettoes are also found in other large cities, and London no longer stands out from the rest of the country for its ethnic diversity. The capital is a world city, humankind in 1,500 square kilometres, in a world country. Towns and villages throughout the British Isles are world towns and villages, some as ethnically varied as any inner-city district. When people in many English villages talk about their heritage, they are more likely to be referring to ancestors from distant continents than to the church steeple or the duck-pond on the green.

Diversity comes in different forms, though. Among wide swathes of the middle classes it is largely a matter of appearances. People look different but behave and think similarly, sharing a common, cosmopolitan culture. Those who have retained traditional beliefs and moral codes mostly find sufficient evidence of shared values in the mainstream for them to feel able to take part in it. The advantages of doing so are immense, for the middle classes are a human internet of information and connections in a world where knowledge is wealth.

Among their servants it is largely a personal matter. Many of the migrants from poor regions of the world earn their living in service, caring and cleaning for the affluent and the infirm. Dispersed around the country to wherever they can find jobs, they rarely have compatriots for neighbours. When they encounter hostility and resentment, as they frequently do, they have to face it as individuals. The most visible tensions are those that arise between different ethnic communities, into which much of what used to be known as the working class is now divided. Urban politics has become a contest between different ethnic groups over

79

resources, in scenes that the politicians who controlled American city halls in the nineteenth and twentieth centuries would have found very familiar. The bourgeois of the world have united; the workers have Balkanised.

Traditional landmarks still decorate the political scene. Parliament is opened by the monarch with as much attendant pomp as ever, and elections are held to choose a proportion of its members. But although political life goes through the old motions, a different order has evolved. Parties continue to exist in name but no longer figure as real forces. Their place has been taken by transient factions that coalesce and fly apart like fish in a tank, coming together across nominal party lines to exploit opportunities and dispersing to take advantage of further opportunities. Some of these formations are showy, branding and marketing themselves like companies; others are shadowy and avoid the public eye.

The sea these shoals swim in is one of consensus. It is not just that almost everybody shares the same assumptions about how the economy or public services should work. Consensus is now seen as a proper and necessary way for society to reach decisions. This feeling has arisen from climate change, a shared predicament that demands collective responses. It is also a reaction to the crowding that climate change has intensified. There is an anxiety about the damage that even minor outbursts could cause in such a densely packed country, the fear that treading on somebody's toes in a crowd could start a riot. At local levels, government goes to considerable lengths to achieve consensus – or failing that, the appearance of consensus – between the various interests involved in decisions about what to build and where to build it. At the national level, efforts to build consensus on major initiatives help to hold the nation together. The more difficult it becomes to define a national identity based on shared traditions, the more valuable it becomes to reach agreements on a case-by-case basis. Instead of trying to agree on what the nation is, the nation defines itself by what it agrees.

Achieving consensus does not necessarily resolve contradictions. On climatic migration there is a consensus of ambivalence. People know that the nation's best opportunities arise from others' climatic misfortunes. They know that they need the migrants, prosperous and destitute alike, who have come in search of a kinder climate. At the same time, they feel threatened by them and fear them. They know that they would be more secure and better off if greenhouse gas emissions had been curbed before it was too late, but they have been left living in a place that is now the envy of the world, and that plays well with their vanities. They are disturbed by simultaneously feeling superior to the rest of the world and dependent on it. In the old days, these contradictions would be fought out by opposing political parties, some trading on xenophobia, others making a case for immigration and closer ties with other countries. Nowadays people feel that they themselves are in two minds.

This inclines them to leave politics to the politicians, but they can be roused now and again by the temporary formations that sweep onto the scene in pursuit of one demand or another. These campaigns focus on issues; they do not project visions. It is not done to call either for a world without borders or one in which foreigners go back where they came from, because people feel that both these options would cause the country to fall apart. Instead the deeper anxieties are expressed in debates whose premise is that here and there the balance has swung too far, usually in recent immigrants' favour. Every so often a group of bewildered Asian or African migrants will find itself facing levies to pay for the treatment of diseases that occur more frequently among them than in the population as a whole, or curfew punishments for going out in the traditional clothes they brought from the old country. The limits of Europe are defined generously, but there the generosity ends.

Europeans themselves are cordial rather than warm with each other. Diplomatic relations among the European Union's members were often fractious even when there were fewer than thirty of them. Its discontents were loud and long. Many influential figures and factions campaigned for, and expected, its disintegration. They made the most of their opportunities to exploit popular reaction against moves to embrace Muslim nations. As the century unfolded, though, the European project gained credibility and momentum. Europeans were not growing to like each other or their neighbours noticeably more than they had, but they were coming to believe that they needed each other more than ever before. The states at the core of the union were convinced that the best way to address the threats caused by insecurity on the borders of Europe was to bring those regions within Europe's borders. Climate loomed ever larger as a cause of insecurity around the Mediterranean and in Eurasia. Integrating states from the Union's periphery would make it easier to tackle climate change across entire regions rather than parts of them. After all, the Mediterranean climate zone doesn't stop at Turkey, even if by convention Europe does.

As climate change inflicted shocks and strains on the economies of regions around the world, Europe's political and business elites pursued security through the expansion of the continent's internal markets. The more disruptions that floods and failed harvests caused to global trade, the more important it was to have as large a European market as possible. Under its roof, the hum of unimpeded trade would keep going whatever happened elsewhere in the world: the larger the roof, the louder the hum. And the larger the bloc, the more resources it can count on. In their historically reflective moments, many European politicians have thanked the Union's lucky stars that the great breadbasket of Ukraine's wheat fields is on Europe's table. Within the Union, the rules of the internal market guaranteed that countries could buy what they needed from each other, while more distant countries were becoming increasingly nervous about allowing unrestricted food exports for fear that poor harvests could leave them struggling to feed themselves.

Sometimes those fears proved justified, especially in African states that had relied on food exports but failed to find alternative goods as farming conditions deteriorated, and people turned upon the governments that they blamed for their hunger. Nations and ethnic groups provoked conflicts with their neighbours in attempts, conscious or otherwise, to gain spoils that would compensate for what they had lost as the climate worsened. Water was a particular cause of grievance, setting upstream regions against downstream ones as the demands of irrigation and sprawling cities rose, while the supply from glaciers and rain declined. In the Andes, melting glaciers revived peasant insurgencies; in China and various parts of Asia, disputes between groups of farmers turned into skirmishes between local militias. Although even antagonistic states had often proved remarkably ready to negotiate agreement over water sources, their arrangements sometimes came under pressure they could not withstand from climate change and the political upheavals it brought in its wake. The treaty between India and Pakistan concerning the waters of the Indus river, which flows through the disputed region of Kashmir, held firm for its first half-century despite two major wars between the states and a series of clashes across the Kashmir 'Line of Control'. It did not, however, survive the break-up of Pakistan. In the late twentieth century, Syria and Turkey had been embroiled in a dispute that combined Syrian anger about Turkey damming the Euphrates and Turkish fury over Syrian backing for Kurdish separatist guerrillas; the prospects for future stability in the region looked increasingly grim as the waters of the Euphrates ebbed, at a rate that would reduce its flow nearly seventy-five per cent by the late twenty-first century. Machiavellian tangles like these, involving diplomatic manoeuvres and attacks by proxy forces, were commoner than open warfare between regular armies. Watching the scenes from abroad, Europe's strategic thinkers were in no doubt that they had to secure the Union's perimeter by bringing the neighbours into the circle, where they would be secure and could become prosperous.

The elite's conviction that this move was vital to Europe's interests was not enough to overcome popular discontent about the blurring of Europe's identity. It took visionary campaigning by some of the Union's most charismatic leaders, who began by propounding the idea of a millennial moment in which the ancient division between Christian Europe and the Islamic belt to its south would be transcended. That got a mixed reception, but Europeans were moved and inspired when the campaigners hit upon a timely metaphor, urging 'Shelter for Our Neighbours From the Storms'.

While they are nowadays diffident or querulous about politics in general, citizens are often ardent in their devotion to civic duties on their own doorsteps. Having accepted that environmental responsibility demands self-discipline and self-sacrifice, they watch their neighbours like hawks for signs of slacking or self-indulgence. Believing also that in crowded communities, harmony depends on the suppression of disturbance or inconvenience, they are ever ready to explain this to neighbours who have left toys in their front gardens or music playing with windows open. New arrivals from overseas receive extensive guidance about local customs, to which they rapidly learn to conform. The compilation of written codes of conduct has become a form of community art, typically baroque in style, and in many neighbourhoods is the highest expression of community values.

Family values have come under the influence of the climate, too. It happened in the earlier part of the century, once doubts about the reality of climate change had ebbed away and the implications had begun to sink in. Now that it looked as though the pursuit of happiness and emotional well-being through spending had reached the end of the road, people were left facing each other and wondering about the quality of the relationships on which, they reflected, their happiness had really depended all along. As people came to accept that the rates at which they burned energy and bought things had been unsustainable, they began to apply the idea of sustainability to their relationships, and came to similar conclusions. Deciding that there might be such a thing as too much choice, they rediscovered the virtues of making the best of what they had. The feeling that too much was changing too fast, including the climate, encouraged couples, families and friends to cling together.

People made explicit connections between the environmental and the personal. If we're supposed to stop being a throwaway society, they would say, we should stop having throwaway relationships. As public sympathies for individuals' rights gave way to concerns about their responsibilities, expectations within intimate relationships moved in the same direction. It was not a retreat to traditional marriage. Although people rediscovered the ideal that partnerships should be for life, they held to the newer principle that partners should be equal – and their ideal of sustainability required relationships to be living things rather than ones that merely persisted.

The tide towards commitment in mainstream, secular society was what brought the middle classes together. It helped people who followed traditional religious ways of life feel that they held values in common with the irreligious majority, which now seemed less chaotic and less threatening to them. Parents became readier to accept that their children could find spouses outside their communities on whose commitment they could depend. Becoming less wary of secular habits and styles, religious minorities felt more at ease and became more deeply embedded within the mainstream. Meanwhile many people brought up without religious faith strove for deeper security by seeking spiritual foundations for their relationships, joining movements that urged marriage for life as a prelude to everlasting life.

All this has had a slight but positive effect upon greenhouse gas emissions. Fewer new homes have been needed because the number of people living alone has risen less than had been expected; people use energy more efficiently living together than living apart; and fewer children need two bedrooms, one in each of their parents' homes.

People move around less altogether. Fuel is expensive and routes are congested. Railways have regained a good deal of the importance they had in transport before motorways displaced them in the second half of the twentieth century. Motorways themselves have become more like railways, and what were once drivers are now passengers. Cars drive themselves, and when they reach major roads, traffic management computers slot them into columns of synchronised vehicles that hurtle along together, bumper to bumper, like trains. Speeds are set by the system, whose programs are configured to keep fuel consumption down, and by the weight of traffic, which is usually about as much as the system can bear. Automation and central control keep the roads moving, but even the most sophisticated software cannot make them go fast. On the other hand, electronically chauffeured cars make cosy little offices, and commuters jovially remark that they get more done on the way to work than when they get there.

That is a telling comment on traffic speeds, for commuting distances are mostly short; especially in London, which is now so densely populated that employers can find all the staff they need within its limits. The London area has become an employment island within the south-east. It has had to reorganise itself, dotting itself evenly with focal points to minimise the distances people travel to work, and to relieve the pressure on the central zone. The old radial Underground system, built to bring commuters from different directions into the centre, still survives as a relic of how the Victorians and Edwardians made the capital work, but it can no longer cope with either the demand or the climate. Deep-level Tube lines with trains running every few minutes would be impossible to keep cool in London summers, even if London Underground engineers were allowed to draw on the groundwater beneath them. The Tube system has become a seasonal railway, changing from a metro stopping service in winter to a pseudo-express line for a limited selection of stations in summer. Its inability to adapt to modern conditions has tipped the capital's transport balance in the opposite direction to the rest of the country. London's railways have lost their grip, and London relies for its transport on the automated vehicles that its traffic system routes as if they were phone calls. The metropolitan travel organisation is called London Transport, like its twentieth-century predecessor, but it is more a computer network than a fleet of vehicles. For those who still hanker after the freedom that wheels can bring, who still want to be in charge of their vehicles, there is a mazy proliferation of cycle lanes.

When it comes to climate change, London leads the country. Although the Thames Valley is generally a touch cooler than the coast to its south, London's heat island makes the capital hotter than Solentside, the conurbation that has swallowed up Portsmouth, Southampton, Bournemouth and Poole. London is more than half a century ahead of Manchester, which by the 2080s was about as warm as London had been in the 2020s, and had taken until the 2050s to reach temperature levels that the capital had experienced by 2000. Further north, Edinburgh did not leave the twentieth century until well past the middle of the twenty-first, when its residents could at last enjoy the kind of conditions that had prevailed in 1980s Manchester.

This temperature gradient has had a marked effect on how people in different parts of Britain see their relationship to each other and to the rest of the world. Watching the rest of the world's climate go by, the Scots count their climatic isolation as another good reason for going it alone. In north Britain and Ireland, distant regions are not easy to see through the Atlantic mists. There is a touch of unreality in the grey air, encouraging people to imagine that they really have been detached from everywhere else. They are inclined to feel that they certainly could detach themselves, or at least semi-detach themselves, from a Europe that no longer feels much like a common home. To them the Continent seems like a vast park whose grass has dried to dust, while their Celtic fringe survives like one last flowerbed on the edge. There once was a time when funds for Europe's poorer regions found their way to the outer parts of the British Isles, but that was long ago. European funds now flow southwards and eastwards. The north and west of the British Isles feel that historically the south has prospered at their expense, and that they continue to be at a disadvantage. People in the north see that the impacts of climate change are falling mainly on the south. As far as many northerners are concerned, the southerners have got the money, so they can pay for it.

That goes especially for the new Thames Barrier, which pickets the estuary just upstream from Gravesend. Rising seas fed by melting ice sheets have left no argument about whether London needs the protection of TB2, as it is known, but Britain has been convulsed to the point of fracture by the arguments about whom it benefits. Westminster asserts that more than national prestige was at stake: if the centre of the capital was knocked out, it would be like a major organ failing. 'Well, they would say that in Westminster, wouldn't they?' retorts the north, where simulated holographic images of the Houses of Parliament succumbing to floodwaters have been a big hit. The northerners have a point. Everywhere is connected to everywhere else now; if one node in the network goes off line, there are plenty more to take its place. London is not the nerve centre it was in the 1960s when Sir Hermann Bondi imagined the consequences of inundation.

London's advocates in national government also point to the immense wealth generated in London; Wales and the north point to the streams of profit flowing from the City around the globe and complain that they see precious little of it. The controversy has lit up all the grievances on both sides of the divide between the south and the rest of Britain

– especially ones to do with water. The pumping of water from Wales to the dry and thirsty south of England is a major source of resentment, strengthening the nationalist movement that began to make its mark, as its leaders frequently remind the people of Wales, after the flooding of a Welsh valley to supply England with water in the 1960s. In turn, southern English partisans call attention to the electricity that courses into Wales from the series of tidal barrages on the River Severn; back and forth it goes. Northern English regions have harnessed TB2 as the engine for a wide-ranging campaign to alter the balance of power and resources between north and south. Westminster is seriously beginning to wonder whether by saving London it will lose Wales.

Londoners themselves feel like Parisians or Berliners, not washed sporadically by warmth but steeped in heat. Their blood is hotter now; they feel the punishment that trapped sunshine inflicts; and they readily recognise themselves as part of the wider climate-changed world. They find it easier to sympathise with their fellow Europeans around the Mediterranean or on the Eurasian plains, and to see that Europe's climatic problems are their problems. A similar outlook is widespread throughout the greater south, which extends to East Anglia and the Midlands, making people more inclined to see themselves as Europeans in spirit and in their common interests. Their feelings remain mixed, however, and they are still tempted to think like islanders. But being on a heat island makes Londoners feel especially Continental.

3

The Cuckmere Delta

As I walked out on a midsummer's morning
For to view the fields and to take the air

This is the freedom implicit in English folk song: the land may not be the singers' land, in the sense of title, but it is theirs to walk out in, theirs to take delight in, theirs in spirit. And in Arcadia they may find opportunity:

Down by the banks of the sweet primroses
There I beheld a most lovely fair.

Several leading voices among English traditional singers took up 'The Banks of the Sweet Primroses' in the 1960s and 1970s. 'All the Southern countryside is here,' declared Shirley Collins. Martin Carthy revelled in 'its idyllic setting of fresh air, flowers and green grass'. Yet this is a country-side with its seasons turned out of joint. It is midsummer, so the primroses should have been and gone by now. Their very name – from the Latin *prima rosa*, first rose – reflects their eagerness to win the flowering race. At Cobham Lodge in Surrey between 1825 and 1850, Caroline Moles-worth included the dates of the first primrose flowers in the nineteen columns of figures she recorded in her journals from observations on her estate. They were out by the last week of March even in years when the average January temperature was less than half a degree Celsius.

As the ballad advances, the narrator offers to bestow happiness upon the fair but melancholy maid. In her distraught rebuff she imagines a fate in which midsummer is turned upside down by some seasonal convulsion:

> *So I'll go down to some lonesome valley*
> *Where no man on earth shall there me find*
> *Where the pretty little small birds do change their voices*
> *And every moment blows blusterous wind.*

The apparent shift from midsummer to a more turbulent season may be an accident arising from the erratic career of a traditional ballad, subject to mishearing or misapprehension as it passed from singer to singer, carelessly edited by its nineteenth-century publishers. Perhaps the primroses started out as the thorned kind of rose, whose sweet smell is noted in the Shakespearean proverb about a rose by any other name. The song ends with a non sequitur of a verse that contradicts both the narrative of failed courtship and the fair weather in which it implicitly begins:

> *So come all you young men who go a-sailing*
> *Pray pay attention to what I say*
> *For there's many a dark and a cloudy morning*
> *Turns out to be a sunshiny day.*

Either half the story is missing, or some broadside hack has stapled a verse onto the end from a different ballad altogether. But the song has settled into its strange disjointed pattern. It appealed to late twentieth-century singers ready to see an ideal England in it despite its contradictions. Now, it sounds like a song that caught glimpses of a future it could not understand. Although it keeps to the rhyme, it struggles to keep hold of the reason in a landscape whose weather, flora and fauna no longer entirely make sense.

Collins, Carthy and their peers owed the song to the Copper Family of Rottingdean, a village pinned to the coast road east of Brighton. 'The Banks of the Sweet Primroses' is one of seventy-three songs listed in the Copper family canon and written out by hand in their songbooks. Some, it is said, are known to have been sung by seven generations of the family. Their chief custodians were 'Brasser' Copper, born in 1845, his son Jim, who lived from 1882 to 1954, and Jim's son Bob, who died in 2004 at the age of eighty-nine. The only instrument to have directed their harmonies is the tuning fork that was struck on the tables of Sussex pubs, on the stage of the Albert Hall, and on Bob Copper's coffin as the family sent him on his final way. It is still the talisman at their gatherings.

The Coppers' family tradition was institutionalised by two encounters with folklorists: one, in the late nineteenth century, led to the formation of the English Folk Dance and Song Society; the second, halfway through the twentieth century, took them onto the airwaves and across the Atlantic. Bob Copper had already made a transatlantic connection years before, when he saw Louis Armstrong in London in 1933, and the family later made a point of noting his warm response to the African-American blues tradition. It was to be understood that his sense of his own local place enabled him to hear what he had in common with others whose roots lay in different continents. The family's most recent patriarch was dubbed 'the King of the Cuckmere Delta'.

There is a grain of truth in the epithet. Unusually for a river on the south-eastern coast, the Cuckmere estuary is inclined to form a delta; but its passage over the beach is something of a blur, and the delta is barely discernible. The estuary does not make its own way to the sea, but is channelled in a straight line along a Victorian watercourse and choked between wooden 'training' walls at the point where it reaches the beach. Now the defences along the artificial channel are losing their political support in the face of rising seas and maintenance costs. Without the banks and walls, the sea will brim over onto the floodplain. According to predictions, the estuary is likely to rediscover its delta; and the lines of the Copper family's kingdom will no longer be greyed out.

The Coppers might have more of a claim to the Ouse, as it is the nearest river to Rottingdean, but its estuary is an industrialised canal around which the port of Newhaven is built. It is the Cuckmere estuary that catches the imagination. The valley mouth and its hinterland are an open space, free of settlement or harbour, on which landscape visions can be projected. Indeed, during the Second World War Newhaven was projected onto it, using decoy lights, to draw German bombers away from the port. In the film of Ian McEwan's novel *Atonement*, the soldier Robbie Turner cherishes a postcard of the coastguard cottages above the beach given to him by his lover Cecilia Tallis. To Turner, waiting at Dunkirk for evacuation to England, it represents the dream that the two of them can be alone together in peace; in the Second World War iconography through which the film sweeps as if it were yesterday, the cottages and the white south-coast cliffs stand both for security and for the part of England that is most acutely vulnerable.

Though driven by climate change, which will cause the seas to swell as the waters warm, Cuckmere Haven's impending transformation is the latest consequence of the coastal processes that have shaped its history since the Middle Ages, if not before. The Atlantic advances up the English Channel and the coastline is turned south-west to face it, taking the full force of the prevailing winds. Along the Sussex coast as a whole, the Atlantic ratchets beaches eastward. When waves hit the shore from a westerly angle, they push the shingle and sediment diagonally landward; as they fall back down the slope of the beach, withdrawing due south rather than back west, the beach-stuff trails down with them, to then be borne diagonally in again by newly breaking waves. The resulting sawtooth movement of swash and backwash, at an angle onto the shore with the incoming waves, straight back down the beach by gravity, then in with the waves again, results in an eastward 'longshore drift' of shingle and silt. Cuckmere Haven is near the eastern end of a 'sediment cell' that carries beach materials the length of the Sussex coast from Selsey Bill to Beachy Head.

Left to take their course, the anglicised Atlantic waves deposit spits that clog the East Sussex estuaries and elbow them eastwards. By the turn of the eighteenth century the Cuckmere had been deflected the entire width of the Haven, and entered the sea under the eastern cliff. The river was left to its own devices until the nineteenth century, by which time it was felt that something should be done about the 'outfall direction and nearly choked up state of the Haven', as well as the river's 'uncommon crookedness'. Eventually, in 1846, rationalisation prevailed: a new straight cut was dug to bypass the meanders, whose uncommon crookedness remains the landscape's signature.

An artist's impression on an information board, planted at a walkers' pause on top of a grassed slope above the road through what was once the village of Exceat, suggests how far the valley has come. It shows chalkland as an Alpine romantic would wish to find it, fresh from the ice, parallel and perpendicular cliffs left behind in the wake of a glacier shouldering its way through. As prehistory heads towards history, the slopes ease and roll into downs, while on the valley floor the river yields to distraction and takes an increasingly roundabout course to the sea. The plain that fills the passage between the downs is covered by saltmarsh, a saline moor covered by hard-bitten plants in seawater shades. In the Middle Ages, as monasteries take control of the valley, confident splashes of meadow green appear to the west, with the draining of marshland by dykes and ditches. Now there are fields by the river in which to take the air.

With the digging of the New Cut and its accompanying embankment in 1846, the conversion of marsh into meadow could be completed. The dykes flanking the cut prevented seawater from flooding the plain, and dammed the lower end of the meanders, turning them into a backwater. Around them the 'salts' freshened into grazing meadows; today only a few faint wrinkles are left as relics among the meanders, though strips of saltmarsh do survive along the lower banks of the estuary. From the vantage point above Exceat, the valley radiates easefulness; the contours seem to settle and the great wayward loop of the meander seems to assume that there is all the time in the world. On the floor, lush alluvial meadow in which to plant cows or sheep; on the eastern slope, a grass firmament twinkling with flowers: here is England.

It took some time to materialise, if one goes by the fictional account by George Gissing in his novel *Thyrza*, which was first published in 1887:

> The country through which the Cuckmere flowed had a melancholy picturesqueness. It was a great reach of level meadows, very marshy, with red-brown rushes growing in every ditch, and low trees in places, their trunks wrapped in bright yellow lichen; nor only their trunks, but the very smallest of their twigs was so clad. All over the flats were cows pasturing, black cows, contrasting with flocks of white sheep, which were gathered together, bleating. The coarse grass was sun-scorched; the slope of the Downs on either side showed the customary chalky green. The mist had now all but dispersed, yet there was still only blurred sunshine. Rooks hovered beneath the sky, heavily, lazily, and uttered their long caws.

This was not a midsummer morning but a September afternoon; quite early, if we assume that the young man whose path took him up the valley to West Dean had maintained a brisk pace on his hike from the 'vulgar hideousness' of Brighton, about fifteen miles away, that he had begun 'not later than eight' that morning. Even in blurred September sunshine, the Cuckmere scene is uplifting, with a breeze of South Downs joy in the air. Yet Gissing finds crows hanging underneath an unsatisfactory vault, and a melancholy vista. The difference between its late-Victorian and its present aspect seems to lie in its degree of saturation, a 'very marshy' expanse left undrained by reed-clogged ditches, in which an upwelling surplus of water festoons the trees with lichen. Over the century these marshes have been dried to a consistency little different from the average meadow inland. Efficient dyking and draining has extended the green vigour of English meadows almost down to the beach. It has become an idealised landscape which has all the southern countryside engineered into it.

Step by step, a pretty order has been installed. In the Middle Ages, or possibly before, a causeway was built from chalk boulders to raise the single main road above the periodic floodwaters. Today it carries coast road traffic between Eastbourne and Seaford. The lie of the land keeps the A259 a mile back from the shore, defining the estuary landscape's northern limit. At the Exceat bend, visitors peel off the road and walk along a concrete track to the Haven. Nearly a third of a million people visited the Seven Sisters Country Park, which starts on the eastern side of the valley, in 2005. Thousands of the visitors are children from schools across the region, for whom Cuckmere Haven is a standard field-trip destination.

With the installation of the Visitor Centre and the Country Park headquarters in the old farm buildings by the road, Exceat has re-emerged with a focus it never had as a settlement, and the very modern function of visitor management. Exceat's principal interest in agriculture today is as a means to landscape conservation, rather than food production. As a building representing authority and expressing values, the Visitor Centre is the successor to the vanished church whose site is marked by a commemorative stone on the hillside across the road. It used to belong to the Church of England, as part of Exceat Farm, and now its environmental vision is about as near as a secular state comes to godliness.

Two other artifices, at diagonally opposite corners of the greater Haven area, complete the arrangement which fills the Cuckmere air with the lark-song affirmation that, as Shirley Collins said of 'The Banks of the Sweet Primroses', all the southern countryside is here. At the south-western corner, on the cliff overlooking the beach, stand a few huddled cottages. Behind the Visitor Centre and the boundary of the main road is Friston Forest, a plantation varied and broadleaved enough to pass from the front as natural. In between there are meadows, sheep grazing, downland hillside, the chalk and the clay; a river running through it all. Above Exceat Bridge the bankside path follows a winding course northward past water meadows, cattle standing at the water's edge, a stream overhung by branches instead of an estuary under a coastal sky; more discreet, more pastoral still, and another story.

The main story is about what will happen to the south of the causeway as the sea rises and the storm surges mount. For the Environment Agency, defending coastlines is an awesomely expensive business – £5 million for a kilometre of rock breakwaters, £6 million per kilometre for rock barriers to protect the toes of cliffs. It can be justified when the defences are holding a line in front of property worth many times more. Almost the entire cliff line from Brighton to Peacehaven has been shielded, protecting the A259 that runs just behind the edge, and several densely built-up patches through which the road passes. Jim Copper worked as a site blacksmith on the first section of sea wall, from Brighton to Rottingdean; the project gave him a wage to replace the living he had lost in the collapse of agriculture after the Great War, when the farm estate of which he had been bailiff was sold for suburbanisation. Like the New Cut on the Cuckmere, dug the best part of a century earlier, the sea wall was the product of pick, shovel and sweat; slow going, which kept men in work from 1921 to 1935. With more than two million out of work throughout Britain during much of that time, it was an example of how public investment could usefully reduce unemployment, as urged by another local man, the economist John Maynard Keynes.

The wall has since had to be reconstructed, as the waves have undermined its foundations. And shielding cliffs makes matters worse for undefended stretches further down the coast. One cliff's erosion is the next cliff's beach: chalk debris and flints are carried eastwards by longshore drift, replenishing the beaches that cover the toes of the cliffs above them: preventing a cliff from crumbling accelerates its neighbour's retreat. Twenty years after the completion of the defences from Brighton to Rottingdean, the cliffs immediately to the east at Saltdean were receding at a rate of 1.3 metres a year. The defences had to be extended, and new sea walls were added further along after subsequent bouts of erosion.

Floodplains are costly to defend, too. In the Cuckmere estuary there is no port at the river mouth, there are no housing estates in the floodplain, and the road is up on a causeway a mile back. By the end of the century the sea could be a metre higher, and rising four times as fast as it is now. Strengthening the defences to cope with the higher seas could cost around £20 million. A floodplain that nobody lives in is not a spot at which to hold the line, but at which to stage a retreat.

Floods on an empty plain could also prevent floods further upstream. The western side of the Cuckmere estuary could hold a million cubic metres that might otherwise cause damage elsewhere. That could prove valuable increasingly often in the future. A study of flood risks for Lewes, Shrewsbury and York, all of which suffered flooding in 2000, calculated that towards the end of the century, the kind of flood that used to happen once in twenty years might happen every couple of years.

The Environment Agency also saw an opportunity to improve its habitat balance-sheet. Saltmarsh and mudflats are being lost around the British coastline at a rate of about 100 hectares a year. They succumb to 'coastal squeeze' as rising sea levels come up against hard defences that prevent the intertidal zones from moving inland with the incoming sea. The squeeze is hardest in the south-east; twenty per cent of the saltmarsh in Kent and Essex disappeared between 1973 and 1988. Holding the line in the lower Cuckmere valley would lead to the loss of the remnant saltmarsh, but letting the sea in could create 112 hectares of new saltmarsh.

This would be a tiny pocket compared with the 8,500 hectares that currently survives either side of the Thames estuary. It could, however, be enough to provoke alarm.

The possibility that malaria could return to Britain was quick to emerge in discussions about the possible effects of climate change on public health. In 2001, the Department of Health predicted that by 2050 the climate might have changed enough to allow malaria to be re-established in Britain, and warned that people living in saltmarsh districts might need to take precautions against mosquito bites. Some scientists have raised the spectre that the disease could become indigenous once again, although others observe reassuringly that outbreaks would likely be confined to one or two people. Rich countries can keep diseases like malaria in check.

People living near saltmarshes in south-east England might not be placated by being told that the risks they might face were trivial compared with those faced in parts of Africa, however. Nor would it help to point out that they could face greater risks holidaying in Florida or Turkey, regions where climatic warming may favour the spread of the potentially lethal *Plasmodium falciparum* form of malarial parasite. English saltmarshes will be more conducive to *Plasmodium vivax*, which is adapted to cooler temperatures and milder in its effects.

History would be repeating itself, prompted by climate change. Up until the twentieth century, malaria was endemic in saltmarsh areas of southern England. The disease abated partly because wetlands were drained, but mainly because living standards improved. People no longer slept in crowded rooms, and put more distance between themselves and their livestock, reducing the opportunities for mosquitoes to transfer malarial parasites.

With rising temperatures and continued international

mobility, the potential for new outbreaks is clear. The risks may grow if climate change leads to more favourable conditions for malaria in parts of Europe, such as an Iberian peninsula that becomes more like Africa, or in other regions that have strong connections with Britain. No vaccine for malaria is yet available, and even if it were, it would be vulnerable in the long run to the emergence of resistant strains. Since the strains that survived it would be the most virulent, a malaria vaccine might even make the disease more dangerous than it already is. Improving people's living conditions is the most effective way to control malaria, but climate change will hamper efforts to achieve the kind of improvements that took people in the English marshes beyond the parasites' reach. Malaria is estimated to reduce economic growth by more than one per cent a year in countries where it is endemic. Between ninety million and two hundred million or more people could be at risk from malaria by the 2080s, depending on how climates and economies change, in countries that struggle to keep the disease under control.

Pathogens and pests will be among the organisms quickest to evolve under the selective pressures of changing climates. They often occur in huge numbers, and the more of them there are, the greater the chances are that some of them will have traits that turn out to confer advantages in the new conditions; they often breed rapidly, so these newly favoured individuals will rapidly multiply. Diseases may make use of organisms they have not previously encountered. Warmer temperatures in Europe have already allowed southern midges to spread further north, carrying with them bluetongue virus, which has found a berth in northerly midge species via which it has caused outbreaks of disease in sheep. As time passes, natural selection may improve the ability of pathogens like these to use local insect species as carriers. A virulent strain of *Plasmodium falciparum* that adapted to make use of northern mosquito species could put the risks around English saltmarshes on a par with those of Florida or Turkey.

Nobody wants malaria hanging in their air. It will not make warming to saltmarsh any easier, and could increase resistance to the deliberate creation of wetland habitats in other parts of southern England. Even if the risk of infection is small, local people will be left thinking about mosquitoes and their bites.

There is also the view to consider. As it changed, the Cuckmere valley would undergo a chromatic shift from rain-green to sea-green, as the grass was replaced by salt-adapted plants. These may be very pleasing in their way. Sea purslane, a low shrub that huddles upon the existing saltmarsh strips, has a soft silvery cast to its leaves. Mats of glasswort form a roasted crimson fringe at the water's edge. Glassworts are a group of succulent plants in the genus *Salicornia* whose name arises from their use in glass-making; *Salicornia* includes marsh samphire, which resembles festoons of tiny green caterpillars when ripe for gathering. But overall it would become a duller vista, saline instead of fresh.

This prospect is regarded with dismay by people who love the place the way it is, with its artificial glow. They are even more dismayed by the prospect that the meadows would first be buried under silt, becoming mudflats on which the salt-tolerating plants would eventually establish themselves. Anybody in or beyond their middle years who had grown to love the estuary in its present state of balance would be forced to contemplate spending the rest of their lives pacing around a demolition site.

For many people, a Cuckmere estuary without meanders would be like a church without arches. The Environment Agency argues that the meanders are on the way out as it is. They have been stagnating ever since the Cut was dug; without the river current to sluice them, they are filling with silt and will gradually disappear over the next thirty or forty years. If the tides were allowed in, the meanders would disappear daily under the incoming sea – but they would reappear as the tides ebbed. In 2008, the EA confirmed that it would opt for a staged retreat. Routine maintenance would continue until 2011. Bulldozers would still go in to clear shingle off the beach for fifteen or twenty years, until the estuary had built up its tidal muscles and the flow of water was strong enough to keep the river's mouth open. After that, the sea would take over.

Invigilators picket the water's edge: herons, alone, in pairs, or by the half-dozen. Most are grey herons, long-established residents, poised like Ronald Searle's caricature schoolmasters, beaky, gowned and menacing. Now, however, many are little egrets, slender and immaculate white. These are recent arrivals, a species that began to gain a foothold on the south coast of England in the 1990s and is now a familiar, almost guaranteed sight on estuaries in Sussex. They are widely thought to be an advance guard of climate-change migrants from the south, and certainly look the part of heralds.

A combined detachment stands motionless in a corner of a grazing meadow on the western side; grey friars and white friars. The Brooks, as the western levels are known, were once the preserve of black canons: black-cassocked Augustinian priests based in Michelham Priory, twelve miles inland, who laboured to manage the waters and hold back the sea.

The two sides of the floodplain are not equal. The east bears the signature of the meanders and draws the visitors down the paved track to the sea. Its features make themselves plain. On the western side, all is just as open, but nothing is as obvious. Seen from its perimeter, along the Cut or the path that skirts the base of the hillside, it hints at an occult structure. Parallel lines divide the meadows east to west: ditches filled with water and shallow grooves that are the remains of ditches long since filled in.

Many of the dykes and ditches that parcel up the Brooks are medieval, the Augustinians' legacy. The gentle vestiges of the extinct channels prompt questions about what went on here in the past. This is the terrain upon which historians have imagined the port and the town that the estuary so conspicuously lacks today. In the absence of supporting archaeological evidence, however, speculations they remain.

Cuckmere Haven was certainly a trading harbour in the eighteenth century – for smugglers taking advantage of the unpopulated estuary. The coastguard cottages on the shoulder of the western cliff overlooking the river mouth are a legacy of the authorities' efforts to suppress smuggling. These two buildings are the figures to which the Seven Sisters act as background: they feature that way in the photograph on the cover of the Ordnance Survey map, and in the film of *Atonement*.

The cottages have a strong claim to historical value, having spent most of the nineteenth century (from 1809 to 1872) in service as a coastguard station. But they were not built for posterity. Along this coast, the going rate for cliff erosion is in the region of half a metre a year. On the other side of the Seven Sisters, the Belle Tout lighthouse was moved back seventeen metres from the cliff edge, using hydraulic jacks, in 1999. The next station to the east in the coastal chain, at Crowlink, fell victim to the retreating cliffs around the turn of the twentieth century. At that stage, the Cuckmere cottages were still a good stone's throw from the cliff edge. They had long gardens then; now they have little more than back yards, the lower ones edged with a railing atop a concrete shield behind which the native rock is invisible.

The concrete should continue to protect the cliff from the bite of the open sea and the lash of the storms that may blow harder as the atmosphere grows warmer. It may also hold together a cliff face that would otherwise crumble in the winter rains that will intensify as the climate changes. Sussex's chalk cliffs do not wear gradually away, like soap. They collapse in leaps and bounds, sometimes falling back several metres overnight. Thousands of tons of chalk avalanched off Beachy Head in January 1999, creating a causeway that almost reached the lighthouse offshore. Often the cliffs succumb to overloading from the top rather than subversion from below: winter rains saturate the chalk, weighing it down, slipping into its fissures and lubricating its internal surfaces so that they slide apart. The efficiency of rain as a lubricant will grow as winters become milder and the water warmer. Summer drought may also weaken the chalk.

A rise in sea level would expose the bases of cliffs to a greater pounding: the deeper the water at the coast, the more energy is transmitted from offshore waves. It would make little difference to the action of waves against protected cliff faces – but with the abandonment of the flood defences, it could outflank the shield in front of the coastguard cottages. The west beach is unstable at present and would move back landward about twenty metres if the defences were gone. That would allow the sea to work away at the slope below the side of the lowest cottage, unless the defences were extended at right angles to cover this eastern flank. With the armour mounting up around them, the cottages would start to look like bunkers.

From the east the sea would be punching with its weaker arm, since the main force of the waves comes from the south-west. But the south-westerly waves will scour away the cliff to the west of the concrete armour, curling around its unyielding edge to wash out a new inlet. The protected section will start to stand proud of the cliff line, and as time goes on, the cottages will look increasingly like the battlements on top of a bastion.

Their fate will depend upon the balance of the political as well as the physical forces that act on them. The regulations governing buildings will become more extensive, and the values sustaining them will alter in ways that would be incomprehensible, and probably absurd, to their original builders. For the coastguards of the nineteenth century, clifftop buildings were functional installations with lifespans that were inevitably limited; if not by the collapse of the ground underneath them, then by the weather or the amount available to spend on their construction. Several cottages were left behind when the Crowlink station ended up on the beach, but an absence of sentiment left them exposed during the Second World War to Canadian artillery, which demolished them by shellfire for target practice. It was not until the later part of the century that the remaining constructions came to be regarded as visual treasures.

At Birling Gap, near Beachy Head, the owners of former coastguard cottages won considerable public support in their campaign for permission to defend their properties with rock armour on the beach; but the courts and the ministry sided with the big conservation organisations, agreeing that it was best not to stand in the way of the sea. The pattern looks set to repeat itself around the coast as rising sea levels step up the pressure on vulnerable stretches. Threatened homes and beauty spots will attract the public's sympathies, but the powers that be will opt for retreat.

At Cuckmere one of the coastguard cottage owners, Nigel Newton, a founder of Bloomsbury Publishing, proposed to raise the embankments along the river south of Exceat Bridge by thirty centimetres, so as to hold the river in place for another fifty years. Newton argued that removing the sea defences would doom the cottages, and that the New Cut was a Victorian artefact that should be preserved. On the other side of the argument, English Nature and the Environment Agency looked forward to the sea flooding in as an opportunity for nature, an authentic greening, better appreciated perhaps by birds than walkers, in place of the unnaturally flushed green of the meadows. English Nature, now renamed Natural England, is bound to welcome chances to let parts of England become less unnatural. Financial considerations rather than the call of the wild have shaped the Environment Agency's position, but the effect has been to make it live up to its name. It has made itself the environment's agent, rather than the environment's manager.

Bodies such as these, with broad horizons, take the longer view of the greater good and risk setting themselves apart from, or sometimes against, local communities. On southern and eastern English coasts householders fear that their homes will fall into the sea. On Welsh or northern uplands the resentment may arise from the visual offence of wind turbines. Measures taken with climate change in mind will add to the litanies of local complaint against decisions taken at a distance.

The Cuckmere plans show how climate change may drive wedges between expert appreciation of environmental quality and popular feeling about the beauty of landscapes. A conventionally pleasing landscape will disappear, to be replaced by one that will require a more specialised aesthetic to enjoy. People might come to like it better – after all, upland moors were once despised as dreary wastes, and saltmarsh is a kind of flat, sea-level moor. But it is hard to imagine that a saltmarsh estuary could ever appeal to the general public as much as the happy contrivance of meanders and meadows. Moreover, the period of transition may be one of decades in which the area is nothing so much as a mile of mudflats. Something that has come to be important to many people will be lost. The post-Victorian estuary is attractive to the public at large. During and after its transformation, the estuary's attractions will become much more dependent on specialised knowledge of nature. There will be treats for those who can tell one kind of mud-wading bird from another, but the rest will struggle to pick out much from the silt. In this and other cases in which nature is granted precedence, the character of the landscape as a public good will change, becoming less of a good for the general public, and more of an abstractly national asset, like paintings 'saved for the nation' in art galleries.

From the far side of the Brooks, on the western edge of the floodplain, it is possible to hear the voices of walkers climbing the slope on the eastern edge. A daytime owl makes a low sortie across the dyke lines; the faint sounds of fellowship drift over from the far side. Waterfowl and waders ply the river in the middle, making occasional interjections as they pass. The illusion of intimacy without proximity, of having a keen awareness of other beings or creatures without having them anywhere near oneself, is a prized feature of Arcadia.

The people on the eastern hillside are walking the Downs; striding across arcs of chalk fleeced with short grass and dotted in summer with flowers. On the coast, the Seven Sisters are a standing wave of chalk cliff that runs from Cuckmere Haven to Beachy Head. The depth of white below the green cap dramatises how thin and exposed chalk grassland is. If it were not, it would cease to be a habitat for the flowers – fifty species or more per square metre – that would otherwise be smothered by coarse grasses, and the insects the flowers support. The shallow layer of topsoil, fifteen to twenty-five centimetres deep, sits directly on top of the chalk, and is itself four-tenths stones. Known as rendzina, it is all that remains of the metre or so of fine silty soil that ran off the hills when Neolithic farmers and their successors cut down the trees. Containing few nutrients, it holds back the coarse grasses and other plants that leap out of the ground when charged up with the right elements.

To maintain the balance between grasses and flowers, the turf must be cropped short by grazing: preferably by sheep, methodically trimming the grass to an even short sward. Rabbits also provide this service to the ecosystem unofficially but enthusiastically. Sheep numbers have dwindled on the Downs as the slopes have been turned over to arable; in the Seven Sisters Country Park, a tenant farmer manages the land in line with the park's ecological aims. Cowslips, orchids and the tangled indigo clusters of the round-headed rampion, 'Pride of Sussex', are among the beneficiaries, as is the Adonis blue butterfly, the male of which has azure wings like flakes of summer Downs sky.

Chalk grassland is characteristically English, and exclusive to north-western Europe, because chalk itself is exclusive to the region. A fifth of Britain's chalk grassland fell victim to agricultural efficiency drives between 1966 and 1980: between 25,000 and 32,000 hectares are estimated to remain; 4,000 of them are on the South Downs. That represents just three per cent of the Downs area. On the South Downs in West Sussex, more than half the unimproved grassland disappeared between 1971 and 1991, yielding in the main to barley and wheat.

Even on the lands that escaped being turned over to arable farming, a rogue agricultural improvement initiative had an unintended impact – through the near-eradication of rabbits by the myxomatosis epidemic, which began with the deliberate release of inoculated rabbits on a private estate near Paris. Although rabbits are once again as numerous in the fields as pigeons in city squares, they cannot recover the ground they lost where scrub invaded in their absence. They now cause damage through the sheer weight of their numbers: grasslands can have too much grazing as well as too little.

Another threat to the balance of grassland is nitrogen, applied deliberately as fertiliser, or emitted as pollution by industry and vehicles. Compensating for the lack of natural nutrients, it allows species such as tor grass to make the most of their capacity to grow fast, out-competing the flowers and the less vigorous grasses. This undoes the defining structural characteristic of chalk grassland, that no single species ever gets an advantage over the rest. On the South Downs, chalk grassland's best defence is gradient. It survives on the steeper north-facing escarpments in the east, unwooded and beyond the reach of tractors; the gentler south-facing dip slopes have gone under the plough.

The new century began with the clearest warning yet that the South Downs were made of the wrong stuff for arable farming as practised over the previous twenty years. A shift to winter cereals, planted in autumn, left hillsides bare and exposed to autumn rains. These ran down the slopes in a cascade of mud, which flooded the outermost houses in the suburbs that extended into the valley floors beneath. This pattern of development had been deliberately chosen in many locations to avoid spoiling the Downs skyline. Much of the expansion had been conducted between the wars; most vigorously around Brighton, on land bought cheaply by the council during the agricultural depression. At that time the houses were overlooked by grassland, which kept the rain to itself.

Between 1976 and 2000, properties on the fringes of Brighton were damaged by muddy floods 138 times. In November 2000 water that had run off fields in north Brighton built up behind a railway embankment, which gave way, flooding the London line. Commuters were re-routed via Lewes along a track now just above the water-line, their trains rolling funereally past the ballooned corpses of drowned livestock. Chalky floodwater also cut the two main roads, giving Brighton and Hove a taste of what it would be like to be an island.

Whether climate change will increase the flood risk may depend on whether autumn becomes more a lingering end to a drier summer or the early advent of a wetter winter. The crucial period is in October and November, when the fields are bare and at risk of flooding. If the winter rains start before the crops have germinated and their roots help to hold the soil together, a grassland cordon could protect the edges of towns that will certainly have expanded further into the downland by then.

Wheat may be favoured by a general climatic shift in favour of lowland agriculture in the British Isles. Winter wheat is likely to grow better in a warmer Britain than a hotter Spain, for example. Farming in the British Isles could very well benefit from climate change, which will deal agriculture in developing countries a meaner hand. The world's population will rise, and farmers in productive regions will see their incomes rise with it.

A modest amount of climate change could be good for agriculture in some parts of the world. Crops might grow better if temperatures rose a degree or two. But once increases reached three degrees or so, harvests would decline. One map of the future, set in the 2080s with high greenhouse gas levels, shows cereal yields down around the entire globe – though Europe stands out as less ill favoured than the rest of the world, with yield losses below ten per cent, compared to losses of up to thirty per cent everywhere else. The one next to it, however, paints a more mixed picture. Africa's predicament is just as bad, but losses are lower across Russia, lower still in much of the Americas, and about the same in eastern Europe. Australia shows a very slight increase in yields; China and western Europe enjoy gains of between five and ten per cent.

These gains are produced by factoring in a boost from carbon dioxide, which is a greenhouse gas in more senses than one. As it builds up in the atmosphere, crops will absorb fertiliser from the air as well as from the soil. Plants use sunlight to convert water and carbon dioxide into carbohydrates; the more carbon dioxide they have available to them, the better they should be able to grow. The catch is that weeds will enjoy the benefits too, as will pests. But crop yields might increase by between five and twenty per cent if atmospheric carbon dioxide levels reach 550 parts per million (roughly double what they were before the rise of industry). The gains will be enjoyed mostly in the north, however, upholding the mercilessly consistent pattern in which the benefits of climate change go to the rich and the costs fall upon the poor. In South Africa, for example, income from farming could fall over the course of the century to just a tenth of what it is today: the smaller and poorer the farmers, the harder they would be hit. South Asia could also suffer badly from falls in crop yields, which are likely to afflict developing countries in general.

The total quantity of crops will have to rise, to feed a growing population, and to meet demands for animal feed that are likely to rise along with the demand for meat that rises with living standards. Wheat production could more than double by 2080. And it will shift northwards: in southern Europe yields could be hit hard, while in northern Europe they will rise as growing seasons become longer and new areas open up for cultivation. These new areas may not be the most fertile, though. The amount of land unsuitable for cultivation is likely to decrease in developed countries and increase in developing ones, but in northern Europe and other wealthy regions the land that becomes suitable will often be marginal. By the 2080s there are likely to be net losses of good farmland through-out Europe, and these losses could be at their highest in the British Isles. The remaining good-quality land will be worked the harder to make up the difference. Prices are expected to rise; modestly for the first half of the century, then more assertively, along with temperatures.

One of the strongest cards in British and Irish farmers' hands will be that extreme weather in the British Isles will be less extreme than elsewhere. Maximum temperatures and torrential downpours could have more of an impact on farm production than average temperatures and rain-fall. Although the weather will give farmers in the British Isles more to complain about than ever, their harvests will be hit less hard than those of their competitors in main-land Europe, exposed to the extremes of the Continental climate. British and Irish farms will be bolstered by the comparative reliability of their crops.

Arable farming on the South Downs could well prosper,

enjoying a benign climate and proximity to Channel ports. The size of the market in the densely populated south-east might also weigh in its favour. But its success would depend upon the supply of water in this heavily populated and thirsty region during increasingly arid summers. Tensions between town and country could be exacerbated if the agricultural consequences of climate change in England include an increase in the leaching of nitrates from farmland into groundwater that is used for drinking and washing. Farmers on the South Downs will certainly have to dose their soil with more and more nitrates to keep up its fertility. It is too thin for crops like maize or potatoes, and it will become stonier as each successive ploughing bites into the underlying chalk, but there should be enough of it to sustain arable farming for another couple of centuries.

If farmers want to relieve the monotony of the cereal rows, vines should offer a profitable alternative. There are already one or two vineyards on the Downs, such as Breaky Bottom, near Lewes. With warmer summers, vineyards in southern England could earn a reputation superior to those of Continental wine regions that will suffer from rising temperatures. Grape varieties tend not to tolerate shifts in average temperature of more than two or three degrees. By the middle of the century, many vineyards may have to abandon their traditional varieties in favour of ones that had hitherto been grown in more southerly regions, and some of the southernmost vineyards might become unsuitable for wine-making altogether. Vineyards in Burgundy could start planting Cabernet Sauvignon grapes that no longer produce classic vintages further south in Bordeaux; vineyards in southern Portugal could find themselves growing raisins. South-eastern England could well become a respected wine-producing region.

The south-east is the sunniest, wealthiest and most conveniently situated part of the country: in the future, it will be sunnier, wealthier and better situated than ever. The land will be under intense demand, for homes, farming and recreation, and all of it will be used unless limits are imposed by the availability of water. In that case, the greater value in built-up land would give the towns the edge in the struggle for their share. If arable couldn't be made to work, there might be no agricultural alternative. Without an improvement in the economics of sheep farming, the prospects for the traditional grassy Downs landscape look poor. The hills would be ploughed for arable where agriculture remained active, and would revert to scrub where farming was abandoned.

Species-rich chalk grassland will survive in refuges on the scarp slope and reservations on the dip slope. A warmer future might make the Seven Sisters park an even better nursery for flowers such as round-headed rampion and the early spider orchid, which are at present pushing their northern limits in the south of England. They may establish themselves more firmly wherever they can find short grass on chalk; already the round-headed rampion could be claimed as the Pride of Wiltshire as well as of Sussex. Meanwhile grasses such as sheep's fescue are already quite well adapted to drought and flourish in the Seven Sisters park. Narrow blades and waxy cuticles help to minimise water loss, as does a short sward: by cutting the length of the plant above ground, grazing trims its wick, reducing the amount of tissue through which water from the roots can evaporate into the air. Other plants found on the Seven Sisters slopes, such as thyme, are also designed for warmth and dryness. Round the back of the Downs, though, the damper, mossier form of grassland on the north-facing escarpment may retreat further into the remaining shade.

At the eastern end of Friston Forest sits a sturdy municipal hall modestly shielded by a screen of trees. It was built on a scale to house beam engines, whose action required a lot of elbow room: this is the site of the plant that pumps water from the chalk of the Downs through to Eastbourne. The pump shaft descends a hundred feet – thirty metres – into an adit, or horizontal shaft, dug by Welsh miners at the beginning of the twentieth century. Measuring two metres by three, it is unlined, so that water can percolate into it through the chalk. After extension it now terminates several kilometres away, well beyond the forest area. In a braver and less automated age, this linear subterranean canal used to be inspected by dinghy.

When the pumping station was built, it looked out on open sheep pasture, clear across to the hamlet of West Dean, the successor to Exceat; and there the water engineers saw a potential problem. Just as rain may seep down through chalk, so may the urine of grazing sheep or other animals. The Eastbourne Water Company conceived the idea of planting a forest to keep the livestock out. In 1926 it sold a lease on the land to the Forestry Commission, which began hacking into the chalk and planting trees, mostly sycamores, in the late 1930s.

Many of these were then destroyed in the war, when the forest was used for tank and artillery training, so the origins of much of today's forest are in the 1950s. It was

then that the beeches which give Friston Forest its character were planted, chosen because they were regarded as
suitable for chalk soils, and anticipated to provide a profitable harvest of timber when mature. But much of the
forest's stock remains a mixture of less distinctive species,
particularly sycamore and ash, and the prospect of climate
change does not bode well for beech woods on the chalk
soils of southern England.

This might seem strange, since beech flourishes on the
Continent. But it does best where it is safe from drought;
in Brittany, for instance, or on German mountains; it may
not be a good bet on thin English soils under an unblink-
ing summer sun. Beech trees would not expire en masse
like unwatered lawns, but their canopies would be thinner,
their limbs would be spindlier, and some of them would
succumb. For foresters, the issue would be how well they
grew, rather than whether they managed to hang on. They
would be felled as their productivity waned, and replaced
by species better suited to the new conditions.

Even in a familiar climate, the Friston beeches' performance has been disappointing. In the shade of the
southern slope they have grown tall, but they have made
slow headway in more exposed areas. Many of the forest's
Corsican pines are in a worse state, their leaves yellow-
ing to the sickly colour of chlorine: they are poorly suited
to chalk soils. Their local difficulties are the least of their
troubles. In 2007 the Forestry Commission imposed a five-
year moratorium on planting Corsican pine, to give it time
to research a fungal disease that has infected the species
across much of England. It is a reversal of fortune for a tree
that had been regarded as a highly promising candidate for

commercial forestry in a warmer climate, and it probably won't be the last of its kind. Milder winters will be a boon to pests; both existing ones and new arrivals. Many trees and other plants that in theory look suitable for a warmer British Isles may fall victim to pests that turn out to be still better suited.

Friston is moving away from plantation forestry anyway. In one part of the forest there are cattle lurking among the trees: a troop of British Whites, representatives of a breed said to be descended from ancient wild British cattle, sent into woods to find pasture as their medieval ancestors did. British Whites are ready to take the rough as well as the smooth: browsers as well as grazers, they will chew twigs, brambles, nettles or the ash saplings that they find in Friston Forest. They are actually there to trample down bushes and break off branches, opening up the woods and creating a mosaic of varied habitats. Although the project to make the forest less like a plantation was not launched with climate change in mind, it could help put it on a better footing to protect plants and animals as changing conditions alter their habitats. The more variety the cattle open up within the original plantation structure, at all levels from the broken branch to the forest glade, the more microhabitats are brought into existence. The more of these there are, and the more varied, the better will be the chances that plants or animals can find new homes if the places they are used to turn against them. Friston Forest and places like it could play an important conservation role as the climate warms.

At a larger scale, the forest would need to be part of an ecological network of large adjoining areas of healthy landscape, through which organisms and their genes can flow. Old-fashioned nature reserves will make less and less sense as climates change. Mobility will become vital, especially in Britain, where so many refuges for wildlife are small islands isolated from each other by suburbs, roads and prairie farms. Many species will need to move north, but will not be able to get there unless they have friendly territory to move through.

Having a better idea than anyone of the complexity of what goes on in an entangled bank, 'clothed with many plants of many kinds, with birds singing on the bushes, with various insects flitting about, and with worms crawling through the damp earth', ecologists are loath to hazard in any detail what might become of habitats and their inhabitants as climates change. They are disinclined to go further than what they always say, which is that scrub and rank grasses will tend to spread. Fair enough. It's far easier and probably more enlightening to pick out a single species and consider its sensitivities to climate and place.

A beguiling example is the early spider orchid, *Ophrys sphegodes*, one of the species that make the coast from Seaford to Beachy Head a Site of Special Scientific Interest. It is vulnerable and easily overlooked; in Britain it is scarce, largely confined to colonies in Sussex and Kent, and erratic in its appearances from year to year. The flowers that can sometimes be seen in the Seven Sisters area amount to an outpost rather than a colony. *Ophrys sphegodes* is regarded as a plant at the limits of its range this far north, the more so for the fact that it tends towards the south in Continental Europe. Between the wars it was more abundant in England; the cooling that followed those sunny decades may have set in train its decline. A warming climate might do wonders for it.

For many years the English centre of botanical interest in the early spider orchid has been the Castle Hill National Nature Reserve, folded discreetly into the South Downs a mile or two beyond the eastern edges of Brighton. Diligent censuses have numbered the plants in the thousands: the degree of diligence required is quietly monumental, for an early spider orchid that is not flowering may put out only a single leaf, covering no more than a square centimetre; and when the orchids do send up spikes, most do not reach more than ten centimetres. In the tangle of grasses and coltish May flowers, the sallow green of the *Ophrys* spikes make them look like plants that stay up too late at night, instead of rising fresh with the dawn chorus. Their pallor helps to conceal them – yet makes them stand out, with that alien quality that is the fascination of orchids, once they have been noticed. It also sets off the deep brandy colour of the pad which forms a lower lip to the flower's mouth. This plush growth could be said to bear a resemblance to a spider's body, but more to the point is that it makes a fair approximation – extending to the fine hairs with which a lens reveals it to be covered – to the abdomen of a bee.

This resemblance is part of the early spider orchid's raison d'être. It has fastened upon a particular species of solitary bee, *Andrena nigroaenea*, manipulating the system by which males find females in order to bring about its own fertilisation. The visual resemblance of the flower to the insect needs only to be passing; the deception is based on a highly refined copy of the pheromone emitted by females to attract males. This scent is a blend of some fifteen chemicals; its mimic contains fourteen of these compounds, in appropriate proportions. The compounds are all natural constituents of the orchid's waxy outer coating: presumably nature has adjusted the mixture by successively selecting variations in the proportion of each substance. Each step defined the plant more closely by its relationship to this particular insect.

Unlike ordinary relationships between plants and the insects that distribute their pollen, this one is not mutual. *Ophrys sphegodes* produces no nectar to reciprocate the service the bee provides it as a pollinator. A male *Andrena* is lured to the flower, attempts to mate with the pad, and all it flies away with are the clusters of pollen stuck to its head. For Charles Darwin, this was beyond credibility as a way to sustain a species. Considering the incalculable number of plants involved, and the large numbers of flowers visited by each insect, he protested that 'we can hardly believe in so gigantic an imposture'. Nevertheless, the imposture extends to a third of all orchid species; several hundred employ sexually deceptive variants. Darwin's objection was based on his estimate of the intelligence of insects, which he confirmed by cutting back some of the nectaries on an orchid spike, and finding that moths discriminated in favour of the intact flowers. However, we know now that sexually deceptive orchids are sustained because their pollinators do not discriminate among potential mates, preferring quantity to quality.

The system does not work especially well for the early spider orchids at Castle Hill. Only about ten per cent set seed each year, whereas nine in ten set seed at Samphire

Hoe in Kent. Samphire Hoe is 'the newest piece of England', an artificial undercliff created on the coast from spoil excavated in the digging of the Channel Tunnel. The difference in fecundity may arise from a difference in temperature: the undercliff is warmer than the downland slopes of Castle Hill, and so may attract *Andrena* more powerfully to the orchids which have germinated there. In 1998 the census at Samphire Hoe found sixty-seven early spider orchids; ten years later, over nine thousand were recorded, confirming the site as one of the largest colonies in the country.

The newest piece of England may be a showcase for a warmer future, and the early spider orchid, given a break by the upheavals around the tunnel entrance, an early beneficiary of continentalisation, climatic and economic. *Ophrys sphegodes* could be a new kind of symbol: not a national flower, like the Welsh daffodil, or a regional one, like the Alpine edelweiss, but one that represents the dispersion of old identities and the illusion that they were fixed.

*

On the morning of Midsummer Day in the year 2100, 24 June, low tide is around half past six. The sea has withdrawn to let the marshes take the air, leaving mats of fingery samphire exposed for harvesting. The longest day was formerly considered the start of the samphire season, but as with so many other plants, the timetable has been brought forward.

It is there because the estuary programme was put back, though. *Salicornia* species colonise bare mud as it emerges between the tides. As time goes by, they should be suc-

ceeded by other plants such as sea purslane, turning mudflats into shrubby marsh that looks like flat moorland. The
process is under way, but it should have been completed by
now. Most of the floodplain is now saltmarsh, dominated
by sea purslane, but the glassworts have yet to be reduced
to waterside fringes.

The delay is partly the result of the debates over the estuary's future, played out in applications, challenges, appeals
and inquiries, until rising seas forced a settlement. There
were shortages of building material too. Saltmarsh grows
as the roots of colonising plants trap particles of silt from
the water, building up sediment. On the lower Cuckmere
plain much of it is carried down by the river – as the silting
of the meanders illustrated, before the dyke was breached
to restore the original channel. The sea also makes a contribution, though. All things being equal, climate change
will tend to speed up the creation of saltmarshes, by
accelerating coastal erosion, which creates sediment, and
washing more of it over the floodplain. But sediment is
in short supply because hard defences have been maintained on urbanised coastlines. The towns to the west of
Cuckmere Haven have held the line, denying it supplies
of fresh shingle and silt. Latterly, though, a local source
of sediment has been restored, and with it the view of the
Seven Sisters as it was before the nineteenth century. The
coastguard cottages have gone, and so has the concrete
armour that helped keep them up.

It was not that they were beyond saving. They could
have been defended. They could have been dismantled
and rebuilt fifty metres inland, where it would take the
cliffs another hundred years to catch up with them. They

could even have been moved back in one piece, like theatre scenery: over the course of the century, more and more coastal property owners have sought ways to keep their houses one step ahead of the sea, and ingenious engineering solutions have prospered, following the course set by the hydraulic jacks and rails used to move the Belle Tout lighthouse just over a hundred years before. These measures are expensive, but then wealth has been accumulating over the century too.

Holding the line lost its credibility as the sea began to gnaw away at the cliff west of the concrete skirting, carving out a diagram of how the armoured face would become a promontory. Large pieces broke away from the upper face from time to time, each a reminder of the need to bolster the cliff from top to bottom. The prospect of a headland bunker, needing more and more concrete and rock armour on three sides, soon came to look like a folly.

The context had changed. No longer was this a landscape in which artifice struck an even balance between the sea and the meadows. Artifice had deferred to the sea. A static scene had given way to an unfolding narrative. And people had come to accept this. Climate change brought home to the English the lesson King Canute was said to have taught them a thousand years before, by demonstrating the futility of trying to command the Channel tides. Around the coast, property owners and public opinion had accepted that holding the line at one place had to be balanced by retreat at another. This was not just a matter of keeping costs down, but of partnership with nature. New saltmarsh along the Cuckmere began to be seen as fair compensation for the loss elsewhere of saltmarsh squeezed between sea walls and rising seas.

Having accepted the principle of accommodating the sea, people began to feel differently about the beauty of the lower Cuckmere valley. Generations who had never known the settlement established by nineteenth-century engineers and builders had no memories of their own to compare with the new vista. They saw a landscape that would improve in appearance as the saltmarsh grew, and a new theme, unfamiliar in southern England and somewhat exciting in that vast suburb, of letting the elements have their head. This was not exactly letting nature take its course, since the elements were whipped up and swollen by the gases emitted by human industry, but it looked as if it was. 'Let the sea decide' became the new theme along the estuary.

In that light, public opinion came to feel that the coastguard cottages had had a good innings. Their passing could now become part of the new story. People stood on the western shoulder of the valley and began to think that perhaps the view of the Seven Sisters would be better unobstructed. Their idea of southern England had changed.

Something had to be done about the cliff armour, too. Like the defences east of Brighton in the twentieth century, it had been undermined by the sea as the decades had passed. By that stage nobody had the heart to propose that it should be repaired, since that would involve extending it even more. The authorities opted for crumbling chalk rather than crumbling concrete. The façade was demolished and the cliff face exposed; the symbolism of particles eroding from the chalk and contributing to the accretion of the marsh was pointed out.

At low tide on a midsummer morning, the meanders shine silver upon the silver grey of the purslane marsh. Above them now wheel birds with tones of sunrise in their plumage, somehow simultaneously a misty orange and a deep nimbus violet. These are purple herons, brought to the south coast by the growing warmth, following in the flight-paths of the little egrets that settled a hundred years ago. The heron family is also represented by a couple of larger species of egret, as well as by the aboriginal grey heron: the likenesses of monks now come in a range of shades and sizes.

The meanders will snake around the eastern marshland until they disappear for a couple of hours at lunchtime, along with most of the valley floor, when the tide turns the valley into a bay. They have been maintained by design, the dyke at the lower end deliberately breached long since to allow the river to flow through them again. And they have been imitated. Once the vision of a valley closer to nature was embraced, and as the new landscape began to acquire its new shapes and textures, the ruled slice down the middle became impossible to ignore. The Victorian cut now looked anachronistic and insensitive, not to say offensive, from the new Romantic perspective through which many people now regarded the lower Cuckmere. Ideally, they would have liked to have stopped up the Cut at each end, leaving the meander channel to carry the entire flow of the river, but as residents of Alfriston upstream were quick to point out, the river needed both channels to accommodate the increased risks of winter flooding and the climatically increased volume of water entering from the sea. Instead, the Cut was made more like the meanders, with artificially introduced curves to take the straight edges off the channel.

Meanwhile the tides have taken the tops off the remaining sections of the old linear dykes between which the Cut ran, and new creeks have began to branch through the marshes. Water collects in the depressions left where ditches on the western Brooks have silted up. They are beginning to turn back into channels: the medieval monks' work is being restored.

On a midsummer's morning it is best to walk out before the dew has risen. The mosquitoes are relatively torpid, and the crowds packing sunscreen and malaria tablets take time to crawl in on the congested roads. South-coast towns and conurbations are pressing against the boundaries of the South Downs National Park, which has passed its ninetieth birthday. New suburbs rarely offer the illusion of a house in its own grounds, however tiny, that lured the middle classes out of the cities in the 1930s. Homes are packed together for energy efficiency. Local parks were built for smaller towns and cannot cope with the increased numbers, so people look to the countryside for their open space.

Although people's access to the open Downs remains secure in the National Park, there are few green slopes for them to walk across. Grassland, and the sheep that maintain it, are confined to the National Trust's reserves. Every other available hectare of open land is planted with cereal crops and doused copiously with nitrate fertiliser. No amount of genetic modification – long since ubiquitous in farmed cereals the world over – can make up for the thin gruel of the Downs soils.

The price the protected areas have to pay for holding their lines is that they have become as organised as any town. The surfaced path from Exceat to Cuckmere Haven, cut into the eastern slope to replace the old concrete path lost to the tides, is now the central highway in a network of defined routes that have replaced the beaten tracks throughout the area. They are in a kind of character, being made out of a sober dark green synthetic material with pseudo-organic properties, draining water – to limit erosion either side of the path – and yielding slightly to the foot. But that is the limit of their generosity. Visitors are not permitted to stray more than a metre either side of them without prearranged permission. There are no fences to enforce the rambling ban: there is no need. Everybody's position is always known, in town or country, thanks to their mobiles. If visitors go beyond the metre-wide buffer zone, they are sent a warning; if they tarry too long before getting back onto the tracks, fines are deducted from their bank accounts.

This happens seldom and is not resented in principle. The watchword of the twenty-first century has been restraint, after all. Generations have been brought up to deplore waste, their ethical sentiments kept keen by high prices and penalties at every turn. Life in Britain has been shaped by the two dominant effects of climate change: the pressure for energy efficiency and the pressure upon space and resources created by the relatively favourable climatic position of the British Isles. People accept that regulation is a necessary response to the imbalance between the demand for resources like open space and the supply – though accepting it is not the same as liking it. By 2100, life in Britain is something like life on a ship in the 1900s.

A lot of people are closely packed together and have to share the same resources: the result is a regime of extensive and detailed regulations, together with a strong moralistic imperative of mutual respect and orderly community. Visitors from Germany and Japan feel quite at home here these days.

Chalk grassland survives at Seven Sisters, with a flora enriched by increased sun and warmth, but the country park has become more like a Victorian municipal park: plenty of flowers, but the public has to keep off the grass. Walkers can view the fields from the paths, but they have to use their mobiles to see the orchids and other blooms flourishing on the warm slopes beyond visual range. Electronic images of a fragile habitat are their substitute for the freedom to roam across it.

Down in Friston Forest the chalk grassland disappeared under plantations a hundred and fifty years ago, so environmental sensitivities are less acute. Much of the area is still covered with trees. The plantations of the twentieth century altered the soil too much for restoration of the grassland to seem viable. Instead, the area has become a post-forest, with animals wandering through what was once a commercial plantation as if it were medieval pasture woodland, reshaping it to make it resemble nature more closely. At the western end, the open woodland pioneered a hundred years before by a small herd of British White cattle has expanded and diversified; there are gaps, clearings, glades and variations in density. Pigs and cattle of various kinds create different varieties of habitat by trampling the ground and wrecking vegetation in different ways – the star performers are the White Park cattle, ancient and looking it, which use their long flaring horns to push trees over.

The uses to which the forest is put are also varied. Demand for timber generally is strong, largely because using it in buildings rather than burning it keeps carbon out of the atmosphere. In an age desperate to redress the carbon balance, this advantage has reinvigorated traditional uses of wood and encouraged innovation in new ones. Friston Forest gains an additional advantage from being located in a densely populated region, since demand for building material is high and transport distances are low. By now carbon has been superseded as the basis of energy for transport – in cars, by hydrogen fuel cells – but the price of mobility is still high and the roads are still jammed with slow-moving vehicles. Traffic problems remain insoluble. As carbon-saving cargoes, Friston timber consignments get priority in the electronic bids that vehicles have to make for access to roads.

Nearly all the beeches have been cleared, debilitated by drought in summer and put out of their misery by the foresters. A few tall specimens remain in the shadow of the southern slope, left in place to sound notes of grandeur and maturity. Some beechwood from these stands has left the valley and returned after a trip to the mills as the timber frame of what looks like an old forge, a curl of smoke drifting from its tall chimney, near the cottages of West Dean.

By now it is seasoned by age, but it was not here in the twentieth century. If it had been, it would just have been a boilerhouse. In the twenty-first century, it has been co-opted as the heart of the village. This is the heat and power plant, supplying energy to the settlement from fuel grown within the forest. One or two older residents can remember the original installation being built, when they were children. They did not actually live in the village themselves at that time, but school parties were shown the coppice-wood burner when they visited the area for lessons in geography and climate. Educationalists wanted to show the children a more clearly positive response to climate change, with tangible domestic benefits, than the abandoned defences on the estuary. Once the sea began to exert its sway over the eastern meadows, however, they found that the children were very taken by the sight of the meander channels reappearing as the tide receded.

The machinery is obsolete, but the villagers are fond of it in the way that they are fond of ancient tractors and carts. They also value it because it draws them together. It would be simpler for them to run their own individual systems, but they have a feeling that without the communal plant, they would be merely residents. In the absence of a shop or a pub, the coppice-burner is what makes them villagers. They share the work of collecting the woodchips and keeping the fire alight. The roads into the village and through the forest have become avenues lined with hazel; the foresters coppice a stretch and leave the chips bagged by the roads for the villagers to pick up as they come and go. Managing heat and power as a community warms the village socially as well as physically; the hazel lanes, radiating to and from the village like the fibres of a nerve cell, provide a visible and literally organic connection with the forest.

It is a self-conscious arrangement in a hamlet that has grown into its role as an educational example. West Dean is a satellite of Exceat, where landscape is interpreted and visitors are managed. Although Exceat still has few residents, it is a busy site and has had to expand. Among the additions to the cluster around the old barn is a pair of buildings that date from the nineteenth century and smack of the sea. There is a place in the new landscape for a couple of the old Cuckmere Haven coastguard cottages after all, and this is undoubtedly it.

4

Suffolk Coastal

Dunwich has grown as the sea has washed it away. The former medieval port on the Suffolk coast has shrunk to a small village, home to about a hundred people, that has found itself an afterlife as an interpretative centre for a non-existent heritage site. In the Dunwich Museum, the centrepiece model depicts successive stages in the sea's advance, like a historical map showing an empire swallowing up a hapless principality in a series of annexations. The more it has disappeared beneath the sea, though, the larger Dunwich has loomed in the imagination. Nine churches dot the underwater street-map; the town was also home to several religious orders, two hospitals and a leper colony. The numbers of these establishments have grown in the telling to more than fifty, and the 'lost city', 'Britain's Atlantis', is ranked as 'one of the most important ports in Europe in the Middle Ages'.

It's said that the bells of the drowned churches can still be heard from under the water at night, and perhaps the more bells there are, the better the legend becomes. Perhaps the sea makes the town seem bigger: when people look at where it used to be, what they see is an expanse that stretches to the horizon. But perhaps the most powerful reason to magnify Dunwich is because its fate expresses the enormity of what the sea can do. You can stand on the beach beneath the puny sand cliffs and wonder how far the town stretched: a mariner used to judging nautical miles could doubtless tell without difficulty, but the question nags at the landlubber's mind. Behind it hovers the real question: how far will the sea stretch? Could it submerge other towns the way it submerged Dunwich? Can it be stopped, or is resistance futile?

These questions are growing more urgent along the East Anglian coast, especially on the shoulder of the Anglian bulge in north Norfolk. At Happisburgh, wooden palisades line the beach, invasion barriers that have been overrun; the sea is behind them now, lashing the cliffs until they collapse, taking with them fences, gardens and houses. Beach Road is being dumped on the beach piece by piece. The coastline immediately south of Happisburgh is also vulnerable; in 2008 there was widespread public dismay at media reports that Natural England was contemplating letting the coastline go along the stretch where the Norfolk Broads meet the sea. If the authorities adopted a strategy like the one proposed for the Cuckmere estuary, half a dozen villages would meet the same fate as Dunwich. Maps of the consequences depicted a bite taken out of the coastline to create a bay fifteen miles long that reached the best part of six miles inland. Hickling Broad and several others would fill with seawater; fens would turn to saltmarsh. According to one report, the leaked draft document suggested that 'by selecting a radical option now, the right message about the scale and severity of the impacts of climate change is delivered to the public'.

Instead it was the public's message about protecting the

Broads that prevailed. Conservationists were expected to conserve. In this case they were expected to protect the results of historical flooding against the effects of flooding in the future: the Broads came into being when the sea rose and inundated land on the banks of waterways that had been lowered by the excavation of peat for fuel. The authorities affirmed their commitment to maintaining the defences for another fifty years, and the final report did not set out the radical option. But the threat still hangs over the Broads. They are in low-lying areas behind a soft coast on which seas are rising. Even if the line of the coast is held, the ecology of the Broads is at risk of salt poisoning, when seas surge over the banks into the fresh water.

In Edwardian photographs, the ruin of Dunwich's All Saints Church stands poised to crumble with the cliff sands onto the beach, its empty arches forming the shape of tombstones. Its last stones were still standing after the end of the First World War, but Dunwich's fate had been sealed more than five hundred years before. Storms in the 1280s left the harbour mouth periodically closed by shingle and sand; a storm in 1328 shut the Dunwich river mouth for good, diverting the channel northwards towards Walberswick, where a new port was built. By the fifteenth century, the town council was reduced on occasions to paying its bills in herrings. The town itself had been shockingly reduced in 1347, by a storm that carried four hundred houses off into the waves. It is almost as if the North Sea chose to make an example of Dunwich that would impress itself on future generations.

Dunwich was the one spot along a coast of low banks and sunken marshes where buildings had been imposed with ambition and purpose. Today that role is taken by a site five miles to the south, a slab on the horizon that is always in the corner of the eye. The nuclear power station at Sizewell is the antithesis of the landscape it commands: massive, solid, rectangular and dense, encasing a kernel of energy powerful enough to rival the sea. It seems like the antithesis of those sandcastle cliffs at Dunwich, too, but it may actually owe some of its solidity to them. The cliffs are more than ninety per cent sand, and erosion releases tens of thousands of cubic metres of it every year, to be carried southward along the coast by the prevailing currents. It piles up on the beaches and offshore sandbanks, helping to cushion Sizewell from the buffeting of the sea.

There are actually two plants on the site: Sizewell A, which shut down after forty years of operation in 2006, and Sizewell B, which went onstream in 1995 and is expected to stop generating electricity around 2035. It is then expected that, like All Saints Church at Dunwich, these edifices will remain standing on the Suffolk coast for a hundred years after they have gone out of use. They may well be joined by a pair of new reactors next door.

Sizewell A already looks lifeless, its connections severed and its concrete trunk darkening like cooled slag. It could stand as a monument to disillusionment with the 1960s, like a tower block laid on its side, brutally indifferent to its surroundings and infused with a Faustian energy. The importance of presentation had come to be appreciated by the time its neighbour was built. Sizewell B is a low pavilion in a vibrant air force shade of blue, midway between sea and sky, topped by a white dome. The nuclear industry's collective noun for a group of power stations is a fleet, and

Sizewell B's livery gives it a passing resemblance to some vast merchant vessel. It looks as though it was made to be modelled in die-cast enamel for boys of the 1960s who still believed in engineering.

Notice boards on the beach in front of the stations proffer tokens to show that the nuclear industry is in touch with its environmental side, warning that ringed plovers nest on the ground, and highlighting the plants that clump in the shingle. 'Flora and Fauna Flourishes At Sizewell', one proclaims; 'This Is A Licensed Nuclear Site'. It notes the sea kale, a cabbage that forms domes pincushioned in May with white flowers, and the tree lupin, an American native with brimstone-yellow flowers that found a home on the beach after escaping from a garden around the turn of the twentieth century. The Westinghouse pressurised water reactor looming over the beach is another American import.

On a May morning, a group of men can be seen taking a breath of fresh air on a staircase outside one of the Sizewell B reactor's ancillary halls. With white plastic domes on their heads and blue technicians' coats, they are dressed to match their workplace. They seem to be separated from the beach only by a bank covered in tousled grass, but the slope conceals the perimeter fences and razor wire below. Although the banks look as though they have been piled up by the tides, they are part of the Sizewell installation. The outer one, five metres high, is made of shingle; it is intended to fall back when battered by a storm surge, piling up against the inner one to reinforce it. At twelve metres above sea level, the rear bank is considered to be well above anything that the sea would be likely to throw at it for at least a hundred years. A risk assessment calculated that the crest of the defences should remain more than seven metres clear of a 4.7-metre surge, which would be expected about once in fifty years by the 2080s. The risk of severe flooding was considered 'not credible'. A report prepared for Greenpeace raised the spectre of inundation by resorting to the extreme scenario of a West Antarctic Ice Sheet collapse, resulting in a six-metre sea-level rise, but its description of the site acknowledged the stability of the area. The banks will be more than enough for the rest of this century.

That does not mean the power stations are safe from the sea, though. They are on a pedestal, with low ground to its north and its landward side. Even today, flood-warning maps show water curling around the back of the site to make Sizewell into a peninsula. From inland, it would look like a moated nuclear castle. The nuclear operators' reports agree that there could be some flooding in this century if the site's defences are not raised. Under Britain's current nuclear decommissioning strategy, these defences will have to secure the defunct stations for a hundred years while the radioactivity inside their hulks decays. If the Sizewell C project goes ahead, the expanded site will have to protect the twin reactors throughout their operating lives, expected to be sixty years rather than the forty achieved by earlier designs, and then through their decommissioning phase. The industry is growing impatient with the old strategy of waiting for the radioactivity to die down, however. Looking ahead to when its planned new reactors come to the ends of their lives, it would like to get on to sites and clear them within twenty or thirty years.

The banks and the site might need to be raised; a causeway might be required to ensure access over flooded hinterland. But that is only earth moving, after all. Though it would add to the costs of the installation, it would be the least of the project's engineering worries. By the time the energy company EdF nominated Sizewell as a site for a pair of EPR reactors, reports suggested that the first example of the design would start generating power three years late and cost fifty per cent more than planned. Nuclear power is not coming back because it is getting cheaper, but because it is a special case. It always was, but now the case is different.

Nuclear power has always been rooted in insecurity. The first of Britain's Magnox reactors were used to make plutonium for nuclear weapons; subsequent units were installed in power stations, including Sizewell A, under a state programme that interconnected civil and military nuclear activities. Costly to build and costly to dispose of, nuclear power stations seemed an underwhelming proposition for a nation that had long thought of itself as resting on a bed of coal – but a source of energy that the miners could not shut down by going on strike had a definite political appeal in certain quarters. Nuclear power re-emerged as an alternative to putting all the country's energy eggs in one basket when the 'dash for gas' in the electricity supply industry led to unease about the relocation of Britain's strategic energy reserves to Russia. Now the nuclear industry has been dealt a new insecurity card. Renewable energy sources like the sun and the wind cannot entirely replace fossil fuels, the industry argues, because they are intermittent: the sun doesn't always shine and the wind doesn't always blow. A source of energy is needed that is continuous and does not burn fossil fuels. After half a century, a bill has finally arrived that nuclear power fits. Even one or two heterodox green thinkers accept the need for it, at least until green ways to work around the shortcomings of existing renewable energy sources have been developed.

A fifth of Britain's electricity is generated by nuclear power stations, and current policy looks forward to an increase in that fraction. All the existing stations except Sizewell B will have shut down by 2023, so an entire new fleet will have to be built. The size of the fleet, and the fraction of electricity supplies that it can deliver, are constrained not just by costs but by location. It is not easy to find places to put the next generation of nuclear power stations. They need large quantities of water to cool them, which in Britain means that they must go by the sea. Rivers will have their work cut out for them to supply the needs of towns and agriculture as summers become drier. Coastal stations must be on solid ground, and have demand for their electricity close enough to avoid overstraining the power grid. It is not surprising that nine out of the eleven sites proposed for the new fleet have already had nuclear plants built on them.

On its little island waiting to be encircled by floodwater, Sizewell epitomises the modern nuclear condition; not exactly isolated – a railway and main road run not far away – but certainly excluded from the urban and industrial districts that power stations are mainly there to serve. Sizewell B is isolated within the electricity industry too, as the only nuclear plant to have gone into service in Britain since 1989, and the only pressurised water reactor in the country. It was built only after a four-year inquiry, and suffered indignities at the hands of anti-nuclear protesters including an invasion in which scores of activists scaled the fences, using rolls of carpet to get over the razor wire. There is room to squeeze in a third development, but no more. That seems to be as far as Sizewell is going to go.

Nuclear enthusiasts would probably disagree. They propound a vision of a global industry invigorated by technological advances and market forces. By the middle of the century, a small band of large engineering companies will supply reactors that are standardised and therefore efficient to operate, the industry foresees, in the same way that a very small number of manufacturers keep commercial aviation costs down by stocking the world's airlines with a limited range of aircraft types. They could send their robots in to clear the Sizewell A and B sites – if they could find somewhere to put the still-radioactive remains – and install new fourth-generation reactors to accompany Sizewell C.

These units may be fast breeder reactors, geared to the conversion of uranium into plutonium, which can then be used as fuel. If enough uranium is transmuted into plutonium, the reactor will produce more fuel than it consumes. But it will leave radioactive waste in the process, and the plutonium could be used for bombs as well as fuel. The more fast reactors are breeding plutonium around the world, the less secure the world is likely to be. States could build up nuclear arsenals or supply the plutonium to favoured clients, who could be other states, insurgent forces or terrorist cells. The prospect would not be so ominous if it looked as though the world would be a safer and more settled place by then, but climate change alone should make sure that it is not.

As states around the world struggle to cope with climatic stresses, diplomatic and trading relationships will become increasingly difficult to count on. Even allies may abruptly decide that they will keep their reserves of radioactive ore to themselves, in order to preserve their energy security during what will be a long transition to a sustainable energy economy. International nuclear energy agencies are upbeat about uranium reserves: they have announced that these are sufficient to keep the world's reactors going for a hundred years at present rates of consumption. They also estimate, however, that world nuclear energy capacity will have increased by between thirty-eight and eighty per cent by 2030. Thorium, a neighbour of uranium in the periodic table, may provide one new source of fuel to meet the increased demand, but countries that lack nuclear ores may prefer to make their own plutonium rather than rely on the good will of other nations. As the international stocks of good will decline, and tensions rise, more and more nations may be tempted to turn their nuclear industries into military-industrial complexes. Counting up the world's nuclear-armed states and its own strategic energy reserves, Britain might look to plutonium both for fuel and for warheads.

One wing of nuclear research offers an alternative that would not spawn bombs and would derive its fuel from the most evenly distributed substance on the planet. Nuclear explosions can be produced by fission, in which relatively large atoms split and release energy, or by fusion, in which the smallest atoms release energy when they fuse together. These atoms give hydrogen bombs their name, and are also the source of the sun's energy, which is produced when hydrogen fuses to form helium. Water is hydrogen oxide, H_2O, so on the face of it fusion on Earth could also be an effectively inexhaustible source of energy – if fusion reactions could not only be triggered but sustained and controlled.

That is the biggest 'if' in the history of electric power. It takes immense concentrations of energy to release energy by fusion. In the sun, temperatures reach fifteen million degrees. Artificial reactors have to reach a hundred million degrees, since they cannot attain the kind of pressure created by the sun's mass. An unearthly kind of fire needs an unearthly kind of furnace, for there is no material that could withstand such temperatures. 'They tell us that they will put the Sun in a box,' one critic has drily observed. 'The formula is pretty. The problem is that nobody knows how to make the box.' Prototypes have been built in which the torrid flux of particles known as a plasma is contained within a magnetic field, but the confinement is imperfect and the plasma is prone to instability. So far, the best that has been achieved in an experimental reactor is a few megawatts of electricity for a couple of seconds.

That was in 1990, and required more energy to heat the plasma than was released in the reaction. ITER (International Thermonuclear Experimental Reactor), an international project intended to demonstrate the feasibility of fusion power, aims to generate 500 megawatts for a few minutes. Originally proposed by the Soviet president Mikhail Gorbachev to the US president Ronald Reagan in 1985, it plans a research programme at its site in southern

France that will take twenty years and will not get under-way before the mid-2020s. If the research is successful, a commercial reactor could follow some time around 2050. The technology would have spent a century in development before it finally went into service. And that will only happen if the researchers manage to solve not only the problems they have wrestled with for more than half a century, but also the new ones that will undoubtedly arise. Sceptics joke that practical fusion is forty years away, and always will be.

If it did work, it would raise nuclear power to a higher plane by lifting its dependence on elements from the infernal regions of the periodic table, but it would not render nuclear energy innocuous. Although fusion would not leave a tail of isotopes decaying for thousands of years, it would leave radioactive scrap and an endemic anxiety about one of its fuel substances. Artificial fusion starts not from ordinary hydrogen but deuterium and tritium, its heavier isotopes. Deuterium can be extracted from seawater, while tritium would be a truly nuclear fuel, bred in reactors from lithium. Tritium is radioactive; being small, it can penetrate concrete and even steel, and being a form of hydrogen, it can readily get itself taken up into water. It would inevitably escape, and inevitably find its way into living tissue. Eliminating tritium is theoretically possible, but the plasma would have to be hotter still. An alternative suggestion is that fusion should be based on an isotope of helium that could be mined on the Moon.

If a fusion plant was built at Sizewell, it would probably dwarf the EPR reactors of Sizewell C. Fusion is big engineering that benefits from large scales: a big reactor is easier to heat than a small one. A power-generating unit would be expected to pump more than a gigawatt of electricity, and possibly several, into the grid. Although it would introduce a new way of generating power into the system, it would be a solidly traditional contribution: a massive concrete edifice housing turbines and channelling steam, centrally planned and incubated in public research institutions.

Instead of larger turbines encased in thicker concrete, environmentally minded technologies offer an alternative vision, of a grid transformed into a fine-meshed and flexible net, powered by countless small generators rather than a handful of giant ones, growing and adjusting itself organically. Streets, houses, vehicles and perhaps even people's clothes will generate power from wind, waste and sunlight, and where they make more than enough for their owners' needs, they will feed the excess into the network. The electricity net will be a myriad sparkling points of light with wills of their own instead of an array of beacons glowing by central command.

The idea of people's power greening the networks and consigning the old grid to history has an obvious appeal to those who look askance at the state and the transnational corporations that now dominate the energy industry. It may also appeal to those who are always on the lookout for ways to minimise state involvement in public services. For now, however, nuclear power can claim that the urgency of the need to reduce carbon emissions overrides all other considerations. The practicality of carbon capture and storage, in which the gases from carbon-burning power stations are funnelled off and pumped underground into aquifers or exhausted oilfields, has yet to be proven. It would also need a staggering quantity of pumps and rigs.

With such immense question-marks over its rivals, nuclear power presents itself as a proven technology ready to curb greenhouse gas emissions during the next couple of decades, during which the world's energy course will be set, and the fate of the world's climate may well be determined. Its capacity to affect the outcome is doubtful. The International Atomic Energy Agency itself estimates that by 2030 nuclear power will meet about the same proportion of world energy needs, around six per cent, as it did in the 2000s. But nuclear power stations are an immediately available option for governments seeking to lower their countries' carbon profiles in the formative decades of the century, and once they are built, they are likely to keep going for most of the century. Sizewell C could still be generating electricity in 2080, long after the renewable energy sources whose shortage justified its construction have wound themselves all over the grid like beans climbing a trellis.

In the end, the future of nuclear power will probably be decided by security considerations. As well as the possible military applications of civil nuclear infrastructure, and the need to reduce or at least spread the risk to energy supplies from actions overseas, keeping the lights on and the country going is a basic responsibility of the state. Any government is likely to see the advantage in having strategic power resources that it can readily control and rely on in an emergency. The people can have their micro-power sources, but the state may want to hang on to its mega-power stations, nuclear ones among them, and the old grid to which they are connected. One way and another, nuclear power is political power.

Across the marshes a couple of kilometres north of Sizewell, the RSPB's Minsmere reserve provides hunting grounds for marsh harriers, a touchdown site for migrant swans, and a home for the elegantly curved, delicately poised avocets that have become the society's emblem. Minsmere was born in war. In 1940, pastures on the banks of the channelled Minsmere river were deliberately flooded in order to reduce the attractions of this long, low coast as an invasion beach. The concrete blocks planted along the beach at the same time still crenellate the bank that shelters the reserve. In 1947, two years after the war ended and 105 years after the avocet was declared extinct as a breeding bird in Britain, several pairs of the waders turned up at Minsmere and further down the coast. Their nests were guarded from egg-collectors by a volunteer squad of birdwatching army officers, who called in the RSPB for assistance. The RSPB remained on the site, and developed it over the years into its flagship reserve.

Minsmere's reedbeds and centrepiece Scrape, a seventeen-hectare islanded lagoon created the way its name suggests, are recent variations on a system of channels and banks that dates back to the early nineteenth century. After shingle and sand dunes blocked the estuary in the eighteenth century, drainage channels were dug into the Minsmere Levels, a clay bank was built behind the dune as a rear line of defence, and the river mouth was fitted with a sluice gate. The sea has moved in closer to the defences since then, and sometimes brims over the top of them.

Sizewell's hazard monitors have an eye on the sluice as a weak spot where a breach could bring flood waters close to the nuclear plant's northern perimeter. A tide a metre above normal sea level would inundate the Minsmere Levels today: the sea level could rise a metre over the century, with fiercer North Sea storms lashing at the banks. At the reserve, it could leave the waters lapping at the doors of the visitor centre, and covering much of the site. To the north, another weak spot could open up as the cliffs recede behind the line of the clay embankment, allowing the sea in round the back. Attempting to hold the cliff line would be undesirable as well as impractical, because cutting off the supply of sand that erodes from them would leave the beaches in front of Minsmere and Sizewell less padded against the sea. Instead earthworks are planned to protect the North Marsh area of the reserve from flooding, but seawater will find its way into the reedbeds all the same.

In the long run, the main defences will retreat to a new line inland, and salt will permeate the wetlands. According to current environmental doctrine, if a valuable habitat is lost as a result of human activities, an equivalent patch of habitat must be created somewhere else. Minsmere's reedbed loss could be the Cambridgeshire Fens' gain. They are within range for bitterns, brindled herons that are rarely seen among the reeds in which they lurk, but can be heard two miles away when males emit their booming foghorn call. The bitterns' toehold in Britain is precarious, and their survival in Minsmere's carefully maintained reedbeds is a point of pride for the reserve. Reedbeds will have to be carefully maintained in the Fens instead.

The greatest climatic impact on what birdwatchers find

at Minsmere will not come from rising seas, however, but from milder winters. Like so much of Britain's coastline, Minsmere is a welcoming lido for birds that cross a continent to escape real winters. In the future many of them will not have to fly so far in order to find winter quarters that to them must seem clement. White-fronted geese coming west from Siberia will land in the Low Countries and stay there instead of pressing on to East Anglia. Birds like these will be absent from British shores because climate change has made their winters easier. Other winter visitors will disappear because climate change threatens their survival in the high north where they breed. Their absence will be a reminder of changes far to the north that will convulse the Arctic and shake the world.

Twelve million birds, including geese, waders, ducks and swans, fly from Arctic regions to spend the winter in Britain, some making their way from the middle of the Canadian Arctic and others from the middle of Siberia. They will not have to come down so far in future to reach winter quarters as mild as those they find on the silt of British estuaries. Their journeys may not be any shorter, though. As warmer climates approach, they may be forced to retreat further north in summer – if there is anywhere further north for them to go. Many birds that breed in the Arctic do not confine themselves to the coasts but occupy belts of territory inland, cushioning their eggs in the tundra. A warming climate will bring forests marching north with it, colonising the open tundra and forcing the birds back towards the coasts. Some populations may manage to regroup on islands such as Novaya Zemlya or the Franz Josef Land archipelago. Others will contract along with their breeding grounds, and disappear with them altogether. More than half the world's tundra, an area that supports more than ten million geese and sandpipers, could be gone by the later decades of the century.

The trees will not be the only new colonists moving into the Arctic. As the ice eases its grip on the northern coastline of Russia, the vast mineral deposits embedded in seams and lodes across Russia and Siberia will become easier and more profitable to exploit, shipped out through Arctic ports that before too long will be free of ice all year round. The Arctic Rim will not only become a new industrial boom zone, but will fuel industry throughout the world. About a sixth of Russia's gas reserves, the largest of any country in the world, are off its northern coasts. The less ice there is in the Arctic seas, the easier it will be to find and extract the gas sealed below them; the more gas that is burned, the more carbon dioxide will build up in the atmosphere, and the quicker the Arctic ice will melt. Arctic ports will also profit as harbours for ships taking advantage of the new routes opening up around the top of the world, as the day approaches when the North Pole becomes a crossroads of shipping lanes. And they will acquire shadows in battleship grey, a steel necklace of naval bases backing national claims to slices of the Arctic and the wealth within it. Some of these installations will be huge, reflecting the scale of Russia's ambitions as a world power, and the extraordinary strategic windfall by which Russia gains, for the first time in its history, a coastline the length of a continent from which to project its military strength.

Many of the birds that visit Britain from the Arctic in winter come from the frontline of Arctic industrialisation.

Over half a million dunlin, small waders with a slight down-
ward curve to their bills that gives a thoughtful cast to their
appearance, spend the winter around the coasts of Britain;
the Blyth estuary by Walberswick is one of their favoured
havens. Most of them are from the Nenets region of Arctic
Russia between the Kola peninsula and the mainland south
of Novaya Zemlya. The Kola peninsula is rich in ores and
pitted with mines, extracting phosphates, iron, nickel and
titanium among many other minerals; the prospectors'
map of the Barents Sea between the peninsula and Novaya
Zemlya is studded with pins marking gas or oil drilling,
either anticipated or under way. Rigs perforate the tundra
too, and pipelines block the paths of migrating reindeer
herds. These are not wild animals, nor has history passed
them by: herds and their herders are known as 'brigades',
a term that has stuck from when they were collectivised
in Soviet times, and over 100,000 still belong to former
Soviet collective farms. They could help the wild birds
survive in the region a little longer, though, defending the
tundra by mowing down the advancing tree shoots. This
rearguard action against climate change could slow the rate
at which the dunlin's nesting area shrinks, by a significant
percentage. But the reindeer will not be able to mount it
if they are penned in by pipelines and excluded from large
tracts of land that have been allocated for drilling, or if
the Nenets and other traditional herders have given in to
industrialisation and gone to work for Gazprom.

*

A dunlin picks its way around a shoal of mud in the flooded
plain around the Minsmere river, probing for worms. It

has the spot to itself. The area is shaping up to be a prime resort for waders, now that the sea regularly inundates most of the low lands between Minsmere and Sizewell, dousing the vegetation with salt and clearing the ground to form mudflats. In time it will be ideal: a saline landscape of lagoons and marshes, sheltered from storms and waves by the remains of the old embankment, complete with an estuary at the mouth of the river. But the more like a perfect wetland it becomes, the fewer migrants arrive to enjoy it. Other birds have faded away as the climate has grown unsuitable for them, including the avocet that inspired the creation of the Minsmere reserve in the 1940s.

The dunlin's main concern is with its energy reserves. It weighed about fifty grams when it reached the end of its journey of around 2,000 miles from the Arctic island of Novaya Zemlya. If it can put on twenty grams, that should be enough to get it nearly halfway home again. Its route takes it over the Nenets lands that used to be its ancestors' breeding grounds; now a vast floodlit industrial zone of fulminating mines, clanging wharves and windowless installations that do not care to reveal their purpose, all built with capital from the gas and oil fields whose reserves are long since exhausted. The forests are advancing from the south; there is precious little tundra left for birds on the mainland, nor enough in their island exile.

South of the Minsmere flats, the Sizewell nuclear colony offers a spectacle to remind the dunlin of the scenes that pass below it at the northern edge of the continent: floodlights, windowless buildings, inscrutable purposes. The visual coup of the dome, with its geometrical refinement and grand connotations, has been spoiled by the twin Sizewell

C reactors lined up in front of it, their central vaults more like gasholders or grain silos. From most vantage points on land, it is an anonymous industrial concentration. From the sea, the term 'fleet' seems apposite: the disused plants resemble a convoy of paid-off battleships paused on their way to the breakers' yard.

It is a convoy of three. Sizewell A was demolished well before its hundred years of radioactive decay were up, to make way for new installations. One is a terminal that makes use of Sizewell's sinewy cables to feed power into the grid from several regiments of wind turbines that now stretch out to sea and beyond the horizon. The other is a reactor, the real reason for clearing the site. Like its predecessors, it splits atoms rather than fusing them. Fusion now works, but in the same way that the Concorde airliner worked a hundred years before: at an uneconomic cost after vast amounts of public investment. By the time it was ready for service it seemed redundant: why strain to mimic the sun in a box, when the sun provides limitless energy from fusion for nothing? Indeed, the turbines offshore supply as much current as the region needs; but this is about power, not electricity. The reactor is a fast breeder, and Sizewell has become a plutonium factory.

In consequence it has become a citadel too, screened and plated all around its perimeter. Bushes are no longer tolerated on the shingle; even lupins and sea kale are regarded as potential cover for intruders. Surveillance drones the size of birds patrol the marshes, challenging the harriers for the territory. Between the advancing sea and the expanded security zone, people walking along the shore are left with a narrow corridor to pass through, in which their lives and identities flash before a battery of screening devices. Any personnel that they glimpse will not be engineers taking a break, but armed guards staring back at them through their visors.

The plutonium security command now in charge on the site is delighted by the flooding from the Minsmere gap, which it sees as serving a similar defensive function to the 1940 flooding that was intended to obstruct invasion from the sea. It has even had channels dug to bring the water to the base of the Sizewell Island, and around its landward side through a gap in the raised causeway that provides access to the Sizewell C buildings at the northern end. The gap is spanned by a moveable section of roadway that can be retracted when alert levels are raised. Sizewell has become a nuclear castle, complete with moat and drawbridge.

5

Upper Margins

Beacon Fires

To the east, a patchwork of handkerchief fields stretching into the distance, seamed with profuse hedges; to the west, dark folded banks like petrified rain clouds, caped with acid moorlands. Offa's Dyke Path runs along the border between England and Wales along the last ridge of the Black Mountains, and the view seems to illustrate the difference between the hands that history dealt the two nations. From here, it appears as though the Welsh were left with what the English didn't want. Down in the valley below, on the Welsh side, are the Romantic ruins of Llanthony Priory. It fell into decline after a daughter monastery was established at Gloucester in the twelfth century. One of the monks summed up the position: 'There, fertile meadows; here, barren heaths.'

A weather summary from the late twelfth century also remains valid today. 'Owing to its mountainous situation, the rains are frequent, the winds boisterous, and the clouds in winter almost continual,' noted Giraldus Cambrensis, Gerald of Wales, the archdeacon of Brecon who passed through the area in the course of a recruiting drive for the Third Crusade. It is quite easy to believe that the clouds issue from the hills they seem to resemble, and in a sense they do: westerly winds sweep in from the Atlantic at sea level and are forced upwards when they hit the hills, cooling down as they rise and releasing the ocean moisture they have brought with them. The Black Mountains are actually made of Old Red Sandstone: they must take their name from the sky.

In bygone times, while barren heaths covered the high roofs, impenetrable thickets filled the valley floor. These became part of the pious legends that grew up around Llanthony, where St David was said to have lived as a hermit. According to Giraldus, the monastery's two founders 'would not suffer the thick and wooded parts of the valley to be cultivated and levelled, lest they should be tempted to recede from their heremitical mode of life'. By the eighteenth century, however, modernity had eclipsed eremitical piety, and the valley's impenetrability tried the patience of a less saintly man of the cloth. A successor of Giraldus, Archdeacon Coxe, complained at some length about the appalling state of the road 'which with more propriety might be termed a ditch'. In the whole course, of his travels, he declared, 'I seldom met with one more inconvenient and unsafe'.

Today the road is still edged and overhung by trees along many of its ascending twists and abrupt turns, but most of the woods have long since been cleared for farming. Cattle graze the pastures by the Honddu river, trampling ruts where they gather into mud of a deep old-red hue. Higher up, the sheep have the run of the mountain, dotting both the fields and the moorland that caps the slopes. Giraldus pictured the monks looking up from their cloisters to see herds of wild deer grazing on the summits: that role has now passed to the sheep, and the odd platoon of Welsh mountain ponies that remain on the hill. The company they keep includes ravens, who call out with more pathos in their voices than their crow cousins, and red grouse, lurking in the heather at the southern limits of their range.

Most of these are spread thinner on the high plateau than they used to be. Sheep numbers have fallen since the European Union stopped making payments per head of stock. Local gamekeepers used to record huge numbers of grouse: whether all those birds actually existed may be open to question, but there must have been many more in the past than there are now, and grouse populations in Wales have dwindled to very low levels. Mountain ponies have lost their traditional jobs now that the coal mines have closed.

There is no shortage of demand for the landscape itself, though. The consequences are visible at the northern end of the ridge, towards Hay Bluff, where the path has been paved with flagstones to slow erosion. When it rains, silt flows away in rivulets either side of them, and they begin to look like stepping stones. There is a saddle of peat across the slopes at this end of the valley, but it is shallow compared with the fathoms buried in Irish bogs, and easily shed.

Walkers' boots are not the biggest threat. Without warning, the edges of the path vanish into a zone of lifeless mud strewn with fragments of shattered sandstone. From the air, it looks like a livid bald patch of mange on a dog's pelt. On the ground, it looks as though the hiker has followed a path to Mordor instead of Hay-on-Wye. The apparent arbitrariness of the blight is as eerie as the barrenness: something seems to have picked on this region, and cursed it.

What actually happened was that the moor caught fire and burned into the peat, over an area of forty hectares. That was in 1976, and although some of the scorched earth has begun to recover, parts of it are only getting worse. A metre's depth of peat has gone; exposed to the air, the soil that it had covered is loose and easily lost, blown away by the wind in summer, washed off by the rain in winter.

It was like a warning shot from the future. At the time, the summer of 1976 seemed like the longest and hottest of long hot summers. With hindsight, it looks like a taste of typical British summers to come. Rainfall was halved and temperatures raised by four degrees, as is projected for southern Britain towards the end of this century if greenhouse gas emissions carry on at their present rate. Much of the region went without rain entirely for more than a month. Fires were rife in woodlands and on heaths; they were especially persistent in peat, which harbours fire and lets it spread through the ground. At the time, a heatwave like that could be expected once in three hundred years. In the future, it could become the norm. Wetter winters would lower the fire risk to some extent – the summer of 1976 was the finale of a sixteen-month drought – but smoke would hang heavy in the summer air.

Burned peat is not just a loss to the landscape. Peat is mostly organic matter, and is one of the planet's richest concentrations of carbon. There is twice as much carbon in the soil as in the atmosphere, and three times as much as in the world's vegetation; between a quarter and a third of the soil's carbon is in peatlands, although they cover just three per cent of the Earth's land surface. Peat covers the same percentage of Wales, but it contains more carbon than all the United Kingdom's vegetation. The peats and other organic soils of Scotland and Wales hold the bulk of the United Kingdom's soil carbon. But it is a store rather than a sink: it can release carbon as well as retaining it, and it is vulnerable not just to fire but to warmth.

In any soils, if temperatures rise, evaporation increases and plants draw up more water to make up for what they lose. The soils dry and oxidise, becoming more acidic; the combination of warmth and oxidation stimulates soil microbes, which consume more oxygen and release more carbon dioxide. Peat forms when plants die and sink into water, which prevents them from decaying as they would in air: Britain's peatlands are thought to have developed in wet areas after prehistoric settlers cleared forests for farming. Warmth lowers the water table, exposing the organic matter to air and allowing the oxygen-breathing microbes to feed on it. Like any other creatures that breathe in oxygen, they breathe out carbon dioxide.

Soils of all kinds in England and Wales have been losing carbon since the 1970s, peat soils most of all. Since the losses have happened everywhere, no matter what the land is used for, it looks as though the warming climate is responsible. These could be the early stages of a vicious circle in which carbon from fossil fuels raises temperatures, releasing more carbon from peatlands, which raises temperatures still further. By the 2050s, climate conditions may have become unsuitable for about a third of Ireland's bogs, which make up nearly half of the British Isles' peatlands.

There is one thing worse than the loss of carbon from

dried peatlands, and that is the loss of carbon from wet ones. When oxygen-breathing – aerobic – bacteria are kept out of the peat by water, bacteria that do not use oxygen have the run of the organic matter, and make methane. This compound of carbon and hydrogen is twenty times more powerful as a greenhouse gas than carbon dioxide. It does not last as long in the atmosphere – but as it forms carbon dioxide when it breaks down, the carbon still stays in the air. If rising temperatures disturb peatlands without drying them out, the methane in them may be released.

This happens when frozen peat thaws. Half the world's peatlands – an area bigger than Greenland – are in Russia, most of them in permafrost zones. Canada's peatlands increase the total peat area in the cold north by half as much again. Together they contain over three hundred billion tonnes of carbon, which is more than half the quantity of carbon – five hundred billion tonnes – that humans have added to the atmosphere since they began to industrialise the world. It would take an immense amount of heat to melt them completely, and probably a very long period of time, but already there are warning signs that the thawing of permafrost has begun to release greenhouse gases into the air. Methane is bubbling up out of melting permafrost at the edges of lakes that are spreading as Siberia thaws: emissions rose nearly sixty per cent as the lakes multiplied between 1974 and 2000. Similar rises were recorded in Sweden over the same period. Meltwater is pooling into new lakes across western Siberia as a million square kilometres of frozen bog begin to thaw. Humans have emitted half a trillion tonnes of carbon, and now the earth itself is joining in.

*

On a warm November afternoon in 2100, a young man called Gerallt is following in the footsteps of his namesake Giraldus, who tramped this path eight centuries before. Like many of his generation, he seeks harmony in his relationship with the environment, and like a number of his peers, he has become a Buddhist monk. Travellers in robes and sandals, or even bare feet, are a common sight in these parts. To the amazement of more conventional folk, and the displeasure of the police, they spurn mobiles and stride electronically naked through the land. If everybody had lived as they do, they point out, the world would not be in its current mess. After jailing many of them under anti-privacy laws, the authorities have decided they are an affront to a surveillance society but not a menace to it.

Gerallt pauses at a crossroads incised into the ridge above the midsection of the valley, where a trail folds downwards towards the ruin of Llanthony Priory. It is known as the Monks' Path, but he does not follow it. This is not just because his ascetic discipline keeps him to his chosen path, but also because entry to the valley is restricted. With their dense woods the valley sides look from above much as they must have done to Giraldus, and the road along the valley floor is as difficult to negotiate as it was for the discomfited Archdeacon Coxe in the eighteenth century – but the obstacles are permits rather than potholes. The valley is private and residents-only. Visitors have to be guests; passing trade is barred.

These restrictions on public access to the valley have been imposed because climate change restricted public access to the mountains., by drawing the thickets up the valley slopes. Alongside the scrub, large tracts of which have matured into woodland, broad rustbelts of bracken spread in phalanxes down into the fields and up into the moor. Heather has vanished, plagued by the heather beetles that thrived in warm weather, and suppressed by the kindness of mild winters that fail to provide the cold spell that sets it up for germination; seedlings that did make a tentative appearance were throttled by summer drought. Grouse have disappeared too: there are none to be found anywhere south of the Scottish Highlands.

The changes have not made the view from the top of the slope any less beautiful, nor have people complained that they have. Indeed, nature organisations across England and Wales have enjoyed considerable success in reshaping public perceptions about the twiggy green tide of scrub, which they have renamed 'youngwood', that has taken over many beauty spots. But whatever it is called, it gets in the way. When people are surrounded by it, their paths and their views are obstructed. Public access was one of the legs on which the National Park status of the Brecon Beacons stood, and the more that public access was hampered by scrub, the shakier the park's status looked. As in other areas of outdoor beauty, the principle of public access itself became increasingly difficult to sustain in the face of increasing pressure from visitors. Eventually National Park status was revoked and building restrictions relaxed; the property-owners took control of access, keeping the road clear for themselves. From up above, parts of the valley floor still looks like farmland, but the trees conceal long ribbons of new buildings, and the fields are devoted to the outdoor recreations on which the valley's economy is now based. Visitors now come in parties and stay for a week or two, as people did in the days before they all had cars.

Pressing on, Gerallt reflects upon the illusions of surface appearances. This has nothing to do with his spiritual insights. It is prompted by what he sees when he leaves the path, which is a broad, sturdy and synthetically surfaced pedestrian highway. Along its sides run discreet embankments coxcombed with moor-grass, sloping gently enough to suggest natural undulations and low enough not to obscure the longer view. Their purpose, however, is to block the scenes of desolation that line much of the route. Striking out, Gerallt finds cracked mud and weathered lozenges of sandstone under his bare feet: he sees the blackened battlefields of recent fires and the denuded aftermaths of old ones. The seasonal double-act of summer drought and winter rain has oxidised and sluiced what has not been burned. A century after industry's ravages in the Welsh valleys were grassed over, this stage of the industrial revolution has scourged a part of the uplands that seemed to have been above industry. Unlike the green of the valleys, the sombre green of the moors cannot be put back.

Little has been done to prevent this. In typical twenty-first-century heatwaves, water is scarce and fires break out across the whole of southern Britain. When an empty Black Mountains hilltop catches light, the firefighters tend to be fully occupied elsewhere, stopping walls of flame from racing into housing estates, or cordoning fields to protect harvests. And there seems little point in trying to defend southern peatlands from fire, since they are oxidising in the warm dry air even when they are not aflame. When the Black Mountains are black in summer it is with smoke, not

167

the toppings of black Atlantic cloud that used to keep them in their own private world.

The New Estate

In the forbidding privacy of steep North Yorkshire valleys, men hacked and tunnelled for lead, the basest of metals; grey, dense, sluggish but toxic, the gloomy clinker left when the sub-atomic fireworks of radioactive decay are spent. The miners worked veins of galena, a compound of lead and the equally infernal element sulphur. When they smelted the ore, in fires of peat dug from the moors, they poisoned themselves with both lead fumes and acrid sulphur dioxide. They charged up the flames with bellows driven by the running waters that lace the valleys, and they dammed becks to create liquid avalanches: when the dams were breached, the water cascaded down the slopes, ripping away their surfaces to expose the veins of ore. The mines had almost all given up the ghost by the end of the nineteenth century, but the stains of these 'hushes' are still splashed across the faces of valleys like Gunnerside Gill in Swaledale.

The ruins of mine buildings also remain, pointing up the rugged strength that underlies the landscape's beauty. But as the River Swale flows down the next valley towards the village of Muker, after meeting the tributary stream that comes down past the old mines in Swinner's Gill, it passes from a mineral landscape to a floral one. Instead of tumbling rocks there are flat meadows, neatly parcelled by stone walls. In early summer, these fields dance with flowers: wood cranesbill, a geranium with flowers of a fine mauve, exuberant buttercups, pignut with its froth of white blossoms. By August the flowers are gone and so are the grasses they grow among, cut to make hay.

Muker's meadows are considered to be among the best remaining examples of their kind. There are less than a thousand hectares of upland hay meadow left in northern England; their rich diversity – thirty species of plants or more in a square metre – is dwindling as farmers strive for efficiency. That was also how they emerged in the first place. The fields are equipped with small stone barns, in which cattle traditionally spent the harsh Pennine winters, eating the hay that had been cut on their doorsteps. Farmers saved themselves the trouble of carrying hay to farmyards, and manure back out to the fields.

The jostling flowers are a happy by-product of circumstances, in which farming practices were adapted to make the best of meadows that were colder, wetter and two or three hundred metres higher than their lowland counterparts. Muker itself must have been cold even by Pennine standards: many of the houses were built without windows at the back to help keep the winters out. Now that farmers have moved on from scythed hay to silage, fertilisers and herbicides, they are offered grants to manage their meadows in broadly traditional ways. Since they struggle to make a profit from their sheep and cattle even with fertilisers and herbicides, many of them take the offers up. In the Muker meadows the grazing is controlled with an eye to the flowers, as is the amount of manure allowed onto the fields; baling the hay rather than bagging it is encouraged, because it gives the flower seeds in it a better chance of being shaken down into the sward.

As in the chalk grasslands of the south, diversity depends on keeping down the grasses that would naturally take over. Cattle keep them down from above; an apparently insignificant plant keeps them down from below. Yellow rattle, which looks a bit like a yellow-flowered nettle with leaves narrowed to blades, is a hemi-parasite: it has roots of its own, but it lives mainly by helping itself from the roots of other plants, especially the kinds of grasses that otherwise tend to dominate. The plant communities of the upland hay meadows are an intricate balance that can easily slip if any one of a number of their knots are loosened. They are already slipping in many places; they are weakening as they become fragmented and isolated from each other; they depend on farming managed and funded for their benefit; and their balance will be tilted further by a changing climate.

The wood cranesbill, a species ecologists welcome as a sign of good health in a hay meadow community, is already in steep decline. Average summer temperatures in Yorkshire could rise more than four degrees by 2080, and summer rainfall could fall by more than a quarter. At that rate, the wood cranesbill would be gone by 2050. The yellow rattle might do better and it might do worse, depending on how it is affected by changes in the climate at different times of the year. In dry summers its hosts might wilt before it did, and it might have less competition; but mild winters could cramp its style, as it needs to spend two or three dormant months between two and six degrees. The story will surely be similar for many other plants, as well as insects, fungi and other forms of life. They will be affected in various ways by climate change, but it's impossible to tell whether on balance they will gain or lose. And all these individual changes of fortune must surely have an impact on communities of species such as those found in meadows, hedgerows or ponds, although it's impossible to say what the changes will be.

Nobody will get to see how the balance of forces plays out in the warming sward if farmers are no longer cutting the meadows for hay in summer, though. British fields may grow greener in warmer and more carbon-rich air; demand may strengthen with rising populations and living standards, but until then, upland farmers will have to count on subsidies. Their sons and daughters may not be willing to take the risk of taking over the farm, and few others may be prepared to start a career in an unprofitable business that may not be able to count on state payments indefinitely, even for providing ecological services. By the time the climate and the market became favourable, the farmers could be long gone. A few could be paid to keep farming in traditional ways, but they would be not so much farmers as museum staff.

*

The Swale now flows from the lead moors to fields of gold. Instead of the gay yellows and whites of buttercups and pignut, the riverside plain flashes with shards of light from golden solar panels and canopies of glass. The meadows have been replaced by buildings and courtyards: the land became free for development once the flowers had dwindled away and the grasses took over. Perhaps it was the yellow rattle, perhaps it was any one of a thousand other knots that became loosened in the heat. Nobody has troubled to find out. They are too dazzled by the glittering reflections.

Muker has been transformed into a new kind of settlement for a new and powerful class. Industry has returned to the Dales two hundred years after it died here, and it has returned in its highest form. Base metals and their primitive extraction have been transmuted into knowledge and the noiseless synthesis of abstract ideas. Knowledge estates like these house the cream of the world's scientists, technologists, financial experts and administrators. They are ensconced in many beautiful and secluded spots around the British Isles, whose climate is now considered equable and particularly conducive to refined thought.

The new Muker is a campus of villas, pocketed with laboratories and the courtyards which express its ideals: they are intended as public open spaces where minds may meet, with distant echoes of ancient Greece. Its population is small as well as select. These people expect luxury and ample living space, and they can state their own terms. One crowded corner remains: the original village has become Muker's old quarter, and also its servants' quarters.

Several powerful forces have combined to bring such settlements and the class that occupies them into being. The most powerful is the ongoing ascent of industry, from making things to selling services and on to the production of knowledge. Now that knowledge is the most valuable kind of commodity, its elite producers enjoy rewards that lift them into a new estate of the realm above the crowds. They are known as the gnostocracy, among themselves as well as among the humbler ranks below them.

They have the means to live where they choose, as well as the wealth, thanks to the development of telecommunications to a level where it is almost as good as being there. As travel has become more difficult, tiresome and inefficient, telepresence has matured into more than a substitute. In the past, there were two great disadvantages to working across distance. One was that intangible but vital information – body language and the subtle shifts in it that occur when people are in each other's presence – was not transmitted. The other was that people were excluded from the buzz of informal chat and gossip on which their ability to collaborate with others and to advance themselves depended.

The latter consideration is irrelevant to the knowledge elite, because they can collaborate among themselves on their estates, and they have advanced themselves into a region where they are untouchable. Telecommunicated imagery is now lifelike enough to evoke the same nuances that emerge in face-to-face encounters, so executives can plan corporate strategies and lawyers can advise their clients without any loss of effectiveness or authority. Much of the world is run from nerve-centres like Muker, in temperate locations that allow the privileged to rise above climate change.

6

A New Caledonia

Deforested, overgrazed, burned and degraded, by the twentieth century the Scottish Highlands had largely become, in the view of the ecologist Frank Fraser Darling, 'wet desert'. In the 1950s two of his contemporaries, Harry Steven and Jock Carlisle, turned their attention to the remaining fragments of the ancient Caledonian forest. 'Even to walk through the larger of them gives one a better idea of what a primeval forest was like than can be got from any other woodland scene in Britain,' they wrote in their book *The Native Pinewoods of Scotland*, published in 1959. 'The trees range in age up to 300 years in some instances, and there are thus not many generations between their earliest predecessors about 9,000 years ago and those growing today; to stand in them is to feel the past.'

Between Darling's phrase and the forest ecologists' observation, Glen Affric found its modern meaning. At the east of the glen is one of the largest and least disturbed fragments of native Scottish pinewood; in the west is a wet expanse scarcely disturbed by trees. Glen Affric became the focus for a new appreciation of native Scottish forests, and for a movement to restore them. Around it a debate arose about the nature of nature in Scotland.

The valley runs north of the Great Glen, the diagonal fault

that separates the top of Scotland from the rest of Britain. It spans the region's two climatic zones, the western side dominated by winds coming in from the Atlantic, with its temperate currents from the south, and the more Continental eastern side, chilled by polar winds; rain, cloud and muffled temperatures in the west, a clearer distinction between winter and summer in the east. The result is a steep gradient in annual rainfall, from 2,800 millimetres in the west of the glen to 1,600 millimetres in the east. In 'this wettest corner of Europe' winters are mild and summers are cool: Steven and Carlisle recorded a mean annual temperature of 6.1°C; the mean for July was a wan 12.2°C.

These conditions combine with the soils – mineral with a thin layer of peat in the east, peat most of the way down in the west – to form a landscape of two halves. The woodlands are in the east, massed above Loch Beinn a' Mheadhoin. They are woods of broad leaves as much as needles, birch and alder in countless number, hazel and juniper among others besides, but the Scots pines are older. The very oldest are around 350 years old, though you cannot tell by looking at them. These 'grannies', as they are known, do not sprawl and bulge with age like other kinds of tree; nor are they necessarily thicker or taller than pines two hundred years younger. The pines become sparse towards the head of Loch Affric to the west; beyond which is another country, wet and desert, defying trees to advance. There's a forest, an open peatland, and an awkward pause in between.

For a wilderness it is easily accessible; less than an hour's drive from Inverness. The turning into the eastern end of the glen is at the Fasnakyle hydro-electric power station,

a handsome and purposeful building which began operating in 1951, the year that the Forestry Commission took
over the surrounding woods and those of east Glen Affric.
Between them these state enterprises industrialised the east
of Glen Affric. Loch Beinn a' Mheadhoin was dammed,
turning it into an immense fuel tank for the power scheme,
and a tunnel was run down from it to the station at
Fasnakyle. They were enlightened industrialists, though.
The Forestry Commission did plant non-native conifers,
but it did not obliterate the hillsides under geometric
blocks of Sitka spruce. The North of Scotland Hydro–
Electric Board (known as the Hydro Board for short) went
to great lengths to limit its impact on the loch – about five
kilometres, in fact, linking Loch Beinn a' Mheadhoin by a
tunnel to Loch Mullardoch, where a much larger dam was
built. The alternative would have been a bigger dam on
Loch Beinn a' Mheadhoin, and periodic falls in the water
level that would have left an unsightly bare rim around the
entire lake.

The Hydro Board's considerate approach reflected the
opposition to an earlier hydro-electric scheme, in the
1940s, which would have raised the water level so high that
the two lochs would have merged. Among its opponents
was an English MP, Noel Baker, who declared that 'the
Highlands are the spiritual heritage of the whole people'.
After it had finished its work, which raised the level of the
loch by six metres, the Hydro Board claimed that public
opinion felt the beauty of Glen Affric had been increased
by 'some hundred per cent'. Their efforts to moderate
the impact of their engineering certainly made a powerful
statement about the prime importance of natural beauty

in Glen Affric. Economic activity there would become increasingly subject to spiritual considerations.

In 1959 the Forestry Commission decided not to cut down the mature forest. Attempts to nurture and extend the wooded areas began in the 1960s, led by the Forestry Commission's District Officer, Finlay MacRae, who observed nature taking advantage of an opportunity provided by industry, as a miniature forest arose upon spoil from the dam and the tunnel. 'Given mineral soil, abundant seed, the right balance of moisture and warmth,' MacRae realised, 'the old native woodland would flourish as strongly as a well groomed lawn.' Advised by Harry Steven, he began a restoration programme. Deer were the main threat to new saplings, and still are: neighbouring estates continue to revolve around shooting.

At the end of the 1980s, forestry in Glen Affric gained a new dimension that was both practical and spiritual. Alan Watson Featherstone, a member of the Findhorn spiritual community that had grown up on the coast to the east of Inverness, had first visited Glen Affric in 1979. 'What struck me the most was the relative wildness of the glen,' he later recalled. 'There, it seemed to me, Nature was closer to free expression – what is known in the language of deep ecology as self-willed land – than anywhere else I had come across in the UK.' Yet he was also struck by a sense of what had been lost, there and elsewhere in the Highlands where the trees had retreated. The exposed glens seemed to him to be calling out for help.

Watson Featherstone spent more time in Glen Affric, some of it in the company of Finlay MacRae, and visited the neighbouring Glen Strathfarrar, where the Nature

Conservancy Council's warden Hugh Brown was doing similar work. It was in India, however, that he experienced a decisive epiphany. At Auroville, a sister community to Findhorn in the state of Tamil Nadu, he worked in a tree nursery, contributing to a community effort that planted two million trees in a desertified landscape where summer temperatures reached forty degrees. If a forest could be restored in a place like that, he decided, it should be possible to do the same in the Scottish Highlands.

In 1986 he stood up at a conference titled 'One Earth: A Call to Action' and, somewhat to his own surprise, spontaneously committed himself to a project to restore the Caledonian forest – despite having no relevant experience beyond tending the Auroville tree nursery and the Findhorn vegetable garden. The following year he founded Trees for Life, whose volunteers took up the work that MacRae and the Forestry Commission had begun. The project became a formal partnership between a New Age NGO and a government agency. The Forestry Commission's mission is to increase the forests' 'value to society and the environment'; Trees for Life's vision is 'to restore a wild forest, which is there for its own sake'.

Alan Watson Featherstone saw Glen Affric as the nucleus of a far larger renewed Caledonian forest, covering an area of 1,500 square kilometres north of the Great Glen. That would be ten times the size of the total remnant forest area, but would still only be a tenth the size of the original forest, which covered most of the Highlands. Trees for Life began to work in other parts of the target area, and in 2008 acquired land of its own for the first time, buying the 4,000-hectare Dundreggan estate in Glen Moriston, south of Glen Affric. By that time, it claimed to have planted over 750,000 trees.

It has also inspired another group to attempt a similar exercise in the Southern Uplands. The Carrifran Wildwood project sought to re-create a forest in an area denuded by over-grazing and over-burning. Over a third of a million pounds had to be raised to buy the 600 hectares of hillside where the forest was to grow. Relying on donations, the project took up a longbow to capture the public's imagination. The weapon, made of yew, had lain preserved in peat at the head of the Carrifran Valley for 6,000 years until its opportune discovery by a walker in 1990. It was used to trace an arc back to the time when forest cover was at its maximum, and thus to emphasise the idea of recreating a prehistoric environment.

As ever more of the planet is cleared, fenced, planted and built on, people are likely to be drawn to the vision of recreating a landscape as it was before humans made any great difference to it. But if human influence starts to change the climate, the vision has the ground cut from under it. Planning to roll back a landscape to a particular moment in prehistory and hold it there looks foolish if the climate has set off on a different track. Like Trees for Life, the Carrifran Wildwood Project and its parent organisation the Borders Forest Trust now talk down the idea that they are seeking to recreate the past. The idea of re-wilding is shifting away from a return to the past and taking on a new mission: to help nature re-invent itself for the future.

Over a timescale of decades, climate change may not make a huge difference to the way that the new Scottish forests grow, especially in the northern Highlands. But

Alan Watson Featherstone's timescale is set by the time it takes for a pine tree to reach maturity: 250 years. The Trees for Life volunteers who plant 100,000 seedlings each year might well wonder what kind of world their trees are going to grow up into. There are veteran trees around the country that have lived through changes of climate – the 'Little Ice Age' that ended in the nineteenth century, and in some cases the Medieval Warm Period before that too. But they are a small band of survivors, and they did not have to adjust to changes as rapid as the ones that are probably on their way. The scale of change could be in a different league too. In the time it would take for a pine to mature, the climate may change beyond anything experienced by a tree in Britain for many thousands of years.

In 1993 the National Trust for Scotland bought the 4,000-hectare West Affric estate, making the environment and its beauty the principal management priority in the west as well as an increasingly important one in the east. The new owners were faced with the question of why the west is so open while the east is so thick with trees. At that time, climate change had yet to become a serious consideration for land managers, and it had not intruded on the plans of the NTS or the Forestry Commission. As awareness grew that the climate could change, the NTS warmed to the idea that knowledge about climate change in the past could cast some light upon what the future might bring. Together with the Millennium Forest for Scotland Trust, it funded an investigation by Richard Tipping, a palaeoecologist based at the University of Stirling.

Tipping brought in two postgraduate students, Althea Davies and Eileen Tisdall, who devoted their doctoral theses to the prehistoric ecology of West Glen Affric; another doctoral student, Helen Shaw, complemented their work with research in the east. They drove corers into the peat and silt to extract deposits dating from the end of the last Ice Age to the present day. Davies and Shaw examined samples under the microscope for pollen grains; Tisdall studied changes in rainfall by measuring changes in the saturation of peat and in the level of a small loch. Between them they reconstructed 11,500 years of plant life and peat history.

At first, Tipping had expected to find evidence that West Glen Affric had been denuded by prehistoric settlers. After a few years of research, though, he and his colleagues had become persuaded that climate change was a prior and much more significant cause. The findings in Glen Affric were of a piece with what is known of the prehistory of Scottish forests. These spread rapidly after the last retreat of the ice; by 10,000 years ago, West Glen Affric was healthily wooded. Birch, rowan, hazel, alder and willow were longstanding residents; pine made inroads when climate permitted. Up to about 4,000 years ago much of the central spine of Scotland north of the Great Glen was covered by a block of pine-dominated forest, flanked by birch cover to the west and oak on the north-east coast. Then the climate changed, and the forests collapsed. They may have succumbed to stresses arising from an accentuation of the seasons, causing the temperatures to swing more sharply and the storms to blow more fiercely.

They certainly disappeared to an extent far beyond the means of the small human groups that had settled in the region. Farmers began to cultivate land in the Highlands about 6,000 years ago, but they made little impact on the forests. When climate changed and the trees fell, new opportunities opened up for the farmers. There was more room for livestock, and less cover for wolves. Farmers did not take over Glen Affric when the forests broke down. But they gradually made their presence felt, the first hints appearing at the end of the Stone Age, and reached the peak of their influence around the eighteenth century.

The investigators found no trace of a pine Atlantis in West Glen Affric. It had once been wooded, but with broadleaved trees; pines had ventured westwards during climatically favourable spells, but they had always been guests. Pollen cores extracted by researchers in East Glen Affric confirmed that the division between the halves of the glen was ancient. Pine made its first appearance there nearly 10,000 years ago, and has been a constant presence since 8,300 years ago. East Glen Affric seems to have been a Caledonian forest fastness insulated from the climatic pressures that destabilised forest cover across Scotland as a whole.

Tipping and his colleagues argued that their research had challenging implications for the vision of foresting West Glen Affric. It had been argued that 'wild woodlands' should replace the open landscape that was considered less than natural, but their data showed 'that future woodlands will not replace a landscape less wild and natural, because the heath and blanket peat that will be displaced is itself natural in origin'. The evidence from the peat cores refuted Frank Fraser Darling's 'emotive but rather wayward and misinformed' belief that dank bogs and dour heath were scar tissue on lands forced to labour beyond their capacity by humans indifferent to both nature and the future. Fraser Darling's 'wet desert' was natural; the nutrient-impoverished peat was not the result of human mismanagement but 'what nature deals'.

They also had their doubts about whether introduced trees would survive in the watery bedding of West Glen Affric. That has not stopped Trees for Life – which is, after all, based in a community that cherishes the legend of how its founder grew prodigiously large vegetables in meagre coastal soils, by following the instructions she received from the plants' 'overlighting spirits'. Trees for Life has set up a series of exclosures reaching far into West Affric, in which both planted trees and self-sown ones are safe from deer. Alan Watson Featherstone anticipates that woodland cover could become quite dense on parts of the slopes, but acknowledges that bogs and mires will remain open, and that broadleaved species stand a better chance on wetter ground than pines. The vision is one of a landscape varied in its textures and diversity. No one imagines that West Affric will ever be covered in a mantle of Caledonian pine.

Having documented how climate change had alternately permitted and extinguished trees in West Glen Affric over thousands of years, Tipping and his colleagues also questioned the wisdom of planting trees there in the face of climate change over a matter of decades. If trees had died in the past because they could not cope with increasing storminess and temperature swings between the seasons, the outlook was poor.

The ground in the west might become wetter still in winter. Climate changes could accentuate the difference between the two ends of the glen, with winter rainfall increasing several times more in the west than the east. And while the western trees struggled against water in winter, summer rainfall in the east could decline by a quarter, exposing the trees there to the risks of fire. According to Oliver Rackham, pine woods are the exception to the rule that British woods 'burn like wet asbestos', and fires are already capable of spreading through Highland pinewoods despite the wetness of the ground. Particles of charcoal in lake sediments at a number of sites, including one in Glen Affric, have shown that fires have burned sporadically on Highland ground since the ice last retreated. They appear to have cleared the land for heath and mire to form.

Average annual temperatures could rise by around three and a half degrees. The increases would be higher in summer and lower in winter, a pattern that looks rather like what the trees would choose if they could. By and large they appreciate increased warmth, which lengthens the growing season. Scots pines, however, need a period of winter cold to prepare them for resuming growth in spring. The relatively modest warming projected for winter is as if designed to take their needs into account. If it did prove too mild for them, however, the birches would stand to benefit, as they need relatively little chilling, and could start their springs earlier. Warmer summers could favour the colonisation of pinewoods by birch, together with other broadleaved species such as rowan and oak.

During the rest of the year, the pines may find themselves enjoying conditions they would have preferred all along. Although *Pinus sylvestris* as a species can cope with all the climatic conditions it encounters across a range that stretches from Siberia to the Mediterranean, it is divided into variants adapted to different regions. Northern trees sometimes grow faster in climates warmer than those they naturally occupy. It seems possible that the pines in Glen Affric could quicken their pace as the climate warms.

As in the woods and fields of the south, the catch is that mild winters are kind to insect pests, sparing vast numbers to emerge in spring that would otherwise have succumbed to cold. In north-western America, warmer winters and drier summers have helped the mountain pine beetle to move northwards and higher. It now infests much of British Columbia, blighting forests with a kind of false autumn in which trees turn red the year after they have been killed, before fading to a skeletal grey. Carbon wafts into the air from dead trees as they decompose, or as their dry wood catches fire. Before the pine beetle outbreak, British Columbia's forests were a modest carbon sink, but now they have become a major source of carbon emissions. In one year, the beetles were responsible for emissions equivalent to three-quarters of those produced by forest fires across the whole of Canada. Climate change may also make life easier for pathogens that kill trees. In Scotland, these may include *Phytophthora* micro-organisms that attack the roots of firs and spruces, as well as those of broadleaved trees including birch, alder and oak. Mild winters and wet springs will favour *Phytophthora*; dry summers will weaken the trees' ability to resist the pathogens. Half the Scots pines in the River Rhône's Swiss valley died in the space of a few years around the turn of the century. They may have succumbed to infestations by nematode worms and bark beetles, the pests invigorated by high temperatures and the trees weakened by drought in an already dry region.

Visitors encounter fragments of the story of the Glen posted on notices and panels scattered around the area; picketing the car parks, hung on deer-fence gates, mounted upon a bulky pedestal which now looks as neglected as the shed huddled next to it. They recapitulate the decline of the woods, the post-war revival, and the vision of a neo-natural future. Part of their role is to prepare public opinion for the reintroduction of mammals long gone from Scotland. 'Perhaps one day Glen Affric's pinewood will be large and healthy enough for the reintroduction of some of its extinct wildlife like beaver and wild boar,' muses a board at Cougie, to the south of Loch Beinn a' Mheadhoin.

Trees for Life helped to run a project there to investigate the possible impact of wild boar upon the forest. At high densities they can wreck pine forests, uprooting trees and stripping their bark or roots, but in suitable numbers can be expected just to clear small patches of ground, relieving the monotony of bracken and opening space for tree seedlings. This study is just a first step, says Trees for Life's founder Alan Watson Featherstone in a video about the project. As he makes crisply clear, his ambition for rewilding is maximal: 'I want to see the wild boar, the lynx, the brown bear and the wolf back here in their rightful habitat,' he declares.

They are not going to return to the Glen by claiming their rights, though. As Trees for Life's involvement with the Guisachan Wild Boar Project implicitly acknowledges, they will have to pass a risk assessment. They will also have to win public support and, because they cannot be guaranteed to remain confined to the area in which they are released, allay the fears of stakeholders across the region, notably forestry, farming, fishing and shooting interests.

Boar already have a reputation for throwing their weight around in the south of England, where escapees from farms have built up a population of two hundred animals in an area straddling the border between Kent and Sussex. Smaller colonies, with numbers closer to fifty, have established themselves in west Dorset and the Forest of Dean. Other small groups have also found room around the edges of Dartmoor – for which responsibility has been claimed by the Animal Liberation Front. Boar are blamed for trampling crops and digging up bluebells; they are feared to be capable of worse. 'These are wild, aggressive animals,' an East Sussex man called John Cook told the *Daily Telegraph*, after dispatching one with a single shot. 'You shudder to think what might happen if they came across a kid playing in the woods.'

The only children likely to be playing in the woods are ones in old-fashioned story books, contemporary parents' fears of human predators being what they are, but the risk of collisions between vehicles and animals which, like John Cook's victim, may weigh well over a hundred kilograms, is a genuine concern. In the south, 'large and wild' means 'out of control and dangerous'. Mr Cook's perception, which harmonises perfectly with the *Telegraph*'s vision of a properly fenced countryside, is a reminder of the distance between southern England and the Scottish Highlands. In southern England, it is just not possible for a large and vigorous mammal to avoid damaging property for which somebody will have to pay. In Scotland their rooting and trampling may have a welcome effect on land that is being offered back to nature, but if animal engineers are needed to break up woodland for the sake of biodiversity in the south of England, as in Friston Forest near the Cuckmere estuary, cattle provide a more tractable alternative.

As well as size and vigour, boar have fertility on their side. They reach sexual maturity quickly and have large litters, sometimes twice in a year. Yet in southern England they have been unable to capitalise on their potential. A study in the 1990s suggested that the Kent and Sussex population could grow to 3,500 by 2012, but today it remains not very far above the minimum estimate of 130. It would appear that John Cook is not the only good shot in the Kentish borderlands. In the Forest of Dean and Ross-on-Wye area boar numbers do not rise much above fifty, and sometimes drop sharply, suggesting that here also local vigilance is keeping the numbers down.

Culling cannot be the sole explanation, though. Boar are multiplying in much of Continental Europe despite their popularity as targets among hunters. Across France and Germany their numbers are estimated at about a million. England may be too much of a mosaic, tight and bound, for even such a robust animal to spread. It also lacks the woods where boars naturally belong. A quarter of the land is wooded in most of the countries where boars are on the increase, whereas less than a tenth of England is under trees. Of that, most of the ancient woodland suitable for boar is in the south-east: Sussex, Hampshire, Surrey and Berkshire. If the boars survive – which is by no means certain – they may be confined within an archipelago of southern woods.

In Scotland the space for them is there, but the welcome may not be. Just as southern Britain stands out in Europe as a region that has largely contained its boar insurgency, northern Britain stands out as peculiarly resistant to the return of the European beaver, *Castor fiber*. Across Europe the story has been much the same: beavers were extirpated by hunting, mostly in the nineteenth century, and reintroduced or protected in the twentieth. In seventeen countries, re-founded populations now number a hundred or more, and in some cases tens or hundreds of thousands. Beavers were eradicated in England much earlier, during the twelfth century, though they may have survived in Scotland until the sixteenth century, when they also appear to have died out in Italy.

By the time of a survey published in 2002, these three nations were the only ones in Europe whose history records the presence of beavers but which had made no official attempt at reintroduction. Scottish Natural Heritage conducted a public consultation on the possibility in 1998, and submitted an application for a trial release in Knapdale Forest, Argyll; but in December 2002 the Scottish Executive parried it with a request for further information about the potential impact on farming, forestry and salmon fishing. These interests were represented by the Scottish Rural Property and Business Association, which set its face firmly against the proposal. In 2005 the Executive refused permission. After elections in 2007, however, the Labour administration was replaced by the Scottish National Party, which turned out to be friendlier to beavers. In May 2008, ten years after the Scottish public was first consulted, the Scottish Government (as the

Executive had renamed itself) finally granted permission to release what its Environment Minister, Michael Russell, called these 'charismatic, resourceful little mammals'.

The pioneers came from Norway, to comply with an International Union for the Conservation of Nature (IUCN) rule that reintroduced animals must come from stocks that most closely resemble the extinct population. Norwegian beavers were identified as the best match by comparing preserved Scottish beaver skulls with specimens from around Europe. Eleven of the animals were finally released into Knapdale Forest, in Argyllshire, in May 2009. They were fitted with radio tracking tags, and would be kept under surveillance for five years. The project has been costed at £850,000, which does not include the expense of the ten-year campaign for permission. Trees for Life regards the beaver as 'perhaps the simplest and least problematical' of all Scotland's extirpated species as a candidate for reintroduction. If this is what it takes to get a couple of electronically tagged beaver families into an Argyll forest for five years of monitoring, it will be a long time indeed before Scotland can accommodate the wolf and the bear.

On the other side of the argument, the rural business lobby challenged the idea that the Argyll release would be a reintroduction. Beavers had been absent from Scotland for so long, and habitats had been altered so much since their extinction, that *Castor fiber* is now an 'effectively alien' species. As if echoing commonly voiced observations about other recent migrants from Europe, its spokesman warned that the proposed new arrivals would prove more industrious than anticipated. In Poland, European beavers had 'constructed over 20 dams in little over a kilometre of river'.

In Bavaria, such industry had led to extensive flooding and a reduction in the output of hydro-electric stations on the Danube. But for the beavers' sponsors, the animals are constructive 'waterway engineers', whose dams can actually counter flooding by creating pools that act as overflow tanks. In their role as foresters they uphold the widely admired tradition of coppicing, and also keep wetlands free of scrub.

As with immigration, the underlying anxiety is about containment. The record of captive beaver domains in Britain will have done little to inspire confidence: over the course of a year, beavers escaped from three of around five sites. They are unlikely to stay free and multiply, though. The real issue is what may happen when the species is deliberately given the chance to find its own level. On a Continental and historical scale, the beaver has demonstrated a spectacular capacity for expansion, from a remnant of about a thousand at the turn of the twentieth century to well over half a million today. If beavers are cleared to become part of Scotland's wildlife once again, they will leave their naturalist minders behind and strike out for ranges of their own choosing. Their standards are demanding, and the first pioneers will trek along watercourses until they find high-quality habitat; later arrivals will have to turn back and settle in what is left. This modus operandi produces a dispersal pattern in which beavers quickly establish distant outposts, and then gradually fill up the reaches between these and their point of departure. A few may travel well over fifty miles, though the average distance is more like fifteen. They could appear to be all over the place quite quickly, which might stimulate public unease about re-wilding.

Their horizons will be narrower than those of their Continental counterparts, however, and their numbers correspondingly lower. Beavers follow watercourses easily, but are slow or unable to cross watersheds – the ridges that separate river systems. On the Continent they can follow the great river systems, the Danube and the Rhine, where the watersheds are barely perceptible irregularities on the vast Eurasian plain. In the Highlands, though, they would face a battery of mountainous ridges, and might be deterred from following watercourses by the gaps between fragments of woodland. A study covering much of the Highlands calculated that the area contained sufficient lengths of wood-lined watercourse to support up to 390 beaver families, totalling a couple of thousand individuals. But in practice it takes more than woods and water to make a decent beaver habitat. Most of the sites the study looked at lacked abundant vegetation; in others, the water flowed too fast or rose too high.

When searching for new places to make their homes, beavers have one great psychological asset. Like other rodents, they are not afraid to get close to humans. In Vienna they live on shores overlooked by high-rise buildings, swimming among bathers and canoeists. Perhaps it isn't surprising that they are unfazed by large artificial structures, since they make those themselves. Dams built by humans present beavers with obstacles that daunt but do not unnerve them: in France, some hydro-electric barrages have been fitted with beaver ladders; elsewhere, in the absence of such aids, beavers have been observed to walk round dams.

Their questing resolve could be significant in the Highlands, where dams or natural obstacles frequently stand in the way of potential beaver oases. One of these is Glen Affric, parts of which look highly suitable for beavers. If beavers were to reach Loch Ness – around which a sixteenth-century author claimed they were to be found – they could head inland along the River Enrick, which would eventually take them less than a forested mile away from the confluence near Cannich where the River Affric becomes the Glass. Upstream, the Affric is joined by the Abhainn Deabhag, which flows down through the Guisachan Forest, parting a curtain of obsolescent pines and threading a ribbon of their broadleaved successors. A beaver that followed the Abhainn Deabhag up to Cougie and prospected to the north-west – there is a swampy stream to lure it in that direction – would find the small and placid Loch nan Gillean, fringed with a woody salad of young trees. From the northern end of the loch, the Allt an Laghair stream would take it the short distance to Loch Beinn a' Mheadhoin, conveniently close to the narrow junction with Loch Affric, an easy point of departure from which to explore the rich habitat potential on both sides of the major lochs. But in between the confluence with the Affric and Cougie the Abhainn Deabhag passes through a gorge of Alpine proportions, with pines spearing up from sheer cliffs and the Plodda Falls cascading down into it from a height of thirty metres. On the northern course, the Affric is stopped up at Benevean Dam, then driven head-long through a natural sluice at Dog Falls. At either point it is easy to imagine a beaver gazing up and turning back to make the most of the calmer reaches downstream.

Getting that far would also require rising to challenges. The Great Glen is filled in the north-east by Loch Ness and by a companion sequence of glacial lochs to the west, joined up in the early nineteenth century by the Caledonian Canal to form a continuous waterway from the North Sea to the Atlantic coast. Any creature that happened upon it would find itself on a corridor wider than any highway and as straight as a Roman centurion could wish. It would also find itself with abundant supplies if the Great Glen were to become part of a habitat network connecting Scotland's currently fragmented forests, as conservationists urge. But the beaver would have to be able to cope with a succession of locks, such as the series of eight that comprise Neptune's Staircase, which raises and lowers boats nearly twenty metres. Across the Highlands as a whole, the number of concrete scarps that would confront pioneering beavers is likely to increase as Scotland pursues its goal of generating half its electricity from renewable sources by 2020. A study submitted to the Scottish Government in 2008 identified over a thousand sites where new hydropower schemes would be technically feasible and financially viable.

The point at which beavers might be faced with such obstacles would depend upon what they encountered as they spread from the places where they'd been released. The more fragmented or meagre the woods along the banks proved to be, the more likely the animals would be to press on further than the naturalists had envisaged. Their range in a mediocre environment might expand more quickly than in a rich one. From a re-wilding point of view, this is another argument for bigger and better woodlands.

Those on the side of the beaver are upbeat about its potential impact. One report puts the potential annual cost in the thousands and the potential benefit, from tourism, in the millions. While unease about the uncontrolled spread of the rodents persists, however, Glen Affric's dam and falls strengthen claims that the area is suitable as an adoptive home for *Castor fiber*. Beavers released around the main lochs would find plenty of territory to fill up, and when a lack of suitable waterside did begin to prompt their descendants to look elsewhere, they would be obstructed by the heroic engineering and the roaring natural gauntlets from venturing downstream towards the River Glass. A beaver colony set up in the Glen would probably stay in the Glen. The barriers that would reduce the chances of beavers making their own way to Loch Beinn a' Mheadhoin could improve the chances that, thanks to an official reintroduction scheme, they might reach it by four wheel-drive.

Suggesting that a place is suitable for animals because they could be confined in it runs counter to a key idea about how to protect species from climate change. Birds have evolved to migrate between regions of suitable climate; now the climates themselves are migrating. As the climate warms, animals and plants adapted to particular climatic conditions will have to follow those conditions as they shift northwards. In Europe, they may be severely impeded by the fragmentation or complete absence of suitable habitats in the areas into which their climates are moving. Conservationists now call for a drive to connect up spaces for nature. Reserves stand to become beleaguered outposts unless they form part of a chain of 'stepping stones' for wildlife, made up from sizeable patches of semi-natural land. Even these might not be enough if plants and animals cannot move quickly enough. A study in France found that

between 1989 and 2006, birds moved their ranges 91 kilometres north – but the temperatures they were used to
shifted 273 kilometres in the same direction, leaving the
birds 182 kilometres behind. While many species will not
be able to move quickly enough, others may not be able to
move at all. Many British butterflies have declined, even
though the higher temperatures of recent years suit them
better than traditional British weather, because their habitats are disappearing and they have not been able to reach
new spots that may now be warm enough for them. Others
could die out because they cannot cope with the warming
climate, but are unable to reach cooler habitats further
north. Naturalists may face the choice between watching
species decline and vanish, or gathering them up and carrying them to new homes.

Such desperate measures may be needed especially for
species whose breeding areas are being ruined elsewhere
in Europe. The memorably cold winter of 1963 finished
off all but a handful of Dartford warblers, little russet birds
with jaunty tails, in southern England. That was a matter
of regret for British birders, but in ecological terms merely
a peripheral trimming of a species vulnerable to cold on the
northern margins of its climatic range. Nowadays about
1,600 pairs live in southern England, out of a world total
estimated at over two million pairs. They have become less
vulnerable on the northern side of the Channel as frosts in
southern England have become less harsh and less frequent
than they used to be. Dartford warblers have the smallest range of any birds that nest in Britain. Their heartland
is Spain, where more than three-quarters of them breed:
almost all of that region may become too hot for them.

By that time, in the later stages of the century, most of England, Wales and Ireland will have a climate to suit them. The British Isles could become the main refuge for the Dartford warbler. But that would depend on whether suitable habitat was available, and whether the birds could get to it. Most of the heathland the warblers used to frequent is already long gone. If they failed to reach remaining or newly created sanctuaries under their own steam, human intervention might be necessary to save the species.

This is not what conservationists want to do. They want to help nature help itself, in the same way that international campaigns against poverty aim to help the poor to help themselves. But they may be forced to act as nature is stifled by the pressures piling up on it. In Europe, it will face a hotter and more arid south as well as sprawling towns, hurtling traffic and expanses of modern farmland that are barren wastes for all but the crops that grow on them. With growing populations, and the possibility that the demand for food will lead to more intensive farming in areas that remain or become suitable for agriculture, the pressures are only likely to mount.

At the same time, climate change will threaten to pull the ground from under conservationists' feet. Up till now, nature conservation has been based to a large extent on reserves, areas that are protected for the benefit of the wild species that live in or visit them. At present they can be preserved by careful maintenance, and often enhanced by sympathetic artificial features such as the Scrape at Minsmere. If the climate changes around them, though, no amount of fencing, digging or draining may be enough to keep them suitable for the species they were set up to protect. It will be all the more important to make reserves part of large habitat networks if the species need to find ways out of them as well as ways in.

If climate change weakens the links between particular places and particular sets of species, while intensifying the threats to wildlife in others, conservationists could be forced to look at habitats differently. Instead of judging a spot according to the importance of the plants and animals already found there, they might judge it according to its potential for plants and animals elsewhere that are in desperate need of new homes. Conservationists could find themselves becoming habitat brokers, searching the continent to identify species in need and places to put them in.

If that were to happen, sites in the British Isles would shine brightly on their maps, offering a reassuring combination of recently acquired warmth and Atlantic shade. Britain can also offer a spectacular example in which relocation has done wonders for at least one charismatic creature, the kind of success story that can win political favour by taking the fancy of public opinion. Its success is visible in skies across Britain. At the beginning of the 1990s, conserving the red kite was a covert operation. Their nesting sites deep in Wales were kept secret, overseen by video cameras, and were said to have been guarded from egg collectors by the SAS. ('The Regiment' lent only its reputation to the defence of the eggs; the soldiers deployed to watch the nests were from mainstream units.) Offa's Dyke was regarded as a wall of death: any kite that drifted across the border would fall foul of the gamekeepers who policed the English estates. To get kites back into England, naturalists clandestinely released chicks from Spain in the Chiltern woods east of Oxford. Before doing so, they conducted a hearts-and-minds exercise among local residents and land-owners, assuring them that the birds would do no harm and encouraging them to welcome the presence of these striking new residents.

Within a few years, the project came out into the open as the kites, pointed and sweeping, became a familiar sight to drivers on the M40 between Oxford and High Wycombe. Before long, wheeling kites were as reliable a presence near the Stokenchurch microwave communications tower as seagulls on a pier. Having been driven to extinction at the turn of the twentieth century, and still confined like a remnant guerrilla band in their Welsh mountains a decade before the end of it, red kites have breezed through south-ern England with sublime indifference to the transforma-tion it has undergone since they were last there. They have settled the M4 corridor and range along the South Downs in Sussex; they are venturing into London, as far east as Hackney. Birds from the Chilterns population, which grew to around 350 pairs, were taken north to Aberdeen and the Derwent Valley near Gateshead, where some of them demonstrated their urban resilience by padding their nests with clothes taken from washing lines. They were beginning to reprise the role of city scavengers they took in Shakespeare's London, and Shakespeare's *The Winter's Tale* – 'My traffic is sheets; when the kite builds, look to lesser linen.' Although the middens around which they used to flock have been replaced by containers with lids, kites can once again be seen crowding the air over open rubbish dumps. In the Chilterns, conservationists found to their dismay that about ten per cent of householders were luring kites to their gardens by putting out food, much of it unsuitable. Ideally suited to the contemporary demands of celebrity, the red kite combines a noble appearance – in French it is the *milan royal*; the adjective is not exaggerated – with plebeian tastes.

Red kites have also been released in several other parts of Scotland, the East Midlands, Yorkshire and Northern Ireland; they now number 1,100 or 1,200 pairs across the United Kingdom. By being put in the right place, which in their case meant an area where they would be at low risk of poisoning or shooting, red kites thrived across huge tracts of urbanised and mechanised British landscape. Given the opportunity, they made straight for the nearest motorway.

Over roughly the same period, the buzzard has also spread across much of southern England. The pocket eagle of the western woods has advanced steadily and rapidly eastward, taking over from the kestrel as the region's principal raptor. Its ability to spread unassisted probably arose not just because it was already common in the west of Britain, unlike the isolated kites, but also because of its robust musculature, which gives it the strength to plough through Britain's hanging maritime air. Kites, by contrast, are not built for the familiar British climate. They are, in fact, kites by design: they lack power and rely upon rising thermals to carry them aloft. Like the Dartford warbler, the red kite was at the northern limits of its range in Britain, and not really at home in the sodden Welsh hills, where fewer of their eggs hatch and fewer of their nestlings survive than almost anywhere else. Kites raise far more young in the drier Chilterns, and may possibly have benefited from the warmer seasons that coincided with their reintroduction to England. A substantially warmer climate will certainly agree with them, and their readiness to see opportunities in built-up areas will stand them in very good stead as the country grows ever more crowded. Britain could support 50,000 pairs, more than double the present world population. Meanwhile their core breeding areas on the Continent could succumb, like those of the Dartford warbler, to increasingly hot and arid conditions. Most red kites breed in Germany, towards the north-eastern end of a diagonal belt extending from the Baltic coast through south-eastern France and across the Iberian peninsula. In the *Climatic Atlas of European Breeding Birds* map showing the projected red kite range for 2070, almost the whole of this belt has disappeared. Britain could become the red kite's ark and its new heartland.

The *Climatic Atlas*, based on data collected before the English kite reintroductions, may be unduly pessimistic. Many other factors besides climate may influence where a species is to be found, especially in Europe, which humans have filled so full of hindrances to other species: the kites' success in England shows that sometimes such hindrances can be worked around. Nevertheless, the implication of a catastrophic collapse in red kite numbers across the Continent is too stark to dismiss – especially as the map is based on a scenario in which greenhouse gas emissions are relatively moderate. One study calculated that the red kite could lose between forty-two and eighty-six per cent of its range. The British reintroduction projects launched late in the twentieth century may turn out to have assured the red kite's survival through the late twenty-first.

The red kite's popularity among Britons today bodes well for its relations with their grandchildren; but their good will cannot be taken for granted. If the birds do fade out of mainland Europe, their contrasting success in the British Isles may be a source of national pride. The bird will surely continue to be admired for its thrilling silhouette: a sail and streaming pennants; the human admiration for the raptor's form seems to be universal and immune to fashion. But familiarity could breed irritation. It is one thing to admire a pair of peregrines that have nested high on a tower block, or to observe ospreys through telescopes at Loch Garten in the Highlands; another to glance out of a suburban kitchen window to see a bird that will eagerly congregate, as it has already demonstrated in the Chilterns, in flocks of two hundred. If it becomes common, it will no longer seem noble. Its distinctiveness will be further diluted if, as ornithologists expect, increasing warmth brings the less finely rendered, more corvine black kite across the Channel to join it. Once the novelty has worn off, householders may be annoyed rather than charmed when kites help themselves to socks and teddy bears (on which they appear keen) for their nests.

A more serious risk is the possibility that farmers and shooters will come to suspect kites of killing game birds. A study of the feeding habits of kites in the Midlands found that although much of their diet comprised a welcome contribution to pest control – rats, rabbits, pigeons – a significant portion of it was pheasant or partridge. Kites prefer corpses to live prey, and these ones may well have found their pheasants dead by the sides of roads; but they are known to kill young crows and are capable of killing game birds during the breeding season. When game declines, predators get the blame. After Spanish rabbit populations collapsed by half or two-thirds under the impact of viral haemorrhagic disease in the early 1990s, rabbit hunters turned on red kites, harrying them in important rabbit-hunting areas, and eliminating them from some altogether. Many hunters maintained that predators, rather than parasites, were the main cause of the rabbits' decline, and felt that there were 'too many kites' in Spain. They did not distinguish between the 3,500 pairs of nesting red kites and the 20,000 pairs of resident black kites or the tens of thousands of red kites that came to Spain for the winter. It is not hard to imagine game-bird breeders in a crowded future British landscape seeing flocks of hook-billed kites and blaming them for lost fledglings. As for people, so for kites: climate change helps to increase population density by improving conditions in the British Isles and worsening them on the Continent; it becomes harder to avoid treading on each other's toes, and tensions readily arise over real or imagined competition for resources.

The consequences for kites of finding themselves on the wrong side of rural business interests are all too apparent in the Highlands, the glaring exception to the pattern of kite multiplication across Britain. Highland kites are laying eggs and raising chicks in healthy numbers, yet the number of breeding pairs has remained in the tens instead of expanding to the hundreds achieved elsewhere. In 2001 the RSPB estimated that poison set out illegally in bait had killed a third of the kites released in Scotland since the reintroduction programme began in 1989. Both motive and means are present. Grouse shooting is an economically dubious proposition, so shooting enterprises want to maximise target numbers. This appears to have encouraged an attitude on some estates of maximum, if illegal, intolerance for birds of prey. The Highlands provide abundant space in which to get away with such offences.

As scavengers, red kites are unlikely to be priority targets, but as scavengers they are particularly vulnerable to poisoned bait. And they may still be vulnerable to the kind of reflexive rural hostility that led to the shooting of a red kite six weeks after Ireland's environment minister released it in Wicklow, south of Dublin. Like the foxes that have become as urban as pigeons, red kites may come to find safety in human numbers.

The beaver, exclusively vegetarian, was kept out for ten years by a business lobby and government foot-dragging. Kites, predominantly scavengers, still fall victim to poison laid to kill birds of prey. What chance do real predators – wolves, bears and lynx – have of roaming Scotland once again?

Of the three, the lynx would blend most easily into the landscape. It is not known to attack people, and where it survives in Europe its impact on livestock appears tolerable – with the aid of compensation payments. The Eurasian lynx, whose range extends from western Europe to eastern Siberia, relies largely upon roe deer as its prey, and upon forests to provide cover from which it can ambush them. Adequate supplies of both are available in the Highlands, according to research by David Hetherington, an ecologist at the University of Aberdeen. Hetherington and his colleagues assessed the regions of Scotland according to lynx standards, ruling areas out as unsuitable for occupation if motorways or dual carriageways ran through them, and assuming that dispersal routes would not have gaps of more than 1,000 metres between patches of wooded cover. They calculated that the Highlands contained about 15,000 square kilometres of suitable habitat, much of it connected together by the axis of the Great Glen. Although they are secretive, lynx are not shy of approaching human settlements, so the Great Glen would offer a line of communication reaching Argyll in the south-west, Strathspey in the east and far into the northern Highlands, taking in Glen Affric on the way. The region could support about 400 lynx, and a separate belt in the Southern Uplands, 5,000 square kilometres in size, could accommodate about fifty more. Only three of Europe's existing nine lynx populations are larger; and the potential north British numbers could be further increased by the expansion of the Southern Uplands zone to include 800 square kilometres of suitable habitat on the English side of the border.

Hetherington has also advanced the case for the lynx by showing that it had remained part of the British fauna until the early Middle Ages. Hitherto scientists had believed that the lynx had become extinct thousands of years ago, and some had suggested that this was the result of a change to a colder and wetter climate. Dating tests on fossil lynx bones have since shown that they were present at the same time as the Romans, however, and Hetherington's sampling indicated that a specimen from north Yorkshire was only about 1,500 years old. This allowed him to take sides in a longstanding scholarly argument about an elusive word in a poem of the period, 'Pais Dinogad' (Dinogad's Smock), arguing that *llewyn* in the Cumbric language should be translated not 'fox' or 'wildcat' but 'lynx'. It also enabled him to argue that, since these recent dates ruled out natural climate change as the cause of the lynx's disappearance, human actions such as the felling of forests and deliberate persecution were implicated, and therefore 'the Eurasian lynx qualifies ethically as a candidate for reintroduction'.

For some scientists, the rapid pace of climate change demands much more radical steps. In July 2008 a group of ecologists published an article in the journal *Science* arguing that those responsible for conservation must contemplate moving species to regions where they have no presence or history. 'This strategy flies in the face of conventional conservation approaches,' they acknowledge. One of the paper's authors, Chris Thomas of the University of York, suggested several species as possible candidates for introduction to Britain. Among these was the Iberian lynx, which may have been confined in prehistory to the south of the peninsula when the rest of its range was covered by ice, and certainly became confined to that area as its Spanish range shrank over the course of the twentieth century. Its numbers are now in the low hundreds, and fragmented into small groups. The Red List rates it as 'critically endangered' and has warned that it is 'close to becoming the first wild cat species to go extinct for at least 2,000 years'.

The Iberian lynx is not only scarcer than the Eurasian lynx but smaller; it is half the size, and hunts accordingly. Iberian lynxes eat rabbits, and little else; each lynx needs to eat a rabbit a day. When rabbit numbers collapsed during the myxomatosis epidemic of the 1950s, lynx numbers crashed with them. By the 1990s lynxes faced continuing food shortages, and death on the roads that diced up their remaining patches of habitat. Although climate change is not the threat that looms largest, its effects could finish off a species that has already been brought to the verge of extinction. The Doñana National Park in south-western Spain is chronically vulnerable to drought and rainfall in the park will steadily decline as Iberia becomes more like Africa: few of the parties struggling to cope with the failing supply of water will be worse placed than the lynx.

If they were taken north, Iberian lynxes could in theory co-exist with their Eurasian relatives, the larger Eurasian lynxes ambushing roe deer and the smaller Iberian ones pouncing upon rabbits. And rabbits are not the only nuisance animals that Iberian lynxes could control. At about twice the size of domestic cats, they are large enough to kill foxes. At the same time, they would be too small to arouse fear among their human neighbours. But if they were released in Scotland, they could pose a threat to Scottish wildcats, should any still survive by the time their distant cousins arrived.

The Spanish imperial eagle survives in roughly the same area as the Iberian lynx. It also relies heavily on rabbits and numbers a few hundred at best. The region may grow too hot for these birds, and Professor Thomas suggests that they might also benefit from introduction to Britain, where they could spend their afternoons thinning the crowds of rabbits in the fields of southern England. It might make a droll historical bookend; an introduced imperial raptor hunting prey introduced by bygone imperialists (Romans, accordingly to recently discovered remains, and also from Spain). But whereas a red kite above a suburban shopping precinct only lacks the appearance of credibility – it looks as though it should be on station above a mountain ridge, but is actually where it historically belongs, close to humans and their refuse – an eagle playing at buzzards would be about as natural a spectacle as a falconry display in the grounds of a stately home.

Welcoming exotic newcomers like the lynx and the eagle would also undermine the widespread assumption that native species are good and aliens are undesirable. Indeed, Thomas invites British conservationists to cherish the rhododendron, rather than working their fingers to the bone – and spending £45 million in Snowdonia National Park alone – in efforts to save native greenery from being extinguished by the waxy gloom. *Rhododendron ponticum*, the form that has turned invasive in the British Isles, was introduced from southern Spain in the eighteenth century. It is still found there in small, sheltered pockets. Once it grew in evergreen rain forests that spread across much of Europe; today their vestiges cling tenuously on in refuges where they are spared the arid extremes of the Mediterranean climate. They may not be spared much longer. *R. ponticum* has already been classified as endangered in Andalucía. In a few decades' time, the Iberian rhododendron may have vanished from a region that was nominally its natural home, but to which it was basically unsuited, while continuing to thrive in the Atlantic shade of the British Isles. Britain should perhaps regard the rhododendron as a plant in need of a haven rather than as an invader. Thomas points out that Iberia is likely to lose species as it becomes hotter and more arid, while Britain will find itself holding a higher proportion of Europe's biodiversity than before.

The British Isles are not exactly the Galápagos Islands, either. The species they harbour tend to be globally widespread and not threatened: the risks are low, Thomas argues, that an introduced species would harm anything rare – and any damage that did occur would be confined to the island on which it took place. Britain and Ireland are relatively low in biodiversity not just because they are northerly but because the last ice age cleared much of the land; and new species were prevented from coming in by the rise in sea levels that cut the land bridges to the Continent.

As a result, the British Isles have little wildlife that is exclusively theirs. The only bird found in Britain and nowhere else is the Scottish crossbill – which, however, is so hard to distinguish from other kinds of crossbill that DNA analysis has been used to support the claim that it really is a species. It is found only in the Scots pine woodlands of the Scottish Highlands (including Glen Affric); its population is estimated at between 300 and 1,250 pairs, and it may not be found anywhere at all before long. The area suitable for it disappears from Scotland in the *Climate Atlas* models, and the only alternative emerges in northern Iceland, far beyond the reach of a small woodland bird.

Chris Thomas's provocative praise of the rhododendron and his less than reverential assessment of British biodiversity may be a foretaste of major ideological clashes among conservationists, fuelled by climate change. Traditional conservationists try to make the public care about the fate of plants and insects that most people have never heard of, and will certainly never see. They feel the loss of a fish from an upland lake or a flower from a hillside even if the species is common elsewhere. They see changes like these as losses of heritage that make a difference to the country even if they do not matter to the world in general.

If one of the arguments for assisting colonisation in the British Isles is that, frankly, British and Irish nature isn't that special, the traditional conservationist message could be seriously undermined. While public opinion could well warm to the image of the British Isles as an ark in the Atlantic for plants and animals threatened with extinction by climate change, a glamorous new role like that would make the job of persuading people to care about the fate of obscure native species even harder.

Re-wilders would also be dismayed. Instead of bringing in wild animals to make British landscapes resemble the distant past – as much as possible, weather permitting – the colonisers would be bringing in rival wild animals that fitted the new climate but were not what nature in Britain would have intended. In a stable environment, being native offers guarantees that a species will thrive and will fit in with other species. As the climate changes, those guarantees will expire. Alien species may fit in better. And they may get preference over native species if, as in the case of the Iberian lynx, their needs are obviously more urgent. Climate change may indeed force conservationists to change their view of life in radical ways, though it may be asking too much to expect them to start with the rhododendron.

Among the suggested candidates for introduction to Britain, Eurasian brown bears stand at the other end of the scale. They are not exclusively carnivorous, eating grasses, nuts and berries as well as meat or fish; but they are too big – up to two metres tall on their hind legs, and 250 kilograms – and too unpredictable to be safe. In North America they occasionally kill people. Nor are there any pressing conservation arguments to override the risks. Although all but a few have been extirpated from western Europe, the world's population is over 200,000, about 100,000 of them in Russia, and 14,000 in easterly parts of Europe outside Russia.

Attempts to dot the slopes of the Pyrenees and the Alps with a few more bears have triggered collective local hysteria. After a hunter killed Cannelle, one of the last native bears in the French Pyrenees, President Chirac ordered the translocation of five Slovenian bears by way of compensation to the environment. They were greeted with protest demonstrations and shards of glass coated with honey. One of them, Franska, was blamed for killing 150 sheep. 'The entire population is living in fear of the bear,' claimed the leader of the local farmers' union. After Franska was run over, the head of the Association for the Protection of Pyrenean Heritage threatened that her people would 'set fire to the mountain' if the bear was replaced.

In Scotland, the bear faces an obstacle of the imagination. It is not part of Scottish history, unless one counts a solitary, and grisly, reference by the Roman author Martial to the use of a Scottish bear to dispatch a condemned criminal. Wolves, on the other hand, jostle for attention in the histories that Scottish people have told for themselves. 'Each district has its last wolf, and the legend of the hero who slew it,' a Victorian commentator observed. Some accounts claim that the last wolf was slain well into the eighteenth century, when some of Glen Affric's pine 'grannies' were already in their prime. It seems more likely that the wolf was extirpated by the end of the seventeenth century, but that is still recent enough for the story to be continued.

Like the bear, wolves are numerous in North America and Eurasia, but have largely been eradicated from the western end of the European continent. The challenges they face in returning are illustrated by the case of the pair that succeeded in establishing themselves deep inside Sweden, 1,000 kilometres from their parents' apparent point of departure in the Russo-Finnish border region. They were the first wolves to benefit from the legal protection established in Sweden in the 1960s, the species having previously been hunted to extinction. Their numbers have swelled to over a hundred, and are estimated to be growing by twenty per cent a year – but it is also estimated that a similar proportion is shot each year. This armed rural resistance has a political wing. According to Petter Hedberg, an ecologist, the wolf has become 'a symbol for the way the political power in Stockholm dictates the way people live in rural areas'. Rural anger, and its electoral repercussions, may force the central government to allow culling. The Norwegian government has already taken such measures to contain a small offshoot from the revived Swedish wolf population, and illegal hunting may well finish it off altogether.

The passions aroused by the Scandinavian wolves might seem to suggest that western Europeans are as hostile to wolves as they are to bears. Popular reactions do seem to follow the messages handed down about these beasts in folk tales. But the most intense manifestations of lupophobia arise from competition for prey. The grey wolf is a class up from the Eurasian lynx in size and chooses its prey accordingly, targeting red deer or other hoofed animals of similar proportions. In Scandinavia, that places them at odds with human hunters whose target is reindeer. An additional source of grievance arises from the wolves' view of dogs as competitors to be eliminated, as lynxes in Spain regard foxes.

In Scotland, however, the value of deer to humans is significantly different. Venison remains a minority taste, and hunters are interested mainly in antlers. The market is for stags, to be shot for trophies; large numbers of hinds are surplus to requirements and are culled to keep deer densities under control. A study published in the *Proceedings of the Royal Society of London* argued that wolves in Scotland would actually do deer estates a favour by saving them the expense of culling, a procedure that barely covers its costs even with trophy shooting incorporated. They would thin down the density of deer in the Highlands, perhaps by more than half, which would help to increase the density of the forests. Climate change adds force to this argument. The general rule that milder winters favour forest pests applies to large mammals as well as to tiny invertebrates. Deer numbers are likely to increase as the effects of cold are eased. A report by Forestry Commission Scotland also notes that, as trees will be more vulnerable to fire and wind in a warming climate, the scrub that fills the resulting gaps will provide extra cover for deer.

While the wolves' effect on the woodlands would be positive, they would inevitably pose a threat to livestock. Sheep are medium-sized, hoofed, and not very fast. Wolves made their renewed presence in eastern Germany impossible to ignore when they slaughtered thirty-three sheep in two attacks on a single flock. But as the authors of the paper on wolves and deer point out, the loss of a sheep does not mean the same to an upland farmer today as it once would have done. Like deer and grouse, sheep are barely profitable, if at all; upland farm balance sheets depend on subsidies rather than sales at market. With compensation payments for killed stock, it should be possible to make farm finances indifferent to wolves.

In Germany, where wolves returned after an absence of nearly a century, a group called Sicherheit und Artenschutz (Security and Species Protection) not only protested against the threat to animals that humans hunt or keep, but raised the old spectre of a threat to humans themselves. The threat is minor but the fear is understandable. According to a study published in 2002, the risk is 'very, very low' in Europe and North America. The researchers found nine records of lethal wolf attacks on humans in Europe, excluding Russia, during the previous fifty years, eight of them in Russia, and none in North America. Five involved rabid wolves; the other four were confined to one area, Galicia in north-western Spain. Similar numbers were recorded from Russia. Across most of Europe, the threat of the wolf lies beyond living memory, before the twentieth century, in the days when children tended flocks and gathered mushrooms or berries in the forests.

Nevertheless, the attacks of the past few decades provide frightful reminders of how the wolf got its place in the folk tales. All the Galician victims were young children. In 1957, a wolf attacked two five-year-old boys who were walking along a road, killing one of them; another five-year-old was critically injured in a similar attack nearby the following year, and a four-year-old was killed the year after that. In July 1974, a wolf snatched a child of eleven months in one incident and a three-year-old in another; both died. When wolves prey on humans, they prey on the weakest. Over ninety per cent of victims are under eighteen, and most of those are under ten. Attacks by rabid wolves, on the other hand, are indiscriminate. An infected wolf may be driven great distances by its viral rage, which is especially furious in wolves, biting every human and animal it can find. People bitten on the head or face are in particularly grave danger, as the virus is likely to reach the brain before treatment can check it.

Rabies has been limited in western Europe by vaccination programmes; it is kept out of the British Isles by quarantine and sea. The Galician attacks were geographically isolated and have not been repeated for over thirty years. It is abnormal for a wolf to regard humans as prey. In the Scottish Highlands there are abundant deer and relatively few people, making the chance of mishaps even more remote. But in a culture increasingly fearful of risks in general and risks to children in particular, even a remote chance might be felt to be too high.

There is also a psychological difference between accepting the natural return of a species and assenting to its artificial reintroduction. Even if people would rather not have wolves back in the woods near them, they may be inclined to feel that if nature has managed to take such a course despite all the obstacles humans have placed in its way, it has earned the wolves at least a conditional right to be there. An artificially introduced wolf, however, would not qualify for a claim on natural justice. In Scotland, the matter would be clear: wolves could only resume a legitimate existence in the wild with official permission. The government would only take on the implied responsibility for the wolves' subsequent actions if it was confident that it could say it was enacting the people's will.

Any re-wilding scheme has to find its own way of resolving the problem that the term is an oxymoron. Only nature can recreate nature. Everything else is engineering. Trees for Life mitigate the contradiction by drawing upon patience and a long time horizon. Although they fence and plant, their ideal is for the seeds to sow themselves. Although they insist that the large mammals must return, they are also clear that there is a natural order to be followed. First the trees must grow and the habitats form, then the animals can come back. This patient respect for nature's timescales also has the political advantage of deferring the need to negotiate reintroductions. By the time Trees for Life are ready to release beavers around Loch Beinn a' Mheadhoin, the political battles will likely have been fought and precedents set elsewhere.

Not all re-wilders are so patient, though. In 2003, Paul Lister bought the 9,300-hectare Alladale estate, fifty miles north of Inverness, and set about turning it into the Alladale Wilderness Reserve. The son of the man who founded the MFI furniture retailing chain, Lister came up from the south with a businessman's view of how things should be done. He had money to invest and he wanted to see results. The first birches, rowans, pines and alders that his workers planted – leaving the Caledonian forest to regenerate on its own would take too long for him – were still saplings when he brought in a small herd of wild boar and followed them up with a couple of elks from Sweden. At Alladale, mammals come first.

Not only are they given priority over the development of their habitat, but they are also to be given precedence over humans. Paul Lister is captivated by wolves, but also impressed by the potential dangers they pose. His proposed solution is a sixty-kilometre electric fence, the longest in Europe. Alladale is conceived as a 'controlled Wilderness and Wildlife Reserve'. There is no embarrassment about the oxymoron 'controlled wilderness'. It is simply the compromise necessary to get paws on the ground. In time, Lister envisages, those could include the paws of bear and lynx as well as wolves.

Within the fenced perimeter, Alladale would be run as an animal tourism enterprise centred upon Alladale Lodge. It would be a park, in which the forestry – and the number of large animals in it – would be decided by management rather than nature. Alladale's scientific credibility has been boosted by the instigation of a partnership with Oxford University's Wildlife Conservation Research Unit, but management decisions must inevitably be guided by commercial considerations, such as the pressure to increase visitors' chances of seeing the estate's charismatic but elusive inhabitants. Pragmatic business-minded measures, such as increasing the numbers of photogenic mammals or luring them into view at feeding stations, would make the reserve still less like a wilderness and more like a zoo.

The priority Lister gives to the formerly native beasts requires what he calls 'sacrifice', meaning that members of the public should have their rights of access to his estate curtailed. Describing himself as a 'custodian', he pointed out to the Glasgow *Sunday Herald* that Alladale is less than one per cent of the Highlands. 'There are lots of places where people can walk in Scotland,' he observed. This went down poorly with the Ramblers' Association of Scotland, which saw it as a challenge to a law passed only five years previously that had 'established for Scotland some of the finest access legislation in Europe'. The Ramblers took a distinctly insouciant view of the risks posed by large carnivores, suggesting that evidence from elsewhere 'does not really support' the idea that bears or wolves are dangerous, and noting that the presence of such animals does not prevent people from going walking in central and eastern Europe. The implication appeared to be that the right to roam should be extended to wolves, not withdrawn from humans.

Lister's claims also raised the hackles of the comment-groundlings who posted responses on the *Sunday Herald*'s website, scornfully dismissing the landowner's argument as a bid to keep out the 'peasants'. Putting animals before people has powerfully emotive resonances in the Highlands: one commentator was quick to caricature the project as a new phase of the Clearances – 'First sheep, now wolves.' Ventures such as Paul Lister's will be seen by many as the pursuit of private privilege rather than justice for wild animals.

Others, however, may be persuaded to judge them by the numbers of visitors they attract to their areas and the numbers of jobs they create. If Alladale or a like-minded project managed to sustain itself, its economic effects would probably win it local support, and it might become a model that other estates or entrepreneurs would consider following in the Scottish Highlands. It would help to naturalise the idea that there can be value, of one kind or another, in the renewed presence of formerly native species.

One of the most notable things about Paul Lister is that he has bought a Highland estate but has not bought into the tradition of stalking, shooting and fishing. He is inspired by the Pleistocene epoch rather than the Victorian era. If the economics of the Victorian recreational industries continue to lack lustre, landowners may be less inclined to play the deer-stalking laird. As the prestige of conservation grows, along with the scarcity value in a warming climate of misty northern peatlands, landowners might become increasingly keen to make the landscapes they control resemble wilderness. They may pick from the post-glacial menu like Paul Lister, or work with what remains to hand in the Highlands. John Mackenzie, whose family has controlled the Gairloch estate in Wester Ross since the late fifteenth century, has covered 3,000 hectares of moorland with more than three million trees, half of them Scots pines and the rest a Caledonian forest mixture of birch, juniper, rowan, cherry, alder and holly. This wilderness has been created with the aid of a £2-million grant and the use of helicopters, which airlifted seedlings into the less accessible reaches of the estate.

Wolves, bears, boar, lynx; red herrings all. The myth that the glens must have monarchs is a beguiling distraction from the truly dominant animal power in the land. Even if every tract of regenerated pine and birch harboured a pack of wolves, they would do less to deter people from roaming the Highlands than the taunting, maddening aerial agitation that is *Culicoides impunctatus*: the Highland biting midge. Impenetrable Caledonian forests, ferocious Pictish tribes and land-clearing lairds have all been blamed for compounding the isolation that arises because Britain's highest mountains are in its northernmost reaches, but insect bites are every bit as credible a population-depressing factor in a region that still contains fewer than ten people per square kilometre. Forestry managers once estimated that up to a fifth of summer working days were lost because midges kept their men out of the forests. Lacking the option of refuge indoors, deer may lose weight through the debilitating effects of midge persecution, and cattle may yield less milk.

As Trees for Life put it, the midge is 'a guardian of wildness in the Highlands'. Nothing provokes it more than a car that has just pulled into a visitors' car park, an egregious superstimulus for an insect configured to seek out large warm objects that emit carbon dioxide. *Culicoides impunctatus* is at home where people are not, breeding in boggy, acid soil that is hard to traverse and cannot be cultivated. In the hanging damp of the Loch Beinn a' Mheadhoin woods, midges are suspended like molecules ready to be precipitated by objects showing signs of animal life. When it rains the air becomes electric with particles of spite. They seem as copious as raindrops, an impression confirmed by studies that recorded the emergence of half a million midges from an area of two square metres, and trapped two kilograms of the insects in a single measuring station nightly.

Midges do not drive out intruders, as wasps or bulls will, but rather force them to keep moving. They do not give walkers long enough to tie their bootlaces or change their outer clothes in response to swings in the mood of the Highland weather. Limbs can be bare if a vigorous stride is maintained, but the consequences of a pause are indicated by observations in which an average of 99 midges, and a maximum of 635, were counted landing per minute upon the exposed arms of dedicated volunteers in Argyllshire. These attentions do not reflect any particular preference for human targets. Deer are the midges' favourites, followed by cattle; sheep blood also forms a major part of their diet, though the lanolin in sheep wool tends to put them off.

In a changing climate, the midges' fortunes will be determined by the balance between the favours they receive in winter, from milder temperatures and heavier rains, and the stresses that drier summers will impose on them. Scotland's midges are sensitive to climate, and people in Scotland are sensitive to midges. If on balance a changing climate inhibits *C. impunctatus*, one of the major impediments to human use and enjoyment will be eased. If a changed climate turns out to suit the Highland midge better than the one it has been used to, the region's wildness will be guarded all the better.

A more immediate concern is that new relationships between different midge species arising from climate change are thought to underlie the spread of bluetongue virus into northern Europe. Bluetongue's principal victims are sheep, for whom it is often fatal, and its principal vector, the creature that carries it to new victims, is the midge *Culicoides imicola*. Until the late 1990s the disease was known in Africa and occasionally seen on the northern side of the Mediterranean, in Iberia or Turkey. Over the next few years it moved 500 miles north, appearing in Italy, the large islands of the western Mediterranean,

Albania and the former Yugoslavia as far north as Croatia: all places where temperature increases had been particularly marked. Six strains of the virus were involved; one and a half million sheep died.

Bluetongue had now outrun its familiar vector. *C. imicola* lives in a warm, even climate, with dry summers and mean annual temperatures between 12 and 20°C. Forty per cent of the southern European bluetongue outbreaks occurred beyond its range. Then in 2006 the disease broke out in a northern European cluster that took in the Netherlands, Belgium, Luxembourg and adjacent areas of Germany and France. It had spread from the Mediterranean to the North Sea in less than ten years. In the summer of 2007 the first British case was recorded in Suffolk, where the virus soon began to circulate between local mammals and midges.

The new hosts may have been cattle, which harbour the virus without succumbing to it. The new vectors may have been members of the *Culicoides obsoletus* and *Culicoides pulicaris* species groups, which are thought to be the craft in which bluetongue virus has flown north, or possibly *Culicoides dewulfi*, a species suspected of spreading the epidemic that arose in the Netherlands. With some forty-seven species of midge recorded in Britain, there is no shortage of potential future suspects. If one type of midge encroaches upon the range of another that is susceptible to infection, the latter can then spread the pathogens throughout its own range. This is known as the 'baton effect'. It can be augmented by trade or by the elements. Outbreaks may arise from the movement of infected animals, or possibly the transfer of midges in consignments of other goods. In the air, *Culicoides* also has the advantage of size. It is small enough to become 'aerial plankton', borne long distances by the winds. Bluetongue was carried 200 miles across the Mediterranean to the Balearic Islands, from Tunisia or Sardinia, aboard midges.

The winds may blow stronger as the climate changes, and the rises in temperature certainly favour midge-vectored viruses in several ways. Mild winters spare midges, and warm summers make them busier (though the effect is counteracted if the summers are also dry). The viruses will require warmth in order to replicate, because the enzyme upon which their synthesis depends has an optimal working temperature of 28–29°C, and becomes inactive below 10°C. They may also gain an advantage from their vectors' physiology: higher temperatures may render the midge gut 'leaky', allowing the viruses easier passage into the body proper, and thence to the salivary glands where they can mix with the secretions that enter the wounds inflicted by the insect.

As the climate warms further, bluetongue outbreaks may become steadily more common in these new northern territories. Vaccinations may become more effective, and dry summers may reverse the midges' gains, but they cannot alter the fact that bluetongue has arrived in northern Europe or the likelihood that this has been a swift result of climate change. It may not be a solitary arrival, either. African horse sickness virus (AHSV), which kills up to ninety-five per cent of its victims, is closely related to bluetongue virus and is spread by *C. imicola*. It has appeared in Iberia, where it has been found in *C. obsoletus*, the dominant *Culicoides* midge of southern England. AHSV needs more warmth than bluetongue virus; it cannot replicate if the temperature falls below 15°C. It could well become a summer threat in the British Isles, and grow in its menace as the summers warm. Although both these diseases would multiply faster in the south than the north, there should be no barrier to their transport throughout Britain. Midge species such as *C. obsoletus*, *C. pulicaris* and *C. dewulfi* occupy almost all of the island, from the south-east of England to the north of Scotland.

One way to avoid Highland midges is to visit in the spring or autumn, but at those times of year the midge's role is taken by the tick. *Ixodes ricinus* resembles a tiny spider with a dorsal shield, underneath which bulges a sac that, on a good day for blood-sucking, can balloon the arachnid from about three millimetres to nearly a centimetre in size. The requirements of the tick are clear. It needs hosts; small ones like mice or blackbirds will do when it is a larva or a nymph, but when it becomes an adult it needs big hosts like deer or sheep. It needs moisture to prevent it from drying out between meals; woodland floors, leaf-shaded and leaf-littered, covered in deep reefs of organic accumulation, are ideal. In short, it thrives upon deer and dampness. Glen Affric, in its current condition, could have been made for it.

With the discipline of frost easing, the ticks in Glen Affric are remaining active through the winter. As winters in Sweden grew milder and shorter from the 1980s to the 1990s, ticks spread north and became denser in the south. A climate that becomes increasingly indulgent towards ticks could encourage the spread of several diseases. When a tick pierces a host's skin, it injects a cocktail of secretions including a cement to keep its barb fixed in place, an anaesthetic to mute its host's pain alarm, and a vasodilator to open up the blood vessels into which it taps. Pathogens may be an additional ingredient. Sheep ticks are the vector for a virus that causes louping ill in sheep and a number of other species, including deer and cattle. The name refers to the characteristic hopping or 'louping' gait that the infection may produce if it lodges in the victim's nervous system, along with other distressing effects, frequently including death. Although it is possible for humans to catch louping ill, the main threats to human health associated with ticks in Europe are tick-borne encephalitis (TBE), caused by a close relative of the louping-ill virus, and Lyme borreliosis, the 'Lyme disease' that has acquired an unsettling reputation as a woodland hazard in North America and has now reached the British Isles. Lyme disease infections can also enter the nervous system, as well as the heart and the joints, though antibiotics should suppress them before they reach that stage.

TBE is considered unlikely to spread to Britain as the climate changes. The effects of climate change on Lyme disease are harder to foresee, because they cut both ways. Ticks will stir earlier in milder springs, but may find their early advantages reversed by dry summers. They are unlikely to find a better summer haven than the peaty woodlands, introverted and saturated, around the Glen Affric lochs. If it were simply a question of climate, tick densities in the inner Glen might be among the highest anywhere, since few places are likely to be more humid. It is also a question of hosts, though, and if the return of the wild were to drive down the number of deer, the number of ticks would drop as well. But with fewer deer, the ticks would have to spend more time in the undergrowth 'questing' for hosts and latching onto humans.

And what would the humans have been doing all this time? It may seem unduly fatalistic to speculate about the future without including efforts to eradicate or at least repel pests like midges and ticks. Efforts to devise new defences will undoubtedly continue. But the struggle between humans and parasites is an arms race between innovation and evolution. Parasites have the advantage of numbers, putting up a barrage of variation from which, sooner or later, a resistant variant may well get through. This will then multiply, and humans will have to find a new means to counter it. Midges and ticks may be repressed, but they are likely to return.

As the climate changes, natural selection may also restore the organisms' operating efficiency by tuning them to the new conditions. They will face competition from newcomers, but may enjoy an advantage as incumbents. When the British Isles were recolonised after the last ice age, the incomers were competing to establish themselves in virgin territory. Different niches would be occupied by the species best suited to them. With climate change, the situation will be different. Although climatic and other habitat conditions in a particular area may on paper be most suitable for one particular species, it may not be able to displace a species already in occupation.

Midges should stand quite a good chance of seeing off new competitors. They already enjoy the advantage of overwhelming numbers, and rising temperatures will tend to make them more numerous still, by allowing more of them to survive winters, and possibly by giving them the opportunity to squeeze another round of breeding into the year. The more of them there are, the more variants will arise that are better suited to the new conditions, and as these breed, the better adapted the local midges will become.

Elsewhere the benefits of warmth may be reversed as it dries the land in summer, but in Glen Affric the midges should be secure. In the east, the wooded shores are likely to remain immersed in their own private climate, and to the west, the peat will remain safe from desiccation in 'this wettest corner of Europe'.

*

Fasnakyle power station still stands at the entrance to the Glen, still spinning electricity from the river. The turbine machinery has been replaced, but it operates on the same hydro-electric principles that were first applied in the late nineteenth century; and are now applied across the Highlands in hundreds of plants, from stations feeding the national grid to miniature rotors lodged in hillside springs, powering farmhouse kettles. The building that houses the plant is admired; its stone cladding is seen to acknowledge nature's strength, and it seems modest, fitting into its surroundings rather than trying to dominate them. These qualities are appreciated in a society that has been forced to reflect hard upon its relationship with nature. Aficionados of period architecture sometimes contrast Fasnakyle with the contemporaneous South Bank development in London, now condemned not for its brutal appearance but for the carbon profligacy of its concrete masses.

The stewards of Glen Affric have taken up an idea

from a more down-to-earth urban example. They have pedestrianised the Glen. The road that continues westwards from the power station is closed to private motor vehicles, imposing a de facto criterion of physical fitness for admission to the lochs. People entering quasi-wilderness are expected to enter into the spirit of the thing. If they are under any illusions as they cycle or stride in, those are dispelled as soon as they pause for breath and the midges materialise around them. The Highland biting midges are not quite as thick in the summer now that the open spaces are drier, but other species have moved in to keep the air filled with minute slicing blades. All have evolved a considerable degree of indifference to the various repellents and insecticides that have been deployed against them over the years.

Places like these, with no large towns nearby, are not expected to play the mass amenity role imposed upon national parks in England. They have been deliberately constructed to differ in character from such areas. As the effects of climate change began to tell upon Britain, they encouraged Scotland to distance itself from its neighbour's economy. The Scottish public and its politicians became increasingly disinclined to help pay the costs imposed by the climate on the threatened coasts and overheated cities of England. They protested loudly that a small country should not be expected to pay for the problems of a quite large and prosperous one; the argument became a powerful expression of the case for independence. At the same time, climate change enhanced Scotland's opportunities to develop its differences in character from England, and the idea of wilderness became more stirring than ever.

Small nations have had to accept that the extent to which they may be shaped from within is limited. Their stability and prosperity depend upon their relationships with the wider world. The vision of a nation suspended in the world's nets has become as much part of Scotland's self-image as the tartan myths of the nineteenth century. All the same, the fantasy of self-determination remains alluring, and for Scotland there is a powerful symbolic consolation in the way that its Atlantic mantle defies outside climatic influences. Even while Scots liked the idea of being successful citizens of the world, their pulses quickened at the thought of recreating the forests of tribal Caledonia that were said to have kept the Roman legions out. Once the Scottish government started issuing passports, wild irresistibly meant free.

Within Glen Affric, the appearance of wilderness has been achieved by management that sees everything but is itself invisible. Space has not been urbanised in the manner that has become familiar further south. There are no obligatory paths from which visitors may not stray. Instead, electronic monitoring is used to keep people and wildlife apart. Rather than enclosing areas, rangers operate like air-traffic controllers, monitoring the positions of humans relative to animal groups and guiding the former away from the latter when necessary. As with air-traffic control, this demands concentration, for now there are animals in the Glen that could pose a real threat to visitors.

In more remote areas, electronic surveillance not only directs rescuers when people get into difficulties, but monitors where all of them are at any given time. Nobody can remember a time when there was anywhere on the surface of the British Isles where a mobile could not get a signal, and people do not feel that these devices alienate them from the organic world any more than their ancestors felt that the use of maps or guide-books compromised their relationship with nature. Electronic images are now so naturalistic, and the devices themselves so discreet, that they have come to seem almost organic themselves.

Although virtual images have become part of the quasi-natural world, feelings run as high as they ever did in previous generations about intrusions into actual views. There are no new buildings in the Glen at all. Forestry roads have been dug up and left to the forest. Road signs and visitor information boards have gone, made redundant by the road closures and the personalised delivery of electronic information. The deer fences were taken down long ago: the deer are fewer, and the woods now have new forms of protection.

A new threat hangs over the trees, however, and it has already stripped a great tract of forest back to raw carbon. Fires break out more easily in the drier summers, spreading underground through the peat. Dousing them would take effort but would not pose any great difficulty in a valley holding two large lochs. The obstacle is philosophical. Does the principle of letting nature take its course extend to spontaneous burning? Fires are more frequent nowadays, and the increase is attributed to climate change, but how can one say that climate change is the cause of any particular fire? While conservationists wrestle with these questions, the fires are left to burn themselves out.

Greater harm is done by older threats that are no longer held in check by the colder seasons. Unchilled insects survive the winters and quickly set to breeding in the early warmth; fungi flourish in the wet springs. Every so often, swarms of pine sawflies erupt in the glen and strip the needles from pines, weakening them and leaving them vulnerable to pine shoot beetles, which finish many of the trees off. Birches succumb to the *Phytophthora* infestations that brew up in the mild wet conditions. The forest's complexion is left ashen in parts and jaundiced in others. Throughout the woodlands, the effects of climate change can be seen as clearly as they can be felt.

In themselves the warmer temperatures have benefited the trees in the east of the Glen, as has the carbon-fortified atmosphere. The woods are now part of a much larger Caledonian forest – but it stops at the head of Loch Beinn a' Mheadhoin. Attempts to push the forest out to the west faltered and were abandoned as the winter ground became increasingly waterlogged. Re-foresting could not be sustained in the face of obviously deteriorating conditions. A few trees remain, but they are outnumbered by stumps and skeletons.

If Frank Fraser Darling were still alive, he would still see 'wet desert' in the west, but the mystique of Glen Affric has only deepened. Many of the granny Scots pines are still standing, having proved their ability to withstand several centuries' worth of climatic fluctuations and weather extremes; the oldest are now around 450 years old. Visitors who stand in the older parts of the forest feel the past more intensely than ever.

Although the mix of trees is largely the same, re-wilding has added charisma to the animals. The beaver families that have entrenched themselves around the two main lochs each range along several thousand metres of wooded banks. Where they can, they simply tunnel into the soft soils at the water's edge, shovelling out a burrow that opens below the waterline. If there is a danger that the level of the stream may fall and leave the entrance exposed to the air, the beavers dam the course below their den to make the water pool up behind the barrier. In places where the bank is too low for a burrow, they build lodges of stacked branches instead.

It's said that beavers can't stand the sound of running water. The waves along the shores of Loch Beinn a' Mheadhoin are too turbulent for them. Even there, though, sheltered backwaters can be found; all in all, the lochs and their hinterlands make only modest demands on their engineering skills. Like other members of the rodent order, they are can-do animals. In Glen Affric they can find niches where tributaries come down to the major lochs, or around the small lochans in the woodlands; at a pinch, once the better spots are taken, they can make do with the river banks.

Besides calm water, beavers need food, both leaf and wood. When the banks are green they can graze on the understorey; when the trees are green they fell them in order to get at the leaves. In winter they can live off the wood itself, a beaver being a mutualistic system comprising a mammal that does the mechanical work and a hindgut-full of bacteria that deal with the chemistry, breaking down the cellulose of which the wood is made. In autumn they gather branches and store them underwater for winter feed.

As to climate, they are not much perturbed. Before human history began to unfold, beavers occupied territories from the Mediterranean to the Siberian tundra.

They encounter nothing in the Scottish Highlands of the late twenty-first century that they have not encountered before. If anything, climate change has tilted the balance in Glen Affric to their benefit, to the extent that it favours birch rather than Scots pine, for which they have no use. Their preference for birch provides local opportunities for pine, however, which they leave to grow while felling the competition.

Finding all they need around the glen, they have made themselves at home. Their presence is visible occasionally in piled branches, but mainly in the narrow tracts where they have thinned the timber by felling birch and rowan saplings. They will not go far for birch or rowan, fifty metres or so at most, but they will trek ten times further for aspen, their favourite tree. Each of their dwellings houses a single family, numbering five or so: parents, the year's offspring, known as kits, and some older siblings. There is something of the American settler about them, the industrious nuclear family building its home and clearing a space in the woods, laying up stores for the winter; except that in beaver families it is the adult female who is dominant. They have more ancient connotations too, adding to the sense that as the climate changes, the Pleistocene epoch is returning, filling the valley with birch and stocky herbivores of the kind whose rolling lines were the gleam in the Palaeolithic cave artists' eyes.

And following the rounded herbivores have come angular carnivores. As time has passed, the idea that wildness needs tooth and claw has grown more persuasive. The thought of the wolf still provokes a shiver, as it probably always will in places that actually go dark at night, but the edge has been taken off the ancient fears by the embrace of the re-wilding vision. The local human population remains small and some distance removed, while sentiment within it has shifted as people have moved to the area to be near something like a wilderness. But the presence of wolves is not at root a local issue. It is a landscape question. A wolf population large enough to maintain its genetic vigour and be insured against catastrophe – a couple of hundred animals – needs a landscape it can disappear in: perhaps a hundred square kilometres for every two wolves. For a population two hundred strong, that implies over a third of the entire Highland region, which itself covers a third of Scotland.

In political terms this makes it a national question, and it has taken the nation's commitment to bring the wolf back. The Caledonian vision of nature has struck increasingly resonant chords with Scottish people, and governments have done what they can to make it a reality. In the Highlands the state has led, guided and directed the major landowners into a position where they feel that they share the same interests. Like the forests created by William the Conqueror's decree in England a thousand years before, the new Scottish wilderness is a political and bureaucratic construction.

In this new Caledonia the wolf is expected to provide charisma and to cull deer. The beaver has also given it an additional role. Although beavers have long since become an accepted part of the ecological furniture, it is felt appropriate that they should have some neo-natural predators. Around the world wolves prefer to prey on large hoofed mammals, of which red deer are an excellent example for their purposes, but they will readily take beavers too. Polish wolves did much to keep beaver numbers down in the late twentieth century, and may have kept them out of some areas altogether. Wolves' attacks on beavers in other European countries suggested a solution when people began to complain that there were now too many beavers in Scotland. The logic of re-wilding is that new herbivores lead to new carnivores.

A small pack of wolves, at most times about half a dozen strong, has made its base in the densest part of the forest south of Loch Beinn a' Mheadhoin, seeking as deep a belt of cover from humans as it can find. In winter the females retreat into the earth, down tunnels a couple of metres or more to secure bunkered nurseries for their offspring. These dens need to be dry: wolves are built to scrabble rather than to shovel, but even if they could dig the peat and mire out, the water would well back up into the tunnels and drown the pups. Fortunately for the wolves, much of the southern forest grows on brown earth soils that are topped by only a few centimetres of peat, drain well and yield to scratching claws. These areas also suit pines, with their aversion to waterlogging. The emblematic Caledonian tree and the epitome of wild forest nature, toothed and clawed, are thus drawn together for reasons of drainage.

From this heartland the grey dogs set out across the forest to hunt as darkness falls. They are most active at sunset and sunrise, when the red deer are also abroad; their canine eyes are adapted to twilight. In open country they might be forced to range over many miles each night, but the forest attracts deer, themselves in search of food. For much of the time the wolves can meet their needs locally, but the glen is not big enough to contain them entirely. At times they are seen on the road and rumoured near houses; at times they strike out onto the moor and are heard under the moon. They move mainly at night, the forest cover in Glen Affric being too narrow to keep them as far from humans in the daytime as they would like. During the hot spells that descend with increasing frequency upon the glen, the wolves retire to damper corners of the woods. They rest up through the close evenings, preferring to save their energies for the cold dawn.

There are lynx here too, but nobody is ever quite sure they have seen one. In photos ornamental, in practice invisible, they have been slipped into the landscape without alarm or controversy.

7

Mountain Avens

In the folds of the hillsides, walls become hedges; ruins become groves, roofed once again by trees and bushes. Above, on the hills' broad backs, walls and land alike are naked to the sky; ruins gape roofless and the ground is a creased brow of bare grey rock. This narrow pair of walls was a mass house, the map says, and the masonry next door, its only neighbour on the hill, was a shebeen; a place of worship and a place to drink in a plot together. From north to south and from east to west run walls with their craggy arms folded, clenched stones enclosing tracts of stone. A gaunt sense of humour seems to have been at work up here.

The mischief runs from top to bottom. You will get nowhere if you let the walls and the thickets stand in your way, but then again you may not get to where you think you are going either. British notions like rights of access or rights to roam do not apply here. There are few paths and few rights, but custom generally allows wanderers to wander where the land takes them. It can be slow going. Although the slope ahead might look green enough from down below, its sward may turn out to be a rug covering rubble. Every step has to be tentative: test or twist.

Around the seaward face of the hill there is a green road instead, following the same course as the paved and brisk coast road, but higher up and arcaded with flowers through spring and summer. Easy as the path is, though, the hill makes sport with gravity, exerting an upward pull. On the green road you would go smoothly round the headland, but you would never find out what was at the top. The texture of the slope is intriguing too; made of boulders yet preposterously abundant in vegetation. These plants seem to have forgotten about their natural habitats, jostling for space on limestone rocks on the west coast of Ireland, moorland heather and meadow orchids side by side. What's the attraction? Maybe the answer is at the top of the mountain.

Above the tangled bank the flowers yield en masse to the rock, which now appears as great tables of pavement, deeply fissured. These clefts, some of which run as straight as the pavements lie flat, now serve as deep havens from which blooms and fern fronds uncurl. Wherever the limestone cracks or shatters, there is an opportunity for delicate petals: the pink dabs of saxifrage, the lapis-lazuli blue star of spring gentian, the mauve blush of the hysterically misnamed bloody cranesbill. These flowers' attachment to the rock is fervent.

At certain moments, even in sunshine, the rock seems to release shade that it has absorbed: every now and then there is a hint of foreboding, of warning. A glance up, and there is a hare a few yards away on the skyline, but not for long. Irish folklore maintained an unhealthy suspicion of hares. 'There's no doubt at all there's some that's not natural,' a man from this part of the world averred to Augusta Gregory, who collected folklore in the west of Ireland during the early decades of the twentieth century.

'There's something queer about them, and there's some that it's dangerous to meddle with, and that can go into any form where they like.'

Even the one emphatic stamp left by human labour halfway up the mountain seems to have something about it that eludes explanation. On a cracked apron of limestone flags looking out to the west, towards the whale-convoy of the Aran islands, a curtain of piled rocks has been drawn around a space twenty-odd paces across. Only a narrow gap has been left unshielded, on the inland side looking up towards the top of the mountain, as if in fear of the sea. Its height and its heavy-shouldered embrace imply defences, but against what? Thomas Westropp, founding father of the region's archaeology, was mystified: 'The approach from the north is so steep as to be practically inaccessible; indeed, it seems wonderful that anyone took such a wind-swept, waterless brow for a residence, or, having done so, took pains to strengthen almost impassable crags and grassy slopes of rock, with a wall 12 feet high, on a ridge 647 feet above a harbourless and stormy shore.' The fort's name, Cathair Dhúinn Irghus, itself further mystifies the site. It claims the ruin for Irghus, a chieftain of the Fir Bolg, one of the mythical ancient races of Ireland.

Now the hill sweeps up to a low abrupt cliff and shelves into a series of terraces, like the weathered remains of some vanished civilisation. The cliffs that separate them are mostly only a few metres high, and have crumbled at so many points that it is a simple puzzle to find a route from one level to the next – and on the way back down, there is a succession of thrills in venturing up to cliff edges and peering over, trying to retrace the route. This mountain, ground into its present shape by great masses of ice that last retreated ten thousand years ago, plays the kind of game that computers have now spread around the world. It lures players irresistibly on to the next level.

With each successive one the texture changes. The competition among the plants is thinning out; wiry grasses have the run of the high ground, or such of it as will let roots bind. Mountain flowers are more in their element and more assertive in their presence: clumps of saxifrage and mats of mountain avens, a dwarf shrub with a pale moon flower and tough little wrinkled leaves, proofed against the cold of the high Arctic where it more typically occurs. This tundra primrose seems to have moved in as the glaciers retreated, while the ground was still cold, and to have remained here ever since. About 700 other kinds of plant, four-fifths of all the species that occur in Ireland, also find a home here in the Burren region of County Clare. 'Burren' comes from the Irish *boíreann*, a rocky place, but the area and its conundrums are better expressed by the Latin dedication attached to the abbey at Corcomroe, somewhere in the haze to the east: *Sancta Maria de Petra Fertilis*, Saint Mary of the Fertile Rock.

Geographers draw not on Irish or Latin but German to describe the Burren landscape. It is known as karst, after the Austrian name for a region of Slovenia. Karst is limestone whose flaws are enlarged and elaborated upon by water. Rain is faintly acidic because of the carbon dioxide in the atmosphere, which combines with water to form carbonic acid; it dissolves calcium carbonate, of which limestone is an immensely compressed form. The rain weathers exposed surfaces and finds the weaknesses in them, eroding its way into the rock. In the Burren it reveals the long stress-lines, carving them down into the deep fissures known as grykes. The slabs in between them are called clints; both words come from the Pennines of northern England, which also have limestone pavements.

As the rain falls, it slips through the surface fissures and percolates rapidly away through the underground cavities and ducts that it has dissolved for itself. In karst country watercourses are subterranean and caves are numerous, but ponds and streams are scarce. Across the four hundred square kilometres of the Burren there are just four kilometres of surface river; the Caher, which flows along the western base of the heights defended by Irghus's fort, through a valley known as the Khyber Pass. There are lakes in the region, but only in winter; these turloughs, as they are known, dry up in summer. They are almost unique to Ireland; there is just one outside it, in Wales.

An early report, by an Englishman named Thomas Dineley who travelled through the area in 1680, summarises the Burren as 'one entire rock with here and there a little surface of Earth'. It can certainly seem so, on the scalped pates of the upper mountainsides, but there is more to the Burren than that. A modern survey, using satellite images, shows that about a fifth of the Burren is limestone pavement, half of which is bare and half to a significant extent vegetated. Most of the region is grassland; much of it moor and heath on the high ground; much of it improved, from the farmer's point of view, in the valleys. What is not grassed or bare is mostly in the close-knit grip of hazel thickets.

These are a recent development. They were conspicuous

by their absence in the seventeenth century, when Thomas Dineley and another Englishman who passed through the region both repeated a local saying about the Barony of Burren. According to Edmund Ludlow, the Burren was said to be 'a country where there is not water enough to drown a man, wood enough to hang one, nor earth enough to bury him'. He added that soil was 'so scarce, that the inhabitants steal it from one another'.

A country that lacked the wherewithal to hang a man must have seemed a desert indeed to Edmund Ludlow, who was a senior commander in the forces that broke the last coherent Irish resistance to the power of the English Parliament. The remaining Irish garrisons were besieged, Limerick falling in October 1651 and Galway in April 1652; the surrounding country became the scene for operations against Irish fighters who now resorted to guerrilla attacks upon the invaders. An absence of trees would have been a distinct inconvenience for soldiers who seem to have habitually reached for the rope to dispose of captured 'tories', as the insurgents were known. Counter-insurgency operations in those days did not trouble themselves with winning hearts and minds.

Ludlow also noted a logistical nuisance that his troops encountered on the rocky terrain. After a march of less than three miles, most of the horses had lost their shoes. By the end of the day, the stock of spares was so depleted that a horseshoe fetched five shillings. Dineley told a tale of how a traveller, reaching into a cleft between rocks that had twisted a shoe from his horse's hoof, found not just the missing one but dozens more besides. He observed that local inhabitants left their horses unshod, and also that they dispensed with harnesses: ploughs were tied to the tails of the horses that pulled them, so that the beasts halted when they felt the plough hit a rock, avoiding damage to the flimsy tackle.

Two centuries later, after the Great Famine of the 1840s, local people were said to gather brambles, ferns and the stems of mountain avens to burn. They would not have resorted to such meagre fuel if the hazel bushes had been allowed to assert their natural dominance. The glaciers had scoured the land in antiquity; latterly its human population scoured away what little was left on its surface. The local saying about the wood, the water and the earth not only enumerated scarcities, but spoke with ominous power about the violence that these scarcities engendered.

In the first quarter of the twentieth century the conflicts revolved around cattle. It was the land rather than the livestock that was at issue, but cows lend themselves to theft: a herd is easier to take than a field. Cattle-raiders drove herds off land in order to drive out the graziers, many of whom were outsiders, enabling local smallholders to take over the vacated tenancies. In the 1900s cattle drives might involve hundreds of people and had the character of popular demonstrations; they were used by the nationalist United Irish League to pursue land reform. Their character changed as the national struggles became wars; in the 1920s graziers were threatened not by torch-bearing processions but by masked men brandishing revolvers.

In the light of these struggles, what look at first like gaunt jokes start to make a bleak sense. Although it remains hard to imagine what natural threats might have induced the builders of Cathair Dhúinn Irghus to make an eyrie of it halfway up a mountain, it is exceptional only in its size and dramatic setting: there are five hundred other ring forts dotted across the Burren. They are also known as cashels, and despite varying degrees of elaboration they were essentially fortified cattle folds, used to defend livestock from the cattle drivers' early medieval predecessors. Above the Caher valley, the mass house and the shebeen were forced up the mountain together by threats of a different kind: in the early nineteenth century, Catholic worship and unlicensed alcohol were both against the law.

After the surrender of the Galway garrison in 1652 allowed the English to declare victory over the Irish Confederates, Parliament took steps to pay for the war by seizing Irish land. The dispossessed landowners were obliged to 'transplant' to the western province of Connacht or to County Clare. Some of the first transplanted persons were allocated land in the Burren: officials expressed fears that sending them to a place 'generally reputed and known to be sterill' would obstruct the project by 'disheartening' subsequent transplantees. Yet the Burren's reputation was not exclusively for sterility. There was always the redeeming paradox of the fertile rock. The earth might be so sparse that the inhabitants stole it from each other, and yet, Edmund Ludlow went on to report, 'their cattle are very fat; for the grass growing in turfs of earth, of two or three foot square, that lie between the rocks, which are of limestone, is very sweet and nourishing.' That was why it made sense, after all, to draw stonewall lines between one field of stone and another.

Assembling upon the rocks in their profusion, their unique diversity and their sublime indifference to their proper place, the flowers of the Burren have come to suggest a spiritual fertility. The Belfast poet Michael Longley vests them with a symbolic power to transcend conflict across Ireland in his poem 'The Ice Cream Man'. On a visit to the Burren, at the suggestion of a botanically minded friend, he made a list of all the plants he had seen that day. Later, when the man from whom his daughter bought ice creams was murdered by the IRA, she spent her ice-cream money on a bunch of carnations, which she laid outside his shop on the Lisburn Road. Longley added his own memorial by taking his list of flowers, meadowsweet to mountain avens, and setting it in his poem as a verbal wreath.

Another of his poems, 'Burren Prayer', is also garlanded with mountain avens. It ends with an appeal to Our Lady of the Fertile Rock – a remarkable invocation for a Belfast Protestant to make, as Longley himself is the first to point out. The Burren is no longer an eerie wasteland at the western limits of the British Isles that outsiders thank their gods they don't have to live in. It is seen as a place whose unique qualities are thrown into ever-sharper relief by the state of the world beyond; a place of which outsiders are in awe, and on which they feel they have a claim.

The map to use in the Burren was made by Tim Robinson, drawing by hand and surveying on foot, amassing knowledge so detailed, comprehensive and intimate that he seems capable of producing not just a two-inch scale map but a complete replica of this and the allied places – the Aran islands, geologically speaking an outstretched arm of the Burren, and Connemara on the northern side of Galway Bay – to which he has devoted himself.

Robinson suggests that in these landscapes, the usual

connotations of geometry are reversed. In most other places, straight lines signify artefacts and curves show nature's legacy. 'Here, though, it is as if the ground itself brings forth right angles.' It is the circular cashels that impose artifice, while the linear grain of the underlying rock is revealed by the grykes that cleave it. Cathair Dhúinn Irghus, the fort on the 'wind-swept, waterless brow' looking out towards the Arans, is an exception that proves the rule. It is not strictly a ring fort but an irregular form whose curvature has been partially straightened; aerial views show that one of its edges follows the line of a fault scored across the topography, like the thoughtless scratch left by a knife when it cuts through card into the table underneath.

Ancient occupiers have left behind plenty of lines and angles as well as circles. There are seventy-five Neolithic wedge tombs, so called because their walls and roofs are angled inwards: a wedge tomb is lower and narrower at the back than at the entrance. More imposing, as their somewhat pompous name suggests, are the portal tombs. They make the most of their entrances by framing them with massive flanking slabs and even larger capstones, overhanging and sloping down towards the back; the effect from the side is a little like a primitive statue of an elephant. The most famous is the one at Poulnabrone, in the middle of the Burren. It always seems to have at least a few visitors inspecting it – and in many cases probably thinking that it is quite a bit smaller than they had been led to expect.

In 1985 a crack was discovered in one of the slabs, and the repair work provided an opportunity for excavation. The major discovery was that of the remains of over twenty people, which spanned 600 years but seemed to have been placed in the tomb together as a single jumbled mass of bones, around 5,200 years ago. As significant in its own way, however, was what was found underneath the cairn on which the tomb is set: a layer of soil, about ten centimetres thick, on top of the limestone pavement. Thin layers of soil like this have also been found elsewhere in the Burren between the remains of ancient stone walls and the underlying rock.

The implication is that the Burren was once far less bare than it is now. To some researchers this suggests a familiar story, in which prehistoric farmers cleared the land of trees, exposing it to the elements, which then washed the soil away. In this light, the Burren should be seen as an artificial landscape rather than a glacial one. It became a scalped stone cranium in late prehistoric times for the same reason that in recent historic times its occupiers were hard put to find two sticks to rub together: because of the pressures to which it was subjected by the people who depended on it.

Not everybody is convinced that what is now mostly grey rock was once mostly green woods, though. David Jeffrey, a plant ecologist who made his first field trip to the Burren in 1958, points out that the soil must have gone some-where, but no trace of it has been found. In karst limestone country, water disappears underground through the open-ings in the rock, and that is where it would have carried the soil. The caves and tunnels underneath the Burren have been extensively explored, but there is no sign of the soil in the form of accumulated sediments.

Nevertheless, the few centimetres of soil trapped between natural pavements and Neolithic walls do imply that it would once have been easier to find the earth to

247

bury a man who did not qualify for a stone tomb. Pollen samples taken in the area suggest that for the past three thousand years, the past few hundred years excepted, the landscape bristled more thickly with hazel than it does today. At present about fifteen per cent of the Burren's surface is hazel-clad; the percentage will rise to the extent that grazing declines. In other places a vigorous eruption of hazel might look promising as a carbon-neutral fuel crop, but on this wheel-tormenting terrain it would probably take more energy to harvest than it released when burned.

The Burren's flowers need its cattle, who not only keep the hazel back but graze the fast-growing grasses that would otherwise choke out the flowers. Traditional farming practice in the area gives the cows an unusually long time in which to promote floral diversity. The kindly Atlantic ensures temperatures mild enough for the cattle to spend their winters on the mountain, living off vegetation that continues to grow for much of the period, unimpeded by frost or snow. In the Alps and elsewhere cattle are sent to high ground in summer; in the Burren it is the other way round, the winters as well as the rock being fertile.

Feral goats, with scimitar horns of biblical proportions, perform a similar service. But grazing alone would not allow seven hundred kinds of flower to bloom. Nor would it explain why the place is home to plants typically found in the Arctic, the Alps and the Mediterranean. They have been recognised as the puzzle at the heart of the Burren since the area first became a magnet for botanists in the nineteenth century. No definitive explanation has yet been agreed, tempting people to suggest that the puzzle cannot be solved.

For several scientists who have risen to the challenge, the key to the answer lies in the soil. Richard Moles, an environmental scientist, and his brother Norman, a geologist, combined their expertise in a series of studies on the Mullach Mór (Mullaghmore) and Sliabh Rua (Slieve Roe) hills in the south of the Burren. Quartering the terrain, a long tilted mound, they built up a picture of how the ice floods had advanced over the rock, scouring terraces and tearing faces off cliffs. They found tracts of soil containing granite pebbles, ground out and carried here by glaciers from Galway to the north. Other patches were a rusty orange colour, stained by high levels of iron. At first the brothers supposed that these soils had also been carried in by the ice, but on returning to the mountain after a break in their field studies, they noticed that a new flush of this rusty earth had appeared on a spot where goats had trampled the grass away. The orange soils were, the brothers realised, the filings of underlying shale deposits, rich in iron, that had been exposed by the inexorable ice. Looking at an 'erratic', one of the thousands of boulders left sitting like dragons' eggs upon the limestone shelves after the melting of the glaciers that bore them in, Norman Moles realised that if such a rock were made of shale and succumbed to weathering, it might leave a dab of rust upon the lime background.

Processes such as these have left the Burren with a mineral surface that appears uniform but is chemically variegated. Limestone gives rise to alkaline soils, whereas soils from the shale and the Galway granite are more acidic. The effect of the glacial bulldozing has thus been to dapple the alkaline surface with acidic pockets. Weathering

249

adds to the variety, as the Moles brothers showed on Sliabh Rua. Rain leached the lime out of the top layer of soil, which then slid down the hillside and accumulated at the bottom, while leaving the limestone soil exposed on the slope. Norman Moles also notes that Rua translates as red: perhaps the name came from a coating of shale soil that has since disappeared.

On Sliabh Rua, only a few paces separate alkaline patches from acidic ones. Acid-loving plants and acid-loathing ones can grow happily next to each other, each in soil that suits them. In itself this is not a unique feature of the area; the same effect can be seen in acid heath near the Cuckmere valley in Sussex, where remnants of glacial silt allow heather to grow on a chalk hill. It has taken a conspiracy of factors, acting largely upon the soil, to bring the Burren's flowers together. As well as the varied mineral combinations and the resulting motley chemistry, there is the Atlantic's influence, through the rains that erode the Burren's outer skin. There are also the natural bunkers provided by the cracks and gaps in the rock, in which the flowers can hole up, safe from grazing. Even the goats tend to keep off the pavement slabs and carpets of shattered rock, giving plants lodged there a better chance of surviving long enough to set seeds, which can then disperse to replenish areas nearby that have been depleted by rough tongues and hoofs.

For David Jeffrey, the key to the survival of the Burren's flowers is the thinness, acidity and poor fertility of the soil, together with the summer droughts that set in as the rain percolates away through the meagre soils and the karst limestone. All of this keeps competitors at bay. As on the chalk hills of the South Downs and in the hay meadows of the Yorkshire Dales, what keeps the grasses down brings the flowers out.

As in the English beauty spots, too, there is particular unease about whether grazing of the right kind can be sustained at levels that will help to keep the space open for flowers. When farming was governed by local needs, it seems from the old reports that every last twig was either grazed as soon as it sprouted, or gathered for firewood. Nowadays local farming is at the margins of a global market, unprofitable, and dependent on European subsidies. About half the Burren's farmers have other jobs, running their farms in what time remains to them outside their paid hours. Many of them have abandoned the traditional practice of turning their cattle out onto the high 'winterages'; cows are now fed on silage and kept in sheds with slatted floors, through which their waste passes to form slurry. Local residents complain about the risk that their water supplies will be polluted by these concentrations of effluent; conservationists worry that if the cows are not out grazing, the hazel will seize its opportunities. Between 2004 and 2009 a number of farms took part in the BurrenLIFE project, which pioneered modern farming techniques that keep the cattle out on the rock during the winter.

In principle there might be no reason why most Burren farms could not adopt such practices, but the prospects for farming must be as uncertain as they are in the British uplands. Farming could be slightly better placed in the Burren than in Britain to take advantage of the conditions that might develop later in the century, as the effects of climate change combine with those of economic and population growth. But, as in Britain, farms might have to endure through many difficult seasons before they reached a sunnier climate.

Winter in the Burren, mild and largely innocent of frost, is ahead of its time. It has never been a sharply distinct season, whereas in other parts of the British Isles the distinction has only become blurred since around the turn of the century. As the climate warms it will become even less of a gap in the green cycle. Burren summers, on the other hand, will be stuck in the past. The area began the century with mean daily July temperatures around 15°C. Even if these have risen three degrees by the century's end, as projections suggest they might, summers in the west of Ireland will offer a nostalgic reminder of how things used to be.

They will not be as wet as they used to be, though. While the pattern of wetter winters and drier summers may not be as marked in the Burren as in neighbouring areas, or in other parts of Ireland and Britain, the decrease in summer rainfall is likely to be significant. The effects on the balance of the Burren's plant communities will remain to be seen. It could prove too dry for the flowers of the High Burren, but on the other hand, it could give them added protection against the grasses that might compete with them more vigorously if the summers were wetter. The possibility that climate change might take a unique habitat further in the right direction is a novel addition to the catalogue of reasons to feel that the Burren has rules of its own.

Three of the plants, the ones suited to Mediterranean conditions, would very likely prefer the climate that may develop in the future. Only one, the dense-flowered orchid, is considered a truly Mediterranean species, while wild madder and the maidenhair fern are classed as Mediterranean-Atlantic. An Atlantic habitat that acquired a slightly more Mediterranean ambience would favour all three, and would probably allow other plants with similar preferences to move in. There would be many more of the Mediterranean plants whose presence is such a celebrated part of the Burren's fascination.

The idea that the Burren is special because Mediterranean plants mingle there with Arctic and alpine ones is not based on a large number of species. On the one hand there are the three with Mediterranean affinities; on the other is a single Arctic-alpine, the mountain avens, though the pyramidal bugle also belongs to the far north and the spring gentian to high mountains. Despite being a plant that belongs to cold regions, mountain avens may be able to cope with markedly higher temperatures than those of the Burren. It is found at much lower latitudes, in Romania and Greece, though at much greater heights – it lives up to its name. An Asian subspecies which survives in isolated pockets upon Japanese mountains is known to encounter summer temperatures above 30°C. One study exposed mountain avens plants to simulated warmer conditions at four tundra sites spanning thousands of kilometres, from Svalbard in the high Arctic to low-Arctic latitudes in Sweden and Alaska, together with an alpine spot near Boulder, Colorado. Mountain avens responded by unfolding earlier to greet the artificial spring, growing taller, and producing more seeds. The more southerly specimens responded more vigorously, suggesting that mountains avens populations at lower latitudes may have adapted to warmer climates, and are better able to deal with warmer climates still.

Although mountain avens has woven itself into ground from Svalbard to Greece and from Japan to Colorado, nowhere has it found itself such a comfortable niche as the Burren. What passes for winter here is as warm as summer in the high Arctic; what pass for mountains would barely count as foothills in the Alps. The plants have surely been here long enough to adapt to a more relaxed climate, as their cousins in Sweden and Colorado appear to have done. Although there are no pollen records to prove that the Arctic and alpine plants of the Burren have been in position since the last glaciers retreated, ten thousand years ago, it is hard to see how they could have got there any later. During what is known as the Atlantic warm period, between about nine and five thousand years ago, temperatures were higher than they are today. If the cold-tolerant plants are indeed survivors from the aftermath of the last ice age, they have already proved their ability to cope with a warmer climate.

If the change of climate were the only consequence of climate change, the prospects for the cattle on the high pastures would also look favourable. The cows would enjoy more clement weather out on their winterages, and richer grazing in longer growing seasons. Traditional breeds as well as traditional husbandry would be encouraged by increasing winter rain. The Continental stocks that have recently been introduced to the Burren – the Limousins and Charolais – are bigger than the longhorns and short-horns they have supplanted. Treading more heavily, they would be more likely to trample wet ground into mud, which the rains could then sluice off the hills.

But whether there are cattle to go up to the winterages will be decided by the state of the world rather than local conditions in the Burren. Population growth and economic growth both favour cattle farming. As the world's population rises and much of it becomes more wealthy, more meat is being eaten. Like the car, meat seems to be something people feel they must have as soon as they can afford it. And like the car, meat warms the planet. As the head of the IPCC, Rajendra Pachauri, has pointed out, a kilo of beef is responsible for the equivalent of the amount of carbon dioxide emitted by a typical European car driving 250 kilometres. On the Irish map, that's roughly the distance from the Burren to Dublin. Meat is also a grossly inefficient way to feed a burgeoning population. Pachauri noted that land used to grow crops can feed up to six times as many people as land used to raise livestock. Felling forests to use the land for cattle replaces carbon stores with carbon sources; nowhere more destructively so than in the Amazon region, where cattle occupy four-fifths of the land already stripped of trees, and where more than half the forest could be gone by 2030.

Within Ireland, climate change may shift livestock westward. Agricultural contrasts between the east and the west of the country are likely to be sharpened, with livestock dominating west of the River Shannon and arable dominating to the east. Grass will grow better in the west than it does today, whereas in the now lush east it is likely to struggle more for lack of water, with summer rainfall down as much as thirty or forty per cent on the southern and eastern coasts by the 2080s. Dairying, the most profitable kind of farming in Ireland for the past forty years, will become more difficult in the eastern regions where dairy farms have long prospered. Although farmers will be able to grow maize and perhaps soybeans to supplement cattle feed, the west will become more clearly suitable than the east for livestock. The Burren will never be prime beef country, but it could benefit from a global background of strong demand for beef and a national concentration of cattle-farming in the west.

It is not inconceivable that the higher powers of the world might try to rationalise the global diet by taking measures to inhibit meat-eating, for the sake of human health as well as that of the environment. As more people around the world become prosperous enough to feel that it is worth taking care of themselves, in order to enjoy the comforts and opportunities of a long life in an affluent society, their attitudes towards meat may develop the degree of ambivalence that already infuses attitudes to sugar and alcohol. But the taste for meat is the kind of fundamental appetite that only religion can suppress, and most of the world's religions are comfortable with most kinds of meat. An environmental conscience may make it a guiltier pleasure, but the demand will still be there.

The ethical light that plays on livestock grazing the upper margins is a lot kinder than that which illuminates the herds growing fat on more versatile land. In the Burren, as in Britain's uplands, livestock makes use of land that farmers could not use for anything else, and helps to make it richer in its wild variety than it would be if left to its own devices. Conservation farming has been pioneered in Ireland by the BurrenLIFE project, and the Burren will continue to be among the strongest of candidates for funds to support agriculture that serves environmental ends. If there is the wealth and the will in the future to bring regions of several hundred square kilometres under environmentally enlightened management, in contrast to the twenty-six square kilometres covered by the twelve farms in the initial BurrenLIFE scheme, the Burren will be among the first in line.

What goes for the upland farming regions of Britain goes also for the Burren. The economic conditions for farming may become more favourable and the climatic ones remain tolerable. The world's population will increase, for decades at least, and the demand for food will increase with it. If much of the world's population grows more prosperous, as the IPCC's scenarios suggest it will, the demand for meat is likely to increase. One study has calculated that the amount of meat people eat per head in developing countries each year could reach thirty-seven kilograms by 2050, an increase of about a third over the twenty-eight kilograms eaten in 2000 – the figure would be four kilograms higher if not for climate change, which is expected to increase meat prices by driving up the cost of livestock feed. The Burren might well have something of an edge over the British uplands, not only because of its unique convergence of flowers and rock, but because there is generally more call for beef than lamb. But as in the Yorkshire Dales and other British uplands, farmers may have left the land by the time that the prospects for hill farming start to look brighter.

If it proves true that places of wild beauty become more precious and more desirable to visit, the proof will pose relatively unfamiliar challenges for the Burren. Celebrated as it is, it has not experienced the influxes that pour into areas such as the Lake District – or the kind of crowds drawn just to the west by the Cliffs of Moher, where the land meets the ocean with a wall of grave promontories sheer enough that a person falling from the top would plummet almost directly into the sea. To reduce that risk, the authorities have paved the hinterland with paths and terraces that smooth the circulation of tourists. Visitors still can reach the very edges of the cliffs, and some do; but no longer by accident, as they now have to climb over the walls that warn them not to. The artificial landscape is sinuous to a fault, avoiding obtrusive right angles and bunkering the 'New Visitor Experience' within the grassed hillside that rises up to the cliff. It is made from sympathetic materials. But it is still a traffic management scheme, and looks like it. The Cliffs of Moher were once as wild as Black Head, guarded by Cathair Dhúinn Irghus, but now they are guarded by a stone gatehouse with windows at which car park tickets are validated.

The Burren does not yet have any single spot where weight of numbers might be seen to justify similar measures. At the moment visitors are borne through the karst in sleek coaches that turn out, as they do on so many lanes and mountain passes around the world, to be more manoeuvrable than they look. Jeff O'Connell, editor of *The Book of the Burren*, observes in his introduction to it that tourists who only set foot in the Burren at brief coach-stops often 'express disappointment or bewilderment'. A synopsis is not available. You have to get off the roads, finding ways in yourself, over the shattered rubble and the fissured pavements, to make as much sense of the place as you can or wish. At the extreme, Tim Robinson insists that the hazel thickets are very beautiful, if you are determined enough to prise your way into them.

There has, however, been one attempt to usher visitors into the landscape through an interpretative centre. It provoked ten years of bitter disputes and eventually failed. In the process, it illustrated the tensions that arise between differing views of the value of land, and exposed weaknesses in civil society that do not bode especially well for the future of political responses to climate change.

The centre was proposed in the late 1980s as an interpretative gatehouse for the Burren National Park, owned by the state and covering 1,500 hectares in the south-east of the region. It was to be sited at the foot of Mullaghmore, where Norman and Richard Moles subsequently studied the legacy of the glaciers in the soil. The initiative was welcomed by local residents, who saw it as an injection of capital – IR£2.7 million, three-quarters of it from the European Union – and a way to develop tourism in the area. Opposition came from people who saw it as an intrusion upon the landscape; an offence against or even a desecration of it. Joined by academics from Dublin and Galway, the opponents of the centre worried that the numbers of visitors it would draw in – 60,000 a year were anticipated – would be too much for a fragile wilderness. Supporters of the project saw the place very differently. A farmer who lived near it told Eileen O'Rourke, who spent a year in the area observing the controversy, that the mountain was 'as solid as a rock, as rough a spot as God ever made, and the rougher one is with it the better'.

259

Although the opponents were locally based, the involvement of people from further afield encouraged the centre's supporters to depict the dispute as one between the community and outsiders. One local councillor dismissed the opposition as 'blow-ins, hippies, homosexuals, drug smokers, intellectuals and non-meat-eaters'. ('Blow-ins' was part of the roll of cultural enemies in the indictment: the term is used in the west of Ireland for people who find themselves there and end up staying.) Opponents whose roots in the community could not be questioned were ostracised from it instead. Neighbours whom they had grown up with stopped talking to them; they were not welcome in local shops or pubs and were ignored at football matches. The assistance that neighbouring farmers normally provide for each other was withheld: on their farms, the centre's opponents were on their own. Struggle over Burren land is no longer violent, but here it remained passively aggressive.

O'Rourke emphasises the cultural inferiority complex she perceived among the locals who supported the centre. Many of them had left school at fourteen, and felt their rural heritage as a source not of pride but shame. Assuming themselves to lack the skills for political action, they saw politics as the levering of resources from distant centres of power, and they looked up to the politicians on whom they counted for the leverage. At the same time they demonstrated their determination and ability to control political activities among themselves. Two local farmers took part in legal action against the centre, and were ostracised, but other critics fell into line under pressure. One woman who took part in a march to protest against the scheme was visited, for no immediately apparent reason, by a number of her neighbours the week before a march in support of the plans. 'Sure we will see you in the march on Saturday,' they said as they left. She took the hint and counter-marched against herself.

Insisting that 'you are either with us or against us', the centre's supporters imposed a view of the community as a monolithic unit that demands conformity as the price of inclusion. There was no sense of the community as a group that could, or indeed should, contain different views conversing with each other. Nor did there appear to be much sense that views from outside, blown in with the intellectuals and the homosexuals, had anything to offer the community. The lines were drawn up according to the familiar old dogma of the group, that it is us against them, and that 'us' is singular rather than plural.

O'Rourke also emphasises the absence of conversation in the decision to build the centre, which she sees as being in line with the Office of Public Works's 'DAD' approach to planning – 'Decide, Announce, Defend'. In the historical background, she suggests, lies the choice of the Free State government at the beginning of independence, in the early 1920s, to take over rather than replace the pre-existing apparatus of power. Being colonial, the appropriated British institutions did not promote participatory democracy, or do very much to bring peripheral areas closer to the centre. But the most striking thing about the workings of power, democracy and community she describes is how typical they are. The Burren is hardly the only rural area in the British Isles where people feel remote from the capital city. Deciding, announcing and defending is a standard operating procedure for officialdom. And dividing people into us and them is ingrained as a standard operating procedure in human nature.

As the climate changes, weaknesses and tensions like these will leave society vulnerable to civic damage. Climate change demands action at the highest level, to address global problems, to reconcile different interests in the present and the future, to take the broadest and the longest views possible. There is nothing about it that inherently favours democracy or participation. Unless those processes are already healthily developed, climate change is likely to encourage the issuing of orders from above. They are the easiest ways to fill a civic vacuum, and often the most tempting ones. In the imagined future sketched earlier for London, consensus had become a premier civic ideal. But it is far less likely to develop, either as an ideal or in practice, where it has not traditionally been sought and there is little of it to build on. And consensus can be a façade for coercion anyway. Being a process that obscures differences of opinion, it can help the powerful to impose their will on the weak without the differences escaping from the room.

The Mullaghmore controversy is a good example of the complexities of the interests that have to be reconciled in environmental decision-making. Although it was presented by the centre's supporters as a dispute between locals and outsiders, the locals implicitly supported the interests of a wider group of outsiders: the people who would visit the area if the centre were built. It was not as though the development in question was a hamburger restaurant or a golf course, after all. This was to be a place that would allow people to approach the hard core of the Burren even if they were not fit or field-wise enough to find their own way in, and would allow them to learn about the mountain's environment while standing on its threshold and in its awe. The centre's opponents were not against a Burren visitor centre in principle and had nothing against the one established in the village of Kilfenora: it was the intrusion of a building into a wild place that offended them. Although they were cast as outsiders, they were campaigning to keep outsiders away from the mountain.

Since they did not yet exist as a group, the potential visitors had no effective voice in the dispute. Their interests were one element in the public interest that is ultimately the government's to decide. Sometimes the government that decides is local, sometimes national, and increasingly it will be supra-national. Climate change will tend to draw decision-making to higher levels, because the sphere of interests is so large. The common good involves the whole planet and generations yet unborn.

Whether they are housing estates or areas of outstanding natural beauty, places will have to be managed with climate change in mind. Sometimes the main concern will be to minimise greenhouse gas emissions; sometimes it will be to protect living species from the effects of global warming; sometimes it might be to make the most of a habitat as a haven for threatened species. The interests implicated will always be much wider than the interests of the parties immediately involved, such as residents and landowners. If those parties are bad at reaching agreement over how a place should be managed, the increasing urgency of the situation will encourage power to assert itself and impose its will in the name of the common good. The more that happens, the more it will become the norm for resolving issues and implementing policies of all kinds. And the more that power asserts itself, the more it is likely to abuse its strength. By obliging the higher powers to compensate for civic weaknesses, climate change may tempt them to exploit those weaknesses.

With its bleak historical landscape of raiding, conquest and coercion, and its thin civic soils that offer little to the grass roots of participation, the Burren is a good place to make out the shadows that climate change casts over civil society. Some of the Burren's own shadows will fade, though. People in peripheral areas may always feel themselves to be at a disadvantage in their relations with metropolitans, but that feeling will diminish as they spend longer in education and where they live becomes increasingly irrelevant to their access to information. Already old certainties and traditional authorities no longer fill the sky the way they used to do. People may continue to believe in them at some levels, but come to see them less reverently at others. The point was made with unsurpassed verve by the 1990s television comedy *Father Ted*, which made fun of the clergy and sport with its characters' provincial naivety, while affirming that its audience was at home with ideas that not long previously would have been regarded as the preserve of a metropolitan elite. This was the new Ireland at play, catching the world's eye with its aptitude for seizing the opportunities offered by hectic modern economics and technologies, while finding artful ways to bring its past with it.

The show added a new note of levity to the Burren too. While the grievances mounted at Mullaghmore, a few miles away the television crews were filming at the farm that played the part of the Parochial House in the exterior shots. The Burren had always had its gallows humour, but now it was ready to reveal its funny side.

Carbon dioxide plus water makes carbonic acid; carbonic acid dissolves calcium carbonate: rainwater erodes limestone. Elementary karst chemistry would seem to imply that the more carbon dioxide there is in the atmosphere, the more acidic the rain will become, and the faster the limestone will erode. More sophisticated analysis shows, however, that the concentration of carbon dioxide in the atmosphere has a relatively minor effect on how quickly limestone dissolves, and that increases in temperature actually reduce the rate. The major factor is the amount of rainfall. Projections applied to the Burren suggest that net annual rainfall could increase over the next few decades, and the rate at which the limestone dissolves could increase by up to nearly ten per cent. But the annual increase in rainfall will only be a finger's breadth or two, and the annual increase in erosion will be a few hundredths of a millimetre. Climate change will have an effect on the rock, but you couldn't really call it an impact.

Though the karst will endure, one of its characteristic features may not. Turloughs, the seasonal lakes that fill when water wells up in winter from the underground cavities in the limestone, and then dry up in summer, could lose forty-five per cent of the area climatically suitable for them by the middle of the century. But if the glacial plants do prove capable of holding their ground in warmer conditions, and ways are found to keep the cattle on the hills, so as to keep the hazel off, the High Burren may hang on to its flowers in more or less their present variety. Whether it is more or less remains to be seen. A report published in 2008 reflects upon the possibility that the major effects of climate change upon Ireland will lie in such changes of tone and texture. Entitled 'Changing shades of green', and produced by the Irish American Climate Project, it is particularly mindful of the imbalance in rainfall that is likely to develop between summer and winter. Instead of an even mist of soft rains throughout the year, summers will be deprived and winters drenched. The great raised peat bogs, the island's soft centre, will dry up and crack in summer, allowing the winter's downfalls to penetrate nearly down to the bedrock, weakening the bog to the point that in places it bursts into muddy gouts. Floodwaters coursing down rivers will rip the jelly of incubating salmon from its pockets in the riverbeds, while droughts will leave adult salmon loitering exhausted near river mouths as they wait for flows sufficient to allow them to make their heroic final journeys upstream.

The vividness with which calamities like these are described is matched by the intensity with which the report dwells upon the possible effects of climate change upon how Ireland will look. 'Changing shades of green' imagines the shades of brown that will appear as grass dies back in summer, and the parallel lines of cereal crops that will be ruled across former pastures. It contemplates Ireland through the misted prisms of an Irish culture that it sees as an organic product of the land. Dermot Somers, a filmmaker, observes that the light and textures of the landscape are the product of the soft and measured rains. He likens the tones to those of tweed: the shades must be subtle and harmonious. And the pace must be slow, to the point where it suggests timelessness: 'a kind of seeping absorption, followed by a slow release of light and sensory images'. That, he says, is what Irish lyric poetry expresses and traditional *sean-nós* singing evokes.

The report is addressed to 'the eighty million Irish living around the world – only five million of whom live on the island of Ireland'. As far as it is concerned, the shades of green in Irish identity can be disregarded. It considers that the Irish diaspora 'tends to hold zealously to images of green hillsides, flowing rivers and soft rains'. An Irish person living in Dublin, it suggests, will not be unhappy to hear that the south-east of Ireland may find itself with a Mediterranean climate. 'But when an Irish person living in San Francisco hears of the projected change, the response is often an expression of heartbreak.'

This claim does more than induce puzzlement about why somebody living in fog-haunted San Francisco would nurse any kind of fondness for cold, damp, overcast weather. It opens up the question of what a country means to its people by opening up the question of who its people are. Only the most elastic interpretation of identity permits the assertion that there are eighty million Irish people around the world. The SeventyMillion Project, whose ambition is to seek out seventy million people of Irish heritage and explore 'what their Irish link means to them', accepts claims based on a grandparent, a great-grandparent, or even a more distant ancestor. Many of those millions doubtless think of themselves as being in some significant sense Irish, but they also think of themselves as being many other things besides.

If people's links to a country are through ancestry, the

affinities they feel may be for the imagined ancestral land rather than the one it has become. 'Sometimes in Ireland we make the mistake of assuming that because so many communities in the United States, Australia or elsewhere celebrate St Patrick's Day or embrace an aspect of Irish culture, that they are automatically affirming a connection to modern Ireland,' observed Mary McAleese, the President of Ireland, in a speech celebrating the 'global Irish family'. The less of the old country that is perceived in the new one, the less keenly some of those overseas communities may feel their connection to the country that actually exists.

It's questionable whether the effects of two or three degrees' worth of climate change would be enough to weaken those ties, though. Visitors of the future are not going to complain that it isn't constantly raining, and with the advent of reliably fine summer weather, Ireland's tourist industry will gain the one advantage it now signally lacks. And, like northern Britain, it will still look very green indeed compared with what people in other parts of the world see around them. If the westerly and northerly parts of the British Isles come to be seen as places that have escaped being torn from their roots by drastic climatic change, people of Irish heritage will be even more entranced by the green of Ireland.

When Irish-Americans visit the west of Ireland and see the remains of abandoned cottages, or walk the green 'famine roads' built to provide the starving and destitute with some sort of an income, they are reminded of why there are so many Americans of Irish descent. Emigration remained a constant of Irish life through the twentieth century, and even now there are a million Irish-born people living abroad, despite the recent transformation in which Ireland has become a net importer of migrants. If Ireland fails to sustain the economic advances it has made since it became part of the European Community in 1973, it will remain an object of sympathy for its diaspora. But if it finds ways to build on those advances, it will cease to be special in one sense. Historically, the Irish diaspora's view of Ireland was steeped in the poignancy of the contrast between the relative prosperity attained by many emigrant communities and the hardship that persisted in the country they came from. If Ireland sustains its development, it will be confirmed as one among a number of countries where Irish people have eventually prospered.

And the Irish who live on the island of Ireland will become a steadily more varied nation. The small town of Gort, a few kilometres west of the Burren National Park, is a quirky showpiece of the future. In the streets many of the people look as though they are not from round there. Guessing where they are from would be tricky without extra clues, such as the posters in Portuguese and the Brazilian flags hanging in windows. One local meat-processing plant began hiring Brazilian migrant workers in 1999, and within a few years they were estimated to make up nearly a third of the town's population. In time this will be typical, though not all the new minorities will be conveniently Catholic like the Brazilians, or the Poles who contributed so much to the inward migration surplus after the European Union enlarged in 2004. Most will leave as quickly as they came, but many will settle and become Irish.

For Ireland, population projections seem to evoke the

past more powerfully than the future. Observing that
the population could reach eight million cannot help but
remind listeners that it peaked at that figure before the
Great Famine killed a million people and forced another
million overseas. And the fact that Ireland is now a developed European nation at no seriously conceivable risk of
hunger does not quell the resonance of the prediction that
climate change is likely to put an end to the cultivation
of potatoes. Like bog bursts and the disruption of salmon
fisheries, this is predicted as a consequence if Ireland's year
divides into a wet and a dry season. Potatoes will be difficult to plant in the wet spring soil, difficult to harvest as
the winter rains set in during October, and will need irrigation to keep them going through the dry summer. It will be
possible to grow them, but probably not worthwhile.

That will be a commercial decision, not a matter of life
and death; yet the thought is still unavoidable. 'Memory
Awakened: Again the Potato is Threatened', broods the
headline in 'Changing shades of green'. In Ireland memory
has never really gone to sleep: the continuing ache of emigration has kept it awake. Ireland will truly have changed if
its population passes the eight million mark and abandons
the potato without seeing the past in front of the present.
How it responds to the effects of climate change, direct
and indirect, will depend on how successful it is at sustaining its prosperity. But Ireland now belongs to a different
world. Its west coast could well become dotted with new
clusters of abandoned buildings – empty houses and hotels
left standing as monuments to the mistaken economic
optimism of the property developers who put them up. As
the climate warms, there will be many villages abandoned

because of hunger, but those will be in the other world, beyond Europe, to the south.

The Burren is often taken to be a relict of the past, a refuge whose ecological quirks have saved some of its plants from retreating north with the glaciers, but it offers an image of the future. As temperatures rise, there may be many other places where plants left behind from a colder climate mingle with plants that have moved in along with a warmer climate. Many of these incongruous juxtapositions will not last long, as the species left behind yield to their new competitors, but the example of the Burren shows that species can occasionally turn out to be more resilient than scientists would suppose. Its paradoxical rocks may come to be seen not just as a vestige of an ancient environment, but as a prototype of habitats to come.

8

Younger Dryas

The naturalists who marvel at the flowers of the Burren are not the only scientists for whom the mountain avens is special. It has given its name to an ancient period of coldness whose sudden onset and abrupt end are a source of ominous fascination for climate scientists. Naturalists may see the mountain avens of the Burren as an example of survival and the possibility of refuge. Climate scientists see the preserved traces of mountain avens further north as a sign of convulsive, inescapable change. The records suggest that when the cold phase ceased, temperatures may have leapt by about five degrees in about as many years. That is how fast and how far the climate of the northern hemisphere can move. If it could happen once, it could happen the day after tomorrow.

To the people who experienced the start of the chill in northern Europe, nearly 13,000 years ago, it must have seemed as though winter had decided it would no longer make way for spring, and henceforth would be the only season. A climate that had been on a warming upswing after the last great ice age was interrupted by a snap freeze that lasted around 1,300 years. In Scandinavia, the trees that had advanced back north in the wake of the glaciers were toppled, and the peaty soil in which they had taken root turned to tundra. Scientists first became aware of this in the 1930s, when researchers in Sweden found layers of sand and silt above peat sediments that contained fossilised tree remains. In the layers above the peaty deposits were the remains of mountain avens, which had taken over the tundra in the way that heather takes over moors. Its leaves were preserved, and gave the cold period its name. Mountain avens is known to botanists as *Dryas octopetala*: *dryas* is Greek for oak, the leaves of which bear a tenuous resemblance to those of the mountain avens, crimped against the cold. *Dryas* remains have identified more than one ancient cold phase. This one has become known as the Younger Dryas.

Its advent was abrupt and its departure even more so. Most scientists are inclined to believe that the Younger Dryas came about because vast amounts of fresh water disrupted the great North Atlantic currents that transport warmth around the northern hemisphere. The centre of what is now Canada was one great reservoir of glacial water, Lake Agassiz, which drained into the Mississippi. Its outflow then shifted through ninety degrees, draining eastwards along the line of the St Lawrence River.

A surge of meltwater into the Atlantic would have intruded into the great procession of water that circulates up the coast of North America at the surface and back down south in the ocean's depths. The course the waters follow contains an oval that spans the ocean between the continents and a plume that arcs up towards the polar seas. The oval is known as the Gulf Stream and is driven by the winds that prevail at different latitudes: trade winds blowing from east to west in the tropics, and westerlies crossing

273

the ocean in the opposite direction further north. Not all of the Gulf Stream follows the route eastwards; part of it continues northwards in the direction of Greenland. Here the circulation is shaped by changes in the warmth and the saltiness of the water. As the current travels north, water evaporates from the surface of the sea. The salt does not evaporate, so the remaining surface waters become saltier and therefore denser, which makes them tend to sink. In the high north, cold and salty waters collect in deep pools – there is one in the Labrador Sea between Greenland and the Canadian coast, and a couple more to the east of Greenland – from which they well up and flow through the depths back southwards.

Intercepting the northern plume near the beginning of its course, an outflow from a glacial lake would have kept the northbound waters fresher, and thus kept them from sinking; the pools of cold dense water would cease to form, and the circle of currents would not be completed. Deprived of those warm currents, northern temperatures would have collapsed. The scale of the heat loss would have been as vast as the ocean itself. Today the Atlantic circulation conveys a million gigawatts of heat in Europe's direction.

This heroic story, with its great masses of water that the ancients would undoubtedly have personified as mighty deities had they known of them, is not fully polished or accepted. Doubts have been raised about the timing of the events and the course of the waters. But what is not in doubt is that the Younger Dryas took place, that it took the north by surprise and held it for well over a thousand years, and that its disintegration swept the climate most of

the distance from the ice age to its modern state within a
few decades. The Younger Dryas shook itself apart within
half a century; the story that Greenland ice records tell is
that most of its final throes occurred in a single five-year
bout. Temperatures appear to have leapt by between five
and ten degrees.

The idea that the Atlantic circulation could be switched
off, and that the surrounding lands could be chilled as a
result, caught the imagination of scientists and the public
alike. It was dramatically visualised in the film *The Day After
Tomorrow*, whose scenario combined two other ideas that
have come to shape how people imagine things happen: the
tipping point and the perfect storm. No scientific model
has generated a scenario like that of the film, in which a
catastrophic combination of events envelops most of the
Northern Hemisphere in ice more or less overnight. The
effects of a collapse in the Atlantic circulation would probably take more like a century to unfold. And that is the day
after tomorrow in the history of the changing climate: the
time when people find out just what forces their ancestors
unleashed. That day may never come, if climate change
is the gradual process assumed in the IPCC projections
on which the sketches of the future in earlier chapters are
loosely based, if it turns out to be more moderate than the
higher projections warn, and if it levels off without taking
the Earth past critical tipping points. But if cornerstones
of the planet's climate have been tipped over the edge –
ice sheets in meltdown, the Amazon forests oxidised into
the air, or the Atlantic circulation collapsed – it will make
all the chaos and turmoil hitherto seem like mere bad
weather. People in the British Isles will no longer be able

to tell themselves that climatic disasters are something that happens to other countries.

The Younger Dryas and the idea that Atlantic currents could stop going round are reminders that what happens in British and Irish air – how warm or wet or windy it becomes – depends on what goes on in the depths of the Atlantic. They are also reminders that the Atlantic could turn from a protector to a scourge. In the British Isles, the idea that an oceanic circulation failure might usher in an ice age played upon the widespread understanding that the Isles owe their mild and moderate climate to the Gulf Stream.

It is only part of the picture, though. Richard Seager, who grew up in England and now works as a climate scientist in the United States, has challenged the belief that the Gulf Stream is responsible for the striking climatic differences between the American and European sides of the Atlantic, such as the fifteen to twenty degrees that separate the temperatures of New York and London in January. He identifies the source of this belief as an American naval officer called Matthew Fontaine Maury, who published an influential book on oceanography in 1855. 'It is the influence of this stream upon climate that makes Erin the "Emerald Isle of the Sea", and that clothes the shores of Albion in evergreen robes; while in the same latitude, on this side, the coasts of Labrador are fast bound in fetters of ice,' Maury wrote.

Computer modelling by Seager and his colleagues, however, suggests that the Rocky Mountains have more to do with it. The scientists took the circulating Atlantic currents out of their model, but the temperature difference across the Atlantic stayed just the same. When they removed the Rockies, half of the difference vanished. Wind blowing in from the Pacific hits the North American mountain spine and is forced upwards, where it meets a layer of the atmosphere that acts as a kind of lid, deflecting it southwards across the middle of North America, a move that draws Arctic air down to chill the east coast; the current of air that has crossed the continent then swings northwards over the Atlantic, forming atmospheric waves that draw up warmth from the ocean and carry it onwards to Europe.

The other half of the temperature difference between the two sides of the ocean is the difference between a continental and a maritime climate. Water can store more heat than earth or rock, and because the waters are stirred around by the winds, the sun's heat diffuses much further down into the sea than into the land, where it can penetrate no more than a metre or two below the surface. Sea temperatures therefore vary less from season to season than do temperatures on land, so where prevailing winds blow in from the sea, winters are milder and summers warmer.

In challenging the widely held view that the British and Irish have the Gulf Stream to thank for their weather, Seager affirmed that the Atlantic is responsible, one way and another: storing heat, warming the atmospheric waves swirling round from the Rockies, blowing mild winds across the coasts. He also affirmed that the Atlantic circulation does warm the lands that it passes: his point was that it warms the European and American coasts equally, and so cannot explain the difference between evergreen England and icebound Labrador. His model indicated that if the Atlantic circulation were to shut down, temperatures on the land that had been under its influence would fall by around three degrees.

That is very unlikely to happen during this century, according to the IPCC. None of the simulations it has looked at predicted a collapse by 2100, though others have. Some experts discount the possibility, though others consider the risk could be significant if global temperatures were to rise by several degrees during the twenty-first century. When a group of a dozen were quizzed about probabilities, a couple rated the risk for a three-degree rise at thirty or forty per cent, and three put the risk for a four-degree rise at forty per cent or more.

The more significant risk is that a tipping point will be passed during this century, beyond which a collapse of the circulation in the following century becomes inevitable. Tim Lenton, a scientist who has focused attention on tipping processes in climate change, reckons that the point of no return could be passed if global temperatures rise by three degrees, which is well within the conventionally accepted range of possibilities for the coming century. It might take as much as five degrees, but even that is within the accepted envelope.

Already there are signs that the circulation may be being subverted. Greenland's ice sheet is thought to be melting at a rate of fifty cubic kilometres a year. Flows through the six largest Russian rivers that drain into the Arctic Ocean increased by an average of 128 cubic kilometres a year between 1936, when they first began to be measured, and 1999. That amounts to an increase in the supply of fresh water to the ocean of about seven per cent: by 2100, it could be more like fifty per cent. Between them the Russian rivers could deliver a sizeable fraction of the quantity of fresh water that would stop the deep water pools from forming. The ice melting around the circumference of the Arctic basin would provide the rest.

It would not, however, lead to another Dryas-like ice age. If the Atlantic circulation weakens as a result of climate warming, it will offset the warming on the lands either side of it. Europe is still likely to be warmer than it was, just not as warm as it would have been if the Atlantic currents had maintained their vigour. The IPCC considers it very likely that the circulation will weaken over the course of the century, possibly losing a quarter or half its strength; but its models still show overall warming around the North Atlantic and Europe. However, when the experts who were invited to put odds on the circulation's failure were asked about the possible consequences, without taking the possible effects of greenhouse gases into account, they suggested that a weakening of thirty per cent could reduce annual mean temperatures by as much as four degrees in the region where the cooling effect was strongest – which most of them thought could include the British Isles. The implication is that temperatures in the British Isles could stay more or less the same while global average temperatures rose several degrees, amplifying the differences between the British Isles and the rest of the world far beyond those suggested earlier in this book.

A weakening of the circulation would not just cancel out greenhouse warming and leave the British Isles undisturbed, though. Changes on such an immense oceanic scale could bring turbulence in their wake, visiting floods and storms upon the coasts. They could also raise the seas higher up the coasts permanently. The dense waters sinking in the North Atlantic draw the ocean surface down with them: if the deep water stopped forming, coastal sea levels could rise by between half a metre and a metre. These increases would be on top of the general expansion caused by global warming and whatever contribution melting ice sheets made to the depth of the sea. They would happen much more quickly too. Within the oceans, plankton would be deprived of the nutrients that well up from the bottom with the deep waters. Plankton densities could be halved or worse, with catastrophic effects upon the fish, and whales, that feed upon the floating creatures.

Nor would the effects stop at the equator. Oceans have no borders, and the North Atlantic currents are only part of a much larger circulation that loops elaborately around the globe. The higher latitudes' heat loss would be the lower latitudes' heat gain. Tropical regions would warm, monsoons might fail, and droughts might strike parts of Asia and Africa. Looked at from a northern point of view, the effects of an Atlantic circulation breakdown would be a climate change anomaly in which warming triggered a cooling process. Looked at in a global perspective, it would be an entirely typical climate-change effect, in which the impacts fall hardest upon the regions whose people are least able to cope with them. The south would have to bear the heat that the north was spared.

But the north would not be spared the waves and the storms, and the previously cosseted British Isles would be hit by the full force of the turmoil. The story so far has been one of gradual change, moderated off the north-western coast of Europe by the Atlantic, as greenhouse gases steadily turn up the temperature. It follows the IPCC's graphs to the end of the century, where they stop. But that only takes us up to the first climate-change horizon, when there will still be people living who are alive today, and it stays within a model of climate change that cannot factor abrupt changes or tipping points into its calculations. It does not show the long unfolding of the effects of climate change over centuries, or depict a climate system melting down rather than gradually warming up. The cameos of Britain's future and the discussions to this point about the effects of climate change on the British Isles have been set in a scientifically plausible world, based upon consensus science that is reluctant to venture beyond what it can model; but other worlds are possible.

If abrupt upheavals such as the collapse of major ice sheets start setting the pace, the world will enter a grave new phase of change, and the British Isles will start to feel out of their depth. They will begin to understand what climate change really means, not only on the coasts and in the air around them, but in their relations with the rest of a world thrown into permanent crisis by the tensions between states and within societies. Squalls will turn into hurricanes and cracks into canyons.

Even the conventional storyline could leave the world on the verge of a future like this, if the business of greenhouse gas emissions were to carry on as usual. The uppermost of the IPCC's graphs, pointing to a maximum temperature rise of 6.4°C by 2099, is a stark warning of what is already considered possible – though it is based on a storyline of relentless and unabated fossil fuel use that might seem beyond even human folly. Whatever level the temperature reaches, it is likely to stay there, and there is no rule that says nations or economies will eventually get used to it. People in Britain and Ireland will look back on the twenty-first century as a phoney war, and realise that 2100 marks only the end of the beginning.

9

The Shade of the Future

Among the grim procession of security measures that have rolled out in the years following the terrorist attacks of 9 September 2001, a rare note of charm was struck by a set of images designed to make British passports harder to forge. The new biometric passports are not only fitted with antennas but also emblazoned with engravings of birds: red kite, curlew, avocet, merlin, red grouse and Scottish crossbill. According to the Home Office, they symbolise freedom to travel.

As expressions of national identity, rather than confirmations of personal identity, these documents will look quaint, and perhaps a little poignant, when they turn up in the effects of the elderly deceased at the other end of the century. As symbols of freedom to travel the birds are not an ideal selection: the grouse and crossbill do not leave British territory, and British kites are more sedentary than their Continental cousins. The Scottish crossbill, evidently chosen because it is the only species exclusive to Britain, does not even leave Scottish territory; and if it cannot cope with a changed climate, its inability to reach a newly suitable habitat far across the sea to the north may have led to its extinction by the time Scotland starts issuing its own passports. On the other hand, the merlin and the red grouse may retreat northwards to become exclusively Scottish residents within the British Isles.

Curlews may also breed largely in Scotland instead of across the British Isles, as they do now, and ones that breed overseas may not bother to visit British coasts as winters become milder closer to their homes. Although the avocet has become a reliable prospect for birdwatchers along the East Anglian coast, and the Exe estuary in Devon, it may turn its back on southern England as the climate changes. But the red kite could make Britain its own, while being forced to abandon its German heartland. It could end up as an eloquent symbol of a new British nature, defined not by heritage but by contemporary conditions, not static but developing; not what it used to be, but rich in new ways nonetheless. It might even stand for a new United Kingdom, answering to the same description.

Once the temperature has risen by more than a couple of degrees, the United Kingdom will have no choice but to accept that the ground is shifting under its feet. People lucky enough to be able to get out into the countryside may enjoy taking the warm summer air in a South Downs valley, or standing in the shade of a Scottish glen and pretending that nothing much has changed. But in a world enveloped by permanent and inexorably worsening climatic crisis, the illusion of Arcadia will evaporate as soon as they return to the world they really live in, of volatile prices, precarious employment, unpredictable shortages and international tension.

They will be able to see further by then. The far horizon, a thousand years away, will be coming into view. The seas will continue to rise, taking bite after bite out of the coastline. Landscapes and the communities of natural life in them will mutate under the sustained pressure from a climate that refuses to cool down again – unless the Atlantic circulation collapses, lowering temperatures but punishing the British Isles with storms and floods instead. As more and more of the species committed to extinction by the heat succumb, people will find out what happens to the living world when a large fraction of its variety is destroyed. People will already have learned what invasive pests can do with heat on their side, after a constant succession of blights in woodlands, waterways, fields and gardens. They will watch apprehensively as tropical diseases advance northwards, as climatically fuelled conflicts erupt in one region after another, and as more ecosystems follow the Amazon rainforest into oblivion, threatening new shocks to the world's climate in the wake of their collapse. There is no end to this in prospect, and no way of stopping it. These will not be countries at ease with themselves.

Nor are they likely to be at ease with the rest of the world, which will have scant sympathy for the problems of the few countries lucky enough, so far, to have got off lightly from climate change. If they start to act like islands, distancing themselves from the rest of the world's climatic problems, they will earn the world's contempt. They got the benefits of burning carbon, other countries will say: now they can pay their share of the bills – after all, it was Britain that had the idea of basing an economy on fossil fuels in the first place. Having spent the past century struggling to alleviate poverty while trying to cope with the climatic ravages to which poverty left them exposed, recently industrialised countries might be particularly indignant. Some of them, notably China and India, will be very powerful, and it will hardly put them out to punish any small nations they see to be cheating. The economic opportunities that the British Isles will enjoy, attracting labour and investment to a benign climate, will only make matters worse. Foreigners will see the islanders not as a nation of shopkeepers but as a nation of spivs, profiteering from global crisis like black-market dealers in the Second World War.

Picture some of these islanders – some of them our grandchildren – looking towards the rest of the world from receding white cliffs. 'Do they mean us?' they ask with wounded bewilderment. Knowing the answer is yes, they cast about for someone else to blame. They look towards the far horizon of climate change, inexorable centuries away, and they turn around to fix on the generation that committed the world to this future. 'What were they thinking?' they ask; and yes, they mean us.

Acknowledgements

Being keen to encourage scientists and other specialists to speculate about the future, while being conscious that this was asking them to wander beyond their professional norms, I adopted a policy of acknowledging help but not attributing views except by agreement. I likewise thought it best not to give affiliations, since some people gave information on behalf of their organisations, some gave their own opinions, and others gave both. However, I feel I should acknowledge a number of these organisations, including the Borders Forest Trust, Brecon Beacons National Park Authority, British Energy, Defra, East Sussex Historical Environment Record, Environment Agency, Forest Research, Forestry Commission, London Climate Change Agency, Moors for the Future, National Farmers' Union, National Trust, Natural England, Royal Parks, Royal Society for the Protection of Birds, Scottish Natural Heritage, South Downs Joint Committee, South East Water, Sussex Wildlife Trust, Trees for Life, UKAEA Fusion, United Kingdom Climate Impacts Programme, Yorkshire Dales Millennium Trust and the Yorkshire Dales National Park Authority.

For advice, discussion, practical assistance and hospitality I am grateful to Philip Ashmole, Phil Baarda, Pearl and Ray Banks, my editor Neil Belton and his colleagues at Faber, John Best, Stuart Blackhall, Alison Blackwell,

ACKNOWLEDGEMENTS

John Boardman, Aletta Bonn, Tatiana Bosteels, Mark Broadmeadow, Lindell Bromham, Niall Burnside, Anne Byrne, Ruairidh Campbell, Chris Carpenter, Frank Chambers, Greg Chuter, Kevin Clark, Dennis Clarke, Rosalind Daniels, Althea Davies, Brendan Dunford, Martin Eade, Colin Edwards, Conor Fahy, Stuart Findlay, Hayley Fowler, Dusty Gedge, Jeremy Gordon, Penny Green, Karl Hardy, Adrian Harrison, Philippa Harrison, David Hill, Paul Holt, Jo Hughes, Nick Humphrey, Kenneth Ip, David Jardine, David Jeffrey, Keith Kirby, Kenneth Knott, James Lamb, David Lang, Irina Levinsky, Catherine MacCulloch, Grahame Madge, Sue Mallinson, Loraine McFadden, Willie McGhee, Diana McGowan, Pippa Merricks, Jane Millar, Paul Mitchell, Norman Moles, Ian Mure, Ann Murray, Matt Neale, Eileen O'Rourke, Duncan Orr-Ewing, Fintan O'Toole, Howard Parker, Sharon Parr, Martin Pearce, Rona Pitman, James Power, Ivor and Noreen Prentice, Dan Puplett, Rupen Raithatha, Pippa Rayner, Tim Reeder, Jerry Rehfeldt, Mark Rehfisch, Jeremy Roberts, Iain Ross, Adam Rowlands, Jonathan Scurlock, Rob Shaw, Adrian Shepherd, Paul Sinnadurai, David Skinner, Roger Smith, John Stafford, Stuart Sutton, Colin Taylor, Stewart Taylor, Chris Thomas, Mark Thomas, Richard Tipping, Eileen Tisdall, Colin Tudge, Stewart Ullyott, Richard Wallace, David Ward, Mark Wasilewski, Jim Watson, Alan Watson Featherstone, Chris West, Richard Westaway, Duncan Westbury, Tony Whitbread, Clive Williams, Malcolm Wolf, Tracey Younghusband, the organisers of the Burren Spring Conference 2009 and all who took part in it.

I am more than grateful to my wife, Sue Matthias Kohn, for everything.

Notes

I ATLANTIC SHADE

2 'Central England has warmed by a degree Celsius since the 1970s . . .' The climate of the United Kingdom and recent trends, www.ukcip.org.uk/images/stories/08_pdfs/Trends.pdf

2 'The North Atlantic . . . have been decreasing.' Wood, 2008; Keenlyside et al., 2008; Next decade 'may see no warming', 1 May 2008, http://news.bbc.co.uk/1/hi/sci/tech/7376301.stm; Rich nation greenhouse gas emissions rise in 2007, 23 April 2009, www.reuters.com/article/environmentNews/idUSTRE53M41R 20090423?feedType=RSS&feedName=environmentNews

3 'about what we've got.' Mallon et al., 2008; 7 Years to Climate Midnight, Carlos Pascual and Strobe Talbott, 28 August 2008, www.washingtonpost.com/wp-dyn/content/article/2008/08/27/ AR2008082703108.html

3 'Emissions fell by about three per cent . . . two-year pause in emission increases.' Fatih Birol, International Energy Agency: World Energy Outlook 2009 Climate Change Study, press briefing, 6 October 2009, http://unfccc2.meta-fusion. com/kongresse/090928_AWG_Bangkok/templ/ovw_page. php?id_kongressmain=91; Carbon emissions will fall 3% due to recession, say world energy analysts, www.guardian. co.uk/environment/2009/oct/06/carbon-cuts-recession-iea; International Energy Agency, 2009.

4 'Nicholas Stern pointed out . . .' Stern, 2006.

4 'With the onset of recession, Stern urged . . .' Nicholas Stern, Green routes to growth, www.guardian.co.uk/commentisfree/2008/ oct/23/commentanddebate-energy-environment-climate-change

5 'In 2000, the world had warmed . . .' Hansen et al., 2005.

6 'The most ominous warning . . . on the ocean floor.' Allen et al., 2009a,b; Solomon et al., 2009; Matthews and Caldeira, 2008;

Archer and Brovkin, 2008. Although the last is published in a scientific journal, it reviews the research and explains the issues in an accessible style.

8 'an extra three degrees could raise the seas by fifty metres . . .' See also '"Scary" climate message from past', http://news.bbc.co.uk/1/hi/sci/tech/8299426.stm, which reports findings that between twenty and fourteen million years ago, when temperatures were 3–4°C higher than at present, sea levels were twenty-five to forty metres higher than they are now.

8 'The authors . . . a good innings for a civilisation.' Lenton et al., 2008.

9 'likely to lose five hundred times as many years of healthy life . . .' McMichael et al., 2008.

9 'Democratic Republic of Congo, . . . a couple of decades.' Liu et al., 2008; CIA – The World Factbook – Country Comparison: GDP – per capita (PPP), https://www.cia.gov/library/publications/the-world-factbook/rankorder/2004rank.html

9 'half of southern Africa's crop seasons may fail.' Philip Thornton, 4+°C: What might this mean for agriculture in sub-Saharan Africa? 4 Degrees and Beyond: International Climate Conference 28–30 September 2009, Oxford, www.eci.ox.ac.uk/4degrees/programme.php

9 'Worsening storms . . . tropical cyclones.' Ministry of Environment and Forests, 2008.

10 'The average death toll from disasters . . . under twenty-five.' Renton, 2009.

10 'There will be losses . . . Irish skies.' Hossell et al., 2000; K. Sweeney et al., 2008.

11 'Alexis de Tocqueville . . .' De Tocqueville, 2004, 611.

11 'Spain, half of which could become semi-desert . . .' Gao and Georgi, 2008.

13 'the world's largest emitter of greenhouse gases.' Global CO2 emissions: increase continued in 2007, Netherlands Environmental Assessment Agency, www.mnp.nl/en/publications/2008/GlobalCO2emissionsthrough2007.html; Carbon Budget 2007, www.globalcarbonproject.org/carbonbudget/index.htm

13 'in China's view . . .' Government of China, 2007.

14 'eighty-five million by 2081.' UK population may double by 2081, BBC, 27 November 2007, http://news.bbc.co.uk/1/hi/

uk/7115155.stm;

14 'Spain and southern France . . . more than six degrees . . .' IPCC, 2007b, ch. 12.

14 'heatwaves in much of France . . . twenty times as long.' Beniston et al., 2007.

15 'nine million before the middle of the century.' Two million in Northern Ireland by 2031, nine million in the Republic of Ireland by 2041: Northern Ireland population set to be over 1.8 million people by 2011, 23 October 2007, www.nisra.gov.uk/archive/demography/population/projections/popproj06.pdf; Central Statistics Office, 2008.

15 'Egypt . . . desert to encroach.' Agrawala et al., 2004; '. . . twice as many people in Cairo as in London, packed twice as closely together . . .' Demographia, 2009.

16 'People living on low-lying coasts . . . will be threatened by rising sea levels.' IPCC, 2007b, ch. 10.

16 'Two million people could be forced to leave the Mekong delta . . . end of the century.' Pamela McElwee, Social vulnerability and adaptation possibilities for Vietnam in a 4+°C world, 4 Degrees and Beyond: International Climate Conference, 28–30 September 2009, Oxford, www.eci.ox.ac.uk/4degrees/programme.php

16 'The Philippines . . . to droughts and landslides.' Yusuf and Francisco, 2009.

16 'The snows and ice-sheets of the Himalayas . . . rely on it for water.' Yakubowski and Meindersma, 2009. IPCC statement on the melting of Himalayan glaciers, www.ipcc.ch/pdf/presentations/himalaya-statement-20january2010.pdf'

17 'nearly half the population of western Europe may be over sixty.' Lutz et al., 2008, give a figure of forty-six per cent.

18 'a map of Europe . . . flecks of ivory.' Change in mean annual temperature and precipitation by the end of the century, http://peseta.jrc.es/docs/ClimateModel.html

19 '"By northern Britain . . . frontier towns."' Smout, 2000, 7–9.

19 'A map of Britain's uplands . . .' Environment Agency, n.d.

21 '"The sky is foul with continual rains and mists; severe cold is absent."' *'Caelum crebris imbribus ac nebulis foedum; asperitas frigorum abest.'* Tacitus, *Agricola*, Book 1(10),www.sacred-texts.com/cla/tac/ago1010.htm

21 '"Most of England is a thousand years old."' Hoskins, 1977, 303.
22 'verderers' etc. Forests and Chases in England and Wales, c. 1000 to c. 1850: A Glossary of Terms and Definitions, http://info.sjc. ox.ac.uk/forests/glossary.htm; The Verderers of the New Forest, www.verderers.org.uk/index.html
23 'temperatures will probably rise . . . maximum is 6.4°C . . .' Nakicenovic et al., 2000; Humans blamed for climate change, http://news.bbc.co.uk/1/hi/sci/tech/6321351.stm
23 'A four-degree rise . . . 2070s or even earlier.' Mark New, opening remarks, Richard Betts, Regional climate changes at 4+°C, 4 Degrees and Beyond: International Climate Conference, 28–30 September 2009, Oxford, www.eci.ox.ac.uk/4degrees/ programme.php
23 'world's population rises . . . staying at that level.' Nakicenovic et al., 2000, ch. 4; UN Population Division, 2004.
24 'As seas rise . . . cholera as well.' Nicholls et al., 2008.
25 'The one that sets the scene . . . their own courses.' The IPCC's high-growth, globalising scenarios are labelled A1. The variant in which the world carries on regardless is called A1FI, for *F*ossil fuel *I*ntensive. A1B represents more of a balance between fossil fuels and other sources of energy. The scenario in which regions and nations pursue growth separately is called A2.
25 'In Britain . . . the south-west.' The UK figures in this book are derived from or broadly consistent with the High Emissions scenario, 2070s–2099, from the UK Climate Projections, http:// ukclimateprojections.defra.gov.uk issued in June 2009. The studies cited mostly used the previous set of projections, issued in 2002.
25 'climb into the forties.' Secretary of the State for the Environment Hilary Benn, Hansard, 18 June 2009, col. 445, www. publications.parliament.uk/pa/cm200809/cmhansrd/cm090618/ debtext/90618-0006.htm#09061861000004
26 'growth rates of between two and three per cent . . .' IPCC special report on emissions scenarios: 4.4.4. economic development, www.grida.no/publications/other/ipcc%5Fsr/?src=/climate/ipcc/ emission/
26 '3.6 per cent a year.' K. M. Campbell et al., 2007, 84.
26 'First World War . . . destruction in Europe.' Jaeger et al., 2008.

27 'The IPCC . . . Greenland ice.' Stefan Rahmstorf, The IPCC sea level numbers, 17 March 2007, www.realclimate.org/index.php?p=427

27 'United Kingdom's environment ministry . . . earlier figures.' DEFRA, 2007.

27 '1.5 degrees . . . thaw in Greenland.' Tirpak et al., 2005.

27 'Stefan Rahmstorf . . . 1.4 metres by 2100.' Rahmstorf, 2007.

27 'upper limit to two metres . . . glaciers melted.' Pfeffer et al., 2008.

28 'the Netherlands should be ready for the North Sea to rise between two and four metres by 2200.' Deltacommissie, 2008.

28 'James Hansen . . . metres within this century.' Hansen et al., 2007a; Hansen, 2007.

28 'Greenland ice sheet . . . seven metres.' Lowe et al., 2006.

28 'West Antarctic . . . by some estimates.' Bamber et al., 2009, estimate a maximum 3.3 metres, though earlier ones have been 5–6 metres: Tol et al., 2006.

28 'change the shape of Britain . . . a new island.' Flood maps, http://flood.firetree.net/?ll=50.6111,-1.9775&m=7

2 THE ISLE OF LONDON

32 'dense woods and forests' Larwood, 1872.

32 'leprous maidens', The Bailiwick of St James, www.british-history.ac.uk/report.aspx?compid=40542

32 'a nursery for deer.' Hutchings, 1909, vol. II, 732.

33 'is full of wild animals . . . pursuit of the dogs.' Braybrooke, 1959, 133–4.

34 'the natural simplicity . . . impart to it.' Braybrooke, 1959, 156–7.

34 'nature appears . . . regards to order.' Larwood, 1872, 446.

35 'much as Nash left it . . . faithful to his spirit.' St James's Park: From pigs to processions, www.royalparks.org.uk/parks/st_james_park/landscape_history.cfm; History and architecture, www.royalparks.org.uk/parks/st_james_park/history.cfm

35 'average summer temperatures in the Greater London area . . . forty-five per cent in summer.' Austin et al., 2008.

36 'London could have a climate similar to that of Marseille . . .' Hacker et al., 2005.

37 'tall buildings . . . trap the sun's energy . . .' Wilby, 2003.

37 'London is Britain's most prominent heat island . . .' Watkins et al., 2007.

38 'London's heat island intensity reached nine degrees.' Greater London Authority, 2006.

38 'thermal map of London . . . City of London.' Watkins, 2002.

38 'Parks . . . paved interior.' Wilby, 2003.

38 'Gothenburg . . . St James's Park.' Upmanis et al., 1998.

39 'Heat islands reduce the costs of heating . . .' Kolokotroni et al., 2007.

39 '600 excess deaths . . . forty-five per cent in London.' Greater London Authority, 2006.

39 'fifty-four per cent rise in France . . . 22,000 and 35,000.' Schär and Jendritzky, 2004.

39 'By the 2050s . . . ten degrees.' Wilby, 2008.

40 'In Latvia the official threshold is 33°C, but in Malta it is 40.' Meze-Hausken, 2008.

40 'heat seems to cause deaths . . . 19°C.' Hajat et al., 2002.

40 'A step as simple . . . three or four degrees lower.' Watkins et al., 2007.

41 'growth in carbon emissions.' Akbari et al., 2008.

41 'Paints . . . coloured and cool.' The Cool Colors Project, http://coolcolors.lb.gov/

42 'As Tom Clarke of the London Wildlife Trust . . . worth little to developers.' People, politics, plants and parties in King's Cross . . . , formerly at www.wildlondon.org.uk

43 'Olympic Park . . .' London 2012 unveils brand new type of park for 21st century, www.london2012.com/news/media-releases/2008-11/london-2012-unveils-brand-new-type-of-park-for-21st-century.php

44 'blends into the original intentions of Nash's 1828 park design.' Inn the Park, www.royalparks.org.uk/press/current/press_release_64.cfm

44 'continue the park . . . seamless curve', Case study - Inn the Park, St. James's Park, London, www.livingroofs.org/livingpages/caseinnthepark.html

44 'Modelling studies in North America . . .' Banting et al., 2005.

47 'among the world's driest capital cities . . . as Israel.' London

Climate Change Partnership, 2002.

47 'Demand may exceed supply . . . dry year.' Supply and demand, updated with 2007/8 map: Figure 3, www.environment-agency. gov.uk/research/library/publications/103016.aspx

47 'Londoners use 168 litres . . . leaks out of them.' Greater London Authority, 2008.

48 'concreting over their front gardens . . .' Paving your front garden, www.planningportal.gov.uk/england/genpub/en/1115316438436. html

48 'London's water foundations . . . North Downs.' Fry and Kelly, 2009.

48 'By the 1960s . . . new wells.' Rising groundwater in central London, www.groundwateruk.org/Rising_Groundwater_in_ Central_London.aspx

49 'too many pumps . . .' Impeccable source, June 2007, www. building.co.uk/story.asp?storycode=3088490

50 'London's population . . .' GLA demography update 16-2008, www.london.gov.uk/gla/publications/factsandfigures/dmag- update-16-2008.pdf

50 'density of dwellings in London.' Ravetz, 2008.

50 'Richard Rogers . . . Notting Hill.' Greater London Authority, 2003.

50 'Carefully designed and properly managed . . . dense packing.' Rosbottom, 2007; PRP, 2002.

51 'superdensity.' Rosbottom, 2007; Derbyshire et al., 2007.

51 'London Plan . . . four hundred dwellings per hectare.' Mayor of London, 2008, 69.

51 'Parisians . . . five hundred dwellings per hectare.' Palmer et al., 2006.

51 'windows . . . compromise decency.' Derbyshire et al., 2007.

53 'One Brighton . . . "three planets to live on".' One Brighton, www. onebrighton.co.uk; One Planet Living, www.oneplanetliving.com/ index.html; BioRegional, www.bioregional.com

56 'Timber-framed buildings seem to be quieter . . .' Derbyshire et al., 2007.

56 'cement production . . . five per cent of global carbon dioxide emissions.' Mahasenan et al., 2003.

56 'Portobello Farm.' Portobello Farm by E. Adveno Brookes –

19th century, www.rbkc.gov.uk/vmgallery/general/medium.asp? gallery=vm_then_now_portobello_road&img=then_and_now/ small/vm_tn_0028.jpg&size=medium&caller=vm%5Fthen%5F now%5Fgallery%2Easp&cpg=3&tpg=3

57 'Over a fifth of English homes . . . before 1945.' Arup and Three Regions Climate Change Group, 2008.

57 'Britain's homes . . . quarter of the country's greenhouse gas emissions.' Office of Climate Change, 2007.

57 'the newest are the most efficient.' Roberts, 2008.

58 'Nearly seventy per cent . . . outlay and disruption.' Adults moving house each year: by tenure before and after move, 1991–1996: Social Trends 30; www.statistics.gov.uk/STATBASE/xsdataset. asp?vlnk=517

58 'People will build their lives upon the capital embodied in their homes.' Scott, 2004.

59 'current rates of demolition . . . national housing stock.' Palmer et al., 2006; Office of Climate Change, 2007.

60 '*Zukunft Haus*'. Power, 2008.

60 'BedZED eco-village has cut water use to half the national average . . .' BedZED, www.bioregional.com/what-we-do/our-work/bedzed/; Building Research Energy Conservation Support Unit, 2002

60 'houses dating from the first half of the twentieth century or earlier . . . makes the rooms smaller.' Eco-refurbishment of solid wall house, http://home2.btconnect.com/eco-refurbishment/, is a site in which a Brighton couple describe how they overhauled their Victorian family home with insulation on as many surfaces as possible, wall heating, new windows (plastic, on cost grounds) and six new south-facing windows.

63 'over half of London's shop floorspace . . .' Austin et al., 2008.

63 'Horsa huts . . .' Burke and Grosvenor, 2008, 96. The name stood for Hutting Operation for the Raising of the School-leaving Age.

63 '75 watts per teacher and 60 watts per pupil.' Jenkins et al., 2008.

65 'the zone at risk from tidal floods . . .' Thames Estuary 2100, 2009.

66 'Sir Hermann Bondi . . . nerve centre of the country' Baxter, 2005; Thames Estuary 2100, 2009.

67 'Not all governments . . . once in a thousand years.' Nicholls et al., 2008.

67 'Bondi's report . . . Thames Barrier.' Baxter, 2005; Risk Management Solutions, 2003; Thames Flood Barrier (Hansard, 9 November 1970), http://hansard.millbanksystems.com/commons/1970/nov/09/thames-flood-barrier

67 'What happened in 1953 . . .' Baxter, 2005.

68 'Another metre . . . 650 square kilometres.' Dawson et al., 2005.

68 'Thames Estuary 2100 project . . . tide-blocking barrages.' Thames Estuary 2100, 2009.; 'More defences needed' against Thames flooding, www.edie.net/news/news_story.asp?id=14171; DEFRA, 2006.

69 'Peak summer daily temperatures are nearly seven degrees hotter . . .' Key findings for London, 2080s. High emissions scenario, http://ukclimateprojections.defra.gov.uk/content/view/2203/528: central estimate for increase in summer mean daily maximum temperature is 6.7°C.

78 'Africa south of the Sahara . . . shortened or failed altogether . . .' Thornton et al., 2006.

81 'In the Andes, melting glaciers revived peasant insurgencies . . .' Such tensions have already arisen in Peru, which has a history of mountain insurgency: Water wars come to the Andes, *Scientific American*, 19 May 2009, www.scientificamerican.com/article.cfm?id=water-wars-in-the-andes

84 'in China . . . skirmishes between local militias.' In 1999, farmers used military weapons, including mortars, in a conflict over water in the Hebei and Henan provinces: Ben Small, Mythical water wars, *Columbia Political Review*, December 2008.

84 'Although even antagonistic states . . . break-up of Pakistan.' Barnaby, 2009; Briscoe et al., 2005; Stephan Faris, The Last Straw, *Foreign Policy*, 2009, www.foreignpolicy.com/articles/2009/06/22/failed_states_index_the_last_straw

84 'Euphrates ebbed . . . nearly seventy-five per cent . . .' Kitoh et al., 2008.

89 'London's heat island makes the capital hotter than . . . Portsmouth, Southampton, Bournemouth and Poole.' Austin et al., 2008, present scenarios for the 2080s in which London's mean summer temperature is 5.5°C higher than a century before, while Southampton's is 5.7°C, but suggest that London's temperatures could exceed Southampton's because of the heat island effect.

89 'London is more than half a century ahead of Manchester . . .' Hacker et al., 2005, investigated how much more uncomfortable buildings in cities could become as a result of warming: Manchester in the 2050s resembled London in the 1980s, and Edinburgh in the 2080s resembled Manchester in the 1980s. They used a 'medium-high' climate change scenario rather than the 'high' scenario that would correspond better to the storyline in this book.

3 THE CUCKMERE DELTA

92 'All the Southern countryside . . . green grass.' 'The (Banks of the) Sweet Primeroses', www.informatik.uni-hamburg. de/~zierke/shirley.collins/songs/thesweetprimeroses.html
92 'At Cobham Lodge . . . half a degree Celsius.' Molesworth, 1880.
94 'seven generations of the family.' The Copper Family, Coppersongs: Song Index page, www.thecopperfamily.com/ songs/coppersongs/index.html
95 'Cuckmere estuary is inclined to form a delta.' V. J. May, Beachy Head – Seaford Head, in May and Hansom, 2003, www.jncc. gov.uk/pdf/gcrdb/GCRsiteaccount1850.pdf
95 'According to predictions . . . greyed out.' Jacobs Babtie, 2007, Appendix 8, pp. 15, 68.
96 'entered the sea under the eastern cliff.' South Coast Harbours 1698: report by Edmund Dummer and Thomas Wiltshaw, www. geog.port.ac.uk/webmap/dummer/dumd_cuc.htm
97 'outfall direction . . . uncommon crookedness.' Bannister, 1999, 25.
98 'The country . . . long caws.' Gissing, 2003.
99 'In the Middle Ages . . . a third of a million people . . .' Jacobs Babtie, 2007; Comparison of annual visitor numbers to the Seven Sisters Country Park, via www.sevensisters.org.uk/rte.asp?id=57
100 'what will happen . . . as the sea rises and the storm surges mount.' Jacobs Babtie, 2007.
100 'defending coastlines is an awesomely expensive business . . .' Beach Sustainability in East Sussex: Interim Report of the BERM Project, 2001.

100 'Jim Copper . . . suburbanisation.' James 'Jim' Copper, 1882–1954, www.thecopperfamily.com/past/family/jim.html

101 'two million out of work . . . Maynard Keynes.' Stevenson, 1984, 266. Keynes spent considerable time at Charleston Farmhouse, a few miles north of Seaford, and owned a house nearby.

101 'Twenty years after . . . bouts of erosion.' ROCC Coast Protection, formerly at http://sesis.eng.bton.ac.uk/environment/research/earth_systems/agru/rocc_coast_protection.htm

101 'a metre higher, and rising four times as fast . . .' Defra, 2006.

102 'Floods . . . hold a million cubic metres . . .' River could go back to nature, *Argus* (Brighton and Hove), 23 January 2002, http://archive.theargus.co.uk/2002/1/23/164549.html

102 'A study of flood risks for Lewes . . .' Huntingford et al., 2003.

102 'Saltmarsh and mudflats . . . 1973 and 1988.' Habitat Action Plan: Coastal Saltmarsh, www.ukbap.org.uk/UKPlans.aspx?ID=33#1

103 'precautions against mosquito bites.' Expert Group on Climate Change and Health in the UK, 2001. The advice was omitted from the 2008 revision of the document; Kovats, 2008.

103 'could become indigenous . . .' Chin and Welsby, 2004.

103 'confined to one or two people.' Lindsay and Willis, 2006.

103 'Rich countries can keep diseases like malaria in check.' Reiter, 2001; Hunter, 2003.

103 'Florida or Turkey . . . malarial parasite.' Rogers et al., in Kovats, 2008, ch. 3.

104 'a malaria vaccine even might make the disease more dangerous . . .' Modelling malaria virulence, http://malaria.wellcome.ac.uk/doc_WTD023856.html

104 'two hundred million or more people could be at risk from malaria . . .' van Lieshout et al., 2004.

105 'Glassworts . . .' Mabey, 1996, 98.

105 'This prospect is regarded with dismay . . .' Local people's views are presented in Hopkins Van Mil, 2009, and Jacobs Babtie, 2007.

107 'Many of the dykes . . . speculations they remain.' East Sussex County Council Monument Full Report 26/10/2007, SMR Number MES1719; Bannister, 1999.

107 'The cottages . . . half a metre a year.' Longstaff-Tyrrell, 2004; Dornbusch et al., 2008.

108 'Belle Tout lighthouse was moved . . .' Managed relocation: an assessment of its feasibility as a coastal management option, 2003, http://goliath.ecnext.com/coms2/gi_0199-2678824/Managed-relocation-an-assessment-of.html

108 'Thousands of tons of chalk . . .' Haslett, 2000, 36.

109 'Several cottages . . . target practice.' Longstaff-Tyrrell, 2004, 86.

110 'Birling Gap . . .' Coastal erosion, House of Lords debates, 7 June 2000, www.theyworkforyou.com/lords/?gid=2000-06-07a.1165.0; Citation: Seaford to Beachy Head, Site of Special Scientific Interest, www.english-nature.org.uk/ citation/ citation_photo/1002008.pdf; John Aldworth, Government Office for the South East, letter, March 2001, www.databases. odpm.gov.uk/planning/data/callins/birlngap.pdf; Convention for the Protection of Human Rights and Fundamental Freedoms as amended by Protocol No. 11, with Protocol Nos. 1, 4, 6, 7, 12 and 13, Council of Europe, www.echr.coe.int/NR/rdonlyres/D5CC24A7-DC13-4318-B457-5C9014916D7A/0/EnglishAnglais.pdf

110 'Nigel Newton . . . should be preserved.' LW/04/0662, Seaford, 30.03.04, Raising height of flood protection banks by 300mm, relaying footpath surface material and construction of bird hide at land & riverbanks south of Exceat Bridge off A259 for Mr N. Newton, Lewes District Council, www.lewes.gov.uk/Files/plancttee_060628_LW_04_0662.doc; Minutes of meeting held on 15 April 2003, Environmental Review Board, Lewes District Council, www.lewes.gov.uk/Files/erb_030415_mins.pdf. Lewes and Wealden District Councils welcomed Newton's planning application but withheld support after English Nature and the EA objected that it had not evaluated the risks sufficiently.

112 'a habitat for the flowers . . . even short sward.' Boardman et al., 2003; Chalk Grassland, www.sevensisters.org.uk/rte.asp?id=58

113 'A fifth of Britain's chalk grassland . . . barley and wheat.' Burnside et al., 2003.

113 'myxomatosis epidemic . . . Paris.' Ross et al., 1986.

114 'On the South Downs . . . under the plough.' Beldon et al., 2000.

114 'damaged by muddy floods . . .' Boardman et al., 2003; also Robinson and Blackman, 1990.

114 'In November 2000 water . . . flooding the London line.' Butler, 2005.

115 'early advent of a wetter winter.' UK Climate Projections data (http://ukclimateprojections.defra.gov.uk) suggest – and at this stage they can do no more than suggest – that south-eastern autumns late in the century could be dry until November, with the winter rains then setting in away from the coast.

115 'Winter wheat . . . a meaner hand.' National Farmers' Union, 2006; Parry et al., 2005.

115 'A modest amount . . . harvests would decline.' IPCC, 2007b, Summary for Policymakers. See also Nelson et al, 2009.

115 'One map of the future . . . five and ten per cent.' A1FI scenario. Parry et al., 2004.

116 'crop yields . . . the rise of industry.' Tubiello et al., 2007.

116 'South Africa . . . a tenth of what it is today . . .' IPCC, 2007b, ch. 9.

116 'South Asia . . . developing countries in general.' Nelson et al, 2009.

117 'Wheat production . . . open up for cultivation.' Ewert et al., 2005.

117 'By the 2080s . . . make up the difference.' Fischer et al., 2002.

117 'Prices are expected to rise . . . along with temperatures.' Schmidhuber and Tubiello, 2007. Parry et al., 2004, calculated that under a business-as-usual storyline of vigorous growth and globalisation, cereal prices would rise by about sixty per cent by 2060, then decline as the world's population fell. They would still remain strong, however – and if the population didn't fall, as the storyline in this book goes, neither would the prices.

118 'agricultural consequences . . . drinking and washing.' Olesen et al., 2007.

118 'vineyards . . . wine-producing region.' Jones, 2007; Jones et al., 2005. Richard Selley, emeritus professor of geology at Imperial College London, predicts that southern England will actually become too hot for cool-preferring varieties like Chardonnay and Pinot Noir, which will be grown in the north, while Merlot and Viognier will flourish in the south and Midlands: www.winelandsofbritain.co.uk/book.htm

119 'Species-rich chalk grassland . . . remaining shade.' English Nature, 1997.

121 'beech woods on the chalk soils of southern England.' Broadmeadow and Ray, 2005.

121 'Corsican pine . . .' Forestry Commission suspends Corsican pine planting, www.forestry.gov.uk/NewsRele.nsf/web-allbysu bject/5E8A8246143878B38025729500510FB6

123 'Many species will need to move . . . territory to move through.' Warren et al., 2001.

123 'clothed with many plants . . . damp earth.' Darwin, 1996, 395.

124 'early spider orchid . . . year to year.' Lang, 2004, www. britainsorchids.fieldguide.co.uk/?PP=species_account&SPID =59&SHC=3&PSD=1

124 ' . . . most do not reach more than ten centimetres.' Hutchings, 1987.

125 'we can hardly believe in so gigantic an imposture'. Darwin, 1877, 37.

125 'we know now . . . quantity to quality.' Ledford, 2007; Schiestl et al., 1999; Schiestl, 2005.

125 'the newest piece of England.' The Newest Piece of England – the Orchid – Publications, Kent Downs, www.kentdowns.org. uk/orchid_1_3.asp

126 'low tide is around half past six.' Newhaven, England, WWW Tide and Current Predictor, http://tbone.biol.sc.edu/tide/ tideshow.cgi?site=Newhaven%2C+England

126 'The longest day . . . samphire season.' Mabey, 1996, 97.

127 'sediment is in short supply . . .' Orford and Pethick, 2006.

133 'British White cattle . . . White Park cattle . . .' British White Cattle - Ancient Breed History of the polled park cattle of the British Isles, J. West Cattle Company, www.jwest.biz/ AncientBreedHistory.htm; Jessica Hemming, *Bos primigenius* in Britain: or, why do fairy cows have red ears?, *Folklore*, April 2002, http://findarticles.com/p/articles/mi_m2386/is_1_113/ ai_86063329

4 SUFFOLK COASTAL

137 'Dunwich has grown as the sea has washed it away . . .' Map of Dunwich and the Lost City, Heritage House, n.d.; 'more than fifty . . .', 'one of the most important ports . . . Middle Ages',

Sebald, 2002, 155; Underwater city could be revealed, http://news.bbc.co.uk/1/hi/england/7187239.stm

138 'leaked draft document . . .' Climate change: Surrender a slab of Norfolk, say conservationists, *The Times*, 29 March 2008, 139 'The authorities . . . did not set out the radical option.' Natural England Climate Change project and report, www.naturalengland.org.uk/regions/east_of_england/ourwork/climatechangeproject.aspx; Defra comment on Norfolk Broads, 23 June 2008, www.naturalengland.org.uk/Images/defra_statement_on_norfolkbroads_tcm6-2720.pdf

139 'Storms in the 1280s . . . new port was built.' Suffolk landscape character typology: Open coastal fens, www.suffolklandscape.org.uk/landscapes/Open-coastal-fens.aspx

139 'paying its bills in herrings.' Kermode, 1993.

140 'The cliffs are more than ninety per cent sand . . . helping to cushion Sizewell . . .' Pye and Blott, 2006; Guthrie and Cottle, 2002.

140 'Sizewell A . . . new reactors next door.' Nuclear Decommissioning Authority, 2006; Sizewell A, www.nda.gov.uk/sites/sizewella/; Nomination details, Nominated Sites: Sizewell, Suffolk, www.nuclearpowersiting.decc.gov.uk/nomination/sizewell/; Allen, 2008; EDF Energy welcomes Government announcement on nuclear sites, www.edfenergy.com/media-centre/press-news/EDF_Energy_welcomes_Government_announcement_on_nuclear_sites.shtml

142 'seven metres clear . . . not credible' Halcrow Group, 2007; see also Gallani, 2007.

142 'A report prepared for Greenpeace . . .' Middlesex University Flood Hazard Research Centre, 2007. An animation on the Greenpeace website, based on the report, vaults beyond scientific credibility with the claim that sea levels could rise six metres by the end of the century. Most scientists believe that if the West Antarctic Ice Sheet were to collapse, the rise in sea levels would take centuries. The likely total rise has been taken to be up to six metres, but a more recent study puts it at half that: Threat from West Antarctica less than previously believed, www.bristol.ac.uk/geography/news/2009/110.html

142 'Under Britain's current nuclear decommissioning strategy . . .'

radioactivity inside their hulks decays.' Institution of Engineering and Technology, 2008, notes that Britain's strategy was developed for its Magnox reactors but could be applied to pressurised water reactors, the type installed at Sizewell B, though the timescales could be different.

142 'The industry is growing impatient . . . twenty or thirty years.' Ernst & Young, n.d.

143 'the first example of the design . . . fifty per cent more than planned.' Possible new delay for Areva Finnish EPR – papers, www.reuters.com/article/rbssUtilitiesElectric/idUSLH21344720081017

143 'used to make plutonium for nuclear weapons . . .' The United Kingdom's Defence Nuclear Weapons Programme, http://tridentplacement.net/fils/historical_accounting.pdf.   Nuclear Power in the United Kingdom, www.world-nuclear.org/info/inf84.html; Nuclear power's uneasy history, www.telegraph.co.uk/finance/economics/2809389/Nuclear-powers-uneasy-history.html

144 'heterodox green thinkers accept the need for it . . .' Mark Lynas, Why greens must learn to love nuclear power, www.marklynas.org/2008/9/19/why-greens-must-learn-to-love-nuclear-power; George Monbiot, Nuked by friend and foe, www.monbiot.com/archives/2009/02/20/nuked-by-friend-and-foe/

144 'A fifth of Britain's electricity . . . increase in that fraction.' John Hutton, New nuclear build: How do we make progress? www.berr.gov.uk/aboutus/ministerialteam/Speeches/page45417.html

144 'which in Britain means that they must go by the sea.' Only one British nuclear power station has been built inland, on a lakeside at Trawsfynydd in North Wales; it shut down in 1991.

145 'an invasion in which scores of activists scaled the fences . . .' Campaigners in power station protest, www.telegraph.co.uk/news/1410143/Campaigners-in-power-station-protest.html

145 'fast breeder reactors . . . bombs as well as fuel.' How do fast breeder reactors differ from regular nuclear power plants? www.scientificamerican.com/article.cfm?id=how-do-fast-breeder-react

146 'uranium reserves . . . by 2030.' Uranium resources sufficient to meet projected nuclear energy requirements long into the future, www.nea.fr/html/general/press/2008/2008-02.html

147 'put the Sun in a box . . .' Quels matériaux pour emprisonner le soleil?, www.cea.fr/jeunes/themes/l_energie_nucleaire/fusion_

controlee/quels_materiaux_pour_emprisonner_le_soleil

147 'ITER.' The ITER Project, www.iter.org; ITER fusion reactor faces new delay, Science Insider, 19 November 2009, http://blogs.sciencemag.org/scienceinsider/2009/11/iter-fusion-rea. html.

148 'forty years away, and always will be.' Nuclear fusion must be worth the gamble, *New Scientist*, 7 June 2006, www.newscientist. com/article/mg19025543.300-editorial-nuclear-fusion-must-be-worth-the-gamble.html

148 'Artificial fusion . . . into living tissue.' Nuclear fusion power, www.world-nuclear.org/info/inf66.html

148 'mined on the Moon.' Mining the Moon, www.technologyreview. com/energy/19296/

149 'The practicality of carbon capture . . . pumps and rigs.' Smil, 2006.

150 'by 2030 nuclear power will meet about the same proportion of world energy needs . . .' International Atomic Energy Agency, 2007, 25.

151 'Minsmere . . . flagship reserve.' Samstag, 1988, 67; Cocker and Mabey, 2005, 193.

151 'Minsmere's reedbeds . . . brims over the top of them.' Pye and Blott, 2006; Recent coastal changes and future management options for the Dunwich to Sizewell area, Suffolk, www.kpal. co.uk/Minsmere.htm; Environment Agency, 2009; Guthrie and Cottle, 2002.

151 'After shingle and sand dunes blocked the estuary . . . reedbeds all the same.' Samstag, 1988, 67; Cocker and Mabey, 2005, 193.

153 'geese, waders, ducks and swans . . . middle of Siberia.' SPA review – Introduction, www.jncc.gov.uk/page-1416

153 'More than half the world's tundra . . . later decades of the century.' Zöckler and Lysenko, 2000.

154 'Over half a million dunlin . . . Novaya Zemlya.' Beale et al., 2006.

155 'Rigs perforate the tundra . . . collective farms.' Dallmann and Peskov, n.d.; Stammler and Forbes, 2006; BBC –Tribe – Nenets, www.bbc.co.uk/tribe/tribes/nenets/index.shtml

155 'slow the rate at which the dunlin's nesting area shrinks . . .' Zöckler et al., 2008, calculate that under a B2 scenario, corresponding to the UK's 'medium-low' scenario, and without the influence

of reindeer, the area occupied by dunlin in the Barents Sea region would decrease 24.5 per cent between 1990 and 2080. With the reindeer, the decrease would be 20.4 per cent.

156 'It weighed about fifty grams . . . halfway home again.' Goede et al., 1990.

157 'the disused plants resemble a convoy of paid-off battleships . . .' illustration in Allen, 2008.

5 UPPER MARGINS

159 'There, fertile meadows; here, barren heaths.' Hopkins, 1979, 13.

159 'the rains are frequent, the winds boisterous . . . Third Crusade.' Giraldus Cambrensis, 1997, ch. 3; Notes on Llanthony Priory, www.ewyaslacy.org.uk/doc.php?d=nw_lty_3003%20

160 'westerly winds sweep in . . . releasing the ocean moisture they have brought with them.' Price, 1981.

160 'Archdeacon Coxe . . . inconvenient and unsafe.' Bellows, 1868, 12–13.

162 'summer of 1976 . . . lets it spread through the ground.' Great weather events: Summer hot and summer even hotter in 1976, www.metoffice.gov.uk/corporate/pressoffice/anniversary/summer1976.html; The 1976 drought, www.bbc.co.uk/weather/features/understanding/1976_drought.shtml

162 'a heatwave like that could be expected once in three hundred years.' Kovats et al., 1999.

162 'There is twice as much carbon . . . land surface.' Eaton et al., 2008.

163 'Peat covers the same percentage of Wales . . . United Kingdom's vegetation.' There are 121 million tonnes of carbon in Welsh peat, 114 million tonnes in UK vegetation: Scottish Executive ERAD, 2007.

163 'Soils . . . have been losing carbon . . . climate is responsible.' Bellamy et al., 2005.

163 'By the 2050s . . . British Isles' peatlands.' Ireland contains 0.95 million hectares of peatland: Connolly et al., 2007; Britain: 1.23 million: Beverland et al., 1996.

164 'Half the world's peatlands . . . industrialise the world.' Martini et al., 2006, 2, 19; Allen et al., 2009b.

164 'an immense amount of heat to melt them completely, and

probably a very long period of time.' Archer and Brovkin, 2008; Shindell, 2007.

164 'Methane is bubbling up . . . 1974 and 2000.' Walter et al., 2006.

164 'Similar rises were recorded in Sweden over the same period.' Thawing subarctic perma-frost increases greenhouse gas emissions, http://earthobservatory.nasa.gov/Newsroom/view.php?id=24343

164 'Meltwater is pooling . . . begin to thaw.' Climate warning as Siberia melts, 11 August 2005, www.newscientist.com/article/mg18725124.500

164 'Humans have emitted half a trillion tonnes of carbon . . .' Allen et al., 2009b.

166 'large tracts of it have matured into woodland.' An experiment in Yorkshire shows that woodlands on this kind of ground could mature in about fifty years: 5.11. The Dimbleby Plots: an experiment in recreating native woodland, www.forestry.gov.uk/pdf/Nympart2.pdf/$FILE/Nympart2.pdf

168 'The miners worked veins of galena . . . Gunnerside Gill in Swaledale.' White, 2005; Lead mining in the Yorkshire Dales, www.martinroe.pwp.blueyonder.co.uk/index.htm

169 'There are less than a thousand hectares of upland hay meadow . . . strive for efficiency.' Habitat Action Plan: Upland hay meadows, www.ukbap.org.uk/UKPlans.aspx?ID=11#1; Pacha and Petit, 2008; Jefferson, 2005.

169 'without windows at the back . . .' Cooper, 1948, introduction.

170 'Yellow rattle . . .' Westbury, 2004; Bardgett et al., 2006.

170 'wood crane's-bill . . . in steep decline.' Pacha and Petit, 2008.

170 'temperatures in Yorkshire could rise . . . gone by 2050.' Key findings for Yorkshire & Humber, 2080s, High emissions scenario, http://ukclimateprojections.defra.gov.uk/content/view/2293/528.html; Berry et al., 2002; Holman and Loveland, 2001.

6 A NEW CALEDONIA

174 'wet desert.' Smout, 2000, 117.

174 'Even to walk . . . to stand in them is to feel the past.' Steven and Carlisle, 1959, v.

175 'a steep gradient in annual rainfall . . .' Ogilvy et al., 2006.

175 'this wettest corner of Europe'. Tipping et al., 2004.

175 'These "grannies" . . . two hundred years younger.' Wield and Stevenson, 2004.

176 'The Hydro Board's considerate approach . . . some hundred per cent.' Smout, 2000, 113, 115; The Hydro Story, www. glenaffric.org/heritage_hydro.html

177 'In 1959 the Forestry Commission decided not to cut down the mature forest.' The Agreement between Forestry Enterprise and Trees for Life on Work in the Glen Affric Caledonian Forest Reserve, www.caledonia.org.uk/socialland/affric.htm; Oosthoek, 2000.

177 'Given mineral soil . . . well groomed lawn.' And it came to pass . . . , Finlay MacRae, www.treesforlife.org.uk/tfl.finlay_macrae.html

177 'What struck me the most . . . in the UK.' Watson Featherstone, 2004a.

178 'increase the forests' "value to society . . ."; ". . . for its own sake".' Our mission and values, www.forestry.gov.uk/forestry/infd-6val65; Our vision, www.treesforlife.org.uk/tfl.visi.html

179 'Carrifran Wildwood'. www.carrifran.org.uk

180 'Tipping brought in two postgraduate students . . .' Tipping et al., 2004, 2006; Shaw and Tipping, 2006; Tipping, 2003.

182 'Farmers began to cultivate . . . less cover for wolves.' Davies, 2007; Davies and Tipping, 2004.

182 'Farmers did not take over . . . .early modern times.' Tipping et al., 2006.

182 'Pine made its first appearance . . . since 8,300 years ago.' Froyd and Bennett, 2006.

182 'Tipping and his colleagues argued . . . "what nature deals".' Tipping et al., 2004.

183 'overlighting spirits'. Findhorn Foundation history, www.findhorn.org/whatwedo/vision/history.php

184 'winter rainfall increasing several times more in the west than the east.' Suggested by UK Climate Projections, http://ukclimateprojections.defra.gov.uk/

184 'burn like wet asbestos.' Rackham, 1986, 72; Tipping, 1994.

184 'Particles of charcoal . . . heath and mire to form.' Froyd, 2006.

184 'Scots pines . . . growth in spring.' Carlisle and Brown, 1968.

184 'birches . . . could start their springs earlier.' Skre et al., 2005.

184 'Warmer summers . . . rowan and oak.' Ray, 2008.

185 'Northern trees . . . naturally occupy.' Davis et al., 2005.

185 'mountain pine beetle . . . whole of Canada.' Kurz et al., 2008.

185 'In Scotland, these may include *Phytophthora* . . .' Ray et al., 2008. UK Climate Projections (http://ukclimateprojections.defra.gov.uk/) suggest that with high carbon emissions, British springs in the late twenty-first century would be slightly wetter than at present.

185 'Half the Scots pines . . . an already dry region.' Rebetez and Dobbertin, 2004.

186 'possible impact of wild boar . . . opening space for tree seedlings.' Results from the Guisachan Wild Boar Project, www.treesforlife.org.uk/forest/missing/guisachan200805.html

186 'I want to see the wild boar . . . their rightful habitat.' www.treesforlife.org.uk/about/200806boar.mov

187 'Boar have already a reputation . . . Animal Liberation Front.' Farmers fear further boar damage, 5 January 2006, http://news.bbc.co.uk/1/hi/england/devon/4583098.stm

187 'These are wild, aggressive animals . . . a kid playing in the woods.' Wild boar is shot dead amid fears for public safety, 19 June 2001, www.telegraph.co.uk/news/uknews/1313721/Wild-boar-is-shot-dead-amid-fears-for-public-safety.html

188 'As well as size and vigour . . . keeping the numbers down.' Moore and Wilson, 2005; Defra, 2008a.

189 'beavers were extirpated . . . attempt at reintroduction.' Halley and Rosell, 2002.

189 'the Scottish Executive parried it . . .' No go ahead for beavers in Scotland, 20 December 2002, www.scotland.gov.uk/News/Releases/2002/12/2837

189 'the Executive refused permission.' Executive rejects proposal to reintroduce beavers, 1 September 2005, www.scotland.gov.uk/News/Releases/2005/09/01131458. Its grounds were possible damage to a Special Area of Conservation and uncertainties about the legality of killing the beavers if they got out of hand.

190 'charismatic, resourceful little mammals.' Beavers to return after 400 years 25 May 2008, http://news.bbc.co.uk/1/hi/scotland/glasgow_and_west/7419183.stm

190 'The piomeers came from Norway . . . in May 2009.' Beavers return after 400-year gap, http://news.bbc.co.uk/1/hi/

scotland/8072443.stm; Royal Zoological Society of Scotland and Scottish Wildlife Trust, 2007.

190 'perhaps the simplest and least problematical'. Response from Trees for Life to the public consultation (1998) about beaver reintroduction to Scotland, www.treesforlife.org.uk/beaver_reintroduction.html

190 'effectively alien . . . on the Danube.' SRPBA responds to consultation on a proposal to introduce the European Beaver (*Castor fiber*) on a trial basis for 3–5 years in Knapdale Lochs, Argyll (Full consultation response); Transcript – Beavers, 9 October 2007, both at www.srpba.com.

191 'waterway engineers'. Royal Zoological Society of Scotland and Scottish Wildlife Trust, 2007.

191 'beavers escaped from three of around five sites.' Macdonald and Burnham, 2007.

191 'A few may travel . . .' Macdonald et al., 2000; also R. D. Campbell et al., 2007.

192 'A study . . . flowed too fast or rose too high.' South et al., 2000.

192 'In Vienna . . . walk round dams.' Halley and Rosell, 2002.

193 'Glen Affric, parts of which look highly suitable for beavers.' Parker et al., 2000.

193 'Loch Ness . . . to be found'. Kitchener and Conroy, 1997.

194 'a habitat network . . . as conservationists urge.' Fowler and Stiven, 2003.

194 'new hydropower schemes . . .' Forrest, 2008.

195 'cost in the thousands and the potential benefit . . . in the millions.' R. D. Campbell et al., 2007.

196 'birds moved their ranges 91 kilometres north . . . behind.' Devictor et al., 2008.

196 'Many British butterflies have declined . . .' Warren et al., 2001.

196 'Dartford warblers . . . two million pairs.' A6.101 Dartford warbler *Sylvia undata*, www.jncc.gov.uk/pdf/UKSPA/UKSPA-A6-101.pdf

196 'Dartford warblers have the smallest range of any birds that nest in Britain.' Cocker and Mabey, 2005, 370.

197 'Spain . . . may become too hot for them.' Huntley et al., 2008b, 711–12.

199 'To get kites back into England . . . east of Oxford.' I became aware of this after one flapped out of a tree and glided low over my head in the Warburg Nature Reserve near Henley-on-Thames. I phoned the British Trust for Ornithology and said that I knew it sounded ridiculous but I had seen a red kite in woods near Henley. 'Well, you shouldn't have!' retorted the ornithologist.

199 'they are venturing into London . . .' Red kite delight as bird of prey makes flying visit to London, 13 January 2006, www. telegraph.co.uk/news/uknews/1507698/Red-kite-delight-as-bird-of-prey-makes-flying-visit-to-London.html

199 'padding their nests with clothes taken from washing lines.' Pants found in red kite nest, 13 August 2008, http:// environment.uk.msn.com/news/in-depth/article.aspx?cp-documentid=9201492

199 'city scavengers . . . when the kite builds, look to lesser linen.' *The Winter's Tale*, IV.iii; Cocker and Mabey, 2005, 114–19.

200 'luring kites to their gardens . . . unsuitable.' Killing kites with kindness, 13 December 2006, www.zsl.org/info/media/press-releases/null,1848,PR.html

200 'fewer of their eggs hatch . . . anywhere else.' Seoane et al., 2003.

201 'Britain could support 50,000 . . . population.' Cocker and Mabey, 2005, 119.

201 'red kite range for 2070 . . . disappeared.' Huntley et al., 2008b, 196–7. The *Climatic Atlas* map does not identify suitable breeding areas in Britain either.

201 'Many other factors . . . other species.' Beale et al., 2008; Pushing the modelling envelope, *Nature*, 15 September 2008, www.nature.com/news/2008/080915/full/news.2008.1108.html

201 'red kite could lose between forty-two and eighty-six per cent of its range.' Climate change threatens a million species with extinction, 7 January 2004, http://web.archive.bibalex.org/web/20040413091907/http://www.leeds.ac.uk/media/current/extinction.htm

202 'feeding habits of kites in the Midlands . . .' English Nature, 2002.

202 'Kites prefer corpses . . . breeding season.' Valkama et al., 2005.

203 'After Spanish rabbit populations collapsed . . . came to Spain for the winter.' Villafuerte et al., 1998.

203 'the number of breeding pairs has remained in the tens . . .' Conservation: Red kite, www.rspb.org.uk/ourwork/conservation/species/casestudies/redkite.asp

203 'bait had killed a third of the kites released in Scotland . . .' Poisoning kills third of red kites, 3 January 2002, http://news.bbc.co.uk/1/hi/scotland/1739549.stm; Red kite: Threats, www.rspb.org.uk/wildlife/birdguide/name/r/redkite/threats.asp

204 'shooting of a red kite...south of Dublin.' Rare bird of prey recently released found shot dead, 30 August 2007, www.irishtimes.com/newspaper/ireland/2007/0830/1188336377272.html

204 'research by David Hetherington . . .' Hetherington et al., 2008.

205 'Hetherington has also advanced the case . . . "candidate for reintroduction".' Hetherington et al., 2006.

206 'This strategy flies in the face of conventional conservation approaches.' Hoegh-Guldberg et al., 2008.

206 'Thomas . . . suggested several species . . . for introduction to Britain.' Relocation, relocation, relocation to save species, http://news.scotsman.com/world/Relocation-relocation-relocation-to-save.4301677.jp; The Lynx could soon be roaming the Highlands under plan to make Britain a 'Noah's Ark' for endangered species, www.dailymail.co.uk/sciencetech/article-1036133/The-Lynx-soon-roaming-Highlands-plan-turn-Britain-Noahs-Ark.html

206 'Iberian lynx . . . Spanish range shrank . . .' Johnson et al., 2004.

206 'Red List . . . at least 2,000 years.' *Lynx pardinus*, The IUCN Red List of Threatened Species, http://web.archive.org/web/20080216010339/http://www.iucnredlist.org/search/details.php/12520/summ

206 'Iberian lynxes eat rabbits . . . numbers crashed with them.' Calvete et al., 2002.

207 'rainfall in the park will steadily decline . . .' Mitigating climate change in Spain's Doñana National Park, 1 February 2006, www.panda.org/about_wwf/what_we_do/footprint/climate_carbon_energy/climate_deal/news/impacts/?uNewsI; Climate Change will bring Spain more than just lack of rain, www.iucn.org/about/work/intiatives/climate_news/?1264/Climate-Change-will-bring Spain-more-than-just-a-lack-of-rain

207 '. . . Iberian lynxes . . . kill foxes.' Palomares et al., 1996.

207 'Spanish imperial eagle . . .' *Aquila adalberti*, The IUCN Red List of Threatened Species, www.iucnredlist.org/details/144496, http://web.archive.org/web/20071129230848/www.iucnredlist.org/search/details.php/1951/summ

207 'The region may grow too hot for these birds . . .' Climate change threatens a million species with extinction, 7 January 2004, http://web.archive.bibalcx.org/web/20040413091907/www.leeds.ac.uk/media/current/extinction.htm

207 'Romans . . . and also from Spain.' Remains of Roman rabbit uncovered, 13 April 2005, http://news.bbc.co.uk/1/hi/england/norfolk/4439339.stm

208 '£45 million in Snowdonia . . .' Defra consults on further protection for UK wildlife from non-native species, 8 November 2007, www.defra.gov.uk/news/2007/071108a.htm

208 '*Rhododendron* . . . Mediterranean climate.' Mejías et al., 2002.

209 'Scottish crossbill . . . species.' Summers et al., 2007.

210 'Eurasian brown bears . . . outside Russia.' *Ursus arctos* Brown Bear, www.iucnredlist.org/apps/redlist/details/41688/0

211 'The entire population is living in fear of the bear.' 'Psycho' bear tears apart an eco-idyll, *The Times*, 29 July 2007.

211 'set fire to the mountain'. Death of Franska the 'sheep-eating' bear greeted with joy and dismay, *The Times*, 10 August 2007.

211 'Martial . . .' Kathleen M. Coleman, *Martial: Liber Spectaculorum*, Oxford University Press, 2006, 82.

211 'Each district has its last wolf . . .' *The Academy*, 19, 1881, 201.

211 'the last wolf was slain well into the eighteenth century . . . to be continued.' The last British wolves, www.wolftrust.org.uk/a-lastwolves.html

212 'Stockholm dictates the way people live in rural areas.' The Scandinavian wolf dilemma, 4 March 2006, http://theorchidblog.blogspot.com/2006/03/scandinavian-wolf-dilemma.html

212 'The Norwegian government . . . finish it off altogether.' Wolf comeback in Scandinavia stifled by public outcry, 17 August 2006, http://news.nationalgeographic.com/news/2006/08/060817-wolves-sweden.html; Wolf population cut in half, 19 June 2008, www.aftenposten.no/english/local/article2493001.ece

213 'wolves in Scotland would actually do deer estates a favour . . .'

Nilsen et al., 2007.

213 'Forestry Commission Scotland . . . extra cover for deer.' Ray et al., 2008.

213 'slaughtered thirty-three sheep in two attacks on a single flock.' Reinhardt and Kluth, 2004.

214 'the risk is "very, very low" . . .' Linnell et al., 2002.

216 'Alladale estate . . . "controlled Wilderness and Wildlife Reserve."' Wilderness Reserve, www.alladale.com/component/ option,com_docman/Itemid,81/task,cat_view/gid,38/; www. alladale.com/wilderness-reserve/

217 The priority Lister gives . . . one per cent of the Highlands.' Keep out . . . wolves about, 29 October 2007, www.sundayherald. com/news/heraldnews/display.var.1791510.0.keep_out_ wolves_about.php

218 'some of the finest access legislation in Europe.' Ramblers Scotland position statement on reintroductions, April 2008, www. ramblers.org.uk/scotland/ourwork_scotland/access/casestudies/ reintroduction-wolves.htm; see also Mountaineering Council of Scotland, www.mcofs.org.uk/assets/access/summary%20of%20 mcofs%20position%20on%20alladale.pdf

219 'Gairloch estate in Wester Ross . . .' Green light for £2m city of trees, 17 March 2002, Forest to be restored to Scottish Highlands, 7 February 2003, http://news.nationalgeographic. co.uk/news/2003/02/0207_030207_scotforest.html

220 'fewer than ten people per square kilometre.' Mid-2005 population estimates Scotland: Table 9, www.gro-scotland.gov. uk/files1/stats/05mype-cahb-t9-revised.pdf

220 'Forestry managers . . . cattle may yield less milk.' Alison Blackwell and Stephen J. Page, Biting midges and tourism in Scotland, in Wilks and Page, 2003.

220 'a guardian of wildness in the Highlands.' Highland biting midge, www.treesforlife.org.uk/tfl.midge.html

220 'half a million midges . . . measuring station nightly.' Blackwell and Page in Wilks and Page, 2003.

221 '99 midges . . . volunteers in Argyllshire.' Carpenter et al., 2005.

221 'spread of bluetongue virus into northern Europe . . .' European Food Safety Authority, 2007; Purse et al., 2005, 2007.

222 'In the summer of 2007 . . . local mammals and midges.'

Bluetongue in East Anglia. Update: 16.20, 28 September 2007, http://webarchive.nationalarchives.gov.uk/20071104143302/ http://defra.gov.uk/news/latest/2007/animal-0925.htm

222 'The new hosts . . . aboard midges.' Wittman and Baylis, 2000. Purse et al., 2005; European Food Safety Authority, 2007.

224 'AHSV . . . cannot replicate if the temperature falls below 15°C.' Mellor and Hamblin, 2004.

224 'C. obsoletus, C. pulicaris and C. dewulfi occupy almost all of the island . . .' John Boorman, A guide to the British Culicoides, www.iah.ac.uk/bluetongue/culicoides/index.html

224 'As winters in Sweden grew milder . . . ticks spread north . . .' Lindgren et al., 2000.

225 'ticks . . . TBE . . . Lyme disease . . .' David Rogers et al., Vector-borne diseases and climate change, in Kovats, 2008; Sarah Randolph in Kovats, 2008, 112; Huss and Braun-Fahrländer, 2007; Randolph, 2000.

227 'this wettest corner of Europe.' Tipping et al., 2004.

231 'pine sawflies . . . pine shoot beetles . . . Phytophthora infestations . . .' European Forest Institute et al., 2008; Pine shoot beetle (Tomicus piniperda (L.)), www.mnr.gov.on.ca/en/ Business/Forests/2ColumnSubPage/STEL02_166995.html; J. F. Webber and J. N. Gibbs, Phytophthora Disease of Alder in the UK, www.forestresearch.gov.uk/pdf/Phytophthora_Diseases_ Poster15.pdf/$FILE/Phytophthora_Diseases_Poster15.pdf

233 'favours birch rather than Scots pine, for which they have no use.' Parker et al., 1999.

233 'They will not go far for birch or rowan . . . aspen, their favourite tree.' Parker et al., 2000.

234 'perhaps a hundred square kilometres for every two wolves.' Wilson, 2004.

235 'Polish wolves . . .' Halley and Rosell, 2002.

235 'brown earth soils . . . scratching claws.' Bell, 2003, 51.

236 'During the hot spells . . . cold dawn.' Theuerkauf, 2003.

7 MOUNTAIN AVENS

238 'There's no doubt at all . . . any form where they like.' Gregory, 2007, 277–8.

239 'The approach from the north is so steep . . . stormy shore.' Archaeology of the Burren: Prehistoric forts and dolmens in North Clare by Thomas Johnson Westropp. Part III: Northern Burren: Black Head; Caherdooneerish. www.clarelibrary.ie/eolas/coclare/archaeology/arch_burren/part3_black_head.htm

240 'About 700 other kinds of plant . . . Burren region of County Clare.' Sweeney et al., 2003.

241 'They are almost unique to Ireland; there is just one outside it, in Wales.' Gunn, 2006.

241 'one entire rock . . . of Earth.' Journal of Thomas Dineley, 1681, www.clarelibrary.ie/eolas/coclare/history/dineley_1681/1681_burren.htm

241 'A modern survey . . . hazel thickets.' Parr et al., 2006.

242 'a country where there is not water enough . . . steal it from one another.' Ludlow, 1894, 292.

243 'people were said to gather brambles . . . to burn.' Burren History Post Famine, www.burrenbeo.ie/burren-history-post-famine.aspx?objID=Article

244 'In the 1900s cattle drives . . . brandishing revolvers.' Campbell, 2005, 143–4; Breandán Ó Cathaoir, 'Violence in the Burren', talk given at the Burren Spring Conference 2009.

246 'generally reputed and known to be sterill'. Prendergast, 1868, 98.

246 'Here, though, it is as if the ground itself brings forth right angles.' Robinson, 2008, 81.

247 'Ancient occupiers . . . limestone pavement.' Clare 1986:11 Poulnabrone Portal tomb M235010, www.excavations.ie/Pages/Details.php?County=Clare&Year=&id=3647

247 'Thin layers of soil . . . washed the soil away.' Drew, 1983.

248 'Pollen samples . . . more thickly with hazel than it does today.' Jelicic and O'Connell, 1992.

248 'At present about fifteen per cent . . . grazing declines.' Parr et al., 2006.

249 'Richard Moles . . . tongues and hoofs.' Moles et al., 1999; Moles and Moles, 2002; Moles et al., 2003.

250 'For David Jeffrey . . . karst limestone.' Jeffrey, 2003.

251 'About half the Burren's farmers have other jobs . . .' O'Rourke, 2005b.

251 'BurrenLIFE project . . .' Burren Life, www.burrenlife.com

252 'Burren summers . . . be significant.' Burren Climate Overview, www.burrenbeo.com/burren-climate-overview. aspx?objID=Article; Sweeney et al., 2003; Viles, 2003.

253 'the dense-flowered orchid . . . Mediterranean-Atlantic.' Webb and Scannell, 1983, xxx.

253 'An Asian subspecies . . . above 30°C.' Wada and Nakai, 2004.

253 'One study exposed mountain avens . . . warmer climates still.' Welker et al., 1997.

254 'Atlantic Warm period . . . temperatures were higher than they are today.' David Jeffrey, in correspondence.

255 'a kilo of beef . . . raise livestock.' Compassion in World Farming - Lecture calls for dietary change, www.ciwf.org.uk/news/factory_farming/lecture_calls_for_dietary_change.aspx

255 'cattle occupy four-fifths of the land . . . gone by 2030.' Greenpeace Brazil, 2009; Nepstad, 2007.

255 'Within Ireland . . . to the east.' Sweeney et al., 2003.

256 'Dairying . . . have long prospered.' J. Sweeney et al., 2008.

257 'amount of meat people eat . . . cost of livestock feed.' Nelson et al., 2009.

258 'Cliffs of Moher . . . up to the cliffs.' Cliffs of Moher, www.cliffsofmoher.ie

258 'express disappointment or bewilderment.' O'Connell and Korff, 2002, 12.

259 'covering 1,500 hectares . . . of the region.' Burren National Park, www.burrennationalpark.ie

259 'as solid as a rock . . . the rougher one is with it the better.' O'Rourke, 2005a.

265 'the faster the limestone will erode . . . hundredths of a millimetre.' Annual effective rainfall is projected to increase by between 16 and 39 millimetres, with an increase of only 11.7 millimetres for the warmest (2050 High) scenario; projected increases in dissolution rates are between three and nine and a half per cent. Limestone typically erodes at a rate of about fifty millimetres per thousand years. Viles, 2003.

265 'Turloughs . . . by the middle of the century.' J. Sweeney et al., 2008.

266 'A report published in 2008 . . .' K. Sweeney et al., 2008.

267 'The SeventyMillion Project . . .' The SeventyMillion Project,

www.seventymillion.org

268 'Sometimes in Ireland . . . global Irish family.' Remarks by President McAleese at 2008 Irish Diaspora Forum, University College Dublin, 10 November 2008, www.president.ie/index. php?section=5&speech=565&lang=eng

269 'Brazilian migrant workers . . . a third of the town's population.' Claire Healy, Carnaval do Galway: The Brazilian community in Gort, 1999–2006, www.irishargentine.org/healy_gort.htm

270 'Potatoes will be difficult to plant . . . probably not worthwhile.' Sweeney et al., 2003.

8 YOUNGER DRYAS

272 'A climate that had been on a warming upswing . . . heather takes over moors.' Committee on Abrupt Climate Change, National Research Councils, 2002, 30.

274 'Atlantic circulation conveys a million gigawatts . . .' Schiermeier, 2006.

274 'Doubts have been raised . . . course of the waters.' Colman, 2007; Seager, 2006; Tarasov and Peltier, 2005; Carlson et al., 2007.

275 'most of its final throes occurred in a single five-year bout.' Alley, 2000.

275 'Temperatures appear to have leapt by between five and ten degrees.' Severinghaus et al., 1998.

276 'Gulf Stream . . . New York and London in January.' Seager, 2006.

276 '"It is the influence of this stream . . .", Maury wrote.' Seager et al., 2002.

278 'That is very unlikely to happen . . . though others have.' Lenton et al., 2009.

278 'Some experts discount the possibility . . . forty per cent or more.' Zickfeld et al., 2007; Kriegler et al., 2009.

278 'a tipping point will be passed . . . accepted envelope.' Timothy M. Lenton, Tipping points in the Earth system, http://researchpages.net/ESMG/people/tim-lenton/tipping-points/

278 'Greenland's ice sheet . . . fifty cubic kilometres a year.' Schiermeier, 2006.

278 'Flows through the six largest Russian rivers . . . stop the deep water pools from forming.' Seager et al., 2002. The projected increase for a 1.4°C rise, at the low end of the IPCC range, is eighteen per cent, and for the opposite end of the range, 5.8°C, it is seventy per cent.

279 'The IPCC considers it very likely . . .' IPCC, 2007a, 774, www.ipcc.ch/pdf/assessment-report/ar4/wg1/ar4-wg1-chapter10.pdf

279 'the experts . . . include the British Isles.' Zickfeld et al., 2007.

280 'if the deep water stopped forming . . . much more quickly too.' Levermann et al., 2005.

9 THE SHADE OF THE FUTURE

283 'they symbolise freedom to travel.' Protecting us from ourselves, www.scenta.co.uk/travel/technology/cit/1702039/protecting-us-from-ourselves.htm

283 'The Scottish crossbill . . . the British Isles.' Huntley et al., 2008b.

Bibliography

Web addresses are given where documents are openly accessible online.

Agrawala, S., et al., 2004, Development and climate change in Egypt: Focus on coastal resources and the Nile, Organisation for Economic Co-operation and Development; www.oecd.org/dataoecd/57/4/33330510.pdf

Akbari, H., et al., 2008, Global cooling: Increasing world-wide urban albedos to offset CO_2, *Climatic Change*, 94, 275–86

Allen, J., 2008, Proposed nuclear development at Sizewell: Environmental scoping report, British Energy; www.british-energy.com/documents/Sizewell_Environmental_Scoping_Report.pdf

Allen, M., et al., 2009a, The exit strategy, *Nature Reports Climate Change*; www.nature.com/climate/2009/0905/full/climate.2009.38.html

—— 2009b, Warming caused by cumulative carbon emissions towards the trillionth tonne, *Nature*, 458, 1163–6

Alley, R. B., 2000, Ice-core evidence of abrupt climate changes, *Proceedings of the National Academy of Sciences*, 97, 1331–4; www.pnas.org/content/97/4/1331.full

Alley, R. B., et al., 1993, Abrupt increase in Greenland snow accumulation at the end of the Younger Dryas event, *Nature*, 362, 527–9; http://earthsciences.ucr.edu/gcec_pages/docs/Alley%20et%20al%201993-Nature-Dryas%20Snow%20Rates.pdf

Allison, E. H., et al., 2009, Vulnerability of national economies to the impacts of climate change on fisheries, *Fish and Fisheries*, 10, 173–96; www.imcsnet.org/imcs/docs/vulnerability_of_fisheries.pdf

Anderson, K., and Bows, A., 2009, Reframing the climate change challenge in light of post-2000 emission trends, *Philosophical Transactions of the Royal Society*, Series A, 366, 3863–82

Archer, D., and Brovkin, V., 2008, The millennial atmospheric lifetime of anthropogenic CO_2, *Climatic Change*, 90, 283–97

Arctic Climate Impact Assessment, 2004, *Impacts of a Warming Arctic*, Cambridge University Press; http://amap.no/acia/

—— 2005, *Arctic Climate Impact Assessment*, Cambridge University Press; http://amap.no/acia/

Arnell, N. W., 2004, Climate change and global water resources: SRES emissions and socio-economic scenarios, *Global Environmental Change*, 14, 31–52

Arnell, N. W., et al., 2004, Climate and socio-economic scenarios for global-scale climate change impacts assessments: Characterising the SRES storylines, *Global Environmental Change*, 14, 3–20

—— 2005, Eliciting information from experts on the likelihood of rapid climate change, *Risk Analysis*, 25, 1419–31

Arup and Three Regions Climate Change Group, 2008, Your home in a changing climate: Retrofitting existing homes for climate change impact, Greater London Authority; www.london.gov.uk/trccg/docs/pub1.pdf

Atkins, W. S., 2002, Warming up the region: The impacts of climate change in the Yorkshire and Humber region; www.ukcip.org.uk/images/stories/Pub_pdfs/Y%26H_tech.pdf

Austin, P., et al., 2008, Climate change – the risks for property in the UK, UCL Environment Institute; www.hermes.co.uk/rpi_report_08/pdf/Climate_Change_Report_web.pdf

Baeza, R., et al., 2008, Carbon capture and storage: A solution to the problem of carbon emissions, Boston Consulting Group; www.bcg.com/impact_expertise/publications/files/Carbon_Capture_and_Storage_Jun_2008.pdf

Baker, T., 2005, Vulnerability assessment of the north east Atlantic shelf marine ecoregion to climate change, WWF; http://assets.panda.org/downloads/climatechangeandseas01.pdf

Bakkenes, M., et al., 2006, Impacts of different climate stabilisation scenarios on plant species in Europe, *Global Environmental Change*, 16, 19–28

Bamber, J. L., et al., 2009, Reassessment of the potential sea-level rise from a collapse of the West Antarctic Ice Sheet, *Science*, 324, 901–3

Bannister, N. R., 1999, Chyngton Farm: Historic landscape survey. South Downs Countryside Management, National Trust

Banting, D., et al., 2005, Report on the environmental benefits and costs of green roof technology for the City of Toronto, Ryerson University; www.toronto.ca/greenroofs/pdf/fullreport103105. pdf

Bardgett, R. D., et al., 2006, Parasitic plants indirectly regulate below-ground properties in grassland ecosystems, *Nature*, 439, 969–72

Barnaby, W., 2009, Do nations go to war over water?, *Nature*, 458, 282–3

Baxter, P. J., 2005, The east coast Big Flood, 31 January–1 February 1953: A summary of the human disaster, *Philosophical Transactions of the Royal Society*, Series A, 363, 1293–1312; http://rsta. royalsocietypublishing.org/content/363/1831/1293.full

Beale, C. M., et al., 2006, Wader recruitment indices suggest nesting success is temperature-dependent in Dunlin *Calidris alpina*, *Ibis*, 148, 405–10

—— 2008, Opening the climate envelope reveals no macroscale associations with climate in European birds, *Proceedings of the National Academy of Sciences*, 105, 14908–12

Beldon, P., et al., 2000, Chalk Grassland Habitat Action Plan, Sussex Biodiversity Partnership; www.biodiversitysussex.org/ file_download/41/

Bell, S., 2003, The potential of applied landscape ecology to forest design planning: Progress in research with special reference to Glen Affric and Sherwood Forest, Forestry Commission; www. forestry.gov.uk/pdf/FCRP002.pdf/$FILE/FCRP002.pdf

Bellamy, P. H., et al., 2005, Carbon losses from all soils across England and Wales 1978–2003, *Nature*, 437, 245–8

Bellows, J., 1868, *Two Days' Excursion to Llanthony Abbey and the Black Mountains*, John Bellows

Beniston, M., et al., 2007, Future extreme events in European climate: An exploration of regional climate model projections, *Climatic Change*, 81, 71–95

Berry, P. M., et al., 2002, Modelling potential impacts of climate change on the bioclimatic envelope of species in Britain and Ireland, *Global Ecology & Biogeography*, 11, 453–62

Beverland, I. J., et al., 1996, Measurement of methane and carbon dioxide fluxes from peatland ecosystems by the conditional-sampling technique, *Quarterly Journal of the Royal Meteorological Society*, 122, 819–38

Bisgrove, R., and Hadley, P., 2002, Gardening in the global greenhouse: The impacts of climate change on gardens in the UK. Technical Report, UKCIP; www.nationaltrust.org.uk/main/w-gardening_global_greenhouse_contents.pdf

Boardman, B., 2008, Home truths, Environmental Change Institute, University of Oxford; www.foe.co.uk/resource/reports/home_truths.pdf

Boardman, B., et al., 2005, 40% House, Environmental Change Institute; www.eci.ox.ac.uk/research/energy/downloads/40house/40house.pdf

Boardman, J., 2003, Soil erosion and flooding on the eastern South Downs, southern England, 1976–2001, *Transactions of the Institute of British Geographers*, New Series, 28, 176–96

Boardman, J., et al., 2003, Muddy floods on the South Downs, southern England: Problem and responses, *Environmental Science & Policy*, 6, 69–83

Bonan, G. B., 2008, Forests and climate change: Forcings, feedbacks, and the climate benefits of forests, *Science*, 320, 1444–9

Bouffard, F., and Kirschen, D. S., 2006, Centralised and distributed electricity systems, *Energy Policy*, 36, 4504–8

Brace, M., 1986, *London Parks and Gardens*, Pevensey

Braybrooke, N., 1959, *London Green: The Story of Kensington Gardens, Hyde Park, Green Park & St James's Park*, Gollancz

Briscoe, J., et al., 2005, Pakistan Country Water Resources Assistance Strategy. Water economy: Running dry, World Bank; http://siteresources.worldbank.org/PAKISTANEXTN/Resources/PWCAS-Title&Intro.pdf

Broadmeadow, M., and Ray, D., 2005, Climate change and British woodland, Forestry Commission; www.forestry.gov.uk/pdf/fcin069.pdf/$FILE/fcin069.pdf

Building Research Energy Conservation Support Unit, 2002, General information report 89: BedZED – Beddington Zero Energy Development

Bullock, D. J., and O'Donovan, G., 1995, Observations on the ecology of large herbivores in the Burren National Park, with particular reference to the feral goat (*Capra hircus*); www.burrenbeo.com/research-article.aspx?article=f16477e7-fbdc-4f0d-9720-3ee1f3f5723d

Burke, C., and Grosvenor, I., 2008, *School*, Reaktion

Burnside, N. G., et al., 2003, Recent historical land use change on the South Downs, United Kingdom, *Environmental Conservation*, 30, 52–60

Butler, J., 2005, Muddy flooding on the South Downs, Institute of Geography, School of Geosciences, University of Edinburgh; www.era.lib.ed.ac.uk/bitstream/1842/830/1/jbutler001.pdf

Calvete, C., et al., 2002, Epidemiology of viral haemorrhagic disease and myxomatosis in a free-living population of wild rabbits, *Veterinary Record*, 150, 776–82; www.catsg.org/iberianlynx/04_library/4_3_publications/C/Calvete_et_al_2002_Epidemiology_of_viral_haemorrhagic_disease_and_myxomatosis.pdf

Campbell, F., 2005, *Land and Revolution: Nationalist Politics in the West of Ireland 1891–1921*, Oxford University Press

Campbell, K. M., et al., 2007, The Age of Consequences: The foreign policy and national security implications of global climate change, Center for Strategic and International Studies; http://csis.org/files/media/csis/pubs/071105_ageofconsequences.pdf

Campbell, R. D., et al., 2007, Economic impacts of the beaver, Wild Britain Initiative; www.beaverinfo.org/download/BMBreport_Final%20271107%5B2%5D.pdf

Canadell, J. G., et al., 2007, Contributions to accelerating atmospheric CO_2 growth from economic activity, carbon intensity, and efficiency of natural sinks, *Proceedings of the National Academy of Sciences*, 104, 18866–70; www.pnas.org/cgi/reprint/0702737104v1

Carlisle, A., and Brown, A. H. F., 1968, *Pinus sylvestris* L., *Journal of Ecology*, 56, 269–307

Carlson, A. E., et al., 2007, Geochemical proxies of North American freshwater routing during the Younger Dryas cold event, *Proceedings of the National Academy of Sciences*, 104, 6556–61

Carpenter, S., et al., 2005, Repellent efficiency of BayRepel against *Culicoides impunctatus* (Diptera: Ceratopogonidae), *Parasitology Research*, 95, 427–9

—— 2008, Control techniques for *Culicoides* biting midges and their application in the U.K. and northwestern Palaearctic, *Medical and Veterinary Entomology*, 22, 175–87

Castles, I., and Henderson, D., 2003, The IPCC emission scenarios: An economic-statistical critique, *Energy and Environment*, 14, 159–85

Central Statistics Office, 2008, Population and labour force projections, 2011–41; www.cso.ie/releasespublications/documents/population/2008/poplabfor_2011-2041.pdf

Chambers, F. M., et al., 2007, Palaeoecology of degraded blanket mire in South Wales: Data to inform conservation management, *Biological Conservation*, 137, 197–209

Cheung, W. W. L., et al., 2009, Projecting global marine biodiversity impacts under climate change scenarios, *Fish and Fisheries*, 10, 235–51

Chin, T., and Welsby, P. D., 2004, Malaria in the UK: past, present, and future, *Postgraduate Medical Journal*, 80, 663–6

Christensen, J. H., and Christensen, O. B., 2003, Climate modelling: Severe summertime flooding in Europe, *Nature*, 421, 805–6

Cocker, M., and Mabey, R., 2005, *Birds Britannica*, Chatto and Windus

Coleman, K. M., 2006, *Martial: Liber Spectaculorum*, Oxford University Press

Colman, S. M., 2007, Conventional wisdom and climate history, *Proceedings of the National Academy of Sciences*, 104, 6500–1

Committee on Abrupt Climate Change, National Research Councils, 2002, *Abrupt Climate Change: Inevitable Surprises*, National Academies Press

Connolly, J., et al., 2007, Mapping peatlands in Ireland using a rule-based methodology and digital data, *Soil Science Society*

of America Journal, 71, 492–9; http://soil.scijournals.org/cgi/
content/full/71/2/492

Cooper, E., 1948, *Muker: The Story of a Yorkshire Parish*, Dalesman

Costello, A., et al., 2009, Managing the health effects of climate
change, *Lancet*, 373, 1693–1733; www.ucl.ac.uk/global-health/
ucl-lancet-climate-change.pdf

Coulcher, P., 1997, *A Natural History of the Cuckmere Valley*, Book
Guild

Countryside Commission for Scotland, 1978, Scotland's
Scenic Areas; www.snh.org.uk/publications/on-line/
scotlandsscenicareas/

Dakos, V., et al., 2008, Slowing down as an early warning signal
for abrupt climate change, *Proceedings of the National Academy of
Sciences*, 105, 14308–12

Dallmann, W. K., and Peskov, V. V., n.d., Monitoring of oil
development in traditional indigenous lands of the Nenets
Autonomous Okrug; www.npolar.no/ansipra/english/Items/
MODIL_En.pdf

D'Arcy, G., and Hayward, J., 1999, *The Natural History of the
Burren*, Immel

Darwin, C., 1877, *The Various Contrivances by which Orchids Are
Fertilised by Insects*, John Murray; http://darwin-online.org.uk/
content/frameset?itemID=F801&viewtype=text&pageseq=1
—— 1996, *The Origin of Species*, Oxford University Press

Davies, A. L., 2007, Upland agriculture and environmental risk: A
new model of upland land-use based on high spatial-resolution
palynological data from West Affric, NW Scotland, *Journal of
Archaeological Science*, 34, 2053–63

Davies, A. L., and Tipping, R., 2004, Sensing small-scale human
activity in the palaeoecological record: Fine spatial resolution
pollen analyses from Glen Affric, northern Scotland, *The
Holocene*, 14, 233–45

Davis, B. A. S., et al., 2003, The temperature of Europe during the
Holocene reconstructed from pollen data, *Quaternary Science
Reviews*, 22, 1701–16

Davis, M. B., et al., 2005, Evolutionary responses to changing
climate, *Ecology*, 86, 1704–14

Dawson, R. J., et al., 2005, Quantified analysis of the probability of flooding in the Thames Estuary under imaginable worst case sea-level rise scenarios, *International Journal of Water Resources Development*, 21, 577–91; www.hm-treasury.gov.uk/d/Atlantis-FloodModellingPaper.pdf

Defra, 2006, Flood and coastal defence appraisal guidance: FCDPAG3 economic appraisal. Supplementary note to operating authorities – climate change impacts, October 2006, Department for Environment, Food and Rural Affairs; www.yhub.org.uk/resources/Climate%20Change%20Micro%20Site/FloodCoastal%20Defence-appraisalguidance.pdf

—— 2007, Flood and coastal defence appraisal guidance: FCDPAG3 economic appraisal. Supplementary note to operating authorities – climate change impacts: questions and answers, Department for Environment, Food and Rural Affairs; www.defra.gov.uk/environment/flooding/documents/policy/guidance/fcdpag/fcd3climateqa.pdf

—— 2008a, Feral wild boar in England: An action plan, Department for Environment, Food and Rural Affairs; www.naturalengland.org.uk/Images/feralwildboar_tcm6-4508.pdf

—— 2008b, Future water: The government's water strategy for England, Department for Environment, Food and Rural Affairs; www.defra.gov.uk/Environment/quality/water/strategy/pdf/future-water.pdf

Deltacommissie, 2008, Working together with water: A living land builds for its future. Findings of the Deltacommissie 2008; www.deltacommissie.com/doc/deltareport_full.pdf

DeLucia, E. H., 2008, Insects take a bigger bite out of plants in a warmer, higher carbon dioxide world, *Proceedings of the National Academy of Sciences*, 105, 1781–2

Demeritt, D., 2001, The construction of global warming and the politics of science, *Annals of the Association of American Geographers*, 91, 307–37

Demographia, 2009, Demographia world urban areas & population projections; www.demographia.com/db-worldua.pdf

Derbyshire, B., et al., 2007, Recommendations for living at superdensity, design for homes; www.designforhomes.org/pdfs/uploads/1/16833/Superdensity.pdf

Dessai, S., and van der Sluijs, J., 2007, Uncertainty and climate change adaptation – a scoping study, Copernicus Institute for Sustainable Development and Innovation, Department of Science Technology and Society; www.nusap.net/downloads/reports/ucca_scoping_study.pdf

Devictor, V., et al., 2008, Birds are tracking climate warming, but not fast enough, *Proceedings of the Royal Society*, Series B, 275, 2743–8, www2.mnhn.fr/cersp/IMG/pdf/devictor_jiguet08.pdf

Devoy, R. J. N., 2000, Implications of accelerated sea-level rise (ASLR) for Ireland, http://web.archive.org/web/20040619041933/http://www.survas.mdx.ac.uk/pdfs/1volirel.pdf

Dik, B., and Ergül, R., 2006, Nocturnal flight activities of *Culicoides* (Diptera: Ceratopogonidae) species in Konya, *Türkiye Parazitoloji Dergisi*, 30, 213–16; www.tparazitolderg.org/pdf/pdf_TPD_188.pdf

Dornbusch, U., 2002, BERM final report: Technical report, University of Sussex; www.geog.sussex.ac.uk/BERM/BERM-final-report-UK.pdf

Dornbusch, U., et al., 2001, Beach sustainability in East Sussex: Interim report of the BERM Project, BERM University of Sussex; www.geog.sussex.ac.uk/BERM/report.pdf

—— 2008, Temporal and spatial variations of chalk cliff retreat in East Sussex, 1873 to 2001, *Marine Geology*, 249, 271–82

Drew, D. P., 1983, Accelerated soil erosion in a karst area: The Burren, western Ireland, *Journal of Hydrology*, 61, 113–24

Eaton, J. M., et al., 2008, Land cover change and soil organic carbon stocks in the Republic of Ireland 1851–2000, *Climatic Change*, 91, 317–34

Edwards, C., and Mason, W. L., 2006, Stand structure and dynamics of four native Scots pine (*Pinus sylvestris* L.) woodlands in northern Scotland, *Forestry*, 79, 261–77

Eickhout, B., et al., 2007, Economic and ecological consequences of four European land use scenarios, *Land Use Policy*, 24, 562–75

Ekström, M., et al., 2005, New estimates of future changes in extreme rainfall across the UK using regional climate model integrations. 2. Future estimates and use in impact studies, *Journal of Hydrology*, 300, 234–51

Empty Homes Agency, 2008, New tricks with old bricks: How reusing old buildings can cut carbon emissions; www. emptyhomes.com/documents/publications/reports/New%20 Tricks%20With%20Old%20Bricks%20-%20final%2012-03-081.pdf

English Nature, 1997, South Downs natural area profile; www. english-nature.org.uk/science/natural/profiles/naProfile74.pdf

—— 2002, Return of the red kite. The red kite reintroduction programme in England; www.bradfordbirding.org/ARTICLES/ Redkite.pdf

Environment Agency, 2009, Minsmere flood risk management study January 2009; http://Publications.environment-agency. gov.uk/pdf/GEAN0109BPFI-e-e.pdf

—— n.d., Climate change in the uplands: safeguarding vital services; http://publications.environment-agency.gov.uk/pdf/ GEHO0508BOBV-e-e.pdf

Environment Agency (Southern Region), 2007, Planning for the future: Cuckmere Estuary draft flood risk management strategy, Consultation document

Ernst & Young, n.d., Reactor decommissioning; www.berr.gov.uk/ files/file36327.pdf

European Food Safety Authority, 2007, Epidemiological analysis of the 2006 bluetongue virus serotype 8 epidemic in north-western Europe; www.efsa.europa.eu/EFSA/efsa_ locale-1178620753812_1211902675175.htm

European Forest Institute et al., 2008, Impacts of climate change on European forests and options for adaptation http://ec.europa. eu/agriculture/analysis/external/euro_forests/full_report_en.pdf

Ewert, F., et al., 2005, Future scenarios of European agricultural land use I. Estimating changes in crop productivity, *Agriculture, Ecosystems & Environment*, 107, 101–16

Expert Group on Climate Change and Health in the UK, 2001, Health effects of climate change in the UK. Department of Health; www.dh.gov.uk/en/Publicationsandstatistics/ Publications/PublicationsPolicyAndGuidance/DH_4007935

Farrar, J. F., et al., 2000, Wales: Changing climate, challenging choices – a scoping study of climate change impacts in Wales, Institute of Environmental Science, University of Wales,

Bangor; www.ukcip.org.uk/images/stories/Pub_pdfs/wales_tech.
pdf
Farrell, G. J., 2007, Climate change: Impacts on coastal areas, Irish
Academy of Engineering.
Federcasa and Ministry of Infrastructure of the Italian Republic,
2006, Housing statistics in the European Union 2005/2006,
Federcasa; www.federcasa.it/news/housing_statistics/Report_
housing_statistics_2005_2006.pdf
Ferreras, P., et al., 2001, Restore habitat or reduce mortality?
Implications from a population viability analysis of the Iberian
lynx, *Animal Conservation*, 4, 265–74
Field, C. B., et al., 2007, Feedbacks of terrestrial ecosystems to
climate change, *Annual Review of Environment and Resources*, 32,
1–29
Fischer, G., et al., 2002, Climate change and agricultural
vulnerability, International Institute for Applied Systems
Analysis; www.donorplatform.org/component/option,com_
docman/task,doc_view/gid,970
Fish, R., et al., 2008, Sustainable farmland management:
Transdisciplinary approaches, CABI
Fitter, A. H., 1995, Relationships between first flowering date
and temperature in the flora of a locality in central England,
Functional Ecology, 9, 55–60
Fleming, A., 1998, *Swaledale: Valley of the Wild River*, Edinburgh
University Press
Foden, W., et al., 2008, Species susceptibility to climate change
impacts, International Union for the Conservation of Nature;
http://cmsdata.iucn.org/downloads/species_susceptibility_to_
climate_change_impacts.pdf
Forrest, N., 2008, Scottish hydropower resource study: Final report;
www.all-energy.co.uk/userfiles/file/Nick_Forrest220508.pdf
Fortey, R., 1993, *The Hidden Landscape: A Journey into the Geological
Past*, Cape
Fowler, J., and Stiven, R., 2003, Habitat networks for wildlife and
people: The creation of sustainable forest habitats, Forestry
Commission Scotland and Scottish Natural Heritage; www.
forestry.gov.uk/website/pdf.nsf/pdf/habnetpto1.pdf/$FILE/
habnetpto1.pdf

Froyd, C. A., 2005, Fossil stomata reveal early pine presence in Scotland: implications for postglacial colonization analyses, *Ecology*, 86, 579–86

—— 2006, Holocene fire in the Scottish Highlands: Evidence from macroscopic charcoal records, *The Holocene*, 16, 235–49

Froyd, C. A., and Bennett, K. D., 2006, Long-term ecology of native pinewood communities in East Glen Affric, Scotland, *Forestry*, 79, 279–91

Fry, V., and Kelly, T., 2009, Management of the London Basin chalk aquifer: Status report 2009, Environment Agency; www.aselb.com/pdf/2009%20london%20gwl%20report_FINAL.pdf

Gallani, M. L., 2007, Review of medium- to long-term coastal risks associated with British Energy sites: Climate Change Effects; http://british-energy.com/documents/energyEnvironment/BE_2006_siteclimate_v1.12_final.pdf

Gao, X., and Giorgi, F., 2008, Increased aridity in the Mediterranean region under greenhouse gas forcing estimated from high resolution simulations with a regional climate model, *Global and Planetary Change*, 62, 195–209

Garnett, M. H., et al., 2000, Effects of burning and grazing on carbon sequestration in a Pennine blanket bog, UK, *The Holocene*, 10, 729–36

Giraldus Cambrensis, 1997, The Itinerary of Archbishop Baldwin through Wales, Project Gutenberg; www.gutenberg.org/dirs/etext97/itwls10.txt

Gissing, G., 2003, Thyrza, Project Gutenberg; www.gutenberg.org/dirs/etext03/thyrz10.txt

Goede, A. A., et al., 1990, Body mass increase, migration pattern and breeding grounds of dunlins, *Calidris a. alpina*, staging in the Dutch Wadden Sea in spring, *Ardea*, 78, 135–44; ftp://80.57.161.240/artikelen/B/Bonte%20Strandloper5.pdf

Gould, E. A., et al., 2006, Potential arbovirus emergence and implications for the United Kingdom, *Emerging Infectious Diseases*, 12, 549–55; www.cdc.gov/ncidod/eid/vol12no04/05-1010.htm

Government of China, 2007, China's national climate change programme, National Development and Reform Commission, People's Republic of China; www.ccchina.gov.cn/WebSite/

CCChina/UpFile/File188.pdf

Gray, A. J., and Mogg, R. J., 2001, Climate impacts on pioneer saltmarsh plants, *Climate Research*, 18, 105–12

Greater London Authority, 2003, Housing for a compact city; www.london.gov.uk/mayor/auu/publications.jsp

—— 2006, London's urban heat island: A summary for decision makers; www.london.gov.uk/mayor/environment/climate-change/docs/UHI_summary_report.pdf

—— 2008, The London climate change adaptation strategy: Draft report; www.london.gov.uk/mayor/publications/2008/docs/climate-change-adapt-strat.pdf

Greenpeace Brazil, 2009, Amazon cattle footprint, Mato Grosso: State of destruction; www.greenpeace.org/raw/content/international/press/reports/amazon-cattle-footprint-mato.pdf

Gregory, A., 2007, *Visions and Beliefs in the West of Ireland*, Forgotten Books

Gregory, R. D., et al., 2009, An indicator of the impact of climatic change on European bird populations, *PLoS ONE*, 4; www.plosone.org/article/info:doi/10.1371/journal.pone.0004678

Gunn, J., 2006, Turloughs and tiankengs: Distinctive doline forms, *Speleogenesis and Evolution of Karst Aquifers*, 4, 1–4; www.speleogenesis.info/pdf/SG9/SG9_artId3294.pdf

Guthrie, G., and Cottle, R., 2002, Suffolk coast and estuaries coastal habitat management plan. English Nature/Environment Agency

Hacker, J. N., et al., 2005, Beating the heat: Keeping UK buildings cool in a warming climate. UKCIP Briefing Report, UKCIP; www.ukcip.org.uk/images/stories/Pub_pdfs/Beating%20the%20heat%20lo%20res.pdf

Hajat, S., et al., 2002, Impact of hot temperatures on death in London: A time series approach, *Journal of Epidemiology and Community Health*, 56, 367–72

Halcrow Group, 2007, British Energy Generation Ltd: Review of medium to long-term coastal geohazard risks at British Energy sites; www.british-energy.com/documents/halcrow_review.pdf

Hall, J. W., et al., 2006, Impacts of climate change on coastal flood risk in England and Wales: 2030–2100, *Philosophical Transactions of the Royal Society*, Series A, 364, 1027–49

Halley, D. J., and Rosell, F., 2002, The beaver's reconquest of Eurasia: Status, population development and management of a conservation success, *Mammal Review*, 32, 153–78

Hansen, J., et al., 2005, Earth's energy imbalance: Confirmation and implications, *Science*, 308, 1431–5; http://isis.ku.dk/kurser/blob.aspx?feltid=146868

Hansen, J. E., 2007, Scientific reticence and sea level rise, *Environmental Research Letters*, 2; www.iop.org/EJ/article/1748-9326/2/2/024002/erl7_2_024002.html

Hansen, J. E., et al., 2007a, Climate change and trace gases, *Philosophical Transactions of the Royal Society*, Series A, 365, 1925–54; www.planetwork.net/climate/Hansen2007.pdf

—— 2007b, Dangerous human-made interference with climate: A GISS modelE study, *Atmospheric Chemistry and Physics*, 7, 2287–312; www.atmos-chem-phys.org/7/2287/2007/acp-7-2287-2007.pdf

—— 2008, Target atmospheric CO_2: Where should humanity aim?; http://arxiv.org/pdf/0804.11263

Harris, N., 2007, *Castor fiber*, Animal Diversity Web; http://animaldiversity.ummz.umich.edu/site/accounts/information/Castor_fiber.html

Harris, R. B., 2004, Newhaven historic character assessment report, Sussex Extensive Urban Survey; www.lewes.gov.uk/Files/plan_Newhaven_EUS_reportpages1to13.pdf

—— 2005, Seaford historic character assessment report, Sussex Extensive Urban Survey; www.lewes.gov.uk/Files/plan_Seaford_EUS_reportpages1to12.pdf

Haslett, S. K., 2000, *Coastal Systems*, Routledge

Hawkes, J., 1951, *A Land*, Cresset

Herbert, T. J., 2003, Global warming and the relationship of plant canopy structure to latitude; www.srcosmos.gr/srcosmos/showpub.aspx?aa=3834

Hetherington, D., and Gorman, M., 2007, Using prey densities to estimate the potential size of reintroduced populations of Eurasian lynx, *Biological Conservation*, 137, 37–44

Hetherington, D. A., et al., 2006, New evidence for the occurrence of Eurasian lynx (*Lynx lynx*) in medieval Britain, *Journal of Quaternary Science*, 21, 3–8

—— 2008, A potential habitat network for the Eurasian lynx *Lynx lynx* in Scotland, *Mammal Review*, 38, 285–303

Hickling, R., et al., 2006, The distributions of a wide range of taxonomic groups are expanding polewards, *Global Change Biology*, 12, 450–5

Hoegh-Guldberg, O., et al., 2008, Assisted colonization and rapid climate change, *Science*, 321, 345–6

Holden, J., et al., 2007, Environmental change in moorland landscapes, *Earth Science Reviews*, 82, 75–100; http://homepages.see.leeds.ac.uk/~lecmsr/EarthScienceReviews2007.pdf

Holman, I. P., and Loveland, P. J., 2001, Regional climate change impact and response studies in East Anglia and north west England (RegIS), www.ukcip.org.uk/images/stories/Pub_pdfs/ReGIS1.pdf

Hope, J. C. E., 2003, Modelling forest landscape dynamics in Glen Affric, northern Scotland, University of Stirling; https://dspace.stir.ac.uk/dspace/bitstream/1893/49/1/Hope_JCE-PhD_Thesis.pdf

Hope, J. C. E., et al., 2006, Modelling the effects of forest landscape dynamics on focal species in Glen Affric, northern Scotland, *Forestry*, 79, 293–302

Hopkins, G., 1979, *Llanthony Abbey and Walter Savage Landor*, D. Brown (distributor)

Hopkins, J. J., and Kirby, K. J., 2007, Ecological change in British broadleaved woodland since 1947, *Ibis*, 149, 29–40; www3.interscience.wiley.com/cgi-bin/fulltext/118531181/HTMLSTART

Hopkins Van Mil, 2009, Cuckmere Estuary Partnership community engagement report; www.cuckmere.org.uk/wp-content/uploads/cep-community-engagement-report.pdf

Hoskins, W. G., 1977, *The Making of the English Landscape*, Penguin

Hossell, J. E., et al., 2000, Climate change and UK nature conservation: A review of the impact of climate change on UK species and habitat conservation policy, Department of the Environment, Transport and the Regions

Hughes, R. G., 2004, Climate change and loss of saltmarshes: Consequences for birds, *Ibis*, 146, 21–8

Hulme, M., 2007, Climate change: A little problem of technical

forecasting; www.opendemocracy.net/article/climate_change/
the_new_determinism

Hulme, M., and Dessai, S., 2008, Negotiating future climates
for public policy: A critical assessment of the development of
climate scenarios for the UK, *Environmental Science and Policy*,
11, 54–70; www.mikehulme.org/wp-content/uploads/2007/09/
hulmedessai-esp-revised.pdf

Hulme, M., et al., 2002, Climate change scenarios for the United
Kingdom: The UKCIP02 scientific report, UKCIP; www.ukcip.
org.uk/images/stories/Pub_pdfs/UKCIP02_tech.pdf

Hunter, P. R., 2003, Climate change and waterborne and vector-
borne disease, *Journal of Applied Microbiology*, 94, 37S–46S

Huntingford, C., et al., 2003, Regional climate-model predictions
of extreme rainfall for a changing climate, *Quarterly Journal of
the Royal Meteorological Society*, 129, 1607–21

Huntley, B., et al., 2008a, Potential impacts of climatic change
on European breeding birds, *PLoS ONE*, 3; www.plosone.org/
article/info;doi%2F10.1371%2Fjournal.pone.0001439

—— 2008b, *A Climatic Atlas of European Breeding Birds*, Lynx
Edicions

Huss, A., and Braun-Fahrländer, C., 2007, Tick-borne diseases
in Switzerland and climate change, Institute of Social and
Preventive Medicine, University of Basel; www.ispm-unibasel.
ch/uploads/news/ticks_climate%20change.pdf

Hutchings, M. J., 1987, The population biology of the early spider
orchid, *Ophrys Sphegodes* Mill. II: A demographic study from
1975 to 1984, *Journal of Ecology*, 75, 711–27

Hutchings, W. W., 1909, *London Town: Past and Present*, Cassell

Inman, M., 2009, A sensitive subject, *Nature Reports Climate Change*
www.nature.com/climate/2009/0905/full/climate.2009.41.html

Institution of Engineering and Technology, 2008, Nuclear
decommissioning; www.theiet.org/factfiles/energy/nucdec.cfm

Institution of Mechanical Engineers, 2009, Climate change:
Adapting to the inevitable?; www.imeche.org/NR/rdonlyres/
FA401F02-3193-4A19-826A-3FEEFB89DEDE/0/
ClimateChangeAdaptationReportIMechE.pdf

International Atomic Energy Agency, 2007, Energy, electricity and
nuclear power estimates for the period up to 2030; www-pub.

iaea.org/MTCD/publications/PDF/RDS1-27_web.pdf

International Energy Agency, 2009, *World Energy Outlook 2009*, OECD/IEA; www.worldenergyoutlook.org

IPCC, 2007a, Climate change 2007: The physical science basis; www.ipcc.ch/ipccreports/ar4-wg1.htm

—— 2007b, Working Group II report: Impacts, adaptation and vulnerability; www.ipcc.ch/ipccreports/ar4-wg2.htm

Irish Academy of Engineering, 2007, Ireland at Risk No.1: The impact of climate change on the water environment; www.iae. ie/site_media/pressroom/documents/2009/Jun/09/Ireland_at_ Risk_Water.pdf

Ise, T., et al., 2008, High sensitivity of peat decomposition to climate change through water-table feedback, *Nature Geoscience*, 1, 763–6

Jacobs Babtie, 2007, Cuckmere estuary strategy strategic environmental assessment – environmental report. Environment Agency (Southern Region)

Jaeger, C., et al., 2008, Stern's review and Adam's fallacy, *Climatic Change*, 89, 207–18; www.springerlink.com/content/ a01631398670555w/

Jefferson, R. G., 2005, The conservation management of upland hay meadows in Britain: A review, *Grass and Forage Science*, 60, 322–31

Jeffrey, D. W., 2003, Grasslands and heath: A review and hypothesis to explain the distribution of Burren plant communities, biology and environment, *Proceedings of the Royal Irish Academy*, 103B, 111–23; www.ria.ie/cgi-bin/ria/papers/100404.pdf

Jeličić, L., and O'Connell, M., 1992, History of vegetation and land use from 3200 B.P. to the present in the north-west Burren, a karstic region of western Ireland, *Vegetation History and Archaeobotany*, 1, 119–40

Jenkins, D. P., et al., 2008, Will future low-carbon schools in the UK have an overheating problem? *Building and Environment*, 44, 490–501

Johnson, W. E., et al., 2004, Phylogenetic and phylogeographic analysis of Iberian lynx populations, *Journal of Heredity*, 95, 19–28; http://jhered.oxfordjournals.org/cgi/reprint/95/1/19

Jones, C., 2005, *The Burren and the Aran Islands: Exploring the Archaeology*, Collins

Jones, G. V., 2007, Climate change: observations, projections, and general implications for viticulture and wine production, Whitman College; https://dspace.lasrworks.org/bitstream/10349/593/1/WP_07.pdf

Jones, G. V., et al., 2005, Climate change and global wine quality, *Climatic Change*, 73, 319–343; http://people.whitman.edu/~storchkh/clim.pdf

Jump, A. S., et al., 2006, Natural selection and climate change: temperature-linked spatial and temporal trends in gene frequency in *Fagus sylvatica*, *Molecular Ecology*, 15, 3469–80; www.creaf.uab.es/ecophysiology/pdfs%20grup/pdfs/jumpetal2006-Mol-ecol.pdf

Keenlyside, N., et al., 2008, Advancing decadal-scale climate prediction in the North Atlantic sector, *Nature*, 453, 84

Kermode, J. I., 1993, Review of Mark Bailey (ed.), *The Bailiffs' Minute Book of Dunwich 1404–1430*, Suffolk Records Society, XXXIV, *Urban History*, 20, 248–50

Kitchener, A. C., and Conroy, J. W. H., 1997, The history of the Eurasian Beaver *Castor fiber* in Scotland, *Mammal Review*, 27, 95–108

Kitoh, A., et al., 2008, First super-high-resolution model projection that the ancient 'Fertile Crescent' will disappear in this century, *Hydrological Research Letters*, 2, 1–4; www.tau.ac.il/~pinhas/papers/2008/Kitoh_et_al_HRL_2008a.pdf

Kolokotroni, M., et al., 2007, The London heat island and building cooling design, *Solar Energy*, 81, 102–10

Kovats, R. S., et al., 1999, Climate change and human health in Europe, *British Medical Journal*, 318, 1682–5

Kovats, S. (ed.), 2008, Health effects of climate change in the UK 2008, Department of Health/Health Protection Agency; www.dh.gov.uk/en/publicationsandstatistics/Publications/PublicationsPolicyAndGuidance/DH_080702

Krieger, C., 2006, *The Fertile Rock: Seasons in the Burren*, Collins

Kriegler, E., et al., 2009, Imprecise probability assessment of tipping points in the climate system, *Proceedings of the National Academy of Sciences*, 106, 5041–6; www.pnas.org/content/106/13/5041.full

Kunzig, R., and Broecker, W. S., 2008, *Fixing Climate: The Story of*

Climate Science – and How to Stop Global Warming, Profile

Kurz, W. A., et al., 2008, Mountain pine beetle and forest carbon feedback to climate change, *Nature*, 452, 987–90

Ladbrook, B., 2007, Analysis of carbon capture and storage cost-supply curves for the UK, Pöyry Energy Consulting; www.berr. gov.uk/files/file36782.pdf

Lang, D., 2004, Britain's orchids: A guide to the identification and ecology of the wild orchids of Britain and Ireland, English Nature and WILDGuides; www.britainsorchids.fieldguide. co.uk/?P=home&SHC=1&PSD=1

Larwood, J. [pseud. P. L. R. Sadler], 1872, *The Story of the London Parks*, vol. II: *St. James's Park, the Green Park*, Hotten

Ledford, H., 2007, Plant biology: The flower of seduction, *Nature*, 445, 816–17

Lenton, T. M., and Schellnhuber, H. J., 2007, Tipping the scales, *Nature Reports Climate Change*, 1; www.nature.com/ climate/2007/0712/full/climate.2007.65.html

Lenton, T. M., et al., 2006, Millennial timescale carbon cycle and climate change in an efficient earth system model, *Climate Dynamics*, 26, 687–711

—— 2008, Tipping elements in the Earth's climate system, *Proceedings of the National Academy of Sciences*, 105, 1786–93

—— 2009, Using GENIE to study a tipping point in the climate system, *Philosophical Transactions of the Royal Society*, Series A, 367, 871–84; http://eprints.soton.ac.uk/65084/01/rsta.2008.0171.pdf

Levermann, A., et al., 2005, Dynamic sea level changes following changes in the thermohaline circulation, *Climate Dynamics*, 24, 347–54; www.pik-potsdam.de/~anders/publications/levermann_ grieselo5.pdf

Leydecker, S., 2008, *Nano Materials in Architecture, Interior Architecture and Design*, Birkhäuser

Lieshout, M.v., et al., 2004, Climate change and malaria: Analysis of the SRES climate and socio-economic scenarios, *Global Environmental Change*, 14, 87–99; http://ncsp.va-network.org/ UserFiles/File/PDFs/Resource%20Center/Human%20Health/ malaria.pdf

Lindgren, E., et al., 2000, Impact of climatic change on the northern latitude limit and population density of the diseasetransmitting European tick *Ixodes ricinus, Environmental Health Perspectives*, 108, 119–23; www.ehponline.org/members/2000/108p119-123lindgren/lindgren-full.html

Lindsay, S. W., and Willis, S. G., 2006, Predicting future areas suitable for vivax malaria in the United Kingdom, Office of Science and Innovation; www.foresight.gov.uk/Infectious%20Diseases/t8_10.pdf

Linnell, J. D. C., et al., 2002, The fear of wolves: A review of wolf attacks on humans, Norsk Institutt for Naturforskning; www.nina.no/archive/nina/Publikasjoner/oppdragsmelding/NINA-OM731.pdf

Liu, J., et al., 2008, A spatially explicit assessment of current and future hotspots of hunger in Sub-Saharan Africa in the context of global change, *Global and Planetary Change*, 64, 221–34

London Climate Change Partnership, 2002, London's warming: The impacts of climate change on London, Technical report; www.london.gov.uk/gla/publications/environment/londons_warming_tech_rpt_all.pdf

Longstaff Tyrrell, P., 2004, *Reflections from the Cuckmere Valley: 200 years of Industry and Intrigue*, Gote House

Lovelock, J., 2007, *The Revenge of Gaia*, Penguin

Lowe, J. A., et al., 2006, The role of sea-level rise and the Greenland ice sheet in dangerous climate change: Implications for the stabilisation of climate; www.metoffice.gov.uk/corporate/pressoffice/adcc/BookCh4Jan2006.pdf

Ludlow, E., 1894, *The Memoirs of Edmund Ludlow*, Clarendon; www.archive.org/details/memoirsedmundluooludlgoog

Lutz, W., et al., 2008, The coming acceleration of global population ageing, *Nature*, 451, 716–19

Mabey, R., 1996, *Flora Britannica: The Definitive New Guide to Britain's Wild Flowers, Plants and Trees*, Sinclair-Stevenson

Macdonald, D., and Burnham, D., 2007, The state of Britain's mammals 2007, www.surreybiodiversitypartnership.org/xwiki/bin/download/Partners/SurreyMammalGroup/Britain's%20Mammals%202007.pdf

Macdonald, D. W., et al., 2000, Reintroducing the beaver (*Castor fiber*) to Scotland: A protocol for identifying and assessing suitable release sites, *Animal Conservation*, 3, 125–33

Mahasenan, N., et al., 2003, The cement industry and global climate change: Current and potential future cement industry CO_2 emissions, *Proceedings of the 6th International Conference on Greenhouse Gas Control Technologies*, 995–1000

Mallon, K., et al., 2007, Climate solutions: The WWF vision for 2050, WWF; www.wwf.org.uk/filelibrary/pdf/climatesolutionreport.pdf

Manley, G., 1952, *Climate and the British Scene*, Collins

—— 1953, The mean temperature of central England, 1698–1952, *Quarterly Journal of the Royal Meteorological Society*, 79, 242–61

—— 1974, Central England temperatures: Monthly means 1659 to 1973, *Quarterly Journal of the Royal Meteorological Society*, 100, 389–405

Marsh, T. J., and Hannaford, J., 2007, The summer 2007 floods in England and Wales – a hydrological appraisal, Centre for Ecology & Hydrology; www.ceh.ac.uk/products/publications/SummerFloods2007appraisal.html

Martini, I. P., et al., 2006, *Peatlands: Evolution and Records of Environmental and Climate Changes*, Elsevier

Matthews, H. D., and Caldeira, K., 2008, Stabilizing climate requires near-zero emissions, *Geophysical Research Letters*, 35; www.mcgill.ca/files/gec3/MatthewsCaldeira2008_GRL.pdf

May, V. J., and Hansom, J. D., 2003, Coastal geomorphology of Great Britain, Geological Conservation Review Series No. 28, Joint Nature Conservation Committee; www.jncc.gov.uk/page-3012

Mayor of London, 2008, The London plan: Spatial development strategy for Greater London. Consolidated with alterations since 2004; www.london.gov.uk/thelondonplan/thelondonplan.jsp

McGrath, R., et al., 2008, Ireland in a warmer world: Scientific predictions of the Irish climate in the twenty-first century, Community Climate Change Consortium for Ireland; www.met.ie/publications/IrelandinaWarmerWorld.pdf

McMichael, A. J., et al., 2008, Global environmental change and health: Impacts, inequalities, and the health sector, *British Medical Journal*, 336, 191–4; www.bmj.com/cgi/content/full/336/7637/191

Mech, L. D., 1970, *The Wolf: The Ecology and Behavior of an Endangered Species*, Natural History Press

Meehl, G. A., and Tebaldi, C., 2004, More intense, more frequent, and longer lasting heat waves in the 21st century, *Science*, 305, 994–7

Mejías, J. A., et al., 2002, Reproductive ecology of *Rhododendron ponticum* (Ericaceae) in relict Mediterranean populations, *Botanical Journal of the Linnean Society*, 140, 297–311

Mellor, P. S., and Hamblin, C., 2004, African horse sickness, *Veterinary Research*, 35, 445–66; www.vetres.org/index.php?opti on=article&access=standard&Itemid=129&url=/articles/vetres/ pdf/2004/04/V4013.pdf

Metz, B., et al., 2005, *IPCC Special Report on Carbon Dioxide Capture and Storage*, Cambridge University Press; www.ipcc.ch/pdf/ special-reports/srccs/srccs_wholereport.pdf

Meze-Hausken, E., 2008, On the (im-)possibilities of defining human climate thresholds, *Climatic Change*, 89, 299–324

Middlesex University Flood Hazard Research Centre, 2007, The impacts of climate change on nuclear power station sites, Greenpeace; www.greenpeace.org.uk/media/reports/the- impacts-of-climate-change-on-nuclear-power-station-sites

Ministry of Environment and Forests, Government of the People's Republic of Bangladesh, 2008, Bangladesh climate change strategy and action plan 2008; www.moef.gov.bd/moef.pdf

Moles, N. R., and Moles, R. T., 2002, Influence of geology, glacial processes and land use on soil composition and Quaternary landscape evolution in the Burren National Park, Ireland, *Catena*, 47, 291–321

Moles, R., et al., 1999, Radiocarbon dated episode of Bronze Age slope instability in the south-eastern Burren, County Clare, *Irish Geography*, 32, 52–7

—— 2003, The impact of environmental factors on the distribution of plant species in a Burren grassland patch: Implications for conservation, *Biology and Environment: Proceedings of the Royal Irish Academy*, 103B, 139–45; www.ria.ie/cgi-bin/ria/ papers/100407.pdf

Molesworth, C., 1880, *The Cobham Journals. Abstracts and Summaries of Meteorological and Phenological Observations Made . . . at Cobham . . . in the Years* 1825 *to* 1850, Stanford University Press

Moore, N. P., and Wilson, C. J., 2005, Feral wild boar in England: Implications of future management options, Department for Environment, Food and Rural Affairs; www.naturalengland.org. uk/Images/wildboarmplicationsofoptions_tcm6-4511.pdf

Morris, J., 1976, *Domesday Book*, vol. II: *Sussex*, Phillimore

Mossman, K., 2008, Profile of Hans Joachim Schellnhuber, *Proceedings of the National Academy of Sciences*, 105, 1783–5

Mráz, R., 1999, Catalogue of biting midges (*Diptera, Ceratopogonidae*) of Slovakia, *Acta Zoologica Universitatis Comenianae*, 43, 15–58; http://zoology.fns.uniba.sk/acta/interface/05307.pdf

Nakicenovic, N., et al., 2000, Special report on emissions scenarios, Intergovernmental Panel on Climate Change; www.grida.no/climate/ipcc/emission/

—— 2003, IPCC SRES revisited: A response, *Energy and Environment*, 14, 187–214; www.iiasa.ac.at/Research/TNT/WEB/Publications/ipcc-sres-revisited/ipcc-sres-revisited.pdf

National Farmers' Union, 2005, Agriculture and climate change; www.nfuonline.com/documents/Policy%20Services/Environment/Climate%20Change/NFU%20Climate%20Change.pdf

Natural England, 2009, Responding to the impacts of climate change on the natural environment: The Broads; www. naturalengland.org.uk/Images/NE114R-TheBroads-report_tcm6-10436.pdf

Nelson, Gerald C., et al., 2009, Climate change: Impact on agriculture and costs of adaptation, International Food Policy Research Institute; www.ifpri.org/sites/default/files/publications/pr21.pdf

Nepstad, D., 2007, The Amazon's vicious cycles: Drought and fire in the greenhouse, WWF International; http://assets.panda.org/downloads/amazonas_eng_04_12b_web.pdf

Nicholls, R. J., et al., 2008, Ranking port cities with high exposure and vulnerability to climate extremes: Exposure estimates, Organisation for Economic Co-operation and Development; http://masetto.sourceoecd.org/vl=1308689/cl=25/nw=1/rpsv/cgi-bin/wppdf?file=5kzssgshj742.pdf

Nilsen, E. B., et al., 2007, Wolf reintroduction to Scotland:

Public attitudes and consequences for red deer management, *Proceedings of the Royal Society*, Series B, 274, 995–1002; www.carnivoreconservation.org/files/issues/wolf_scotland_ reintroduction.pdf

Nolet, B. A., and Rosell, F., 1998, Comeback of the beaver *Castor fiber*: An overview of old and new conservation problems, *Biological Conservation*, 83, 165–73

Nordhaus, W., 2007, A review of the Stern Review on the economics of global warming, *Journal of Economic Literature*, 45, 686–702; http://nordhaus.econ.yale.edu/stern_050307.pdf

Nuclear Decommissioning Authority, 2006, Sizewell: A site summary lifetime plan; www.nda.gov.uk/documents/loader. cfm?url=/commonspot/security/getfile.cfm&pageid=4012

O'Connell, J., and Korff, A., 2002, *The Book of the Burren*, Tír Eolas

Office of Climate Change, 2007, OCC Household Emissions Project: Analysis pack; www.occ.gov.uk/activities/emissions/ Household%20emissions%20report%20-%20analysis%20 pack%2028March2007.pdf

Ogilvy, T. K., et al., 2006, Diversifying native pinewoods using artificial regeneration, *Forestry*, 79, 309–17

Olding, F., 2000, *The Prehistoric Landscapes of the Eastern Black Mountains*, Archaeopress

Olesen, J. E., et al., 2007, Uncertainties in projected impacts of climate change on European agriculture and terrestrial ecosystems based on scenarios from regional climate models, *Climatic Change*, 81, 123–43

Oosthoek, J.-W., 2000, The logic of British forest policy, 1919–1970; www.eh-resources.org/documents/esee_paper.pdf

Oppenheimer, M., et al., 2007, The limits of consensus, *Science*, 317, 1505–6

Orford, J. D., and Pethick, J., 2006, Challenging assumptions of future coastal habitat development around the UK, *Earth Surface Processes and Landforms*, 31, 1625–42

O'Rourke, E., 2005a, Landscape planning and community participation: Local lessons from Mullaghmore, the Burren National Park, *Ireland Landscape Research*, 30, 483–500

——— 2005b, Socio-natural interaction and landscape dynamics in the Burren, Ireland, *Landscape and Urban Planning*, 70, 69–83

Overpeck, J. T., et al., 2006, Paleoclimatic evidence for future ice-sheet instability and rapid sea-level rise, *Science*, 311, 1747–50

Pacha, M. J., and Petit, S., 2008, The effect of landscape structure and habitat quality on the occurrence of *Geranium sylvaticum* in fragmented hay meadows, *Agriculture, Ecosystems & Environment*, 123, 81–7

Palmer, J., et al., 2006, Reducing the environmental impact of housing: Final report, Environmental Change Institute, University of Oxford; www.rcep.org.uk/reports/26-urban/documents/reducingenvironmentalimpactofhousing.pdf

Palomares, F., et al., 1996, Spatial relationships between Iberian lynx and other carnivores in an area of south-western Spain, *Journal of Applied Ecology*, 33, 5–13

Parker, H., et al., 1999, Landscape use and economic value of Eurasian beaver (*Castor fiber*) on large forest in southeast Norway; http://teora.hit.no/dspace/bitstream/2282/325/1/MNBEVD1.pdf

—— 2000, A gross assessment of the suitability of selected Scottish riparian habitats for beaver, *Scottish Forestry*, 54, 25–31

Parkes, M., 2004, Natural and cultural landscapes. The Geological Foundation: proceedings of a conference, 9–11 September 2002, Royal Irish Academy

Parr, S., et al., 2006, Mapping the broad habitats of the Burren using satellite imagery: End of project report. RMIS 5190c, Teagasc; www.teagasc.ie/research/reports/environment/5190c/eopr5190c.pdf

Parry, M. L., et al., 2004, Effects of climate change on global food production under SRES emissions and socio-economic scenarios, *Global Environmental Change*, 14, 53–67; www.undp.org/gef/adaptation/docs/foodproduction.pdf

—— 2005, Climate change, global food supply and risk of hunger, *Philosophical Transactions of the Royal Society*, Series B, 360, 2125–38

Patz, J., et al., 2005, Impact of regional climate change on human health, *Nature*, 438, 310–17

Peterson, B. J., et al., 2002, Increasing river discharge to the Arctic Ocean, *Science*, 298, 2171–3; http://ecosystems.mbl.edu/partners/pdf/Peterson%20et%20al%20Science%202002.pdf

Pfeffer, W. T., et al., 2008, Kinematic constraints on glacier contributions to 21st-century sea-level rise, *Science*, 321, 1340–2

Pielke, R. J., et al., 2008, Dangerous assumptions, *Nature*, 452, 531–2

Piersma, T., and Lindström, Å., 2004, Migrating shorebirds as integrative sentinels of global environmental change, *Ibis*, 146, 61–9

Pounds, J. A., and Puschendorf, R., 2004, Clouded futures, *Nature*, 427, 107–9

Power, A., 2008, Does demolition or refurbishment of old and inefficient homes help to increase our environmental, social and economic viability?, *Energy Policy*, 36, 4487–501

Prendergast, J. P., 1868, *The Cromwellian Settlement of Ireland*, P. M. Haverty; www.archive.org/details/cromwellianooprenrich

Price, M. D. R., 1981, *Palynological Studies on the Black Mountains*, University of London

PRP, 2002, High-density housing in Europe: Lessons for London, East Thames Housing Group

Purse, B., et al., 2005, Opinion: Climate change and the recent emergence of bluetongue in Europe, *Nature Reviews Microbiology*, 3, 171–81

—— 2007, Incriminating bluetongue virus vectors with climate envelope models, *Journal of Applied Ecology*, 44, 1231–42

Pye, K., and Blott, S. J., 2006, Coastal processes and morphological change in the Dunwich-Sizewell area, Suffolk, UK, *Journal of Coastal Research*, 22, 453–73

Quadfasel, D., 2005, The Atlantic heat conveyor slows, *Nature*, 438, 565–6

Rackham, O., 1976, *Trees and Woodland in the British Landscape*, J. M. Dent

—— 1986, *The History of the Countryside*, J. M. Dent

—— 2001, *Trees and Woodland in the British Landscape: The Complete History of Britain's Trees, Woods and Hedgerows*, Phoenix

Rahmstorf, S., 2007, A semi-empirical approach to projecting future sea-level rise, *Science*, 315, 368–70; www.pik-potsdam. de/~stefan/Publications/Nature/rahmstorf_science_2007.pdf

Rahmstorf, S., et al., 2007, Recent climate observations compared to projections, *Science*, 316, 709

Ramanathan, V., and Feng, Y., 2008, On avoiding dangerous anthropogenic interference with the climate system: Formidable challenges ahead, *Proceedings of the National Academy of Sciences*, 105, 14245–50

Randolph, S. E., 2000, The shifting landscape of tick-borne zoonoses: tick-borne encephalitis and Lyme borreliosis in Europe, *Philosophical Transactions of the Royal Society*, Series B, 356, 1045–56

Rauer, G., 2004, Re-introduced bears in Austria, *Ecos*, 25, 69–72; www.banc.org.uk/Articles/December2004/PDF/Ecos25_34.pdf

Raupach, M. R., et al., 2007, Global and regional drivers of accelerating CO_2 emissions, *Proceedings of the National Academy of Sciences*, 104, 10288–93; www.pnas.org/content/104/24/10288.full

Ravetz, J., 2008, State of the stock: What do we know about existing buildings and their future prospects?, *Energy Policy*, 36, 4462–70; www.foresight.gov.uk/Energy/EnergyFinal/Ravetz%20paper-section%205.pdf

Ravetz, J., et al., 2005, Stabilizing the ecological footprint in the South East Plan: A report to South East England Regional Assembly, Centre for Urban & Regional Ecology/Stockholm Environment Institute – York; www.southeast-ra.gov.uk/southeastplan/publications/research/se_footprint_main_report_july05.pdf

Ray, D., 2008, Impacts of climate change on forestry in Scotland: A synopsis of spatial modelling research, Forestry Commission Scotland; www.forestry.gov.uk/pdf/fcrn101.pdf/$FILE/fcrn101.pdf

Ray, D., et al., 2008, Impacts of climate change on forests and forestry in Scotland, Forestry Commission Scotland; www.forestry.gov.uk/pdf/scottish_climate_change_final_report.pdf/$FILE/scottish_climate_change_final_report.pdf

Rebetez, M., and Dobbertin, M., 2004, Climate change may already threaten Scots pine stands in the Swiss Alps, *Theoretical and Applied Climatology*, 79, 1–9; www.wsl.ch/personal_homepages/rebetez/Rebetez-Dobbertin-TAC2004.pdf

Rehfeldt, G. E., et al., 2002, Intraspecific responses to climate in *Pinus sylvestris*, *Global Change Biology*, 8, 912–29; http://forest.

akadem.ru/Articles/02/tchebakova_9.pdf

Reinhardt, I., and Kluth, G., 2004, Wolf territory in Germany, *Ecos*, 25, 73–7; www.banc.org.uk/Articles/December2004/PDF/Ecos25_34.pdf

Reiter, P., 2001, Climate change and mosquito-borne disease, *Environmental Health Perspectives*, 109 (supplement 1), 141–61; www.ehponline.org/members/2001/suppl-1/141-161reiter/reiter-full.html

Renton, A., 2009, Suffering the science: Climate change, people, and poverty, Oxfam International; www.oxfam.org/en/policy/bp130-suffering-the-science

Rhines, P. B., and Häkkinen, S., 2003, Is the oceanic heat transport in the North Atlantic irrelevant to the climate in Europe? *ASOF Newsletter*; www.realclimate.org/Rhines_hakkinen_2003.pdf

Risbey, J. S., 2008, The new climate discourse: Alarmist or alarming?, *Global Environmental Change*, 18, 26–37

Risk Management Solutions, 2003, 1953 UK floods: 50-year retrospective; www.rms.com/Publications/1953_Floods_Retrospective.pdf

Roaf, S., et al., 2005, *Adapting Buildings and Cities for Climate Change: A 21st Century Survival Guide*, Elsevier

Roberts, S., 2008, Altering existing buildings in the UK, *Energy Policy*, 36, 4482–6; www.foresight.gov.uk/Energy/EnergyFinal/Roberts%202%20paper-%20section%205.pdf

Robinson, D. A., and Blackman, J. D., 1990, Soil erosion and flooding: Consequences of land use policy and agricultural practice on the South Downs, East Sussex, UK, *Land Use Policy*, 7, 41–52

Robinson, R. A., et al., 2005, Climate change and migratory species, British Trust for Ornithology; www.bto.org/research/reports/researchrpt_complete/RR414_Climate%20change_&_migratory_species.pdf

Robinson, T., 1999, *The Burren*, Folding Landscapes
—— 2008, *Stones of Aran: Pilgrimage*, Faber

Rohling, E. J., et al., 2008, High rates of sea-level rise during the last interglacial period, *Nature Geoscience*, 1, 38–42; www.nature.com/ngeo/journal/v1/n1/full/ngeo.2007.28.html

Romm, J., 2008, Cleaning up on carbon, *Nature Reports*

Climate Change; www.nature.com/climate/2008/0807/full/
climate.2008.59.html

Rosbottom, D., 2007, We now have an opportunity to reflect upon
how terraced housing can be reinvigorated, *Architects' Journal*,
18 October, 26–30; www.drdharchitects.co.uk/images/025_045_
AJW_181007.pdf

Ross, J., et al., 1986, The establishment and spread of myxomatosis
and its effect on rabbit populations, *Philosophical Transactions of
the Royal Society*, Series B, 314, 599–606

Rounsevell, M. D. A., et al., 2005, Future scenarios of European
agricultural land use: II. Projecting changes in cropland and
grassland, *Agriculture, Ecosystems & Environment*, 107, 117–35
—— 2006, A coherent set of future land use change scenarios for
Europe, *Agriculture, Ecosystems & Environment*, 114, 57–68; www.
mncn.csic.es/pdf_web/maraujo/Rounsevell_et_al_AEE2006.pdf

Royal Zoological Society of Scotland and Scottish Wildlife
Trust, 2007, Application to Scottish Government by the Royal
Zoological Society of Scotland and Scottish Wildlife Trust for a
licence under section 16(4) of the Wildlife and Countryside Act
1981, as amended, to release European beaver, *Castor fiber*, for a
trial re-introduction in Knapdale, Argyll; www.scottishbeavers.
org.uk/docs/files/general/BeaverApplicationWeb.pdf

Samstag, T., 1988, *For Love of Birds: The Story of the Royal Society
for the Protection of Birds, 1889–1989*, Royal Society for the
Protection of Birds

Schär, C., and Jendritzky, G., 2004, Climate change: Hot news
from summer 2003, *Nature*, 432, 559–60

Schellnhuber, H. J., 2008, Global warming: Stop worrying, start
panicking?, *Proceedings of the National Academy of Sciences*, 105,
14239–40

Schellnhuber, H. J., et al., 2006, *Avoiding Dangerous Climate Change*,
Cambridge University Press

Schiermeier, Q., 2006, A sea change, *Nature*, 439, 256–60

Schiestl, F. P., 2005, On the success of a swindle: Pollination by
deception in orchids, *Naturwissenschaften*, 92, 255–64

Schiestl, F. P., et al., 1999, Orchid pollination by sexual swindle,
Nature, 399, 421–2; http://protist.biology.washington.edu/
biol489/Readings/1-19_Schiestl99.pdf

Schmidhuber, J., and Tubiello, F. N., 2007, Global food security under climate change, *Proceedings of the National Academy of Sciences*, 104, 19703–8; www.fao.org/es/ESD/PNAS.pdf

Scott, P., 2004, Selling owner-occupation to the working-classes in 1930s Britain, University of Reading Centre for International Business History; www.rdg.ac.uk/nmsruntime/saveasdialog. asp?lID=10400&sID=34517

Scottish Executive Environment and Rural Affairs Department, 2007, ECOSSE – Estimating carbon in organic soils sequestration and emissions, Scottish Executive; www.scotland. gov.uk/Publications/2007/03/16170508/1

Seager, R., 2006, The source of Europe's mild climate, *American Scientist*, 94, 334–41; www.americanscientist.org/issues/feature/2006/4/the-source-of-europes-mild-climate/1

Seager, R., et al., 2002, Is the Gulf Stream responsible for Europe's mild winters? *Quarterly Journal of the Royal Meteorological Society*, 128, 2563–86; http://rainbow.ldeo.columbia.edu//papers/qj.pdf

Sebald, W. G., 2002, *The Rings of Saturn*, Vintage

Seoane, J., et al., 2003, The effects of land use and climate on red kite distribution in the Iberian peninsula, *Biological Conservation*, 111, 401–14

Severinghaus, J. P., et al., 1998, Timing of abrupt climate change at the end of the Younger Dryas interval from thermally fractionated gases in polar ice, *Nature*, 391, 141–6

Shackley, S., and Deanwood, R., 2003, Constructing social futures for climate-change impacts and response studies: Building qualitative and quantitative scenarios with the participation of stakeholders, *Climate Research*, 24, 71–90

Shaw, H., and Tipping, R., 2006, Recent pine woodland dynamics in east Glen Affric, northern Scotland, from highly resolved palaeoecological analyses, *Forestry*, 79, 331–40

Shindell, D., 2007, Estimating the potential for twenty-first century sudden climate change, *Philosophical Transactions of the Royal Society*, Series A, 365, 2675–94; http://pubs.giss.nasa.gov/docs/2007/2007_Shindell_3.pdf

Simmons, I. G., 2003, *The Moorlands of England and Wales: An Environmental History* 8000BC–AD2000, Edinburgh University Press

Sinnadurai, P., 2004, A review of current literature on the evidence for climate change and its implications for the Brecon Beacons National Park; www.breconbeacons.org/environment/climate-change/bbnpa-climate-change-information-note

Sistermans, P., and Nieuwenhuis, O., 2001, South Downs, Sussex County (United Kingdom): Eurosion case study, DHV Group; http://copranet.projects.eucc-d.de/files/000167_EUROSION_South_Downs.pdf

Skre, O., et al., 2005, Responses of temperature changes on survival and growth in mountain birch populations. In F. E. Wielgolaski (ed.), *Herbivory and Human Impact in Nordic Mountain Birch Forests*, Springer, 130–45; www.nmvskre.no/doc/Springer%20II%20article.pdf

Slingenbergh, J., et al., 2004, Ecological sources of zoonotic diseases, *Revue scientifique et technique de l'Office international des épizooties*, 23, 467–84; www.oie.int/boutique/extrait/467-484slingenberg.pdf

Sluijs, J. van der, 1998, Anchoring devices in science for policy: The case of consensus around climate sensitivity, *Social Studies of Science*, 28, 291–323

Smart, G., and Brandon, P., 2007, *The Future of the South Downs*, Packard

Smil, V., 2006, Energy at the crossroads, OECD Global Science Forum Conference on Scientific Challenges for Energy Research; http://home.cc.umanitoba.ca/~vsmil/pdf_pubs/oecd.pdf

—— 2008, Long-range energy forecasts are no more than fairy tales (Correspondence), *Nature*, 453, 154; http://home.cc.umanitoba.ca/~vsmil/pdf_pubs/nature2008.pdf

Smith, D. M., et al., 2007, Improved surface temperature prediction for the coming decade from a global climate model, *Science*, 317, 796

Smout, T. C., 2000, *Nature Contested: Environmental History in Scotland and Northern England since 1600*, Edinburgh University Press

—— 2003, *People and Woods in Scotland: A History*, Edinburgh University Press

Solomon, S., et al., 2009, Irreversible climate change due

to carbon dioxide emissions, *Proceedings of the National Academy of Sciences*, 106, 1704–9; www.pnas.org/content/early/2009/01/28/0812721106.full.pdf+html

South, A., et al., 2000, Simulating the proposed reintroduction of the European beaver (*Castor fiber*) to Scotland, *Biological Conservation*, 93, 103–16

Stammler, F., and Forbes, B. C., 2006, Oil and gas development in Western Siberia and Timan-Pechora, *Indigenous Affairs*, 2–3/06 part 2, 48–57; www.iwgia.org/sw29928.asp

Sterl, A., et al., 2008, When can we expect extremely high surface temperatures? *Geophysical Research Letters*, 35, L14703; www.knmi.nl/publications/fulltexts/sterl_extreme_grl_2008.pdf

Stern, N., 2006, The economics of climate change, Cabinet Office – HM Treasury; www.hm-treasury.gov.uk/stern_review_climate_change.htm

Steven, H. M., and Carlisle, A., 1959, *The Native Pinewoods of Scotland*, Oliver & Boyd

Stevenson, J., 1984, *British Society, 1914–45*, Penguin

Stott, P. A., et al., 2004, Human contribution to the European heatwave of 2003, *Nature*, 432, 610–14

Summers, R. W., et al., 2007, Assortative mating and patterns of inheritance indicate that the three crossbill taxa in Scotland are species, *Journal of Avian Biology*, 38, 153–62

Swart, R., et al., 2002, Stabilisation scenarios for climate impact assessment, *Global Environmental Change*, 12, 155–65

Sweeney, J., et al., 2003, Climate change: Scenarios & impacts for Ireland (2000-LS-5.2.1-M1): Final report Environmental Protection Agency; www.epa.ie/downloads/pubs/research/climate/epa_climate_change_scenarios_ertdi15.pdf

—— 2008, Climate change: Refining the impacts for Ireland (2001-CD-C3-M1), Environmental Protection Agency; www.epa.ie/downloads/pubs/research/climate/sweeney-report-strive-12-for-web-low-res.pdf

Sweeney, K., et al., 2008, Changing shades of green: The environmental and cultural impacts of climate change in Ireland, The Irish American Climate Project; www.irishclimate.org/changing_shades_of_green.pdf

Tarasov, L., and Peltier, W. R., 2005, Arctic freshwater forcing of the Younger Dryas cold reversal, *Nature*, 435, 662–5

Tchebakova, N. M., et al., 2006, Impacts of climate change on the distribution of *Larix* spp. and *Pinus sylvestris* and their climatypes in Siberia, *Mitigation and Adaptation Strategies for Global Change*, 11, 861–82

Thames Estuary 2100, 2009, TE2100 plan consultation document, Environment Agency; www.environment-agency.gov.uk/research/library/consultations/106100.aspx

Theuerkauf, J., 2003, Impact of man on wolf behaviour in the Bialowieza Forest, Poland, Technischen Universität München; http://deposit.ddb.de/cgi-bin/dokserv?idn=968912680&dok_var=d1&dok_ext=pdf&filename=968912680.pdf

Thornton, P. K., et al., 2006, Mapping climate vulnerability and poverty in Africa, International Livestock Research Institute; www.research4development.info/PDF/Outputs/ClimChangePovInAfrica.pdf

Tipping, R., 1994, The form and fate of Scotland's woodlands, *Proceedings of the Society of Antiquaries of Scotland*, 124, 1–54

—— 2003, *The Quaternary of Glen Affric and Kintail*, Quaternary Research Association

Tipping, R., et al., 2004, Trees and wild land values in West Glen Affric: A personal view, *Wild Land News*, 61, 14–17; www.swlg.org.uk/61_-_Autumn_2004.pdf

—— 2006, Long-term woodland dynamics in West Glen Affric, northern Scotland, *Forestry*, 79, 351–9

Tirpak, D., et al., 2005, Avoiding dangerous climate change, International Symposium on the Stabilisation of Greenhouse Gas Concentrations. Report of the International Scientific Steering Committee International Symposium on Stabilisation of Greenhouse Gas Concentrations – Avoiding Dangerous Climate Change; www.stabilisation2005.com/Steering_Commitee_Report.pdf

Tocqueville, A. de, 2004, *Democracy in America*, Library of America

Tol, R. S. J., et al., 2006, Adaptation to five metres of sea level rise, *Journal of Risk Analysis*, 9, 467–82; www.fnu.zmaw.de/fileadmin/fnu-files/publication/tol/jrrslr5.pdf

Trudgill, S., 2008, A requiem for the British flora? Emotional biogeographies and environmental change, *Area*, 40, 99–107

Tubiello, F. N., and Fischer, G., 2007, Reducing climate change impacts on agriculture: Global and regional effects of mitigation, 2000–2080, *Technological Forecasting and Social Change*, 74, 1030–56

Tubiello, F. N., et al., 2007, Crop and pasture response to climate change, *Proceedings of the National Academy of Sciences*, 104, 19686–90

Tuck, G., et al., 2006, The potential distribution of bioenergy crops in Europe under present and future climate, *Biomass and Bioenergy*, 30, 183–97

UN Framework Convention on Climate Change, 2007, Climate change: Impacts, vulnerabilities and adaptation in developing countries; http://unfccc.int/files/essential_background/background_publications_htmlpdf/application/txt/pub_07_impacts.pdf

UN Population Division, Department of Economic and Social Affairs, 2004, World population in 2300, United Nations; www.un.org/esa/population/publications/longrange2/2004worldpop2300reportfinalc.pdf

— 2007, World population prospects: The 2006 Revision. Highlights, United Nations; www.un.org/esa/population/publications/wpp2006/WPP2006_Highlights_rev.pdf

Upmanis, H., et al., 1998, The influence of green areas on nocturnal temperatures in a high latitude city (Göteborg, Sweden), *International Journal of Climatology*, 18, 681–700

Valkama, J., et al., 2005, Birds of prey as limiting factors of gamebird populations in Europe: A review, *Biological Reviews*, 80, 171–203

Vaughan, D. G., and Spouge, J. R., 2002, Risk estimation of collapse of the West Antarctic Ice Sheet, *Climatic Change*, 52, 65–91

Verburg, P. H., et al., 2007, Downscaling of land use change scenarios to assess the dynamics of European landscapes, *Agriculture, Ecosystems & Environment*, 114, 39–56

Viles, H. A., 2003, Conceptual modeling of the impacts of climate change on karst geomorphology in the UK and Ireland, *Journal for Nature Conservation*, 11, 59–66

Villafuerte, R., et al., 1998, Extensive predator persecution caused

353

by population crash in a game species: The case of red kites and rabbits in Spain, *Biological Conservation*, 84, 181–8

Viner, D., et al., 2006, Climate change and the European countryside: Impacts on land management and response strategies, Climatic Research Unit, University of East Anglia; www.cla.org.uk:80/Policy_Work/Policy_Reports/Environment/ Climate_Change/5118.htm/

Wada, N., and Nakai, Y., 2004, Germinability of seeds in a glacial relict *Dryas octopetala* var. *asiatica*: Comparison with a snowbed alpine plant *Sieversia pentapetala* in a middle-latitude mountain area of central Japan, *Far Eastern Studies*, 3, 57–72; www3.u-toyama.ac.jp/cfes/FES3/2004WADA.pdf

Walter, K. M., et al., 2006, Methane bubbling from Siberian thaw lakes as a positive feedback to climate warming, *Nature*, 443, 71–5

Warner, K., et al., 2009, In search of shelter: Mapping the effects of climate change on human migration and displacement; www. preventionweb.net/files/9870_climmigrreportjune09final1.pdf

Warren, M. S., et al., 2001, Rapid responses of British butterflies to opposing forces of climate and habitat change, *Nature*, 414, 65–9

Watkins, R., 2002, The London heat island: Results from summertime monitoring, *Building Service Engineering Research and Technology*, 23, 97–106

Watkins, R., et al., 2007, Increased temperature and intensification of the urban heat island – implications for human comfort and urban design, *Built Environment*, 33, 85–96

Watson Featherstone, A., 1997, The wild heart of the Highlands, *Ecos*, 18, 48–61; www.treesforlife.org.uk/tfl.wildheart.html

—— 2004a, Glen Affric: the return of the wild, *Wild Land News*, 61, 12–14; www.swlg.org.uk/61_-_Autumn_2004.pdf

—— 2004b, Rewilding in the north-central Highlands – an update, *Ecos*, 25, 4–19; www.banc.org.uk/Articles/December2004/PDF/ Ecos25_34.pdf

Webb, D. A., 1983, The flora of Ireland in its European context, *Journal of Life Sciences of the Royal Dublin Society*, 4, 143–60; www. botanicgardens.ie/herb/census/webbboyle.htm

Webb, D. A., and Scannell, M. J. P., 1983, *Flora of Connemara and the Burren*, Cambridge University Press

Welker, J. M., et al., 1997, Responses of *Dryas octopetala* to ITEX environmental manipulations: A synthesis with circumpolar comparisons, *Global Change Biology*, 3 (supplement 1), 61–73

Wennerberg, L., 2001, Breeding origin and migration pattern of dunlin (*Calidris alpina*) revealed by mitochondrial DNA analysis, *Molecular Ecology*, 10, 1111–20

Wesolowski, T., 2007, Primeval conditions – what can we learn from them?, *Ibis*, 149, 64–77

Westbury, D. B., 2004, Biological flora of the British Isles No. 236 List Br. Vasc. Pl. (1958) No. 433, 2, *Rhinanthus minor* L., *Journal of Ecology*, 92, 906–27

Westhoek, H. J., et al., 2006, Scenario development to explore the future of Europe's rural areas, *Agriculture, Ecosystems & Environment*, 114, 7–20

Whitbread, T., 2008, *Weathering the Changes: A Living Landscape in a Changing Climate*, Sussex Wildlife Trust

White, R., 2005, *The Yorkshire Dales: A Landscape through Time*, Great Northern

Wield, M., and Stevenson, A., 2004, Forestry and wild land in Glen Affric, *Wild Land News*, 61, 3–10; www.swlg.org.uk/61_-_Autumn_2004.pdf

Wilby, R. L., 2003, Past and projected trends in London's urban heat island, *Weather*, 58, 251–60

—— 2007, A review of climate change impacts on the built environment, *Built Environment*, 33, 31–45

—— 2008, Constructing climate change scenarios of urban heat island intensity and air quality, *Environment and Planning*, Series B, 35, 902–19

Wilby, R. L., and Perry, G. L. W., 2006, Climate change, biodiversity and the urban environment: A critical review based on London, UK, *Progress in Physical Geography*, 30, 73–98

Wilks, J., and Page, S. (eds), 2003, *Managing Tourist Health and Safety in the New Millennium*, Elsevier

Williams, G., 1978, *The Royal Parks of London*, Constable

Wilson, C. J., 2004, Could we live with reintroduced large carnivores in the UK?, *Mammal Review*, 34, 211–32

Winchester, A. J. L., 2000, *The Harvest of the Hills: Rural Life in Northern England and the Scottish Borders, 1400–1700*, Edinburgh University Press

Wittmann, E. J., and Baylis, M., 2000, Climate change: Effects on *Culicoides*-transmitted viruses and implications for the UK, *Veterinary Journal*, 160, 107–17

Wood, R., 2008, Natural ups and downs, *Nature*, 453, 43–4

Wright, G. N., 1977, *The Yorkshire Dales*, David & Charles

WWF et al., 2007, 80% challenge: Delivering a low-carbon UK; www.wwf.org.uk/filelibrary/pdf/80percent_report.pdf

Yakubowski, D., and Meindersma, C., 2009, Water on the Tibetan plateau – ecological and strategic implications for the region, Hague Centre for Strategic Studies; www.hcss.nl/en/publication/1103/Water-on-the-Tibetan-Plateau---Ecological-and-Stra.html

Yusuf, A. A., and Francisco, H., 2009, Climate change vulnerability mapping for Southeast Asia, Economy and Environment Program for Southeast Asia; www.idrc.ca/uploads/user-S/12324196651Mapping_Report.pdf

Zaehle, S., 2007, Projected changes in terrestrial carbon storage in Europe under climate and land-use change, 1990–2100, *Ecosystems*, 10, 380 401

Zickfeld, K., et al., 2007, Expert judgements on the response of the Atlantic meridional overturning circulation to climate change, *Climatic Change*, 82, 235–65

Zöckler, C., and Lysenko, I., 2000, Water birds on the edge: First circumpolar assessment of climate change impact on Arctic breeding water birds, World Conservation Monitoring Centre; www.unep-wcmc.org/climate/waterbirds/index.aspx

Zöckler, C., et al., 2008, Potential impact of climate change and reindeer density on tundra indicator species in the Barents Sea region, *Climatic Change*, 87, 119–30

Author's website: http://homepage.ntlworld.com/marek.kohn

Index

357